CREATING AN INTERIOR

Helene Levenson
A.S.I.D., NHFL

PRENTICE-HALL, INC. / ENGLEWOOD CLIFFS, NEW JERSEY

Library of Congress Cataloging in Publication Data

Levenson, Helene.
    Creating an interior.

    (A Spectrum Book)
    Includes index.
    1. Interior decoration.   I.   Title.
NK2110.L43   729   79-26861
ISBN 0-13-189019-0
ISBN 0-13-189001-8 pbk.

Art director: Jeannette Jacobs
Buyer: Cathie Lenard
Production Coordinator: Fred Dahl

A SPECTRUM BOOK

10   9   8   7   6   5   4   3   2   1

Printed in the United States of America

PRENTICE-HALL INTERNATIONAL, INC., *London*
PRENTICE-HALL OF AUSTRALIA PTY. LIMITED, *Sydney*
PRENTICE-HALL OF CANADA, LTD., *Toronto*
PRENTICE-HALL OF INDIA PRIVATE LIMITED, *New Delhi*
PRENTICE-HALL OF JAPAN, INC., *Tokyo*
PRENTICE-HALL OF SOUTHEAST ASIA PTE., LTD., *Singapore*
WHITEHALL BOOKS LIMITED, *Wellington, New Zealand*

Contents

Preface, xi

Acknowledgments, xiii

How to Use This Book, xv

CHAPTER **1**
The Professional Approach to Interior Design, 1

Begin with a Plan, 1

PART **I**
What Makes a Style, 5

CHAPTER **2**
The French Style, 7

French Style Periods, 8
The Baroque Style (1643–1700), 12
The Rococo Style (1730–1760), 14
The Neoclassic Style (1760–1789), 16
The Empire Style (1804–1820), 18

CHAPTER **3**
The English Style, 20

English Style Periods, 21
The Tudor Style (1500–1558), 26
The Queen Anne Style (1702–1714), 28
The Middle Georgian or Chippendale Style (1750–1770), 29
The Late Georgian Style (1770–1810), 30
The Regency Style (1810–1830), 32
The Victorian Style (1830–1901), 33

CHAPTER **4**
The American Style, 34

The American Style, 35
The Early American Style (1608–1720), 36
The Georgian Style (1720–1790), 38
The Federal Style (1790–1820), 40
The Greek Revival Style (1820–1860), 42

Comparative Furniture Styles, 44–45

CHAPTER **5**
Contemporary Style, 46

Architecture and Interior Design, 46
Industrial Revolution, 47
Arts and Crafts Movement (1860–1900), 48
Art Nouveau (1890–1905), 48
Organic Architecture, 48
European Architecture (Post 1900), 50
De Stijl (1917), 50
The Bauhaus (1919–1933), 50
The International Style, 51
Art Deco, 52
The California School, 53
Architecture Today, 53

CHAPTER **6**
Adapting a Room to Suit Your Chosen Style, 54

The Country Look, 54
The Formal Look, 60
Creating Architectural Changes, 61

PART II
Furniture: Planning and Selection, 67

CHAPTER 7
The Space Plan, 69

Psychological Needs, 69
Space Planning, 71
Making the Floor Plan, 72

CHAPTER 8
Traditional Furniture, 82

Materials Used in Traditional Furniture, 84
Finishes, 91
Upholstery, 96

CHAPTER 9
Contemporary Furniture, 98

Contemporary Designers (1860–1933), 98
Scandinavian Design, 105
American Design, 106
Italian Design, 110
Universal Style, 116

PART III
Color: Unlimited Possibilities, 117

CHAPTER 10
The Nature of Color, 119

The Physics of Color, 119
Psychological Effects of Color, 120
Pigment Theories, 120

CHAPTER 11
Color Schemes, 126

Related Color Schemes, 126
Contrasting Color Schemes, 127
Textures and Patterns in Colors, 129
Breaking the Rules, 130

PART **IV**
Lighting, 131

CHAPTER **12**
Sources of Light, 133

Daylight, 133
Artificial Light, 134
Measurement of Light, 138

CHAPTER **13**
Application of Light, 141

Lighting Classifications, 141
Types of Fixtures, 142
Special Effects, 151
Lighting Plans, 155

PART **V**
Fabrics, Wallcoverings, Window Treatments, 161

CHAPTER **14**
Fabrics, 163

Introduction to Story, 164
How a Fabric Is Made: The Story of Fabric, 165
Fibers, 170
Weaves, 170
Patterns, 174
Flame-Retardant Fibers, 179
Finishing Processes, 180
Fabric Terminology, 182

CHAPTER **15**
Wallcoverings, 187

Wallpaper in History, 187
Wallpaper Today, 188
Other Wallcoverings, 193

CHAPTER **16**
Window Treatments, 196

Drapery Styles, 197
Other Window Treatments, 202
Drapery Measuring, 207

PART **VI**
Floor Coverings, 209

CHAPTER **17**
Machine-Made Carpets, 212

Manufacturing Techniques, 212
Carpet Yarns and Fibers, 217
Dyeing and Printing, 220
Removing Stain from Rugs, 221

CHAPTER **18**
Rugs, 223

Custom-Made Rugs: The V'soske Technique, 223
Oriental Rugs, 229
Other Hand-Made Area Rugs, 237
Carpet and Rug Terminology, 240

CHAPTER **19**
Other Floor Coverings, 244

Ceramic Tile, 244
Vinyl-Covered Wood, 249

PART **VII**
Art and Accessories, 253

CHAPTER **20**
Mirrors, 255

Uses of Mirrors, 256
Mirror Installation, 261
Mirror Terminology, 261

CHAPTER **21**
Graphics, Paintings, and Drawings, 264

Definition of Art Forms, 267
Paintings and Drawings: Unique Works of Art, 273

CHAPTER **22**
Accessories, 276

The Fabric Arts, 276
Sculpture and the Three-Dimensional Arts, 278
Antiques and Objets d'Art, 281

PART **VIII**
Professional Interior Design, 285

CHAPTER **23**
Professionally Designed Interiors, 285

Presentation of a Plan, 286
Finished Interiors, 292
Warren Platner's "Windows on the World," 293
Professionally Designed Interiors, 298

CHAPTER **24**
Professional Organizations, 299

A.S.I.D. (American Society of Interior Designers), 299
F.I.D.E.R. (Foundation for Interior Design Education Research), 302
N.C.I.D.Q. (National Council for Interior Design Qualification), 304
N.H.F.L. (National Home Fashions League, Inc.), 306
Conclusion, 308

Glossary, 309

Bibliography, 321

Index, 324

Preface

Since the beginning of human history, people have hollowed out of their immediate surroundings an environment increasingly more pleasurable, more efficient, and more beneficial to their existence. Interior design was eminent in the human mind from the earliest years, reflecting social, political, and artistic growth. Functional needs and available materials greatly influenced the design and construction of the dwellings that protected early dwellers from the elements. From cave and mud hut to cottage and castle, their shelters continued to change and evolve to meet their demands. Throughout this process, interior layouts became more and more complex, eventually generating a need for individual rooms for individual functions.

Because of the strong bonds between people and their environment, their homes throughout history have been preserved. The study of these interiors provides historians with valuable information about the customs, tastes, and attitudes of earlier eras. From the beginning, the core of creativity was evident. Our changing lifestyles continue to demonstrate the evolution of our imagination and creativity; and today we have the advantage of unlimited resources in material and design. The professional interior designer first appeared in the United States less than a century ago, and the steady progress of this profession is increasingly evident.

Interest in interior design is universal, unaffected by age, sex, or economic level. Everyone responds to a well designed interior. Because a person's needs and personality are directly influenced by his or her surroundings, living and working in a pleasant atmosphere are necessary to one's personal contentment.

This book is written to enable the reader to reach higher goals of creativity by learning the essential language of interior design. I hope to share with you the joy and excitement I derive from creating an interior and to provide you with the inspiration and knowledge to fulfill your own quest for beauty.

The key word in this book is "create"—but what is creativity? Webster gives this definition: "to produce through imaginative skill, to design . . . an original work of art." Well-known interior designers, interviewed during the preparation of this book offered an interesting variety of definitions.

Ben Cook, Fellow of the American Society of Interior Designers (FASID), writes: "Creativity, as applied to interior furnishings, means, to me, an uncommon assemblage of both useful and decorative household goods in such a manner as to offer a refuge to the body and a delight to the eye."

Martin Elinoff, ASID (past liaison officer between the National Student Council (NSC) and ASID), gives his definition: "Creating to me is the fulfillment of an inspiration . . . it is making an idea come to fruition! The excitement engendered by the end result of a creation, makes the field of interior design uniquely satisfying. Imagination, knowledge, and follow-through are the important ingredients for prolific creativity."

Ben Beckman, FASID (former President of the New York Chapter of ASID), says that creativity in interior design is ". . . applying one's talent to arrive at a new solution which is both a practical answer to the problem and a visual pleasure. The professional designer should recognize that 'new or different' is not his primary target and that his creativity has a new meaning in today's world as a tool for social action."

To me, interior design is an art form. Skill, taste, and imagination combine to produce an atmosphere, a multidimensional sculpture composed of various materials, textures, and patterns, and enriched by a palette of unlimited color variances. As creativity is to me the connecting thread of interior design, so will it be the thread that binds this book.

Creating an interior requires knowledge and expertise, as does any other art form. The following chapters will provide you with the basic elements and tools you need to develop your own creative imagination.

HELENE LEVENSON
A.S.I.D., NHFL

Acknowledgments

The list of those whose help and encouragement made the concept of this book a reality is long. I wish to thank:

My husband, *Edward Levenson*, to whom this book is dedicated, for sustaining moral support and unselfish devotion to a project that took precedence in our lives for more than a year;

My daughter, *Leni Levenson-Wiener*, who enthusiastically offered her advice and reviewed every word, and her husband *Fred*, who put up with it; because of her background as an art historian, the chapters on Art and Accessories were written by Leni;

My son, *Barry Levenson*, whose review and commentary kept this book from being 600 pages, and my mother who patiently understood the long hours I took to do the work;

My professional peers in the *American Society of Interior Designers*, a most reinforcing group without whose backing this book would not have been possible;

John Mead, then Executive Director of ASID, whose concern both for my book and for the welfare of the organization were unfailing; *Louis Tregre*, Fellow of the American Society of Interior Designers, for information and guidance on the National Council of Interior Designers Qualification, of which he was National Chairman; *Richard A. Rankin*, ASID, IDEC, then National Chairman for the Foundation for Interior Design Education Research, for his many lengthy letters to me; *Ben Beckman*, FASID, then President of the New York Chapter of ASID, who helped me to obtain excellent color photographs showing work of the New York Chapter's professional interior designers;

Ola Pfeifer, then ASID Public Relations Chairman, who provided both color and black and white photographs; my fellow members of the New England Chapter of ASID individually, for the use of photos of their work and for their continued interest;

The late *Ben Cook*, FASID, whose constant interest and encouragement from the very onset was respectfully appreciated;

Ida Goldstein, associate member of ASID and designer for my

xi

firm, to whom I owe a special debt of gratitude; in helping to run an active business, she divided herself between working with the clients, assisting in my teaching, doing graphs of templates and glossaries, and keeping track of releases for the illustrations;

Edward Jacoby of Architectural Photography Group, for his excellent photographs of interiors.

Many manufacturers gave helpful interviews about their products. For their expert advice on furniture I especially thank *Dave Israel* of Trouvailles, Inc.; *Steven Kiviat* of Atelier International; *Chris Baitz*, New England Manager for Atelier International; *Leon* and *Irving Rosen*, owners and founders of Pace Furniture Company; *Knoll International Furniture*; *Mrs. Walter Gropius* for consenting to an interview on the philosophy of the Bauhaus School;

Derek Lee of Lee/Jofa Fabrics, for his invaluable help with the Fabrics section and for his continued interest in advancing the education of future students;

For expert advice on lighting, *Gertrude Winchel*, NHFL (National Home Fashions League) and *Lee Bierly*, ASID; *Frances Davison*, NHFL, of V'soske Rug, for sharing her knowledge of rugs; my *New England Chapter of the NHFL* for their individual and Chapter support; and the staff of the *DeCordova Museum*, where I am a member of the faculty, for their interest.

To many more valuable contributors of information and material in every area of interior design, and to the people from all over the country who supported my endeavor, thank you.

HELENE LEVENSON
A.S.I.D., NHFL

How to Use This Book

Interior design is a creative art, an aspiration to a higher level of living. But changing a vision into a reality is not an easy accomplishment; to realize such a vision requires skill and knowledge. In laying the groundwork, you need to learn the basic elements of good design. You then add your own imagery and magic to create enchantment.

The sections of *Creating an Interior* are designed to be read in the order in which they appear. If read consecutively they will lead the reader step by step through the thinking that goes into a beautifully designed space. The text of each section is complemented by illustrations which are integral to the overall presentation.

Throughout this book, one central point lies behind all the information that is presented: the person—whether professional designer or individual homeowner—who sets out to make a room more pleasing must *begin with a plan*. The chief elements of the plan are three: awareness of the architectural features of the space to be designed; awareness of the actual tastes and instincts of the persons who will use that space; and awareness of the functions that the space must serve. Chapter 1 explains these elements of the fundamental plan.

Part I contains information in table form about style periods throughout French, English, and American history; following each table are discussions of the most important of those styles. These discussions present each style at a glance, embracing not only characteristics of domestic and institutional architecture, but also salient features of furniture design and developments in fabrics, floor treatments, and the use of colors. Following these three chapters on period styles, a chapter on contemporary style gives the roots and leading figures of modern architecture and furniture design. And finally, a chapter on adapting a room to suit a chosen style suggests ways to incorporate elements of the period or contemporary style that most appeals to a person in rooms that are both interesting and functional.

Part II deals with the planning and selection of furniture: starting with the psychology of space, one chapter tells exactly how to make a floor plan; another chapter describes the many materials and finishes available in traditional furniture; a third chapter traces the evolution of contemporary furniture, and gives examples of outstanding designs and new materials.

Part III tells how the eye sees color, and sets forth the major characteristics of color in pigment form together with the dominant systems of pigment nomenclature. A chapter on color schemes makes it possible for the reader to employ any of a huge number of proven schemes—or to branch out in imaginative variations—with happy results.

Part IV, on lighting, goes into the sources and qualities of light (which has become increasingly a central element in both architecture and interior design) and includes instructions for making lighting plans according to the precise functions of the areas involved.

Thus the plan has been conceived, the style selected, the layout and types of furniture determined, a color scheme and a lighting plan developed. Parts V through VII carry the reader or student farther into the actual planning of an interior.

Part V introduces the wide varieties of drapery and upholstery fabrics, wall covering materials, and window treatments, with sections listing specialized terminology for both fabrics and window treatments.

Part VI, on floor coverings, examines both machine carpet manufacture and traditional hand-weaving of rugs; describes the materials and weaves used in carpets and rugs; explores other floor-covering materials made of ceramic, vinyl, and wood; and contains a listing of floor-covering terminology.

Part VII brings the reader to a consideration of the finishing touches that complete the carefully designed room: mirrors, paintings, graphics, objets d'art, and accessories.

Part VIII will be of particular importance to the student planning a career in interior design: It focuses on the professional interior designer. Through words and pictures a selection of professionally conceived and executed rooms are described; and the history, goals, and functions of the vaious professional interior design organizations are presented in detail.

Glossary: The main glossary at the end of this book gives definitions for all words which may be unfamiliar to the general reader, words which may have two or more meanings, and words from foreign languages which have become part of the language of design. Any technical word encountered in the text (which is not actually defined in accompanying text) may be looked up in the main Glossary.

In addition, special lists of terminology relating to fabrics, window treatments, and floor coverings accompany the chapters which deal with those topics. These specialized glossaries may be used (like the main glossary) for reference; they will also serve as a quick learning aid as the reader approaches the areas they cover.

Bibliography: The bibliography, which will be of particular usefulness to the student of interior design, is organized according to subject category and includes not only books for further reading in all the topics covered in this book, but also a listing of magazines

important to anyone interested in the field.

If read in the order of presentation, the sections of *Creating an Interior* should provide the student or the lay reader with an orderly approach to design, a full array of basic information, and the tools with which to find out more about specialized subjects. The first step of all is the basic plan, and we shall take that first step in Chapter 1.

The Professional Approach to Interior Design

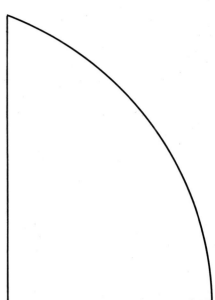

1

We live in an era in which the choices of styles and materials are almost unlimited. Magazine and newspaper articles, shops and antique stores have made the public very aware of fashions in design. Yet the average consumer intent upon furnishing a room has very little information about how and where to begin. Surprisingly, the initial approach is usually the wrong one. Often a single purchase is made with no thought of an overall scheme; and after many such purchases, the desired effect is not achieved.

BEGIN WITH A PLAN

My message is simple: *begin with a plan* and then follow it. There is always room for innovation and interpretation within the plan. A professional designer takes considerable time to capture the essence of the architecture, evaluate the client's instincts for color and style, and plan the entire project—long before he or she takes the first formal step toward achieving it.

Note the Architecture

The first impression of a room is of its overall size and shape. Note the personality of the room itself. Is it light and open, or closed and intimate? Are the ceilings high? What are the wall areas or decorative elements? Does the house communicate with its surroundings?

Many rooms can successfully be designed around their architecture, but they need not be. Backgrounds can be changed to suit personal preference. Whether you are influenced by an appreciation of the past or prefer the contemporary, you can transform a background in a multitude of fashions to create the desired effect.

I rarely find a room that I can't alter in some way or another. Chapter 6 of this book is devoted to such changes.

Know Your Own Taste

The individual has to take time to analyze his or her own taste; and similarly, it is the first responsibility of the professional interior designer to reflect the personality and taste of the client. A successful room is an interpretation of the particular taste and mode of living of the person or family who will use it, and sets the mood for the lifestyle of its inhabitants. It might be necessary for a very busy executive to have a comfortable retreat, a place to relax after a busy day. Such a retreat might be cozy, done in warm, calming colors, perhaps with bookshelves, comfortable seating, and a fireplace. This would differ greatly from the room used by a family enjoying a summer home. Here simplicity might be the keynote, with clear, cool, bright colors, cotton prints, and painted furniture. The choice is individual: a ski lodge, a farmhouse, a country house, a modern apartment, or a formal antique setting. Will the background create a sophisticated setting for formal entertaining, or will it create an informal atmosphere suitable for pets, children, and constant activity?

Your home is more than just a place to live; it should be a visual representation of your personality, filled by your awareness of who you are, a statement of your tastes in art, colors, memorabilia—with rooms that delight your eye and give you the happiness of being surrounded by all the things you love and enjoy.

Learn to follow your own instincts for things that visually appeal to you. You may admire your neighbor's home, but would it really reflect you? If you are a quiet, introverted person who loves to be surrounded by art and music and subtle colors, then follow your natural leanings. Perhaps you are an active, extroverted type, engaged in many activities; then you can be more dramatic, using bright, strong, clear colors. This takes some concentration on the part of each person if the designer is to successfully relate the client's individual taste to his or her environment.

The following example may be helpful. I recall a client who seemed to be successfully defying my conviction that people should be true to their own tastes. My first visit to the home of this genteel lady brought me into an aura of quiet restraint—one that had been assembled many years before and needed a new image. I associated the client with subtle, warm, sophisticated colors that would blend with her charming manner. She informed me that she had just seen a neighbor's home, finished in a striking, contrasting color scheme of black and white, and that she loved it.

Realizing that she was trying to make a new statement and wanting to give her home a new lift, I worked with her desires and planned a new color scheme of contrasting lights and darks. The plan was to paint her French furniture frames stark white and set them against deep chocolate walls. She claimed to love the effect, but somehow she just couldn't bring herself to place the initial order.

After she had made many visits to my office and explored many showrooms, I realized what her problem was. This time I showed her a color scheme of dark brown and white, but added to them many fabrics in soft shades of pale pink, brick, and rust tones. These softened the stark effect. She responded immediately, made her decision with conviction, and couldn't wait to get started. The house was finished with these colors accenting a lovely brick fireplace and illuminated by the sunlight that filled the rooms; and she has been happy with it ever since. The original image she liked was there, but changed to suit her own personality.

In order to accomplish this crucial step of knowing your own taste, do this: at the outset of a job, make a list of the things that you really like. This simple task will force you to think about yourself—or will help the designer to interpret the personality of the client.

Define the Function of the Area

After a total evaluation of your own personal desires, your next important step is to know the function of the space.

The functional requirements of an area would seem obvious to most of us, but it is still likely that an important element could be missing. If your lifestyle follows the usual pattern, it is important to have rooms in your home explicitly designed for their functions. A well-planned, comfortable kitchen, a bedroom retreat, an area for dining, and an area designed for your leisure activities are basic requirements. Your living needs might also include a formal living room, a recreation room, a library, or a studio. Or you might have to combine all of these in a small apartment.

Here again, a list of your personal needs will help determine the functional uses of the areas being designed. Is there a conversation area, whether large or intimate? Do you wish to see the TV from this area? Are the tables placed for the best possible usage? Has the necessity of proper lighting been considered? Where are your paintings, books, or collections to be housed? Does the room function well for your hobbies or activities? Could you serve a meal there? Is there space allotted to write at a desk?

After you have analyzed the functional requirements to your satisfaction, you are ready to envision the decorative possibilities of this functional space, and to select a suitable style. This is a rewarding step. With your overall plan in mind, you can get to know the hundreds of styles there are to choose from, and prepare to make your personal choices.

The style is one of the most important decisions you make as you create the setting for your own living area. In Part I we will summarize the parallel developments of styles in France, England, and America, from the Middle Ages to the mid-nineteenth century, in three successive chapters. In a fourth we shall see how contemporary style evolved from this historical background. The fifth chapter will indicate ways in which a room can be altered to enhance the style chosen for its furnishings and decoration.

PERIOD FURNITURE & DECORATION

History abounds with varieties of style, each with its own unique characteristics. The ability to recognize differences in styles will give you endless choices of possibilities for your own use and will make the study of interior design far more interesting and rewarding to you.

I use the term "style" rather than "furniture period" because my intention is to show you the total look of the period, not just the furniture of the time. The "style" of a room encompasses the room in its entirety, including its architecture, woodwork, wallpaper, fireplaces, colors, furniture, fabrics, floors, art, and accessories—an orchestration of many elements creating the total theme.

5

A working knowledge of important period styles will open new doors of appreciation for interiors—for viewing as well as for creating them. One must understand the old in order to fully appreciate the new. The designs of the great cabinetmakers of the past, for example, are still much loved today and still have a place in the current decorative scene. Many well-known interior designers have taken elements from the past and re-created them with minor changes to suit our present mode of living.

The professional designer's understanding of period design enables him to draw from his experiences and knowledge for the best possible results. As the artist studies the masterpieces of the past periods of art, observing how one style evolves into another, so does the designer study the history of his field. Even when his plan does not actually include period pieces, his working knowledge of the past enables the designer successfully to reach a higher level of contemporary design.

As in art, certain periods of furniture are considered better than others: the test of time is the deciding factor. Good design is lasting and can be appreciated for itself. Personal preferences, however, will enable you to choose the right style for yourself.

In Chapters 2, 3, and 4, study first the tabular listing of period styles. These tables provide basic facts: the dates of the periods, reigning monarchs (where applicable), significant stylistic trends and influences, and some outstanding examples of the styles mentioned. The most important of these styles are discussed in greater detail in the pages following the table: these are the styles that have been loved for centuries—and that remain influential to this day.

Chapter 5, which brings our study of style up to the present, does not contain an historical listing (since it embraces only the period from the late nineteenth century to the present) but follows the schools of art and architecture in Europe and America that have combined to influence and shape "modern" interior design.

Chapter 6 builds upon the familiarity with styles that the preceding chapters have established. In Chapter 6 we look at ways of changing the structural details of a room so that it will become the ideal framework for the style that the person who lives in that room has chosen.

The French Style

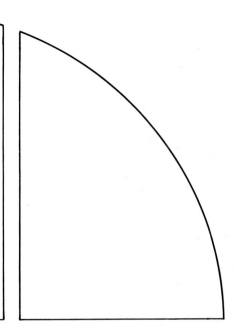

STYLE AT A GLANCE

In this chapter and in the two that follow, we first present a table that lists chronologically the major style periods, giving the dates, reigning monarchs where applicable, distinctive characteristics, and some outstanding examples.

The names and dates of certain periods are printed in boldface letters. These styles will be discussed in the pages following the table so that you can absorb the central information about historical background, architectural characteristics, furniture, fabrics, colors, and floors—all the aspects that combine to make a "style" at a glance.

FRENCH STYLE PERIODS

PERIOD/DATES	REIGNING MONARCH(S)	CHARACTERISTICS	EXAMPLES
MIDDLE AGES (1000–1484) **Norman/Romanesque (1000–1200)**		The Romanesque style began in France; in 1066 it was carried by William the Conqueror to England, where it was known as Norman. Cathedrals, the principal structures of the period, were often built with parts from ancient Roman ruins, or stone brought from distant areas. Rounded arches, separated by heavy columns, were a predominant feature.	
Gothic (1200–1484)		As was true of the Romanesque style, many famous churches and cathedrals were built during the Gothic period. Houses were built for comfort, with rough plaster walls, tapestries from Arras over windows and doors, and enclosures for beds. Ceilings had exposed beams; floors were stone, brick, or tile; huge projecting hoods were placed over the fireplaces. Wall panels of this period were vertical or linenfold (carved to resemble vertically draped linen). Furniture was made of natural wood, almost always oak. Design was vertical in its orientation.	Chartres Cathedral
Early Renaissance (1484–1547)	CHARLES VIII (1483–1489) LOUIS XII (1498–1515) FRANCIS I (1515–1547)	In this period French artists followed the lead of the Italian masters who worked in the new mannerist style. This style continued to influence French design as long as the Renaissance continued—well into the Baroque style of the middle 1600s.	Chateaux of Blois, Azay-le-Rideau, Chambord, Fontaine-bleau

PERIOD/DATES	REIGNING MONARCH(S)	CHARACTERISTICS	EXAMPLES
Middle Renaissance (1547–1589)	HENRY II (1547–1559) FRANCIS II (1559–1560) CHARLES IX (1560–1574) HENRY III (1574–1589)	The Italian Catherine de Medici, wife of France's King Henry II, was instrumental in bringing change to French styles by inviting to her court many Florentine artists. Gothic forms became less evident as the Italian influence increased.	Louvre Palace
Late Renaissance (1589–1643)	HENRY IV (1589–1610) LOUIS XIII (1610–1643)	In the Late Renaissance, the Italian Renaissance influence continued; but the influence of Spanish and Flemish artists and craftsmen emigrating to France brought a grandeur and elegance to the style.	
BAROQUE (1643–1700)	LOUIS XIV (1643–1715)	This was an era of magnificence and splendor. Furniture was massive in scale with heavily carved ornamentation. Rooms featured gilded paneling (*boiserie*) and large-scale tapestries.	Palace at Versailles
Regency (1700–1723)	LOUIS XV (1715–1723) Too young to reign Regent: Phillip II, Duke of Orleans (1715–1723)	These years, a period of transition, saw the beginning of curved forms and more delicate sculptured motifs. A less grandiose style than Baroque, the Regency look was keyed more to domestic taste than to court functions.	

FRENCH STYLE PERIODS (cont.)

PERIOD/DATES	REIGNING MONARCH(S)	CHARACTERISTICS	EXAMPLES
ROCOCO (1730–1760)	LOUIS XV (1723–1774)	Curved forms that had originated in the Regency continued to dominate but in a more delicate, feminine manner. Based on rock and shell motifs, designs became more graceful. New furniture designs made their debut, including the tea table; popular woods were fruit woods. Oriental influence appeared.	Painting by Boucher, Watteau, Fragonard
NEOCLASSIC (1760–1789)	LOUIS XVI (1774–1789)	A dominant influence was the Roman design discovered in new excavations at Pompeii and Herculaneum. Straight classic lines replaced the curved, and a revival of classical architecture became popular.	Petit Trianon Chateau
French Provincial (1610–1792)	LOUIS XIII LOUIS XIV LOUIS XV LOUIS XVI	Simplified versions of Louis XIII, Louis XIV, Louis XV, and Louis XVI furniture were made by local carpenters for the average person of modest means. Economics allowed little ornamentation, but the basic lines were those of the regal designs that the French Provincial style copied.	
Directoire (1789–1804)		In the transitional period following the French Revolution military motifs began to emerge. These motifs led into the Empire style.	

PERIOD/DATES	REIGNING MONARCH(S)	CHARACTERISTICS	EXAMPLES
EMPIRE (1804–1820)	NAPOLEON (1804–1815)	Military themes were created at Napoleon's request by French designers Percier and Fontaine as symbols of his victories. The motifs of the Empire style were taken from classic Roman and Greek designs.	Palais Royal, Tuileries
Restoration (1830–1870)	LOUIS XVIII CHARLES X LOUIS—PHILIPPE NAPOLEON III	In this period, machine manufacturing came into existence, starting a decline of French furniture. Styles were copied from late eighteenth-century designs.	

THE BAROQUE STYLE (1643–1700)
Reign of Louis XIV (1643–1715)

Historical Background

This was a regal age—France was the most powerful state in Europe, both in the military and in the arts. Louis XIV was the master of France. He called himself "the sun king," and under his reign France developed as the cultural center of Europe. The arts flourished, with a magnificent standard of excellence. The supreme architectural achievement of the reign of Louis XIV was the building of the palace and gardens at Versailles. Skilled artists and craftsmen were brought from all over Europe to combine their talents in the embellishment of the palace.

Architectural Characteristics

With classic proportions, and using gilded and heavily carved woods, the rooms at Versailles were of vast dimensions, designed for entertaining large groups. Characteristics of massive size, great splendor, and elaborate details are indicative of the Baroque style. Ceilings were heavily ornamented.

Figure 2-1: Armchair.

Figure 2-2: Massive, carved limestone mantelpiece, Normandy, France, about 1500. (The Metropolitan Museum of Art, The Cloisters Collection.)

Furniture

The furniture, in keeping with Baroque massiveness, was opulent. Some was of pure silver; some was carved and gilded in oak. Chairs were thronelike in design, with high backs. Legs of chairs were turned baluster or curved, usually joining in a crossbar.

Fabrics

In upholstery, as in drapery, fabric patterns were large, with strong figures contrasting in tone to background. Favorite fabrics were brocades, damask, and satin tapestry weaves.

Colors

Colors were strong, with bold reds, blues, and greens.

Floors

Floors were often marble, stone, or inlaid parquetry in a basket-weave pattern. A Savonnerie or Aubusson carpet was often used over a wood floor.

Figure 2-3: Drawing room at The Elms, Newport, R.I., in the style of Louis XV, with 18th-century Savonnerie carpet; Louis XVI furniture upholstered with Beauvais tapestry depicting fables of La Fontaine. (The Preservation Society of Newport County, Newport, R.I.)

Figure 2-4: Flat-top writing desk (bureau semainier).

13

THE ROCOCO STYLE (1730–1760)
Reign of Louis XV (1723–1774)

Historical Background

Under Louis XV, France entered a frivolous and voluptuous period, bringing a wave of fantasy into decoration. Madame de Pompadour, who remained royal mistress to the king for twenty years, exerted the greatest influence in the fields of art, furniture, and cabinet design, ceramics, and Oriental imports. She contributed financially to the excavations in Herculaneum and Pompeii, and patronized many skilled artists in Europe to further her own interests in the decorative arts. The term "rococo" derives from the combination of two French words: *rocaille*, meaning rustic ornamentation, and *coquille* which means shell. The motif of the shell used as decoration in many forms became synonymous with this style.

Architectural Characteristics

An obvious characteristic of Rococo architecture was the use of flowing, curved forms, replacing the straight line. This period saw the emergence of decorative wall panels in the Chinese manner and hand-painted wallpaper. Mantels were made of marble with overmantels (known as *trumeaux*) combining woodwork, mirrors, and painting.

Figure 2-5: Armchair (bergère).

Furniture

Rococo furniture was fanciful, based on rock and shell motifs, and designed to fit the human body, rather than for splendor alone. The characteristic leg was curved, flowing in an unbroken line. Cabinets had flowing, bulging fronts known as *bombé*. Enrichments of marquetry (decorative surface designs made of wood veneer pieces), carving, and lacquer were used. Various types of fruitwood appeared, and painted furniture was used in pale and neutral tones. New styles appeared: the *bergère*, or duchess chair; the chaise longue; and the tea table.

Figure 2-6: Serpentine-front commode.

Fabrics

Textile patterns were small, with ribbons, flowers, and shells in curved harmonious lines that blended with those of the furniture. Brocades, damasks, taffetas, satins, and silks were used. *Toiles*— printed cottons depicting pastoral scenes—were designed by the artist Oberkampk.

Colors

Fashionable colors of the era were light and greyed tones of soft green, blue, rose, and beige.

Floors

Floors of the Rococo style were in parquet patterns, marquetry, or marble. Rugs were usually Savonnerie or Aubusson weaves in Rococo patterns.

THE NEOCLASSIC STYLE (1760–1789)
Reigns of End of Louis XV
and Louis XVI (1774–1789)

Historical Background

The period of Louis XVI produced new furniture designs based on the excavations of Pompeii and Herculaneum, which had brought the study of archaeology into fashion. Architects and artists followed suit with new classical lines. Now straight lines replaced the curved. The foremost work of the day was the Royal chateau, the Petit Trianon, built at the suggestion of Madame de Pompadour.

Figure 2-7: Armchair (bergère).

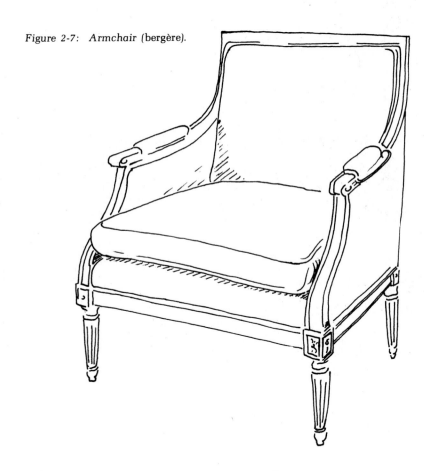

Architectural Characteristics

Architects treated interiors mostly with wood paneling, most often symmetrical in form. Panel centers in some rooms were painted or enriched by stucco relief patterns, most often of classical figures. Wallpaper and textiles were used to cover the walls. Mantels were mostly marble with a *trumeau*. Ceilings were usually left plain, or were painted with a cloud or sky effect.

16

Furniture

In furniture, proportions remained light and delicate, as in the previous eras, but the free curve was replaced with the straight line. The scroll foot disappeared; simplicity was the keynote. Other characteristics were marquetry, ormolu (metal coated with a goldlike finish), painted decorations, and gilt mounts. Chinese lacquer had its place in the finish of many elegant pieces. Cabinets were extremely fashionable.

Figure 2-8: Small table.

Fabrics

Upholstery materials were Aubusson tapestries, moiré, silks, needlepoint, damasks, brocades, and printed cottons.

Colors

Colors of the time were in many light tones, such as pale gold or terra cotta shades: soft tones, reflecting feminine tastes.

Floors

Floors were mostly in parquet patterns of oak, and covered with Aubusson, Savonnerie, or Oriental rugs.

THE EMPIRE STYLE (1804–1820)
Rule of Napoleon (1804–1815)

Historical Background

The Empire style took hold when Napoleon Bonaparte became Emperor of France in 1804. Its style, derived from the Grecian and Roman influences, was increasingly massive and elaborate. Built on heroic proportions, it created a background for Napoleon's power, eliminated both femininity and frivolity, and introduced a dignified masculinity to design. Charles Percier and Pierre Francois Leonard Fontaine were appointed as government architects, and worked on elaborate renovations of buildings such as the Louvre and the palace at Versailles.

Figure 2-9: Armchair with open arms (fauteuil).

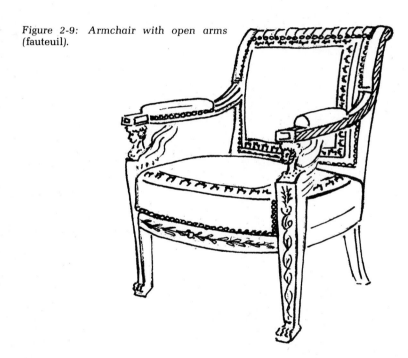

Furniture

Furniture was designed to look as if it had been created for Caesar. In a large, heavy scale, with masculine overtones, wood pieces were in ebony or deep red mahogany and redwood, and highly polished. They were richly embellished with many motifs from antique or military sources, including swans, eagles, lions, laurels, caryatids, swords, and spears. Inlays of wood or silver were used, and gilding was often applied. *Guéridons*—round tables with marble tops—were supported by one central leg. The characteristic Empire bed was shaped in a boat or gondola design. Armchairs of the period had concave backs, straight front legs, and curved back legs. Arm designs were often mythological birds and beasts.

18

Architectural Characteristics

The decoration of Empire rooms was inspired by Pompeiian design, consisting of pilasters, columns, cornices, and friezes. Walls were wood paneling or wallpaper, sometimes painted plaster, decorated with classic motifs and finished in a polished effect. Marble mantels, also classical, were often supported at each side by caryatids (columns that are actually female figures). Windows typically had two or three sets of complicated drapery with elaborate valances, fringes, tassels, and swags.

Fabrics

Fabrics were rich silks, satins, moirés, damasks, velvets, and lampas. Their patterns were victory wreath designs, laurel sprigs, and, typically, the initial "N" with a bee (Napoleon's emblem) surrounding a rose.

Colors

More brilliant, darker colors than earlier were used, as were stronger patterns. Green, yellow, blue, red, and purple were seen; gold thread was used in the weave and also as a trim to the drapery treatment.

Floors

Inlaid parquet floors or black and white marble squares were created in elaborate patterns. Otherwise, an imported Turkish carpet or Aubusson rug usually covered the floor.

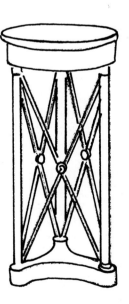

Figure 2-10: Guéridon *table.*

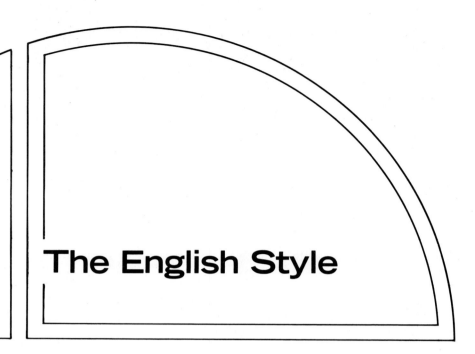

The English Style

3

THE ENGLISH PERIODS

The English periods are sometimes divided according to the woods most prominently used at the time:

○ The Age of Oak, about 1500 to 1680
○ The Age of Walnut, about 1680 to 1710
○ The Age of Mahogany, about 1710 to 1770
○ The Age of Satinwood, about 1770 to 1820

In the table that follows, once again, the names, dates, monarchs, characteristics, and examples of the English style periods are presented in chronological order. The styles named in boldface letters will be discussed in greater detail in the pages following the table.

ENGLISH STYLE PERIODS

PERIOD/DATES	REIGNING MONARCH(S)	CHARACTERISTICS	EXAMPLES
MIDDLE AGES **Norman** **(1066–1154)**		When the Normans invaded England in 1066, they found native Saxons inhabiting wooden huts with little furniture. Stone houses were then built, with rounded arches. The main piece of furniture was the hollowed-out log, used as both seat and bed, as well as for storage.	
Gothic **(1200–1500)**	HENRY VII (1485–1509)	Great Gothic cathedrals were being built 150 years after the Norman invasion, and homes and furnishings were finally given some needed attention. Linenfold carving (wood carved to resemble formalized folds of linen) made its appearance in the latter part of the era. Other carved and heavy-proportioned furniture was added, usually in oak. Trestle tables, benches, stools, and hutches were the principal furnishings. Wall tapestries, designed to keep out drafts, began to be used in this period.	Salisbury Cathedral
EARLY RENAISSANCE **(1500–1660)**		During this period, which opened the Age of Oak, the rebirth of secular culture that had begun in Italy a century earlier began to be felt in England.	
Tudor **(1500–1558)**	HENRY VII (1485–1509) HENRY VIII (1509–1547) EDWARD VI (1547–1553) QUEEN MARY (1553–1558)	The transition from the Gothic to the Tudor period showed in many ways. Castles gave way to country houses of brick and stone in irregular shapes; rooms were spacious and austere; windows were built with pointed arches. Fireplaces were of great importance for warmth, as were tapestries. Walls were paneled in oak.	Hampton Court Palace

ENGLISH STYLE PERIODS (cont.)

PERIOD/DATES	REIGNING MONARCH(S)	CHARACTERISTICS	EXAMPLES
Elizabethan (1558–1603)	ELIZABETH I	This was also a transitional period. During this time, the classic forms of the Roman architect Palladio, brought back to England by the great English architect Inigo Jones, began to be influential. Elaborately carved furniture made of English oak was large and heavy, best described as Gothic with influences of the more gentle forms of the Renaissance.	
Jacobean (1603–1649)	JAMES I (1603–1625) CHARLES I (1625–1649)	Little new furniture was created during this time of political unrest—ending in the Civil War, when Charles I was beheaded and Oliver Cromwell, a commoner, took over the rule of England and made it a Commonwealth. Furniture was similar to that of the Elizabethan style, but of smaller proportions. Oak continued to be of importance in the design of these pieces.	Bromley-By-Bow England Coleshill Birkshire Holland House, London
Cromwellian (1649–1660)	OLIVER CROMWELL (1653–1658) RICHARD CROMWELL (1658–1659)	The Puritan Cromwells' forms of luxury was reflected in homes and furnishings. There was a plainness of line, although cushions and pads were added for seating comfort. This furniture was important because it was the design copied in the American Colonies, now known as Early American.	
MIDDLE RENAISSANCE (1660–1750)		Ushering in the Age of Walnut, this period is marked by the restoration of Charles II to the throne. His taste, shaped by styles of different countries visited during his exile, influenced the development of furnishings in the following years.	Horace Walpole Strawberry Hill Home

PERIOD/DATES	REIGNING MONARCH(S)	CHARACTERISTICS	EXAMPLES
Restoration (1660–1689)	CHARLES II (1660–1685) JAMES II (1685–1688)	This period featured a formality of design. The woodcarver Grinling Gibbons was responsible for much of its beauty. Along with Christopher Wren, he created designs for Windsor Castle. Together they worked on many famous London churches, including St. Paul's, as well as many English estates.	Windsor Castle, St. Paul's Cathedral
William and Mary (1689–1702)	WILLIAM III and MARY II	The Dutch husband of Queen Mary II, William of Orange, introduced to England the Dutch cabinetmakers, including Daniel Marot, favorite cabinetmaker of Louis XIV of France. Mary, with her love of collecting Chinese porcelains, had Marot build opened walnut cupboards to house them. Thus the tastes of both rulers influenced the beautiful furniture designs of this period. Most characteristically known as the AGE OF WALNUT.	Christopher Wren remodeled Hampton Court Palace
Queen Anne (1702–1714)	QUEEN ANNE	The Queen Anne style was one of grace and intimacy, with simplified interiors. The curved line, typically illustrated in the familiar Queen Anne splat-back chair, influenced furniture design. Walnut was now the favorite wood.	
Early Georgian (1714–1750)	GEORGE I (1714–1727) GEORGE II (1727–1760)	This period is the beginning of the golden age of English design, the Georgian era, which lasted from 1714 until 1830. The furniture from the start of the period was a heavier type of Queen Anne, and mahogany was used instead of walnut. Early Chippendale work made its appearance in this period.	Chiswick House England

ENGLISH STYLE PERIODS (cont.)

PERIOD/DATES	REIGNING MONARCH(S)	CHARACTERISTICS	EXAMPLES
LATE RENAISSANCE (1750–1830)		The Age of Mahogany gives way to the AGE OF SATINWOOD in the Late Renaissance period.	
Middle Georgian (1750–1770)	GEORGE II (1727–1760) GEORGE III (1760–1820)	Thomas Chippendale (1718–1779), the first cabinetmaker to have his name associated with a furniture style, dominates English design of the Middle Georgian period. Using elements from all past periods, he was not an innovator, but a borrower. From the French Rococo style he took the motifs of rocks, shells, ribbons, and scrolls. From the Gothic he adapted suggestions of columns. From the Chinese he borrowed the pagoda. These exotic forms, translated into his unique new style, won him great acclaim. Chippendale used chiefly mahogany because of its adaptability to carving.	
Late Georgian (1770–1810) Adams Sheraton Hepplewhite	End of GEORGE III (1820)	Robert Adam was a predominant figure in this period. With his strong belief in an overall unity of architecture and furniture design, he led the classical revival, which paralleled developments in France under Louis XVI during the same period. George Hepplewhite led in building furniture of delicate proportions, cooperating with the Adam brothers by producing furniture they had designed. Thomas Sheraton, designer of original furniture produced by other cabinetmakers, flourished at the same time. The frequent use of satinwood causes this period sometimes to be referred to as the Age of Satinwood.	Somerset House, Church of St. Martin's-in-the-Fields, London

PERIOD/DATES	REIGNING MONARCH(S)	CHARACTERISTICS	EXAMPLES
Regency (1810–1820) French Empire Industrial Age (1830–1837)	GEORGE III GEORGE IV (1820–1830) WILLIAM IV	This period paralleled—and was influenced by—the French Directoire and Empire periods. Simple designs of masculine shapes, with motifs borrowed from the Greek, Roman, and Egyptian sources, characterized this style.	Royal Pavilion, Brighton; Regent's Park, London
Victorian (1830–1901)	VICTORIA (1837–1901)	Bulky, overdecorated, and full of superfluous details, this period is nicknamed the "gingerbread era." These years saw both a Gothic revival in aesthetics and the beginning of the industrial period.	House of Parliament; Crystal Palace, London

Figure 3-1: Dining room from Lansdowne House, Berkeley Square, London, 1765-1792. Designed by Robert Adam, painted gray with white ornament; marble fireplace, mahogany doors. (The Metropolitan Museum of Art, Rogers Fund, 1932.)

25

THE TUDOR STYLE (1500–1558)

**Reigns of Henry VII (1485–1509),
Henry VIII (1509–1547),
Edward VI (1547–1553),
and Mary (1553–1558)**

Historical Background

When Henry VIII broke with the Roman Church, he brought Italian craftsmen to England. This Renaissance influence departed from Gothic forms and introduced softer lines and more decoration to the plain furniture. This was a transitional period, in which Gothic castles gave way to country homes, and the English Tudor style developed.

Architectural Characteristics

Many large houses were built in irregular shapes around courtyards. The rooms were large and austere, often planned in the shapes of letters L, E, and H. Bay windows were used, many still in Gothic style, with diamond-shaped panes separated by strips of lead. Influences of the Italian Renaissance continued in the shapes of pilasters and columns, surrounded by oak paneling. Fireplaces were prominent. The introduction of the pointed Tudor arch was seen in heads of doors, fireplace openings, and other decorative areas. Walls were of rough plaster with oak wainscots, and ceiling beams were exposed.

Furniture

Furniture was still large and heavy and strong enough to hold men in suits of armor. Styling was masculine and simple in effect. Principal pieces were for practical purposes: tables, beds, cupboards, and wardrobes, continuing in the Gothic tradition.

Fabrics and Colors

In fabrics very little color or pattern was used; there were occasionally small patterns with designs of coats of arms. Neutral or natural shades were most frequently seen.

Floors

Flagstone or slate was used on floors, as were oak planks of random widths.

Figure 3-2: Tudor architectural detail.

THE QUEEN ANNE STYLE
Reign of Anne (1702–1714)

Historical Background:

During the rule of Queen Anne (who herself was neither influential nor interested in furthering the development of furniture styles), design in England flourished. This was a time of progress, both economic and political. Falling within the Age of Walnut, this period is chiefly important for the introduction of the curved line in furniture.

Figure 3-3: Slat-front secretary-cabinet.

Architectural Characteristics

In this period, the influential architects Vanbrugh, Hawksmoor, and James Gibbs designed many handsome buildings. Wall treatment often featured white painted paneling.

Furniture

The all-important curved line in the design of chairs was similar to the French style of the same period. The most popular pieces were highboys, lowboys, secretaries, writing tables, and wing chairs. The leading wood carver was Grinling Gibbons. Walnut was used, as well as marquetry, and lacquer pieces came into existence. The splat-back chair became the most distinguished piece of the Queen Anne period.

Fabrics

The Queen Anne style included rich fabrics, damasks stretched over bed frames, chintz, brocades, crewel embroideries, and needlepoint.

Colors

Colors of this period were true, clear tones.

Floors

Area rugs over wood floors are characteristic of this period.

Figure 3-4: Chair.

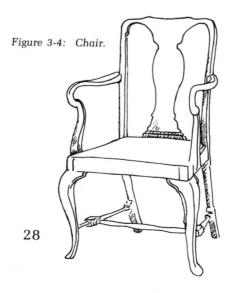

28

Historical Background

Covering portions of the reigns of George II and George III, the Age of Mahogany begins. With the French Rococo movement leading the way, the British aristocracy began to demand an English counterpart. Thomas Chippendale, a cabinetmaker in London, published a collection of furniture designs called *The Gentleman and Cabinet-Maker's Director*. Its popularity made the author the leading furniture authority of his time. He produced work for the greatest mansions in England.

Architectural Characteristics

Architecture continued the early Georgian styling. It was in furniture that the important evolution was taking place, and the furniture's design did not influence its background.

Furniture

Chippendale's designs were influenced by three sources: French Rococo, Chinese, and Gothic. His principal wood was mahogany because of its ability to hold carving and to be polished to a lustrous finish. Touches of gilt are used on his Rococo-inspired tables. Mirrors in the Rococo manner also became popular. Brass hardware and patterned moldings followed. In the Chinese Chippendale style, designs took to chinoiserie such as carved pagodas. The fretwork and Chinese motifs can be seen on most of his chairs and sideboards. Chippendale chair designs are the most renowned. They varied from splat-back to ribbon-patterned back to pagoda and tracery backs. Legs ranged from curved and heavily carved to straight and Gothic. Sofas looked like combinations of two or three single seats. The varieties of tables were almost endless. Chippendale designed drop-leaf tables, extension tables, dining tables, rent tables, tilt-top piecrust, and so on. His work was extensive throughout the period. The third edition of the *Director* made his name a byword in eighteenth-century furniture.

Fabrics and Colors

Middle Georgian fabrics included brocade, damask, leather, needlepoint, tapestry, velour, and velvet. Little change in choices of colors was apparent.

Floors

Rugs often were in Oriental design. Rugs with small patterns and in Chinese designs on blue grounds were typical.

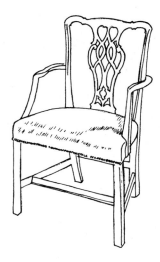

Figure 3-5: *Chippendale chair.*

Figure 3-6: *Breakfront bookcase.*

THE LATE GEORGIAN STYLE
(1770–1810)
Reign of George III
(1760–1820)

Historical Background

The Late Georgian style flowered during the last years of the long reign of George III. Robert Adam, the brilliant English architect who was influenced by the discovery of the ruins of Pompeii, was a dominant figure in the period of classical revival to which he imparted his taste and philosophy. He advocated harmony in the relationship between architecture and furnishings—a perfect example of total style. His inspiration and influence had a strong effect on the leading craftsmen of the time; they, too, turned to the classics for their elegant designs. These craftsmen included the furniture designers Chippendale the younger, Hepplewhite, and Sheraton; the much-loved master potter Josiah Wedgwood; Italian painters; and the Swiss artist, Angelica Kauffmann, whose work can be seen in panel paintings.

Architectural Characteristics

Architects of this time, under the predominant influence of the classic ruins, turned toward designs of great formality and elegance. Adam, using these designs, created unity in walls, ceilings, floors, furniture, and accessories. Wood paneling was replaced by plaster walls, either in their natural white or in pale colors, enriched by applied plaster moldings or plaster relief in contrasting white. Circular and oval rooms were introduced. Slender columns were designed in the Greek style, and the classical motifs of urns, rosettes, swags, festoons, wreaths, and honeysuckle appeared. Mantels were of

Figure 3-7: Hepplewhite breakfront bookcase.

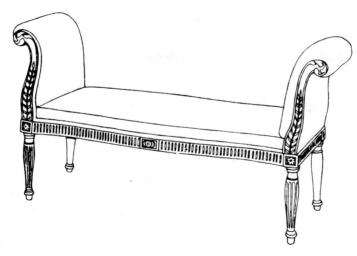

Figure 3-8: *Adam window seat.*

smaller proportion and were enhanced by the use of a decorative projecting shelf, under which might be a frieze of colored marble with a center panel carved in delicate figures or motifs. Ceilings, always in plaster, either plain or with superimposed ornamentation, were designed for a delicate effect. Artists of the time also painted some elaborate ceilings in larger interiors.

Furniture

Furniture designers, in accord with Adam's strong belief in an overall unity of design, strove to enhance their architectural surroundings; and leading cabinetmakers like Hepplewhite and Sheraton began making smaller-scaled pieces, more delicate in proportion than those of Thomas Chippendale. In chairs, straight, tapering legs replaced curved ones, while backs became oval, heart-shaped, and shield-shaped. Some upholstered backs were also used. Console tables made their appearance, gilded and with marble tops, and often decorated by Angelica Kauffmann or ornamented with inlaid woods or Wedgwoodlike plaques. Satinwood was now the popular wood.

Figure 3-9: *Sheraton chair.*

Fabrics

Textile designers produced fabrics to enhance the classic designs, such as figured moiré and satin, ribbon and tassel trims, and damasks.

Colors

Pale tones were fashionable.

Floors

Area rugs over wood floors continued to predominate.

Accessories

For the first time, decorative accessories became widely used. Because of the interest in an overall unity of design, each item from the architecture of a building to its smallest accessory became important. Collections of China, Delft, and Wedgwood porcelains appeared. Popular paintings were portraits, landscapes, and engravings by notables like Hogarth, Constable, and Wolstenholme. Mirrors, clocks, and marble busts helped to create the complete Adam style.

Historical Background

As Napoleon's power ended at Waterloo, England exchanged war for peace, and industrial production once again began to pick up momentum. The newly acquired wealth of the people had a direct bearing on the formulation of a style of opulence.

Architectural Characteristics

In architecture, the classic influence and appeal of the French Empire were still evident. With architect Sir John Soane leading the way, a new interpretation of the Greek style emerged—a bolder, stronger edition of the classic proportions. Plaster walls were painted in deep browns or reds, in contrast with Grecian white Doric and Ionic columns with gilded ornamentation.

Furniture

Classical forms were used in abundance in furniture of larger-scaled proportions, often designed with animal motifs such as lions. The typical "Grecian" sofa, with its scroll shapes and lion's-paw feet made from dark mahogany wood, is a prime example of this period.

Fabrics

Bolder, larger-scaled patterns were used on fabrics and wallpaper.

Colors

Contrasting colors, such as deep reds against clear whites and gilt, created bold effects.

Floors

Wood floors were covered with area rugs.

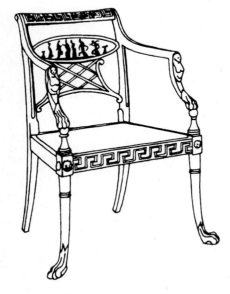

Figure 3-10: Painted armchair.

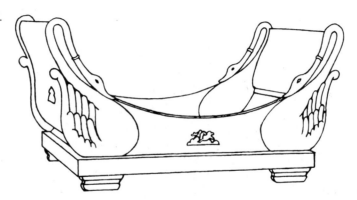

Figure 3-11: Sleigh bed.

32

Historical Background

In an era in which Great Britain reached its peak as a world power, Queen Victoria, ruling from 1837 to 1901, was considered one of her nation's greatest rulers. Her interest in art, however, was of lesser importance. While imperialistic expansion went on abroad, industrial expansion developed on the home front. Many years passed before it became evident that the Industrial Revolution had progressed too rapidly, causing aesthetic levels of architecture and design to decline during this period.

Figure 3-12: Sofa.

Furniture

Victorian furniture reflected many past styles—but the older designs did not adapt well to the new mass production. The French Louis XV style was most often copied, but, characterized by massive proportions and gingerbread ornamentation, the copies became clumsy and overdone. The decline in popular taste and a penchant for false magnificence resulted in a conglomeration of artistically poor furniture design. A variety of materials were used: mother-of-pearl inlays, gilded metal ornamentations, machine carvings, and even chairs made of papier-mâché.

Fabrics

An abundance of strong flower patterns in fabrics, wallpapers, carpets, and curtains prevailed. Well-padded, embroidered upholstery covered most seating units.

Colors

Bright colors were reproduced in machine-made textiles.

Floors

Strong patterns covered Victorian rugs.

Figure 3-13: Corner china cabinet.

The American Style

In this chapter, study first the table, which gives the chronological listing of American styles (without, of course, reigning monarchs). In the pages following are detailed discussions of each style listed in the table.

Figure 4-1: Cedar bedroom, Hunter House, Newport, R.I. Left to right: 18th-century four-post bedstead; Chinese Chippendale Townsend-type card table; Queen Anne tilt-top table; pair of Newport Chippendale side chairs by Townsend; Newport Queen Anne lowboy, c. 1750-1760; American Chippendale mirror, c. 1760-1790; Philadelphia Chippendale daybed with Gothic splat back; Newport Chippendale armchair attributed to Townsend—all in mahogany. (The Preservation Society of Newport County, Newport, R.I.)

THE AMERICAN STYLE

PERIOD	DATES	CHARACTERISTICS	EXAMPLES
EARLY AMERICAN OR COLONIAL	**1608–1720**	The furniture called Colonial, made primarily in Virginia and New England, reflected the English trends of the seventeenth century. With limited tools and facilities, American carpenters produced furniture that was simpler and smaller in scale, and that had less embellishment than that of its English counterparts.	Capitol, Williamsburg, Va. Parson Capen House, Topsfield, Mass. Restoration—Sturbridge Village, Sturbridge, Mass.
GEORGIAN	**1720–1790**	Furniture design advanced in the United States to produce sophisticated copies of English Queen Anne, Chippendale, Georgian, and Hepplewhite. Walnut and maple were the most widely used woods.	Restoration in Williamsburg, Va. St. Paul's Chapel, New York; houses at Charleston and Philadelphia, e.g., the Samuel Powel House, Phil.
FEDERAL	**1790–1820**	The influence of the English furniture designs of Hepplewhite and Sheraton continued, together with that of French Directoire and Empire designs. The Federal American period also took the classic forms of the classic revival. Mahogany, rosewood, and cherry were used.	Samuel McIntire houses, Salem, Massachusetts; Monticello; the Capitol, Richmond. Charles Bulfinch houses, Boston White House plans made by HOBAN.
GREEK REVIVAL	**1820–1860**	The French Empire influence continued to dominate this period, as well as the English Regency. Greek themes were apparent everywhere.	Rufus King House, Albany, N.Y.
VICTORIAN	**1840–1880**	With the beginning of the industrial era, machine-made details became inferior to those that had been produced by skilled craftsmen. Spindles, columns, and grilles became too overdone to be of any aesthetic value.	Trinity Church, Boston by H. H. Richardson

THE EARLY AMERICAN STYLE (1608–1720)
Virginia (1608–1720) and
New England (1620–1720)

Historical Background

Political conditions in England under James I led some people to protest against what they considered to be religious tyranny. This precipitated their migration to North America. These Pilgrims, primarily of modest origins, brought with them their cultures and mores. In their tastes the influence of the English style was clear, even though it had to be crudely adapted to a new environment. The settlers were predominantly English, although North America also attracted people from other nations—Spain, France, Germany, and Holland. However, after the Navigation Acts of 1651, which restricted the colonists' trade with countries other than England, the English style took precedence in America.

Architectural Characteristics

Early colonial houses, built of wood, were purely functional dwellings. The limited available materials and craftsmen created a picturesque style of unique characteristics. Necessity dictated the use of a single area that served as living, eating, and sleeping space. The dominant walled brick fireplace was flanked by plain vertical boards. Building components such as ceiling beams and wall support structures were left exposed and unpainted. Plaster, when it was used, was painted white; windows were small and shuttered, or had small diamond panes.

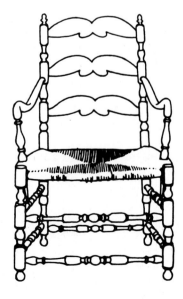

Figure 4-2: Ladder-back armchair.

Furniture

Furniture, executed by local carpenters, followed the pattern of functional necessity, using smaller and more primitive adaptations of English Jacobean and Restoration designs. Indigenous woods of many types—such as oak, walnut, pine, beech, ash, cedar, cherry, and maple—were used, either alone or in combinations in a single piece of furniture. Furniture was solid, with heavy proportions. Great varieties of pieces were available: chests, cupboards, highboys, tables (such as butterfly trestle, gate-leg, chair-table, and drop-leaf), chairs in ladderback, turned, or wainscot style; four-poster beds, trundle beds, and wooden candle stands.

Figure 4-3: Butterfly table.

Fabrics

Handwoven textiles were used sparsely. Imported silks, needlepoint, and embroidery were used on their cushions.

Colors

Room colors followed the natural colors of building materials: brick, stone, wood. Fabrics were in clear primary colors.

Floors

Floors were made of wide wood planks, either left bare or covered with area rugs.

THE GEORGIAN STYLE (1720–1790)

Figure 4-4: Bedroom, Richardson House, East Brookfield, Mass., 1748. (Old Sturbridge Village Photo by Donald F. Eaton.)

Figure 4-5: Highboy.

Historical Background

As prosperity continued and immigration increased, the American colonies sought to express more culture and style. Modeling their work after the taste of the English aristocracy, colonial craftsmen developed a remarkable ability to reproduce or interpret the furniture they saw in the many illustrated manuals published in England. Architecture followed this advancement, aiming toward the more luxurious living of the English Renaissance styles.

Architectural Characteristics

Architecture in various areas followed the same general symmetrical plan, but developed differently according to available building materials. Brick homes in the Southern states became imitations of English Georgian mansions, while the New England style was of stately wood construction; stone architecture took precedence in New York. Paneled rooms with fine detailing, higher ceilings with concealed beams, and large-scaled windows and doors created an open, spacious look.

Furniture

Furniture designs, in keeping with the trend of increased architectural embellishment, were variations of the Queen Anne, early Georgian, and Chippendale styles. Chair characteristics were the cabriole leg with various club, claw-and-ball, or lion's-paw foot. Regional characteristics became evident. For example, Boston furniture was light and delicate; Newport's furniture had a simple look; New York's designs were heavier; and Philadelphia furniture showed more elaborate detailing in famous mahogany chairs, highboys, and lowboys in the early Georgian style. Later, Hepplewhite and Sheraton furniture was produced in mahogany and satinwood.

Figure 4-6: Edenton bedroom, Blair-Pollack House, Edenton, North Carolina, c. 1766; in Museum of Early Southern Decorative Arts, Old Salem Restoration, Winston-Salem, North Carolina. Chippendale side chair and armchair, piecrust pedestal-base table. (Brunschwig & Fils, Inc.)

Fabrics

Many fabrics were used. Some were imported, such as silk damask, brocades, printed cottons, chintzes, and toile-de-Jouy; and many hand-loomed wools, linens, and cottons were made at home.

Colors

Lighter, open, more spacious effects were achieved with light, subtly grayed color tones.

Floors

Stained wood floors were covered with Oriental rugs in the most luxurious homes, while smaller dwellings used home-made hooked or braided rugs.

Figure 4-7: Wing chair.

Figure 4-8: Room from Kittinger Furniture's Williamsburg Collection. Queen Anne wing chair; 18th-century upholstered sofa; Queen Anne tea table. (Kittinger Furniture.)

39

THE FEDERAL STYLE (1790–1820)

Historical Background

The political upheaval during the period leading to the Declaration of Independence and the Revolutionary War strongly influenced the changing architecture of the new nation. Classical styles of Greece and Rome were characteristic expressions of the independence of the republic, as well as of its European heritage. Great men in politics, Jefferson and Washington, were instrumental in reviving Neoclassical as well as Gothic themes. Professional architects and designers made their first appearance on the American scene, and the scientific progress that would give rise to the Industrial Revolution began. These two influences created a great growth period in American style.

Architectural Characteristics

Inspired by the Palladian style, Thomas Jefferson designed the Richmond Capitol in 1789, and Monticello in 1809. Plans for the White House were designed by Hoban in 1792 while Charles Bulfinch of Boston and Samuel McIntire of Salem developed their own interpretations of Adam's classical style. Interiors were formal and symmetrical; circular and oval rooms were introduced. Elegant classical forms were seen in columns, pediments, mantels, and arches. Woodwork included detailed moldings. Predominantly straight lines, reflecting the work of Adam, Hepplewhite, and Sheraton, were apparent.

Furniture

Duncan Phyfe (1768–1854), the preeminent cabinetmaker of this period, left his mark in his delicate interpretations of Sheraton designs in mahogany and satinwood. Chairs with curved back legs, console tables with pedestal flared legs, lyre-back chairs, and sofas were synonymous with his name. The American eagle made its appearance at this time, was declared an official symbol, and began to appear as an ornamental motif everywhere.

Figure 4-9: Sofa-table.

Fabrics

Federal textiles made formal use of silks, particularly in stripes and delicate patterns.

Colors

Clear, delicate colors predominated in fabrics as well as room decoration.

Floors

Stained wood floors covered with Oriental or patterned rugs were popular. (See Figure 4–1 for an illustration.)

Figure 4-10: American Empire-style furniture, of the Duncan Phyfe type. (The Metropolitan Museum of Art.)

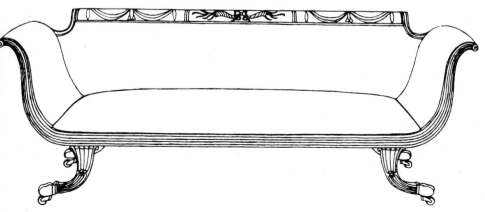

Figure 4-11: Sofa.

41

THE GREEK REVIVAL STYLE
(1820–1860)

Historical Background

The influx of books from Europe on architecture, furniture, and decoration began to influence American architects of the time, and adaptations of the French Empire style emerged in the United States.

Architectural Characteristics

The Greek Parthenon was the inspiration now for residential as well as public buildings. The American Empire style carried the Greek theme into ornamental design in interior trim: large Greek columns flanked doorways to rooms; pediments topped doors and windows; scaling became more massive.

Furniture

Greek Revival furniture developed a heavy, richly ornamented look, sometimes overdone in its efforts to take too much from many past styles, losing the simplicity of good design.

Fabrics

Fully draped silks were much used, in strong prints.

Colors

Strong, resonant colors echoed the French Empire style.

Floor

Made of fine finished woods, usually as background for quality area rugs such as Aubusson in Savonnerie.

Figure 4-12: The Victorian Parlor in the Wickham-Valentine House at the Valentine Museum was redecorated in the 1850s, at the height of the Rococo Revival period, and reflects the fullness of Victorian eclecticism. Medallion-back armchairs and tufted rosewood and walnut sofa are covered in the same deep rose wool damask as the draperies at the gilt-corniced windows. (Brunschwig & Fils, Inc.)

Historical Background

The cultural level of the times was reflected in the architecture and design of the Victorian period in America. With the coming of the machine age, and with manufacturers appealing to the tastes of the masses, this period became a symbol of industry, not art. Anything could be reproduced by machines, and usually was, so that styles overlapped each other. The result was the characteristically Victorian overdecorated and overelaborate style.

Architectural Characteristics

With its confused mixtures of Renaissance, Baroque, Gothic, and Greek, the architecture of the American Victorian period was, for the most part, badly designed. It was derived from many sources. In France, Napoleon had revived the style of the great architect Mansard in the new wings he had added to the Louvre; this was later poorly copied by American architects. One brilliant architect of the time, H. H. Richardson, designed Trinity Church in Boston, using Romanesque forms instead of the much-used Victorian Gothic.

Furniture

In this, the beginning of the age of machine production, furniture was of massive proportions, over-ornamented with superficial detailing and spindles, balusters, moldings, and trims. All-upholstered furniture, with metal springs, made its appearance at this time. These cushioned seats were finished with many elaborate trimmings. John Henry Belter was an outstanding cabinetmaker, and in great demand in the 1840s. His factory-made pieces consisted of frames covered with rosewood veneer, in an early laminated technique for which he held the patent.

Fabrics

Plushes and embroidered fabrics were favored for draperies and upholstery, with overly lush trims.

Color

Dark colors prevailed: black horsehair upholstery was often used, and typical fabric colors were bright red or green, often with gilt trims.

Floors

Because of machine production, rugs with pattern repeats became widely available.

COMPARATIVE FURNITURE STYLES

DATE	FRENCH DATE	ENGLISH DATE	AMERICAN DATE
MIDDLE AGES	NORMAN• ROMANESQUE	NORMAN 1066-1154	
	GOTHIC	GOTHIC 1200-1500	
		Henry VII (1485-1509)	
1400	**EARLY RENAISSANCE 1484-1547**	**EARLY RENAISSANCE 1500-1660**	
	Charles VIII (1483-1489) Louis XII (1498-1515) Francis I (1515-1547)	TUDOR 1509-1558	
		Henry VIII (1509-1547) Edward VI (1547-1553) Queen Mary (1553-1558)	
1500	**MIDDLE RENAISSANCE 1547-1589**		
	Catherine de'medici—Henry II (1547-1559) Francis II (1559-1560) Charles IX (1560-1574) Henry III (1574-1589)	ELIZABETHAN 1558-1603	
1600	**LATE RENAISSANCE 1589-1643**	JACOBEAN 1603-1649	
		James I (1603-1625) Charles I (1625-1649)	**COLONIAL 1608-1790**
	Henry IV (1589-1610) Louis XIII (1610-1643)		EARLY AMERICAN 1608-1720
	BAROQUE 1643-1700	CROMWELLIAN 1649-1659	
	Louis XIV (1643-1715)	O. Cromwell (1653-1658) R. Cromwell (1658-1659)	
		MIDDLE RENAISSANCE 1660-1750	
		RESTORATION 1660-1689	
		Charles II (1660-1685) James II (1685-1688)	
		WILLIAM & MARY 1689-1702	
		William III Mary II	

COMPARATIVE FURNITURE STYLES

DATE	FRENCH DATE	ENGLISH DATE	AMERICAN DATE
1700	REGENCY 1700-1730 Regency (1715-1725)	QUEEN ANNE 1702-1714 Queen Anne EARLY GEORGIAN 1714-1750 Sir Christopher Wren George I (1714-1727) Portion of George II (1727-1760)	GEORGIAN 1720-1790
	ROCOCO 1730-1760 Louis XV (1715-1774)	**LATE RENAISSANCE 1730-1830** MIDDLE GEORGIAN 1750-1770 Chippendale George II George III (1760-1820)	
	NEO-CLASSIC 1760-1789 Louis XVI (1774-1789)	LATE GEORGIAN 1770-1810 Adams End of George III Sheraton (1820) Hepplewhite	**NEO-CLASSIC 1790-1860**
1800	DIRECTOIRE 1789-1804 EMPIRE 1804-1820 Napoleon (1804-1815)	REGENCY 1810-1820 French Empire George IV Style (1820-1830) Industrial Age William IV (1830-1837)	FEDERAL 1790-1820 GREEK REVIVAL 1820-1860 French Empire Style
	RESTORATION 1830-1870 2nd Empire Louis XVII Louis Philippe Napoleon III	VICTORIAN 1830-1901 William Morris Victoria (1837-1901)	**INDUSTRIAL AGE** VICTORIAN 1840-1880 Arts & Crafts 1960
1900	Art Nouveau — 1900	**ARTS & CRAFTS 1860-1900** Art Nouveau Edward VII (1901-1910) Art Deco George V (1910-1936) George VI (1936-1952) Elizabeth (1952-)	ECLECTIC 1870-1925 Art Nouveau — 1900 ART DECO 1925-1940
	CONTEMPORARY	CONTEMPORARY	CONTEMPORARY

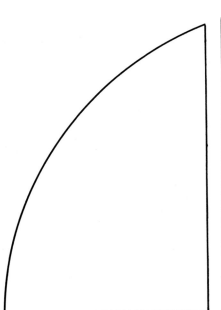

Contemporary Style

In the last three chapters we have summarized some of the most important characteristics of period styles in France, England, and America, through the Victorian era. With the coming of the modern age, national boundaries and historical periods begin to have less clear definitions. "Contemporary" style has its roots in the days of the Industrial Revolution and surrounds us today.

Travel is rapid now, and communication is instantaneous. Schools of art, architecture, and design now cross national boundaries and overlap each other chronologically—in a way that was impossible a mere hundred years ago.

For that reason, this chapter does not begin with a table of style periods. Instead, the schools and the individuals who have shaped both contemporary architecture and contemporary design (the two are now increasingly interconnected) will be discussed in a sequence that is necessarily only roughly chronological.

ARCHITECTURE AND INTERIOR DESIGN

Architecture and interior design throughout history have served a purpose beyond pure aesthetic appreciation. Together, they exhibit the thinking and way of life of the inhabitants. The study of civilization, mirrored in its art and architecture, allow us not only to come in contact with the past and to help in its preservation but also to understand and appreciate today—and tomorrow.

Our progressive technical advancements, coupled with our educated aesthetic values, have led us to the brink of great growth and change in all areas. We can choose from the heritage of the past and partake of the innovations of the future. This is a wondrous age in which to evolve new images in contemporary design.

The most important advancement in interior design in the twentieth century has been the emergence of the creative thinkers who had shaped our current architecture.

Architecture is the art of creating a building in an aesthetically satisfying manner, with an outer facade relating to the complexity of many purposeful interior spaces. A building is a composition of many elements: light, dimension, space—both negative and positive—shapes, colors, and textures.

If successfully executed, the outside proportions enhance the interior spaces. The outer structural forms are translated within, and windows or glass walls integrate the natural surroundings of the building with its interior. Proper use of indigenous materials and awareness of climatic conditions help considerably to determine the design of the interior and to produce harmony of a building with its site.

The character of the home or edifice is determined at the outset by the architect, then by the architect working in conjunction with the interior designer. Because of the necessity for the two professions to interrelate, many architects have become involved in the design of furniture as well as buildings. In order to understand contemporary design, it is imperative to have a working knowledge of its historical background and of the architects who have created it.

INDUSTRIAL REVOLUTION

With the onset of the Industrial Revolution, building materials that were produced by machinery were often badly designed. Gradually these materials took the place of hand-crafted components. It was only when designers of architecture and interior furnishings stopped trying to imitate past styles and started to devise proper uses of materials produced by machinery that architecture began once again to progress. The use of new materials developed through scientific means and engineering inventiveness—such as structural frames of iron, structural steel and concrete, and central heating—facilitated a new expansion of architectural possibilities. Wood and glass later became important elements of the new designs. The new idea that form should fit functional requirements became the criterion for beauty. Moralists cried out for the return of handwork, declaring that machine-made items were all of inferior quality.

Michael Thonet, 1796–1871

A well-known furniture designer, important in the development of contemporary furniture, Thonet was the first to succeed in combining aesthetic design with the processes of mass production. He is known especially for the bentwood chair, which he designed in 1840 and began mass-producing in 1870. The construction of this classic chair was made possible by the process of steaming (to soften) and then gracefully bending beechwood. Thonet's curvilinear wood chairs and rockers continued in production up into the 1920s, when designers of the time began to experiment with the curved line in metal. Thonet's company then was able to produce tubular steel furniture designed by Breuer, Van der Rohe, and Le Corbusier. Today, this company continues to produce well-designed furniture of bent-

47

wood, steel, aluminum, and even plastic. The technique of shaping many layers of veneer into heated molds is also attributed to Thonet. (Also see Chapter 9.)

ARTS AND CRAFTS MOVEMENT (1860–1900)

At the close of the nineteenth century, leaders of the arts and crafts movement urged that hand-craftsmanship should return to architecture and design, in place of machine-made products. Handmade items were more costly than the products of industry, but an ideal was established of honest craftsmanship. This reform movement, backed by many artists and architects, led to the founding of the Arts and Crafts Exhibition Society in 1888.

William Morris (1834–1896)

The leader of this new arts and crafts school was William Morris, who looked to the styles of the Middle Ages for his guidance. His contention was that that period had created craftsmanship of individual beauty that pervaded every aspect of daily life. He made his theories reality when he established his own firm in 1861. There, his craftsmen produced furnishings, wallpaper, and textiles in Morris' designs. In collaboration with architect Philip Webb, Morris designed the famous "Green Room" in 1867. This can now be seen at the Victoria and Albert Museum in London, England.

ART NOUVEAU (1890–1905)

Art Nouveau was style that took nothing from the past but was based on the rhythmic, flowing lines of plant forms. The Paris Exhibition of 1900 showed furniture and stained glass in this style. The Eiffel Tower employed ornamental ironworks in the Art Nouveau style.

James Bogardus (1800–1874), an American, developed a system of substituting iron columns for masonry outer walls. The skeletal structure of iron with glass filled in made the skyscraper possible.

Henri Van de Velde of Belgium was a nineteenth-century architect and furniture designer who is known for mass-produced furniture and graphic art.

Louis Tiffany, another American designer, is best remembered for his decorative art in metal and glass.

ORGANIC ARCHITECTURE

Three men provided the major impetus behind the progress of American organic architecture; in their work we can see the beginnings of fine contemporary residential design.

Henry Hobson Richardson (1838–1886)

Organic architecture grew out of the arts and crafts movement; and architect Henry Hobson Richardson was responsible for the beginning of this tradition, later taken up by Sullivan and Wright. Successfully combining the beautiful with the utilitarian, and conceiving the building as a whole, Richardson was a romantic who created simple, massive masonry forms, often with Romanesque overtones. Trinity Church in Boston is one of his finest works.

Louis Sullivan (1856–1924)

Sullivan was the first to phrase the concept "form follows function," a rule so broad that it has no exceptions. His work combined the strengths of modern engineering and artistic expression.

Steel frame, large expanses of glass, and natural ornamentation were the marks of Sullivan's work. The invention of the elevator and the use of steel were at the core of his skyscraper designs, with accents always on the vertical. After the fire that destroyed much of downtown Chicago, the way was opened for the construction there of many of Sullivan's buildings—including the Auditorium Building, the Gage Building, Walker Warehouse, and the Stock Exchange Building. During the first fifteen years of his career, Sullivan designed over a hundred buildings, but in the remaining twenty-four years he designed only twenty-two.

Frank Lloyd Wright (1869–1959)

A student of Louis Sullivan, Wright is considered the greatest architect of our times. He designed more than 600 buildings in a 66-year period. He carried the traditions of the arts and crafts movement, together with those of organic architecture, to their greatest heights. His genius was demonstrated time after time with each new building he designed, and his work can still be seen in many parts of the United States and abroad. Although Wright's designs date back as early as the turn of the century, his influence on today's buildings is marked, and will remain so in future years.

Wright's architecture was from the very beginning suitable to contemporary life. His original theory, which opened the way for modern building design, stated that architecture should be "organic": that is, it should develop from the inside outwards, incorporating materials, functional needs, and site.

Frank Lloyd Wright's designs are especially appealing because of his use of warm natural materials such as stone, brick, and wood in conjunction with their natural surroundings. His early work included buildings other than residential architecture: examples are the Unity Church (1906) and the Larkin Building (1904). Wright's prairie houses, built from 1893 to 1910, stressed horizontal lines and long, low overhung roofs. To build them he used wood, masonry, and glass. One of the best-known of the prairie houses is the Robie House in Chicago—built in 1909. The first of his Taliesin houses, designed for his mother, was built in 1911, near Chicago on rounded land instead of flat, and its design was based on the premise that the

49

house grows out of the land. Wright was involved with new types of construction, especially in poured concrete and precast concrete blocks. In 1911, he built his own home in Spring Green, Wisconsin and named it *Taliesin*, a Welsh word meaning "shining snow." His commission to do the Imperial Hotel in Tokyo (1916–1922), and its survival after the great Tokyo earthquake, brought still greater attention to him in America.

Wright incorporated elements of Japanese design in later work in his own country; one example, the famous Koufman House in Bear Run, Pennsylvania, was built when he was 70 years old, finished in 1936, it is better known as "falling water." His nonresidential work includes the Johnson Wax Tower in Racine, Wisconsin (1950) and the Guggenheim Museum in New York City, completed in the year of Wright's death, 1959.

EUROPEAN ARCHITECTURE (Post 1900)

Auguste Perret (1873–1954)

Auguste Perret was a French architect and the first person to make reinforced concrete, a material combining steel and concrete. His apartment building at 25 Bis Rue Franklin (1903) was the first completed work using a reinforced concrete framework. Perret's innovation made the creation of new kinds of architectural design possible.

DE STIJL (1917)

A group of Dutch artists and architects who were connected with the magazine *de Stijl* (which means *style*) started a new movement emphasizing clarity and order. This system of clean, abstract line and geometric spaces presented itself in the Dutch school of sculpture, architecture, and art. *Piet Mondrian* was one of the artists of this school; another was *Malewitsch*, a sculptor. The furniture of *Gerrit Rietveld*, also of this group, took nothing from past designs; it was angular, and painted in red, blue, black, and white.

THE BAUHAUS (1919–1933)

After more than fifty years of debate over philosophies of design, the arts and crafts movement at last was succeeded by a new concept— one that aimed for a complete unity of art and technology. This was the German school of design known as the *Bauhaus*. The Bauhaus has been the most significant force in all contemporary architecture that has followed. The main objective in this movement was the pure design of form following function, combined with proper use of the machine.

Walter Gropius (1883–1969)

Gropius founded the Bauhaus school when he combined the Art Academy and the Arts and Crafts School in Weimar. Soon the school moved to new buildings designed by Gropius, in Dessau, and there it became the international center for the arts. Its faculty included such notables as the painters Klee, Kandinsky, Albers, and Feininger; architect and furniture designer Marcel Breuer; textile designers; and scenic designers. Before the rise of Nazi Germany, Gropius went to England, then to the United States in the late 1930s. There he established an architectural practice in New England, and became chairman of the Department of Architecture at Harvard University. After World War II, The Architects Collaborative (TAC) was founded in Cambridge, Massachusetts to further the doctrines of the Bauhaus movement. Gropius was one of the most important figures of our times in his field.

Marcel Breuer (1902–   )

Marcel Breuer was a student of the Bauhaus who became well known for his furniture design. In 1925, Breuer invented the first tubular steel chair frame designed after Thonet's bentwood, and produced by Thonet Industries. (Also see Chapter 8.)

Alvar Aalto (1898–1976)

Aalto, a Finnish architect, continued the work of Breuer. In 1932 he took Breuer's chair of tubular steel frame and added a molded plywood seat and back, using white birch. (Also see Chapter 8.)

THE INTERNATIONAL STYLE

Ludwig Mies van der Rohe (1886–1969)

Ludwig Mies van der Rohe was a German architect who became the director of the Bauhaus after Gropius (1930–1933). In 1937 he came to the United States to become the director of architecture at Illinois Institute of Technology. His doctrine and his much-followed idea that "less is more" are indicative of his architectural style. He began the movement known as the International Style.

Because of steel construction, which allowed nonsupporting wall divisions, the buildings designed by Mies provided open, uncluttered spaces and allowed for large areas of glass or window walls. Not only the exterior but every detail of the interior was designed by Mies, including the furniture, tables, and chairs. The most famous of his chairs is called the "Barcelona Chair." His architectural achievements include the Exhibition Pavilion in Barcelona (1929); the Tugendhat House in Brno, Czechoslovakia (1930); the Farnsworth House in Plano, Illinois (1950); the Lake Shore Apartments in Chicago, and the Seagrams Building in New York. (Also see Chapter 9.)

51

Le Corbusier—Charles Edouard Jeanneret-Gris (1887–1968)

Although he was born in Switzerland, the painter and architect Le Corbusier studied and traveled so extensively that he became known as a French architect. He was directly involved in furthering the existence of the International Style in the 1920s. He was influenced both by de Stijl and by modern painters. Le Corbusier brought to architecture an artist's eye for abstract form and sculptural interest, as well as the Bauhaus philosophy of incorporating industrial technology and art. He wanted to create a functional living house; it was he who defined a house as "a machine to live in."

Characteristic of his style is the functional use of space, as seen in the Villa Savoye, built in Poissy, France (1929–1931). This is a "citrohan" house, the prototype single-family dwelling conceived as part of an entire urban setting. Typical of this house was the use of vertical space. A two-story living area, raised above the ground by free-standing columns or stilts, allowed for an opened plan for the interior. The windows of the Villa Savoye are long horizontal strips of glass. Because the house is raised one story, the ground is freed for circulation, while there is a flat-roofed area used for a garden and reached by an exterior ramp. Other architectural achievements include the Swiss Pavilion (1932) in Cité Universitaire, Paris, and the Carpenter Hall (1962) at Harvard University, Cambridge. (Also see Chapter 8.)

ART DECO

The Art Deco period of the late 1920s and early 1930s was named after the Exposition Internationale des Arts Décoratifs held in Paris in 1925. This was a modernistic but fairly superficial style. In Art Deco the simple lines of the Bauhaus were replaced by dynamic patterns, zig-zags, and energy patterns—all suggesting the explosive aggressiveness and vigor of modern machinery. The use of these patterns in surface decoration quickly reached its height on every machine-made article—from cars, furniture, textiles, paintings, and walls to skyscrapers like the Chrysler Building in New York. This style lacked the more serious intent of other twentieth-century movements. The Art Deco period combined the fantasy and humor of the post–World War I era with the influence of the cubists and dadaists.

Recently there has been a revival of interest in this period. Collectors both here and abroad have become aware of its unique qualities and the influence it has had on subsequent designs. Throughout the United States, preservation leagues are trying to prevent the demolition of buildings in the Art Deco style. Examples of this style of architecture include Radio City Music Hall in New York City, Houston City Hall in Houston, Texas, and older hotels such as the Plymouth Hotel in old Miami Beach, Florida. The Miami Design Preservation League is currently working to have portions of the old Miami Beach area declared an official site for restoration.

THE CALIFORNIA SCHOOL

Richard Neutra (1892–1970)

An architect born in Vienna, Neutra worked with Frank Lloyd Wright before opening his own architectural firm in California. The influence of the International style is obvious in his work, which largely consists of steel-frame construction, glass walls, and hard-edge design. Contrasting natural materials such as wood and bricks are also incorporated in Neutra's buildings. His architectural achievements include the Kronish House and the J. B. Nesbitt House, both in California.

William Wilson Wurster (1895–1973)

The American architect Wurster, along with Neutra, led the California school, and was not associated with any past school. Together they furthered the development of contemporary architecture in this country. Wurster follows the trend of blending the building with its site. Formerly head of the School of Architecture at the Massachusetts Institute of Technology, Wurster started his directorship of the School of Architecture at the University of California at Berkeley in 1960. Never stagnant in his designs, he has been quoted as saying, "There is always more than one answer." Among his better-known works are the residence of I. Schuman in Woodside, California (1949) and the Center for Advanced Study in Behavioral Science in Palo Alto, California (1954).

ARCHITECTURE TODAY

Using these fine examples of great architecture, as guidelines, many other fine architects have contributed to the growth of modern architecture, which continues to evolve into more exciting and complex phases. Although some do not represent specific schools, all phases are either influenced by the past masters or totally innovative in their approach. The following is but a list of prominent contemporary men working and producing our great current buildings of this century. Ongoing study is suggested to keep up with the fast trend of contemporary architecture.

Table 5–1. Architects of Today.

Well Known Internationally	*Now Internationally*
Bulfinch	I.M. Pei
Eliel Saarinen (1873–1950)	Kevin Roche
Pier Luigi Nervi	John Dinkeloo
Skidmore, Owings & Merrill	Arne Jacobsen
Eero Saarinen (1910–1961)	Sven Markelius
(Eliel Saarinen's son)	Richard Meier
Lawrence Perkins	Charles Moore
Philip Will	Robert Venturi
John Lyon Reid	Architects Collaborative
Edward Durrell Stone	Louis Kahn
R. Buckminster Fuller	Buckminster Fuller
Louis I. Kahn	Peter Cook
Kenso Tange	Warren Platner
Phillip Johnson	

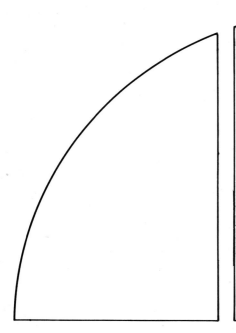

Adapting a Room to Suit Your Chosen Style

6

With the knowledge you have gained from our brief look at the major styles, you are ready to choose the best style for your taste. If you are creating a pure restoration with authentic period furniture and architecture, this is indeed a challenge and more research into your period will be necessary.

But for any other interior setting, pure authenticity is not only unnecessary but undesirable. The look, or essence, of a style is of greater importance. The main characteristics that create the mood are what you need to remember; it is for this reason that a general guide was given in the preceding chapter.

Will the theme of your choice be a country look, a formal French style, or perhaps an Early American decor? Will you search into the past for a Baroque or Empire style? Perhaps you might choose a contemporary look or an eclectic blend of styles.

Whatever your decision, your next step is clear. Now that you are familiar with the characteristics and dominant influences of the furniture style of your choice, look around you. Is the room you are going to design suitable for that style? In most cases the answer will be no. This certainly is not going to limit you, because there are many ways to create your own architectural background and translate your style choice to suit your own interior. This is an exciting challenge. I call it *setting the stage*. Defining the major elements of your style and interpreting them in your room will create your setting. Let's examine two "looks" that may give you an idea of what I mean by creating a setting: the country look and the formal look.

THE COUNTRY LOOK

The country look has been one of my favorites through the years. I have always been fascinated by the beauty and informality of furniture, fabrics, and architectural detail in country homes; in my search for decorating ideas, I inevitably find myself visiting restorations of the earliest homes possible. The appeal of these homes has awakened my appreciation of the simplicity of life in the past. The individual quality and beauty of things made by hand with loving care and skill are of special interest to me.

It was seeing this inspiration from the past that led me one spring to a search through the French countryside looking for a typical rural French farmhouse.

Very late one evening I pulled into a village so small that I never discovered its name. Of the dozen or so houses flanking the narrow main road, I noticed that one was an inn. The facade was nondescript, but I entered in hope of finding a place to spend the night. Reluctantly and apologetically the innkeeper said that there was an attic room, but that it had not been decorated. I was led up three flights of stairs, passing door after door of newly painted bedrooms, all with the same blond modern furniture, which the owners pointed out with great pride. Then we reached the top floor. To my surprise and delight, the attic room had not been modernized, but left in its own original French country style.

The furniture was old with the marks of time and the use of many years. The ceilings were dormer style with exposed hand-hewn, aged wooden beams. Flowing as if it were growing on a vine, a harmonious wallpaper pattern of tiny flowers covered all the walls and ceiling. A patchwork quilt covered the bed. The little old sink that stood in the corner was not there as a decorative element but as a practical one.

Sitting in the old chair with its heavy rush seat, I fingered the painted finish. For years I had been imitating the aged painted finishes of French country furniture, trying to make them look as if they had been painted 200 years ago with the paint worn thin in the areas in which hands had constantly rubbed, exposing the natural wood beneath.

Creating a House with Country Charm

Creating the illusion of a French country home seemed a difficult accomplishment in a suburban split-level home. The pictures show that it can indeed be done, however—even in a small, unpretentious house.

Architectural changes were necessary. With great enthusiasm, the project of transformation began. All moldings and the poor copy of a Georgian fireplace mantel were removed. Wallpaper was stripped and white plaster was used to surface the walls. It was applied in a heavy manner, as in country farmhouses, to let the beauty of the material work for itself. Square doorway openings were slightly rounded for a more natural flow. A fireplace hood was constructed and covered with white plaster, designed to curve gently from the ceiling down to a hand-carved French-style mantel, replacing the old one. This was finished in a white stain, rubbed off to show suggestions of bare wood underneath the surface, to give the effect of many years of use. The personality of the setting was beginning to emerge—a crisp, airy country look with the sunlight reflecting off the white walls.

55

Figure 6-1: Living room with country charm, seen from dining area. (Helene Levenson, ASID. Photo © Edward Jacoby.)

The ceiling was wallpapered in a country French diamond print in navy and white, and hand-hewn beams surfaced the ceiling paper.

The room had now been adapted to suit my decorating needs. To complete the look, an old formal French fruitwood frame sofa was then upholstered in the same fabric as the ceiling, only blue and white, quilted, and with a full-gathered skirt added. Plump oversized pillows were added in many patterns of blue and white cotton. The delicate French bergère chairs were enhanced by the use of a colorful harvest and navy blue print linen fabric, echoed in the drapery treatment. A high-back chair upholstered in a deep blue suede contrasted with the white walls, and the added materials of brass, pewter, glass, Chinese porcelain, and antiques brought the room into full focus. The result was a delightful country setting, comfortable and restful while still maintaining an ambiance of quality.

The Barn Room

A room created for a family retreat became an interior of unique personality and a perfect example of "creating a setting." The transformation of this basement area in a suburban house was influenced by nostalgia for a different type of country style, that of an earlier and more primitive environment.

56

Figure 6-2: The same, seen from entrance hallway. (Helene Levenson, ASID. Photo © Edward Jacoby.)

My intent was to approximate closely the one-room living area of early New England homes, complete with a wood-burning fireplace, cooking utensils, and dining and seating areas furnished solely for comfort and convenience.

Because of the lack of architectural features in this home, major changes were necessary to reach my desired goal. We purchased a 200-year-old-barn in Vermont and took it apart piece by piece, carefully saving all the component parts—including the weathered barn siding, beautiful huge hand-hewn beams, and rugged floor. These special elements were then carefully shipped to the house and prepared for the task of installation.

Many months of work by a competent and highly creative carpenter* were essential to interpret my designs. His ability to find a variety of old and unique building materials, and especially his innovative ideas in working with them, contributed a large measure of the success of this project. An interesting note is that during the entire time of construction, there wasn't a person viewing it who either liked or understood what we were trying to achieve, *until* it was all finished. Now there isn't a person, young or old, who isn't enchanted by the warmth and character of the room.

*Appleton Schneider

57

Figure 6-3: Brick-topped serving counter in the Barn Room. (Helene Levenson, ASID. Photo: Laban Whittaker.)

Figure 6-4: Siding from a hundred-year-old country barn is the background for an informal entertaining area. (Helene Levenson, ASID. Photo: Laban Whittaker.)

The effect upon entering the barn room is part of the charm itself. One follows the natural flow of the house down narrow stairs, passing walls paneled with the old barn floor boards, then a wall of old bricks set in a herring-bone pattern with deep grooving painstakingly dug out for an extreme dimensional effect. The way continues through an opening beneath an arch created from a wagon wheel, to the first view of a rustic setting, a reconstruction of the past, glowing with indirect lighting which highlights the natural rough texture of the aged barn siding set in board-and-batten style. The old beams crossing the ceiling in a pattern of squares greatly add to the charm of the setting. The old brick used on some walls is also used as counter-tops for easy maintenance, and a whole wall of uncut natural fieldstone completes the fireplace.

Half of the room accommodates the sitting area, with a deep, puffy down sofa covered in tobacco-colored velvet, flanked by a carriage seat covered in saddle leather and a loveseat in brown and red paisley. In the center of the sitting area is a huge round coffee table with a circular sawblade from a Vermont sawmill in its center.

Figure 6-5: In the Barn Room, a bar/flower sink in an unobtrusive corner serves both the room and the adjacent deck. (Helene Levenson, ASID. Photo: Laban Whittaker.)

The colors were chosen to go with the architecture, so shades of tobacco and saddle brown are prominent, and the floor is covered in a rug of brick-red color, echoed in the linen paisley in the laminated window shades. Blending with the red and providing accents are smaller amounts of orange and red-violet in toss pillows on the sofa.

A view of the woods behind the house is seen through large windows, and sliding glass doors provide access to a large wood deck to be used for informal gatherings.

The setting turned out to be perfect for primitive antiques. It became a family habit to search the New England countryside for artifacts from past years. The black iron stove, the carriage seat, the saw, pewter dishes, fireplace cooking utensils, antique scales, old paintings and books, and a country-store collection of old cans complete the convincing early New England setting. Added were hand-weaving and hand-crafted pottery.

A page from the past, a virtually indestructible room using materials that had served generations before, integrating all the component parts in harmony: such a room is timeless, waiting to gather new acquisitions introduced in future years.

An air of antiquity has been recaptured in a comfortable, livable room, simply by changing the setting. This room now stands untouched by further designing for almost 20 years.

THE FORMAL LOOK

The formal look, whether it be French, English, or even eclectic, is a style for the person with an eye for luxury and a reason to create an atmosphere that will make use of fine paintings, antiques, crystal, silver, China, and Oriental rugs. In a French setting, a look of beauty and elegance prevails. In an English setting, a quality of tradition and stability evokes thoughts of a lifestyle of culture and refinement.

Figure 6-6: The formal look, in a parlor of the Hunter House, Newport, R.I. Left to right: New England Chippendale pole screen with Florentine stitch needlepoint center; mahogany New England Queen Anne tea table, c. 1730-1740; mahogany Newport-type wing chair, c. 1740-1770; Georgian mirror (probably English) c. 1740-1770; 18th-century Waterford crystal candelabrum; mahogany Rhode Island Chippendale chest of drawers with rounded block front, c. 1760-1780; mahogany Newport-type Chippendale side chair. On walls, marbled pilasters and naturally colored cherubs' heads; on floor, Persian Kirman rug, c. 1850. (The Preservation Society of Newport County, Newport, R.I.)

The eclectic style combines the beauty of all worlds; it is never a purist approach.

To enhance period furniture, the use of proper architectural elements is a must. To adapt your surroundings to suit your chosen formal style takes thought and research.

Walls can be wood-paneled, one of the best backgrounds for a formal setting. French paneling is curved, gracious; English has stronger, straight lines. Beautiful woods are walnut, cherry and mahogany. Molding may be applied to paneling for additional contrast.

The use of fabric on the walls in a formal setting has many varieties. Walls can even be upholstered in silk, applied smoothly or draped in a full, gathered fashion. The use of wallpaper, as well as hand-painted murals, is prevalent in formal settings. Simple architectural moldings can be put onto painted walls; or glass or mirrored walls can reflect the other textures in the room. Doors can be changed, ceiling treatments can be ornamental in keeping with the manner of the period.

Whether you will be sipping champagne or enjoying afternoon tea with friends, the background is essential in a sophisticated formal room. The stage has to be set.

The country look and the formal look have been described in order to suggest how a designer thinks about the various elements of the room. First the style—the overall effect and tone—of the room is selected; then the designer must ask whether the room as it is will provide the ideal setting for that style. Often, this requires changing the actual shape, size, or details of the room.

CREATING ARCHITECTURAL CHANGES

In many years as an interior designer with a special interest in architecture and the general ambiance of an interior, I find that in creating the right background to set the mood or style, some architectural changes are often necessary. This is where your talent and creativity come into focus. Some rooms have no redeeming architectural features to speak of. To these, additions are necessary. Others have too many; sometimes by simplifying you may make the best of a room ("less is more"). In other settings, a designer may play up already good features to their best advantage.

Basic examples of this policy are simple. For the room with no interest, logical steps might be to redesign a fireplace; add beams, moldings, or paneling; or raise an area to become another level, with steps—creating a playpen area for sofas on the lower level. It is possible to change two small windows to a large bay window; lower ceilings, using mirror and lights; add wallpaper, murals, or wall treatments such as round-cornered walls of patterned herringbone brick; remove walls to create open spaces; or add walls or draped areas to create cozy nooks. Basically, if a particular style or period is to be used in the furniture and fabrics, then the architecture should set the pace, using the same elements that characterize this particular style, such as Georgian or Regency paneling, or stucco and beams for rural interiors.

61

For rooms with too many architectural features, removing some and leaving the rest to show to their best advantage is the key. For example, a room overdone with moldings shows off nothing, but you can leave the most effective areas and remove the superfluous ones (as in the Country Room section). Another example of this approach is a home that I recently designed, which had a large top-floor area with a cathedral ceiling and brick fireplace. Within this area were the living room, dining room, and sitting room, with walls separating them. We removed all the walls to create one large open conversation and dining area surrounded by window walls, giving a view of woods and of a full deck running the length of the house. This allowed all the essential architectural features, such as the cathedral ceiling, to be seen at once. A careful lighting plan was executed, using wallwashers, dimmers, and spots. Because the individual areas are divided by furniture groupings, the walls are not missed.

In rooms with beautiful architectural features, the designer can play up these features to their full advantage. For example, when the walls in a large room are painted dark, a white molding gleams like a jewel, showing off every detail. Even in period settings, this is very effective: painting the lovely detailed moldings of an English or Georgian room to set it off is ideal. Gray-blues or greens can pick up the colors of softly patterned papered walls extremely gracefully. On the other hand, if you are adapting a traditional room to suit a contemporary style, there are ways to use detailed moldings to their best advantage. In one such room, the walls were smoothed and painted stark white; all the woodwork that had been stained dark was stripped to light natural color and sealed; and the floor was sanded to natural and lightly whitewashed. The ceilings were also done in white. A great deal of additional background lighting was used. The entire house, once very dark and traditional, was transformed into a light, open contemporary setting. All natural and beige colors were used, even in the furnishings, the only clear color being the huge abstract paintings on the walls of this large interior.

For individual examples, let's take each element to illustrate various concepts:

Ceilings

Ceilings have been neglected for too long. Just think of all the possibilities of ceiling treatment. In a formal French home, ceilings can be painted in sky murals or bas-reliefs, or decorated with dimensional designs. In an informal home, beams, white stucco, wallpaper, tiles, or paneling may be used. Fabric-shirred or pole-tented ceilings or fabric loosely draped are all very effective. In a contemporary interior, ceilings can be low with lucite panels lit from above; or raised ceilings can be left open to show construction beams or natural ceiling peaks, sometimes leaving room for balconies or lofts. Ceilings can be painted in colors or white gloss; wallpapered in copper, bronze, chrome, or mylar; entirely mirrored, reflecting color and light from every area of the room; or left open to expose the room to natural sunlight.

In place of horizontal ceilings, there are many alternatives from
which to choose. Ceilings can be sloped, angled, or sculptured in

Figure 6-7: Reception area for a suite of law offices, combining traditional formality with contemporary overtones to give a sense of youthful energy combined with the solidity and prestige of the past. (Helene Levenson, ASID. Photo: Laban Whittaker.)

dramatic ways. Ceilings can serve practical needs, as well. Acoustical ceilings keep noise at a pleasant level; a ceiling can furnish an entire area of lighting; or lowered ceilings can conceal pipes or air conditioning ducts. Even a ceiling left white so that light from beneath can bounce off it gives an interesting effect to a room.

Varied ceiling heights within one area can also be interesting. Do not forget to do the lighting and air conditioning plan for the area *before* the ceilings are completed.

Moldings

Moldings, like most design elements, originally had a practical purpose. These strips of wood, when set at the joining between top of wall and ceiling, finished the uneven areas. Wall moldings, set at chair height, protected the furniture from marking or breaking the wall surface. Such functional moldings varied from simple to very elaborate designs.

Today, we use moldings in architectural treatments when we are trying to create a traditional feeling. They are, at this time, used solely for eye appeal, and to set one area apart from another. These additional touches can dramatize an area that might otherwise be void of interest.

An example of this is seen in Figure 6–7. In office design today the emphasis is on a comfortable atmosphere. In this reception area, in a suite of lawyers' offices that I renovated in an old Boston building, a contemporary feeling was desired for a progressive young law firm—but also required was a look of stability that a traditional setting would give.

63

The solution lay in the use of surface architectural molding to set the right mood. Mylar wallpaper totally covered the wall, creating a mirrorlike reflecting surface. On top of it were placed thin black moldings in large, severe squares. Within this Georgian style, other moldings were painted a warm off-white. Terra-cotta leather was the upholstery material for the center and the double door.

This wall was set off visually by black ceilings and other walls covered in crinkly black leather. Furniture was upholstered in black leather and white leather. The space is a perfect example of the use of moldings to create architectural changes and to enhance an interior.

Another example of effective treatment of walls is seen in the Captain's cabin aboard this Navy ship. In designing all of the com-

Figure 6-8: Captain's cabin in ship of U.S. Navy. Walls are covered with wood-grain vinyl to create a feeling of warmth; furnishings are contemporary, in red and black; all materials are practical, budget-conscious and fire-retardant. (Helene Levenson, ASID and Leni Joyce, ASID. Photo by Paul Connell.)

partments for an LSD (Landing Ship Dock) a 600′ ship, my problem, and my partner's, lay in the fact that these spaces were historically nondescript, drab and mismatched; with steel-grey furniture upholstered in khaki vinyl it is usually a dreary assemblage. I was to prove that within the same budget I could create an environment more pleasant for the long months the ship was out at sea. Adhering to a strict code of fire laws, for the captain's cabin the walls were covered in a wood-grained vinyl in pecan color and grain, already setting the theme of warmth and comfort. The ceiling was lowered with concealed lighting put in, and the furnishings were a blend of black leather-like and chrome, set on a red and black rug. For the wardroom, which is a lounging center, wood-grained vinyl chosen in a warm deep walnut pattern gave the room a softer more traditional look, achieved also by adding deep blue tufted vinyl chairs and sofas bound with brass nail-heads, wall to wall carpeting, dark shelves and painting on the walls. Truly an example of how changing the walls created a comfortable ambiance of that of a men's club, with no hint of the usual monotonous grey bulkhead walls and exposed overhead pipes.

Fireplaces

Your imagination has to take over here, for the fireplace area is the focal point of the entire room. You may want to remove an existing mantel completely and cover the entire wall with mirror or sheets of copper or lucite. A large, hand-hewn beam can be set horizontally over a fireplace to create a country effect. By elongating the beam, you can add a bookcase area under it. The addition of a hood to the ceiling—sometimes constructed of heavy plaster over a frame—is another effective treatment. Walls surrounding the fireplace are always taken into consideration; they can be covered with textured surfaces such as stone, brick, or wood paneling.

In this chapter we have considered, above all, examples of the kinds of preparation that go into the "setting of the stage." These examples—discussing ways to achieve the country look or the formal look, as well as a consideration of the architectural details that can be shaped to individual needs—are intended to help you open your mind to your own ideas.

In all your planning, remember the three central elements: *awareness of architectural styling; awareness of your own tastes and instincts; and awareness of the functions of your space.* With these principles in mind, let your imagination be your guide. Train your eye to see the many decorative motifs that surround you daily, and be ready to translate these motifs to suit your own interior setting.

In Part II we will leave the general areas of style and mood, and move to specific components of the designer's plan. Planning of space and selection of furniture are important steps in achieving the finished room.

II Furniture: Planning and Selection

This section of Creating an Interior *falls into two general sections. The first, Chapter 7, details the step-by-step procedure required for making a space plan. Before you can choose furniture, wallcoverings, rugs, or any other components of a room, you have to deal with the purposes the room is to serve and the basic dimensions available to you. Furniture on a grand scale will dwarf a room with a low ceiling; furniture that is too fragile will be lost in a huge space. The floor plan will enable you to pick the right location and scale of furnishings without doubt or error.*

Once that plan is made, the selection of actual pieces may begin. Here, again, knowledge of what is available is of the greatest impor- 67 *tance; so Chapter 8 surveys the almost infinite variety of materials and finishes employed in the making of traditional furniture. Chapter 9, on contemporary furniture, emphasizes the designers of today whose new technologies and designs have redefined the very concept of furniture.*

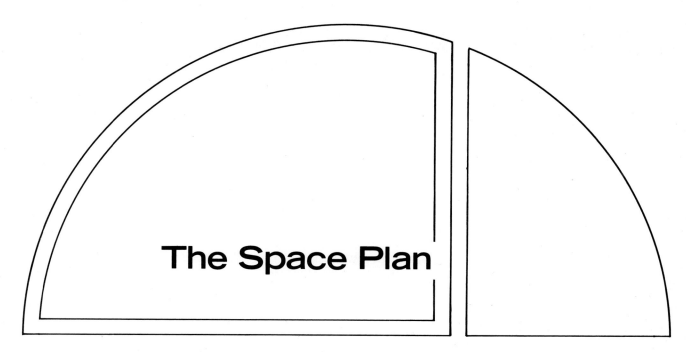

The Space Plan

The single most important element in interior design is the space plan. If this plan is not carefully thought out, nothing else will work well. If you develop a good space plan, you will be well on the way to the creation of an effective and exciting interior. But to be able to do this, you must first understand basic human space needs.

PSYCHOLOGICAL NEEDS

In the past, investigations of the psychological effects of space on behavior have primarily involved animals. But recently there has been a growing interest in human space needs. Studies of psychological space requirements are affecting the design and construction of one-family homes, multiple-family dwellings, workplaces, and public areas—such as airports, hospitals, schools, and theaters.

The psychological needs of individuals for space differ according to many factors. But every human being requires a minimum amount of space for each of his or her varying activities. And the interactions of people are largely dependent on the space in which they are allowed to operate. So to a large extent, the manner in which space is used—for living, learning, working, playing—determines the quality of human interactions.

Territories

There are certain distances, evidently learned at an early age, at which individuals are comfortable with one another. These distances depend to a large degree upon the type of the particular situation and the types of transactions to be carried out. (And it is important to remember here that distance refers not only to physical aspects, but to visual and auditory aspects as well. This is something you, as a prospective interior designer, need to know.)

69

Any *changes* in the distances at which people feel comfortable with one another can be threatening. For example, if you are sitting on an almost-empty bus and someone gets on and sits very close to you, you may feel nervous and anxious; an assault has been made upon your privacy.

In a world that seems to be getting more crowded and less personal every day, it is vital that the space designed for human activities be made adequate to personal needs. Our surroundings affect our feelings; and our feelings affect our behavior.

There are several classifications of space that are relevant to the person concerned with creating viable interior designs:

Personal space is a minimal territory, confined to a few square feet (up to 4 feet) and used for self-contained or lone activities, private or intimate relationships, or close family relationships.

Social space is usually an area of from 4 to 7 square feet. This is the range in which so many of our interpersonal relationships take place—such as dinner conversation, business contacts, and social gatherings. When this social space is extended to more than 10 square feet, it lends itself to the more formal type of business relationship.

Public space of over 20 square feet obviously takes the individual out of the realm of person-to-person involvement. Greater space than this is usually confined to public speakers or actors.

Space Requirements

The interior designer needs to know not only the functional and aesthetic aspects of space, but its psychological ramifications as well. Crowding can produce stress and cause abnormal behavior. In animal populations, severe overcrowding can actually cause death. In human population, overcrowding can cause an explosion of aggression. To avoid this, layouts of every living area from the home to public buildings to communities to cities must be carefully determined. The basic human need for adequate psychological space must be observed.

It is interesting that space requirements differ among social groups, countries, and cultures.

The Japanese experience of space, for example, differs entirely from that of the Western world. The people of Japan give a very special meaning to their personal space. The Japanese concept is of a center around which everything flows: people live and work in close proximity; even their rooms are multipurpose—the walls are usually movable, allowing for eating, sleeping, or socializing, and opening to include the outdoors and their beautiful gardens.

Germans, on the other hand, typically go to great lengths to preserve their private space. Public rooms are soundproof, doors are used seriously, and furniture is rarely moved—this would violate the control of the occupant. Even individual balconies are designed to insure visual privacy.

The French usually live in close proximity, and this tends to develop a high sensory involvement. This is reflected in the layout and design of French homes, offices, buildings, and even their cities.

We need at this point in time to alter our perspective in the study of spatial needs. Designers must leave the old theories on space planning behind and develop new plans to suit the needs of today's behavioral patterns. The "form follows function" principle is a good standard, although until now we have been involved more with the form than with function. The division of enclosed space has to be more than attractive—it must be efficient and comfortable as well. This can be achieved in many ways—for example, we can use wall divisions, or we can use the open plan, creating invisible boundaries by placement of furniture. There is no universal ideal; these decisions must be based on the specific human space needs of the prospective occupants.

SPACE PLANNING

A well-designed room represents the blending of the space and all of its interior elements to achieve a total composition, well balanced and proportioned. In order to achieve the best possible ultimate blend, there must be a plan. Whether the design is for an entire house or for a single room, the approach is the same.

Space Relationships

Make a bubble or circle plan roughly outlining the main areas and the relationships between various spaces. This basic diagram should show circulation patterns and the access from one area to another. This initial plan is the first consideration before we zero in on the more specific floor plan.

Allotment of Square Footage

Each space will give a different impression. What are the architectural features? Is it necessary to increase or to decrease the size? What divisions of the space would be most advantageous to each area in relation to other areas? Provide a circulation area (doors, halls, corridors, stairwells, etc.). Determine the traffic pattern. Note the natural light areas. Is the space oriented to the outdoors? Examine the view from within. Determine the focal point of the area; fireplace, bay window, and so forth.

Function or Purpose of the Space

Is the space to be quiet or active? Make a zone plan for activities— storage, intimate seating, dining, reading, music, major conversation group, collections, study, games, book storage. The lighting plan should be considered both for the needs of activities and for mood change. Daylight also has to be taken into consideration.

Personal Space Requirements

Individual considerations may call for special areas for reading, music (either listening or performing), desk study, plants, workshop, art. Plans should take into account the size of the human figure.

71

Equipment Needs

Be sure to allow for acoustical equipment for music, plumbing, heating ducts or pipes, lighting (indirect or direct), electric wiring, cooking facilities, and so forth.

MAKING THE FLOOR PLAN

The floor plan is an outline of the room to be furnished. It is made to determine the most effective use of all three dimensions of the space. Many nonprofessionals attempt to furnish a space without a floor plan, but the professional interior designer knows that this is a vital step. Looking at the room on the floor plan provides the options of changing architectural features, altering lighting or electrical outlets, and determining the best possible traffic or circulation patterns. It can also show at a glance the balance and proportion of pieces of furniture to be used, and offer the choice at this early stage to change them. Remember, there is never only one suitable floor plan; only the best one to suit the individual's needs.

The following materials are necessary to start your floor plan:

1. Steel tape measure for exact measurement of area
2. Drafting pencils with erasers (suggested: medium H, or soft HB), sharpened fine
3. Graph paper—¼″ or ⅛″ scale, size 8½″ × 11″[1]
4. Tracing paper—usually 18″ × 24″, depending on size of area needed
5. Plain paper—18″ × 24″
6. Triangle
7. T-square
8. Drafting board or 45° cornered backboard
9. Architect's scale rule or 12″ flat ruler
10. Compass
11. Furniture templates in ¼″ scale

Method

1. **MAKE SQUARE-FOOT MEASUREMENTS.** Ascertaining square footage is done either to determine the area (if space requirements are given in square footage) or to best divide an area into the best individual-size room areas (if total plan is in square footage).

The width times the length equals the square footage.
Examples.

- ○ 10′ × 40′ = 400 sq. ft.
- ○ 20′ × 20′ = 400 sq. ft.
- ○ 16′ × 25′ = 400 sq. ft.

Remember: plan individual room areas to allow for standard material lengths and widths, thicknesses of inner construction walls, standard sizes of windows, doors, door openings, sliding glass doors, and so on.

[1]Residential space is usually scaled for ¼ inch to 1 foot. Commercial space is usually scaled for ⅛ inch to 1 foot.

TWO BEDROOM SINGLE LEVEL OR SPLIT LEVEL

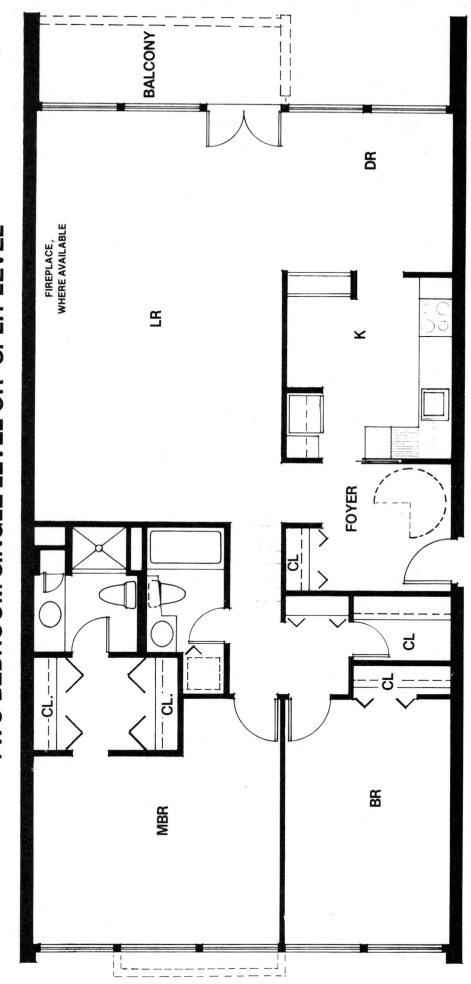

FIREPLACE, WHERE AVAILABLE

BALCONY

LR

DR

K

FOYER

CL

CL

CL

MBR

CL.

CL.

BR

Size and location of certain features, where available, including bay window, kitchen window, terrace, balcony, fireplace, garage, and basement will vary with each condominium home.

Figure 7-1: Basic floor plan for an apartment in the ASID "Hope House" at Cabot Estate, Boston. (Cabot Estate, Franchi Construction.)

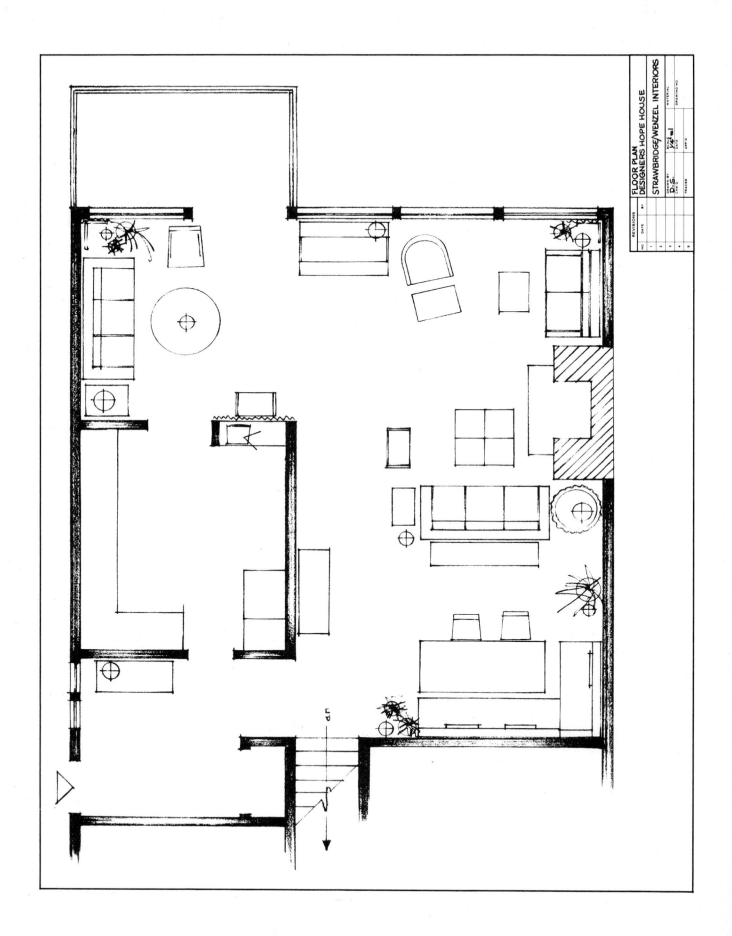

REVISIONS

NO | DATE | BY

FLOOR PLAN
DESIGNERS HOPE HOUSE
STRAWBRIDGE/WENZEL INTERIORS

1
2
3
4
5

SCALE 1/4"=1'
DRAWN BY D.S.
DATE
CHK'D
TRACED
MATERIAL
DRAWING NO
APP'D

DN

Broadloom rugs usually come in 12-foot or 15-foot widths.

Where space is limited, allow the minimum of square footage for circulation—halls, corridors, and stairways.

Average examples of square footages for individual areas in homes are as follows; they can be somewhat smaller or considerably larger:

- Entrance: 40 sq. ft.
- Living room: 250 sq. ft.
- Dining area: 180 sq. ft.
- Bedroom: 180 sq. ft.
- Kitchen: 150 sq. ft.
- Bathroom: 40 sq. ft.

2. MAKE A FREE-HAND FLOOR PLAN SHOWING THE NEEDED MEASUREMENTS.

Going around the room from the entrance hall, measure all walls, window areas, doorways, door openings (with direction of door swing), and so forth. Put all notes and accurate measurements on drawing; measure outside total length and width of room.

3. DRAW AN ACCURATE FLOOR PLAN ON PAPER. Using a scale of ¼ inch to equal 1 foot. With a flat ruler, put measured outline of room on paper. (For beginners to practice: use ¼″ graph paper and measure one square for every foot. *Example:* a 24 foot wall will be designated by twenty-four ¼″ blocks of space.)

Use dark solid lines for walls, open spaces for door openings; indicate windows and fireplaces.

4. MAKE FURNITURE TEMPLATES FOR EXISTING FURNITURE. Measure the outside length and width of each piece, using a scale of ¼″ to 1′. Your templates can be outlined on graph paper or heavy-duty paper to make your own templates.

Use standard template sheet (see Figures 7–3 and 7–4). For the beginner: cut out pieces, place them on the floor plan, and arrange for the best groupings. Place tracing paper over this and trace your plan with furniture. Juggle for a second grouping; put another piece of tracing paper on, and trace the plan again. This way you can compare tracings without making another original floor plan.

For the more advanced: put tracing paper over an accurate floor plan and mark the furniture arrangement on the tracing, to scale, using a template or slide rule. Make two or three separate plans.

Compare tracing plans before marking in the final furniture plan on your floor plan. Remember to leave enough space between pieces for accessibility.

Figure 7-2: *Floor plan showing furniture arrangement in "Hope House" living and dining rooms. Note that L-shaped dining area is used as sitting area, with unusual banquette arrangement for dining at upper right. (Strawbridge/Wenzel Interiors.)*

Figure 7-3: FURNITURE TEMPLATES:
Scale: ¼ inch equals 1 foot. (Ida Goldstein, ASID Associate.)

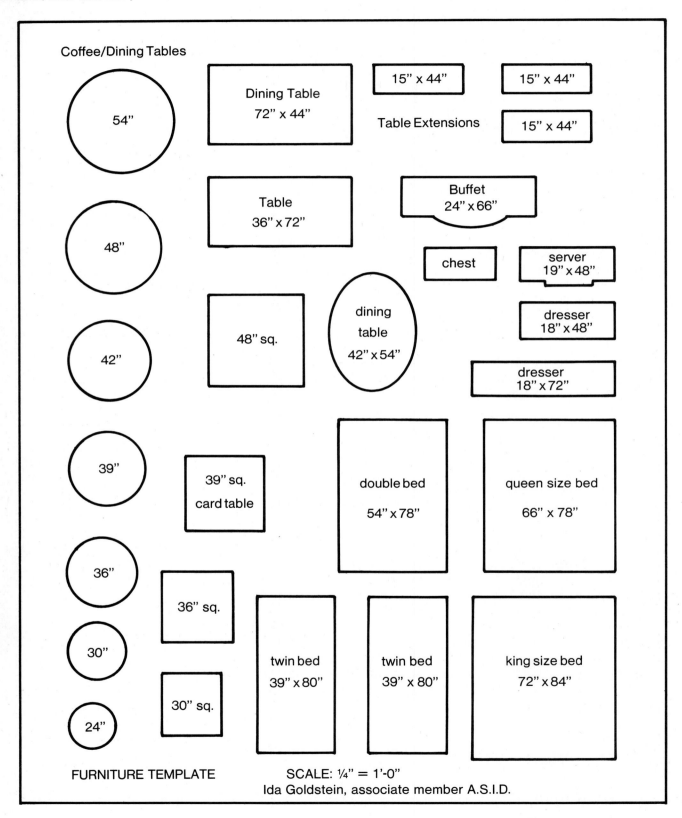

Coffee/Dining Tables

54"

48"

42"

39"

36"

30"

24"

Dining Table
72" x 44"

Table
36" x 72"

48" sq.

39" sq.
card table

36" sq.

30" sq.

15" x 44"

15" x 44"

Table Extensions

15" x 44"

Buffet
24" x 66"

chest

server
19" x 48"

dining
table
42" x 54"

dresser
18" x 48"

dresser
18" x 72"

double bed
54" x 78"

queen size bed
66" x 78"

twin bed
39" x 80"

twin bed
39" x 80"

king size bed
72" x 84"

FURNITURE TEMPLATE   SCALE: ¼" = 1'-0"
                    Ida Goldstein, associate member A.S.I.D.

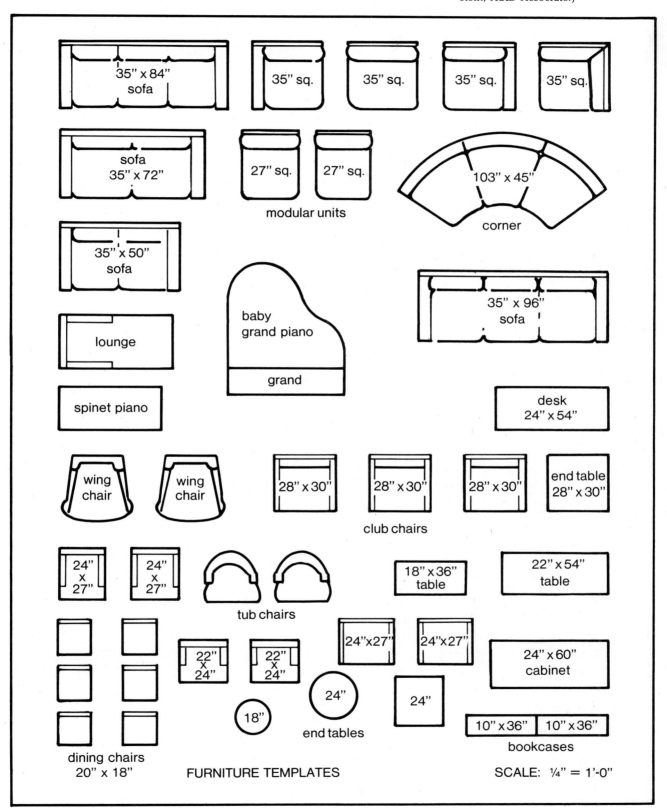

FURNITURE TEMPLATES   SCALE: ¼" = 1'-0"

Figure 7-5: "Hope House" dining area—before designer's work. (Strawbridge/Wenzel Interiors.)

Figure 7-6: "Hope House" dining area turned into finished sitting area. (Strawbridge/Wenzel Interiors. Photo © Edward Jacoby.)

Figure 7-7: "Hope House" living room—before designer's work. (Strawbridge/Wenzel Interiors.)

Figure 7-8: Finished "Hope House" living room. Seating area around fireplace uses warm tones of terra cotta and beige. (Strawbridge/Wenzel Interiors. Photo © Edward Jacoby.)

Figure 7-9: Finished "Hope House" bedroom. Walls are covered in vinyl with inserts of contrasting vinyl; blinds have been painted to follow inserts on walls. Colors are beige and terra cotta, to follow color scheme set in living and dining areas. (Michael Campbell, ASID Associate. Photo © Edward Jacoby.)

List of Standard Furniture Sizes for Reference:

○ Sofa: 72″, 84″, 90″ etc. long, 32″ to 39″ deep

○ Loveseat: 54″ to 60″ long, 30″ to 36″ deep

○ Large chair: 26″ to 31″ wide, 30″ to 34″ deep

○ Small chair: 24″ to 28″ wide, 24″ to 30″ deep

○ Grand piano: 56″ wide, 5′ deep, curve on right side as you face keys

○ Spinet piano: 56″ wide, 22″ deep

○ Cocktail table: 30″, 36″, 48″ or more across (round or square); 18″ wide (at least), 42″, 54″, or more long (rectangular)

○ End table: 22″ wide, 28″ deep (rectangular); 24″, 26″, or 30″ across (round or square)

○ Dining table: 42″ wide, 56″ opening to 108″ long (rectangular); 42″, 44″, 48″ diameter (round) (many other sizes available)

○ Dining chair: 20″ to 22″ wide, 22″ to 24″ deep (many other sizes available)

○ Single bed: 39″ wide, 75″ long

○ Double bed: 54″ wide, 75″ long

○ Queen-size bed: 60″ wide, 75″ long

○ King-size bed: 75″ to 78″ wide, 75″ to 80″ long (using one king-size mattress or two twin-size mattresses)

5. CHECK THE SCALING. Keep vertical as well as horizontal scale in mind. Alternate between short and tall pieces. Overscale furniture makes a room look more important than underscale. Don't line furniture up against walls: seating areas in the center of a room allow the architecture to show. The size and proportion of pieces relative to the other pieces in the room, as well as to its surroundings. Pieces can be light in effect as well as scale.

Plan varied materials (wood, upholstered, and glass pieces, for instance). Use different-size pieces for variety.

6. COMPLETE THE DETAILS.

○ Make an itemized list of all furniture for reference.
○ Add mirrors, plants, room dividers, art, bookcases, sculpture, etc.
○ Most important—*plan all lighting at this stage*, including electrical outlets and dimmers, before any construction begins. (See Chapters 12 and 13 on lighting; make a lighting plan.)

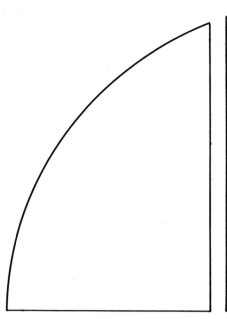

Traditional Furniture

8

In the study of furniture, an understanding of period as well as contemporary pieces is essential to any interior designer. This chapter will cover both.

"Man's first seat was a tree branch, we are told. ... The Romans worked bronze into chairs, the Chinese carved teak wondrously. ... Stone, ivory, deerhorn, iron, willow, rattan, rush, ceramic, silver, and gold—every conceivable material—has been turned by man's hand, into a place to sit, and a way to express his art."[1]

All fine pieces of furniture, covering a wide span of artistic endeavors, are mirrors of their times, reflecting human values and achievements. When used today, the pieces of the past evoke moods, transcend time, and create an atmosphere of past elegance. Examples of fine craftsmanship and quality in period furniture are at home with the most contemporary setting. And in the new furnishings of this century we find new heights of technical and aesthetic achievement.

The making of fine furniture was originally conceived of as an art; the finished object was always considered a luxury product of quality and craftsmanship denoting status. It is only in the twentieth century, with mass-produced furniture—some of very high quality, some of lesser grade—that it has been possible for almost anyone to own furniture. In our society there is a place for both the higher-quality piece that is going to be kept for a long time, usually for a permanent residence, and the one with a short life expectancy—that is, a budget commercial installation.

There is a different philosophy and approach to the use of each type; and it is important that the interior designer know which end of the spectrum he or she is dealing with.

The reason for dealing with the quality or hand-crafted piece is

[1]Reprinted by permission from Trouvailles Furniture catalog, ninth edition.

Figure 8-1: Traditional French furniture in a Louis XVI setting. (Trouvailles, Inc.)

that through it the designer can best express individual talent and individuality: he or she can create something without multitudes of copies being available on the market. This individuality is important if the craftsman is to show taste and designing ability, and this after all is what a good interior designer tries to do.

"A designer essentially creates a conception, an image of a room, that is satisfactory to and expresses the people who live in it." The furniture becomes one of the simplest and most interesting tools the designer can use to realize his or her decorating intent. "One aims finally at universality, at transcending the immediate, evoking atmospheres which by their subliminal stirring of cultural roots welcome the occupants of the room into a particular world ... a world which existed, and will always exist, as eternal as man's proud memory of the best work of his hands."[2]

In order to best express your abilities in design, you must be aware of the multitude of furniture varieties. Until the nineteenth century, every piece of furniture was hand-made and regarded as an art object; and the perpetuation of this tradition is what fine custom furniture companies are involved in today.

Mass-production methods use an entirely different approach, utilizing their material also to the best advantage.

[2]Quotes by David Israel, founder of Trouvailles Furniture. Under the auspices of Mr. David Israel, Owner and Developer of the international firm of Trouvailles Furniture, effort is being made to develop and recreate the wondrous but fast becoming obsolete furniture techniques. Mr. Israel has spent a lifetime of study to reproduce this fine furniture in the hand-skilled traditional methods so that it will not be lost entirely to future generations. These invaluable contributions to interior design and the furniture industry will undoubtedly continue to endure and become the valued antiques of tomorrow.

Because of his vast knowledge and willingness to share it, the information on materials and finishing techniques of furniture was made available.

Mr. Israel shared his knowledge with me in a taped interview on the premises of Trouvailles Furniture Co., whose main office and plant is in Watertown, Mass. Other showrooms internationally are available to designers and architects.

MATERIALS USED IN TRADITIONAL FURNITURE

You can divide traditional furniture rather basically into four groups according to materials: wood, metal, natural fibers, and earth materials. Each of these materials appears in various styles, derived from the countries in which they were originally made.

The following pages explore the uses of these materials; it is necessary to learn these in order to exercise discretion in your future selections.

Wood

Every kind of wood ever used by human beings has been used in furniture; it is still the most common material found in furniture. The important thing is that different woods give a different character to the furniture. A formal air is heightened with mahogany; an informal air is achieved with oak. Basically, the different woods have textural differences; they take finishes differently, as well as polish and surface effects.

Figure 8-2: Beautiful woods appear to their best advantage in these pieces; finishing details include inlays, brass trim, hand painting, and marble tops. (Trouvailles, Inc. Photo: George M. Cushing.)

TYPES OF WOOD. Those used in furniture include walnut, oak, pine, mahogany, ebony, rosewood, palisander, cherry, pearwood, beech, redwood, cedar, satinwood, cypress, butcher block, teak, zebrawood, elm, yew and pecan.

The choice of wood is dictated by the design, by the surface cosmetic impression desired, and by construction needs.

Beech, for example, is often used for chair frames because it's a wood that has strong bonds (ball fibers), is very tough, and will take a great deal of strain—much more, for example, than walnut. Walnut is used often in veneer form for surfaces such as table tops, because the grain is beautiful and can, when it is cut into a veneer, be emphasized even more beautifully. It also takes a lovely finish.

Very often woods are used in combination. In a chair frame, the parts that take the structural strain are often made of beech or birch. The decorative portions, if it's a chair with a finished frame, can be in cherry or walnut or a less expensive wood that can be finished to resemble one of the others.

Actually, in the upper-quality ranges of furniture, the cost of one wood as opposed to another is almost immaterial: hand labor constitutes such a high percentage of cost that the choice of wood is seldom made on the basis of cost but instead is normally made on the basis of usage. Only in lower-priced furniture, where labor is an insignificant portion of the cost as opposed to the materials, is the ratio reversed. Wood seldom increases in price because of scarcity; rather, it becomes more costly according to the difficulty in choosing it by hand.

VENEERS. A veneer is a thin sheet of finishing wood (sometimes also of other materials) that is applied as a surface over a material of coarser consistency.

Veneers are used on flat surfaces by almost anyone making good furniture today; dining table tops are normally veneer, as are the flat surfaces on the sides of a cabinet or on a drawer front. The solid posts and portions of a cabinet are of solid wood; a chair, of course, except in rare cases, is usually made entirely of solid wood. (The rare exception is the veneer detail, such as is found on some English Regency chairs.)

Solid wood construction is not necessarily superior to veneer construction; in some regions the relative humidity inside a house or apartment can drop from 40 to 4 percent in a matter of a few hours, and here veneer furniture is a necessity. Veneer construction was not developed because of cost factors (it actually is *less* costly to make a solid top than to make a good veneer top) but to prevent warping because of sudden humidity changes. Veneer is really an American invention, having first appeared in the 1860s and 1870s. Shortly afterward, the technique was used in Germany, and its use slowly spread to the rest of the world, reaching southern Europe after the Second World War, as a standard method of construction.

There are two or three types of veneer. The kind normally used in furniture construction is called "lumber core plywood." For this the core is made up of a variety of 2- to 3-inch-wide strips of wood glued together. This is sanded and then overlayered with two thicknesses of veneer on either side, for a total of five plys. The two plys on the top and on the bottom are laid across each other at angles; this prevents the grain from telegraphing through and keeps the wood from warping. The core is carefully engineered so that the glued-together pieces will provide extra tolerance (resulting in a much harder and more expensive piece than one solid piece), and the result is a balanced panel that will not warp.

85

KILN DRYING. The entire technology of wood veneer furniture changed with the invention of the kiln drying process, which became important in the first years of this century. It was at this time that the increased use of central heating began to cause problems. Although wood absorbs and loses moisture slowly under *natural* temperature conditions, central heating caused it to do so too rapidly; and consequently wood objects began to suffer—bursting and cracking.

Kiln drying limits the range of moisture absorbency in woods. Once wood is kiln-dried, it will not absorb less than 6 percent or more than 12 percent. It will continue to gain and lose moisture, but only within that range. Non–kiln-dried wood gains from 10 to 20 percent moisture—and in dry heat it can't rapidly throw off that much, so it cracks.

Bentwood furniture is made by applying a steam-with-pressure method to a strong and pliable hardwood, such as beechwood, allowing it to be bent to the desired shape. The Thonet chair is the most famous example of this technique (see Chapter 9.)

Metal

STEEL AND IRON. For today's furniture, many different techniques are employed to shape pieces of steel and iron—from the hand forging method blacksmiths used, to the casting method, which was used commercially for the first time in the Industrial Revolution.

Contemporary furniture made of *polished steel* uses all existing metal-working techniques in order to copy different kinds of antique designs. An example: bakers' racks, made of iron forged by blacksmiths in France in the eighteenth and nineteenth centuries, are being forged the same way today—but of polished steel.

Polished steel furniture was used in Germany in 1920 by the Bauhaus School, to create contemporary designs that are now classics. Breuer and Mies van der Rohe were noted designers in this school.

Cast iron furniture uses copy techniques that were introduced, along with cast iron itself, at the Crystal Palace Exhibition in London in 1851.

Cast iron is made when hot iron is poured into a mold and takes shape; then it is either polished or painted black. Polishing shows the form of the cast iron and its steely gray color. It is grayer than drawn steel, a very much whiter metal whose color changes with the heat and with the composition of the alloy.

Hand forging was the technique of the blacksmith, when he hammered metal over an open fire to get the shape desired. The typical marks of the hammer indicate hand forging, as is seen in horseshoes.

Drawing is a machine process by which iron is forced through a die to form a particular shape such as a rod or a nail.

OTHER METALS. Many metals besides steel and iron are used in furniture.

Brass is used both solid and plated with silver to attain certain kinds of designs, particularly those of the Napoleonic style.

Brass can be cast or it can be drawn. Basic brass-work today is done by machine, except in such cases as bronze sculpture.

Figure 8-3: A variety of traditional furniture types are seen here, including a steel chair with ottoman. (Trouvailles Furniture. Photo: George M. Cushing.)

Bronze is an alloy of brass, an admixture with copper to produce a material different from brass (copper being the basic material of both). Alloys of various metals have been known for thousands of years. The Egyptians and the Etruscans both used metal in making furniture, and some of the earliest Egyptian furniture that survives is metallic. The oldest surviving Etruscan furniture was bronze metal, which was costly but was used for permanence and for strength in such items as chairs and beds.

The whole technology now applied to bronze and iron to create metal furniture grew out of what was learned in arms manufacture in the Napoleonic wars. Following Napoleon, from 1820 to 1830, the vogue for metal furniture characterized the Directoire period and carried on into the Restoration period. Elegant metal tables were done in bronze and in combinations of bronze and iron, or wood and bronze, but with bronze as the basic material.

Pewter is a malleable alloy of lead and tin. It can easily be hammered, and most pewter articles are made by hammering the metal cold over a form. All other metals are worked hot.

Silver plate is used in furniture as it is in table service, over a base of copper—but it is plated more heavily for furniture. It can tarnish, but all metals used for furniture are protected with synthetic

87

lacquers so they will not tarnish or oxidize. These lacquers, if not damaged, will provide a good protective coat for many years. When a metal does start to oxidize it can be relacquered.

Aluminum is also used to make furniture. Some use only aluminum; other pieces use a combination of wrought iron and aluminum. Cast aluminum furniture weighs less than cast or wrought iron.

Natural Fibers

Rattan is a popular natural fiber. Its use began in Europe in the days of the British Empire, when the English brought it home from India. From 1840 to 1900 it was in vogue. This material comes from Indonesia, China, and the Philippines. It is solid, with natural dark markings. It is stronger than bamboo, and can be fastened securely, like wood. A distinctive quality that rattan shares with bamboo is its tough outer coat, which is impermeable to weather. It can be used outdoors—sometimes with a coating of clear polyurethane to protect it further. (Rattan cannot take paint; nothing penetrates it, so it can only be enameled.) Some furniture companies use hardwood frames wrapped with rattan peel. Rattan can be bent under steam and pressure.

Bamboo (hollowwood), like rattan, has a hard outer coat that makes it almost impervious to the weather. The joints of bamboo furniture, however, must be protected from water. Bamboo is hollow, softer, and more absorbent than rattan, and can be painted.

Willow differs from rattan and bamboo. Its thin branches are stripped of leaves; then it is dried and later woven into furniture. The close botanical relative of our familiar willow also grows in the form of canes in many parts of the world.

Cane is the split surface of either rattan or bamboo, usually bamboo, cut into very thin pieces and woven. This can also be done with the smaller branches of rattan.

Synthetic canes made of plastic are used widely in this country. There is an obvious difference from natural cane, which if properly applied is extremely durable. Natural cane should be woven on the piece, one strand after another: this is the old hand-caning method, an almost lost art in this country but still done in many parts of Europe.

Synthetic cane must be spliced onto the object being made. A band of plastic or fiber is glued around the edges to hold a prewoven cane section. To tell this method from hand caning in, for instance, a chair, note that in hand caning there is no band of material around the edge of the chair; instead; each strand disappears into a hole in the frame so that the cane section becomes integral to the structure of the piece.

Rush grows as a grass or weed along the river banks in many parts of the world such as southern Europe. It is usually hand-woven by local people, directly on the piece itself. Rushes are soaked and woven piece by piece into a rope of rush. One rope is then interwoven with another to form a rush seat.

Synthetic rush is a paper product; although it is used by some manufacturers, its life expectancy is much shorter than natural rush.

Wicker is used in much the same way as willow. It is a natural vine, and can be woven into furniture. With a rising new interest in this fiber, more of it will be coming into the market. The quality of wicker, however, can vary greatly. Designed properly, wicker can be very strong. But it is not self-supporting, and must be used in combination with another material. It is usually worked over a wood frame. (Rattan, on the other hand, is so strong that it is its own frame.) There is a method of drying and seasoning wicker so that it retains its natural color.

Earth Materials

Ceramics is a category embracing the whole range of clay-based materials, some of the oldest substances used by human beings. Ceramics are used today, however, in very sophisticated ways—including techniques of manufacture originally worked out for spaceship nosecones, called metallized ceramics. Some of these ideas have been applied to decorative objects.

Strength is produced by this technique when metal powders are put into suspension with the clay, making the clay much harder and stronger. Such a technique allows it to be used, for example, as a table base that can support a 400-pound glass top.

Porcelain, one type of ceramic, can be made very hard. The Viennese used it to make stoves. The Chinese used porcelain as table bases during the Ming Dynasty (1368–1644). Decorative objects of ceramic, such as small tables, have been a feature of the Florentine market since the nineteenth century. Ceramics can be used in connection with iron, copying the old designs with new techniques, which makes an interesting counterpoint.

Alabaster is a natural material. It is quarried and looks like marble when it is removed from the ground in its rough form. The Etruscans, in the second century B.C., developed the technique of boiling alabaster to leach out the minerals so that there would be a translucency to it. (It is not naturally translucent.) There are several side effects, however, to this leaching process: the alabaster becomes quite weak and tends to be light-sensitive, changing from white to brown if exposed to light. A new transference process has been worked out to eliminate this problem. Instead of boiling the alabaster in water, it is now boiled in aniline dyes which chemically transfer their colors. Coloration then is permanent and translucent and goes all the way through, because the aniline dye replaces the mineral that was originally there.

This is a cosmetic trick, of course, but necessary to certain decorative ideas. It also strengthens the alabaster. Large chunks can be used as table bases in the natural form. Treated as marble, alabaster is a very sensual stone, smooth and lovely.

Marble has been used for table tops, chairs, and solid furniture throughout the centuries. It keeps recurring in its natural form and will always remain a favorite. The inlay of marble can be done in several different forms. *Pietra dura* is the Byzantine technique of inlaying bits and pieces of marble (mosaic). The floors in the Cathedral in Siena, Italy are an example of the *pietra dura* technique.

In the Renaissance, this technique was taken a step farther, and *intarsia* was developed. *Intarsia* means carving designs in marble, some parts of which are emphasized with inlaid pieces.

89

The old *scagliola* technique, named for a fifteenth-century artisan of Mantua, Italy, has recently been revived. Scagliola was commissioned to work on the new palaces that the Medicis were building in Florence. With vast amounts of pietra dura work to do, he knew that it would take more than a lifetime to finish the job; so he invented the shortcut that bears his name.

The scagliola technique is to grind the natural marble into powder, then mix it with a binder (which Scagliola also invented). After it dries and is polished, it takes the same grain that it had originally, so there is no visible difference. This technique allowed Scagliola to fashion marble to a thickness of one-eighth of an inch; he could lay in his paste of marble powders, each powder in a different color, and then polish it. The material in its final stage was as hard and gave the same appearance as natural marble, because the grain came back.

This method remained a carefully guarded secret within the stoneworkers' guild for many generations and was done only in Florence at very high prices, entirely by hand.

Today the scagliola technique has been adapted to a planograph carving machine, and the finished marble is coated with a layer of urethane to protect it.

Marble can also be frescoed, using a technique invented by the Romans, called *encaustic*. Roman frescoes of the fourth century B.C. were painted on marble in various bright colors (recreated at the Getty Museum in Malibu). The Roman villas originally looked bright and quite garish, by our standards. The encaustic technique involved painting marble with dyes; because marble is a porous material, the dyes sank into it and remained there for thousands of years. The encaustic technique is used today by artisans from all over the world, and thus ancient artistic traditions remain with us.

Slate is a natural material used for table or chest tops.

Terra cotta is a clay product; it is not very strong and is used mostly for planters and jardinieres.

Other Materials

Glass can be etched, beveled, or leaded; most of these processes are done by hand, although some beveling can be done by machine. Large table tops can be beveled. Tempered glass, largely imported from Europe, is preferable because it is hard to break. Table tops should be ½'' to ¾'' thick. Glass usually accounts for three-quarters of the cost of a piece of furniture that incorporates it. It is not impractical when used correctly, although it will scratch.

Mirrored furniture, first made in Venice, attained its height of popularity in 1900 to 1925, first in France, then in the United States. It is reappearing now in many forms in contemporary styling, and creates a particularly nice counterpart to steel.

Leather is a durable material with an appealing texture and color; it was used for furniture long before furniture was upholstered, starting in the form of sling benches.

Leather is used often in the hand-tooled form called Moroccan work, developed in Spain from the eighth through the eleventh century by the Moors, and continued today as a tradition there. In this technique the leather is worked with a tool to produce a raised design.

Hand-glazed leather is traditionally used in English furniture. In Edwardian days the leather was put on in its raw, bleached state, then hand-glazed with aniline dyes—and hand-tufted if necessary, after the piece was upholstered. Hand-glazing allows for a depth, variation, and richness of color that would not be possible in a pre-dyed material.

Figure 8-4: Leather-upholstered pieces in an "old-world" setting. (Trouvailles, Inc. Photo: George M. Cushing.)

FINISHES

The three main categories of finishes used in wood furniture are stains, paints, and lacquers.

Stains

Water stains can produce interesting wood tones. This technique calls for the use of aniline dyes suspended in water. It is a staining method only rarely used in this country today because it requires a great deal of skill and is difficult to control. The advantage of water-staining is that it enhances the grain of the wood and hides nothing. The dyes in water are applied during the first finishing application; they darken the wood, following the grain and the softness and hardness of the wood.

Water stains are usually applied with a rag and wiped by hand. This is the key process in the finishing of a piece of furniture. By removing or leaving on the desired amount of stain while the piece is still wet, the skilled craftsman can shade as he wipes, capturing the full beauty of the wood. Some top manufacturers still use the water-staining technique.

91

Oil stains are used by most manufacturers today. They contain the same kind of pigment as water stains, except that they are suspended in oil rather than water. The difference is that water stains reveal the grain of the wood more fully. Oil finishes work well with walnut, teak, rosewood, and oak, but not as well with maple, cherry, birch, or mahogany.

Oil stains are usually sprayed on—and can be wiped by hand, as in the water-staining technique. Today, however, oil-staining is often done automatically. A piece of furniture may simply be glazed with a diluted oil stain to the overall degree that is wanted, or spray-gunned for shading. This cuts down the most costly step of finishing wood—namely, skilled hand labor.

After staining—whether with water or oil stain—a sealer is applied. The piece is then sanded, given another coat of stain, and sanded again, with up to four coats of the sealing lacquer (depending on the quality of the furniture). This lacquer can have any one of a number of chemical bases. It can be nitrocellulose-based, polyurethane-based, or vinyl-based, depending upon the lacquer manufacturer and its process. Some believe that the nitrocellulose materials are preferable in custom hand-crafted furniture, because they are more malleable; they make it possible to obtain a more satiny surface than with the other finishes. All are good, however, and all are durable, although degrees of quality vary.

Occasionally, a glaze coat is applied on top of the sealer coat. This is a thinner translucent material, which can darken or lighten at the option of the craftsman. This should preferably be done by brush and by hand, not by gun, to get the exact color depth desired. Hand-glazing and wiping gives a mellowness, with subtle changes and gradations of color not obtained by machine methods.

Paints

Synthetic enamels of many kinds have various chemical bases; they can be vinyl-based or steroid-based. For softer finishes, the degree of gloss can be controlled.

Enamels can be applied evenly, or they may be antiqued to simulate the natural aging and mellowing of an old painted piece. Antiquing can be done with or without physical distressing. An antiqued finish, when it is hand-done, is glazed, and has a great deal of character and interest.

The standard antiqued and distressed piece is first prepared with small holes, worn spots, and other simulated effects of aging. When the glazing is applied, these marks retain the glaze, giving the true effect of an antique piece.

Heavily antiqued wood is first stained, then distressed, and finally the paint is worked off, in places of natural wear, back to the wood. The final finish appears to have had the paint worn or chipped off through use.

Lacquers

Lacquers are completely different from paint. Natural lacquer, as it was used by Japanese and Chinese, was obtained from the dried bodies of a certain insect, or from *lac*, the sap of the lacquer tree. It was built up in fifty or sixty coats into a solid material, often as thick as one-eighth of an inch all the way through.

92

Today lacquer is a chemically produced substitute for natural lacquer. It differs from paint, first in that its color is translucent, not solid; and second, in that it must be sprayed on in many coats and should be dried mechanically to form a hard, smooth, durable finish.

Modern lacquered furniture does not copy the original Oriental techniques. It emulates instead the European techniques inspired by what travelers saw in the Orient or in the furniture sometimes made there for export to Europe in the seventeenth and eighteenth centuries, produced on French and English designs and called *chinoiserie*.

Many techniques of lacquering were used in different parts of the Orient. Today five basic techniques are used.

Figure 8-5: *This exquisite table displays Trouvailles' "Canton" lacquer technique. (Trouvailles, Inc. Photo: George M. Cushing.)*

1. THE LACQUE DE CHINE (CHINESE LACQUER). This technique is most often used in France. Essentially, *lacque de Chine* is different from other lacquering techniques in that it is a knife technique, with decoration made up of thousands of lines cut with a knife. Silver leaf, then gold leaf, then numerous thin coats of lacquer are applied, building up a measurable thickness. A rice-paper pattern is placed on the top and cut through with a knife to place the large outlines of the pattern of the decoration. Then, by knife-scraping, the design is revealed in gold or silver. No brush is used.

2. FAUX BOIS[3] OR LACQUE GRAVÉE (ENGRAVED AND INCISED KNIFE TECHNIQUE). Used in France during the days of the China trade. This, like the *lacque de Chine* method, is also a knife technique, but it is not done

---

[3]*Faux Bois* is a trade name of the Trouvailles Furniture Company. Under the auspices of David Israel, founder of Trouvailles Furniture, efforts are being made to discover and re-create techniques of furniture constructure and finishing that are fast becoming obsolete, so that traditional methods will not be lost entirely to future generations. The information on materials and finishing techniques found in this chapter are made available thanks largely to Mr. Israel's willingness to share his knowledge.

over silver or gold leaf. Instead of cutting down to the silver or gold, the small amount of coloration is done afterwards, and there are many more lines cut. Faux Bois works as a design because it creates a highly textured surface by thousands of knife cuts. This is the only truly Oriental furniture finish: The Chinese used this technique in combination with woods for furniture for themselves. Their other techniques were used on other articles, such as trays.

3. THE CANTON.[4] This technique originated during the China trade days. It copies what is essentially a batik or "lost wax" process, in which the design is applied over gold, but with a brush. The design is blocked out and then protected with wax, which covers the gold wherever the design is to appear. Then a coat of black lacquer is painted on, the wax is washed away, and the gold is exposed. This method was originally used in the Chinese city of Canton, and was brought back by the English.

4. JAPANNING. This technique, much used in the eighteenth and nineteenth centuries, is similar to the Canton technique, except that instead of being gold, the background color is the black, or dark color. The design is done with a brush on top, with gold paint or gold in suspension (gold powder mixed in oil).

5. COROMANDEL. This is the technique of lacquering we see on Coromandel screens. The lacquer is put on in as many as thirty to forty coats, and built up to a measurable thickness—as much as one-quarter of an inch. Then it is cut with a knife, as in other techniques, to develop the design, but in broad strokes, scraped down and then colored afterwards. The color penetrates into the cuts. The name *Coromandel* has more than one definition; it is also used to designate a particular type of Eastern wood and furniture. The Coromandel lacquering technique, however, means something different; it was often used in decorative boxes in the eighteenth century.

These five techniques are all very time-consuming. One piece of furniture, such as a secretary, can require as much as 175 to 200 hours of hand labor. This means that one person could work on a piece for as long as five weeks. Production is very limited because of the time the artisan takes, which is why these pieces are so costly.

Other Finishes

COMMERCIAL OR MANUFACTURED LACQUER FINISHES. In the United States, the lacquering technique used most for furniture is a finish similar to hand-done Japanning. The lacquer color is first sprayed on, in as many as four coats, then hand-decorated with a brush over a stencil design or even with decals. In some better furniture, poncing paper is used: the design is indicated by the many, many pinpoint holes in the paper, which is laid on the piece and sprinkled with a powder. When the paper is carefully lifted, the powder has gone through the holes, leaving the design on the piece. This is followed with the brush on top of the lacquer, and is finally given many protective clear coats.

[4] Trade name of Trouvailles Furniture Company.

GOLD AND SILVER DECORATION.   In the eighteenth century, gold burnishing was done by hand according to a French technique called *dans l'eau*, which means "in water." Burnishing is done by rubbing gold leaf onto a piece of wood with an agate tool until it has the consistency of metal. Actually it is plating the wood with gold, by building up microscopic layers of leaves. This is so extremely costly and difficult that it is almost never done today except on very special custom orders.

GOLD OR SILVER LEAF.   In this technique a special brass alloy called Dutch metal, which is the color of gold and will not tarnish, is laid on in paper-thin pieces, 3 inches square, one on top of another, and rubbed so that the seams disappear, just as with real gold. In this process, however, the sheets are laid over glue, not burnished on. This makes the big difference in time saved.

MARBLING.   A method of surface painting to imitate the veining of marble, the marbling technique is done similar to the application of malachite finishes (below).

MARQUETRY.   A complex hand technique, marquetry uses thin inlaid pieces of various woods to develop a design of many subtle color tones. The wood is cut out in layers. One piece of veneer is laid over another, the design is cut through both of them, then the shaped piece is removed from the bottom layer. The color wanted to replace it then slips into the opening that has been made and is held in with tape until glued. Many small pieces of a great variety of woods are used. In the French Rococo period, marquetry designs were made in tulipwood, kingwood, yew, amaranth, violetwood, palisander, and lignum vitae. Patterns included squares, herringbone, floral, and lozenge shapes. Marquetry is still done today.

Faux (false) marquetry, an imitation of marquetry used in France, Holland, and England in the seventh century, is a technique in which the design is simply painted on to cosmetically simulate the look and feel of wood marquetry.

MALACHITE FINISHES.   This technique involves working on glass or wood with wet reagents. These finishes are created with liquids of different viscosity, which are mixed with aniline dyes and dropped onto the surface of a piece, where they spread, forming the designs. This is a difficult hand process to achieve. Two examples of malachite finishes are the Trouvailles Company's Teapaper and Lapis Lazuli finishes.[5]

To imitate the natural streaky patterns of malachite (a greenish mineral), paint is put on in the form of a paste and a paper comb is drawn through by hand to form the natural design.

INLAID IVORY AND MOTHER-OF-PEARL.   The technique of inlaying mother-of-pearl and ivory originated in Peking, China, and is followed by a few companies in the United States.

[5] Trade name of Trouvailles Furniture Company.

UPHOLSTERY

Methods

The traditional method of furniture upholstery, used since its inception, made the most progress in the nineteenth century. On the bottom of the frame of the chair or sofa seat, jute straps 4 or more inches wide are nailed on in a criss-cross web. On top of this, springs are tied on (in France these were traditionally of copper, but steel replaced copper because it was stronger and springier). These springs are tied with jute rope in an eight-way geometric hand-tie called a *diamond tie*. The purpose of this is to keep each spring rigid in its position in relation to all of the other springs, while still being free to go up and down. On top of the springs is placed a layer of burlap.

On the upper edge of the frame is a *fox-edge*—a built-up edge, ½ to 2 inches thick, made to retain the filling material—normally loose hair, a rubberized hair pad, or cotton felt. The deck is then covered with a cotton cloth tacked around the edges to form a soft surface.

Figure 8-6: A fine example of traditionally upholstered furniture. (Trouvailles, Inc. Photo: George M. Cushing.)

96

The cushion on top, which traditionally was down, or feathers, now is often polyurethane, polyfoam, latex, or a spring-and-down combination, wrapped in soft dacron foam.

Modern upholsterers still sometimes use hand-tied springs; or they may turn to preform metal spring units that are prewebbed and dropped in. (This production method is faster but less durable.) Steel strapping is used today instead of jute because it is stronger. And nails are now replaced with staples shot in under air pressure.

In this chapter, we have concentrated on the wealth of materials and methods that go into traditional furniture of the finest quality available. As you begin to explore the workshops and showrooms of furniture-makers, the knowledge of basic techniques and styles that you bring with you will make your search for the perfect piece both more interesting and more successful.

Chapter 9 will focus on the designers of contemporary furniture—as well as on the innovative materials and techniques that have revolutionized the contemporary furniture industry.

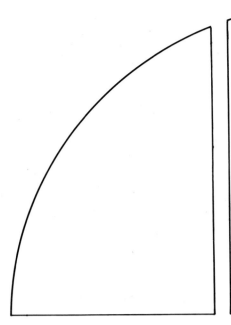

Contemporary Furniture

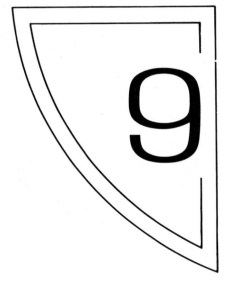

It is necessary here to refer to the sections on architecture in Chapter 4 on contemporary style, because the development of contemporary furniture is intermingled with that of contemporary architecture. Many of the noted modern architects have also been the leading furniture designers of their time. It is the meshing of these two elements that creates the purity of total design, with furniture reflecting the development of many innovative architectural ideas, such as the curtain wall, poured concrete, or tubular steel construction.

Because we have discussed these designers more thoroughly in Chapter 5, the review in this chapter will be mostly pictorial, and will lead up to the most recent designs.

CONTEMPORARY DESIGNERS (1860–1933)

The Arts and Crafts Movement (1860–1900)

MICHAEL THONET (1796–1871). Thonet was the first furniture designer to combine elegant design with the use of mass production. His furniture designs were given the highest awards in 1851 when they were first presented at the World's Fair in London. He is noted for his invention of the process of bentwood—beechwood softened by steam and then bent into curved shapes. First produced between 1860 and 1876, Thonet chairs are still very popular today. He also is credited with having invented the technique of using many layers of veneer, bent and shaped in heated molds. The Thonet family continued to manufacture his furniture designs after his death and are still known today as leaders in the field of contemporary furniture.

WILLIAM MORRIS (1834–1896). Morris established a firm in 1861 to make a reality of his concept of using the styles of the Middle Ages as the criteria for well-designed machine products. Collaborators in his firm were Henry Cole, Owen Jones, and Richard Redgrave, all of whom produced furnishings, wallpaper, and textiles.

Many designers showed their furniture at the Morris Arts and Crafts Exhibition Society in 1890. Among them were Ernest Gimson and Sidney and Ernest Barnsley. Other noted designers of the arts and crafts movement were Sir Ambrose Heal and Charles F. Annesley Voysey.

Art Nouveau (1890–1905)

An aesthetic revival, taking nothing from styles of the past, Art Nouveau became a style itself.

HENRI VAN DE VELDE (1863–1957). This Belgian-born architect and furniture designer was prominent in the Art Nouveau movement. Although he first studied painting, his interest gradually changed from fine to applied arts, and he became the spokesman for the Art Nouveau movement. He accented the use of the curved line as seen in nature, and saw the line as one with the complete form. This flowing line, misunderstood, was used as ornamentation instead of as part of the form itself. Belgium remained the source of this ornamental innovation.

CHARLES RENNIE MACKINTOSH (1868–1928). This Scottish architect Mackintosh designed many buildings using pure lines with no evidence of earlier period styles. He took the ornamentation out of Art Nouveau and simplified it, creating a "perpendicular" look. An example of Mackintosh's perpendicular style is the curved lattice-back chair, de-

Figure 9-1: Furniture designed by Charles Mackintosh. Left to right: ladder-back chair, 1902; curved lattice-back chair, 1904; oval-back chair, 1897. (Atelier International, Ltd.)

signed in 1904. This was fabricated in solid oak with an upholstered
seat cushion and storage compartment. The construction was traditional mortise-and-tenon, and the oak was finished in ebony stain.
The original fabric was a green and beige Indian material. This and
other examples of his work are produced today under license from
the Mackintosh estate by the Atelier International, Ltd. Furniture
Company. (See Figure 9–1.)

de Stijl (1917)

This contribution to the further development of modern design was
originated by a group of Dutch artists and architects associated with
the magazine *de Stijl (Style)*, founded in 1917. Using abstract lines,
verticals, horizontals, geometric shapes, and the primary colors of
red, blue, and yellow, a new creative force manifested itself in paintings (Mondrian), sculpture (Malewitsch), and furniture design (Rietveld).

GERRIT THOMAS RIETVELD (1888–1964). A Dutch furniture designer and architect, Rietveld created a classic chair using simple, square, three-
dimensional elements held together by a series of vertical and horizontal planes. His classic red/blue chair was produced in 1917 from
kiln-dried wood, blind-dowelled and glued. The seat and back are
beech marine plywood, finished in bright primary colors akin to
those of a painting by Mondrian. The beechwood is aniline-stained
with a clear matte lacquer finish. The back is red, the seat blue, and
the framework black—with the tips of the arms yellow or white. This
chair is now produced under license from the Rietveld estate, ac-

*Figure 9-2: "Zig zag chair" designed by
Gerrit Thomas Rietveld. (Atelier International, Ltd.)*

cording to the original design and specifications, stamp-signed and serial-numbered, by the Atelier International, Ltd. Furniture Company. (See Figures 9–2 and 9–3.)

The Bauhaus (1919–1933)

After fifty years, the arts and crafts movement was finally succeeded by a style representing a new harmony between art and technology.

WALTER GROPIUS (1863–1969). Gropius formed the Bauhaus school in 1919, and the philosophy of design changed radically under his influence, with a profound effect on furniture design. Mrs. Walter Gropius described the purpose of the Bauhaus school to me:

He meant the school to be a place where teachers and students could cooperate and experiment together, to develop educational methods and resources which would free the individual from stereotyped prescription-learning of the past, and would set him on the path to find creative solutions for contemporary problems. His emphasis was on search rather than research, and he wanted to steer the students clear of the traps of slavish imitations of established masters, as well as being swallowed up by the expedient solutions of the marketplace. He wanted them to find forms for our twentieth-century world which would emerge from untrammeled, unprejudiced minds, but which were to be based on a solid knowledge of hand-work and visual studies. The Bauhaus challenged them to become conscious of their own needs and their own desires for form.

Figure 9-3: Gerrit Thomas Rietveld's "red and blue chair." (Atelier International, Ltd.)

101

The founding of the Bauhaus by Walter Gropius was the beginning of great contemporary furniture design which was aesthetically pleasing, and simple as well as functional.

MARCEL BREUER (1902–   ).   An architect and furniture designer, Marcel Breuer was born in Hungary and has lived most of his productive life in the United States. He once wrote: "A piece of furniture is not an arbitrary composition, it is a necessary composition of our environment. In itself impersonal, it takes on meaning only from the way it is used or as a part of a complete scheme." (Figure 9-4)

The classic Breuer pieces attest to this philosophy. His light-weight-steel design made an important mark in the history of furniture design. In 1925 Breuer invented the first continuous tubular steel frame, used in conjunction with loose canvas seat and back. The inspiration for this came from the handlebars of a bicycle, as well as from the theories of the de Stijl group. This piece, called the Wassily chair, is the epitome of machine expression. Of his tubular metal pieces Breuer wrote:

I already had the concept of spanning the seat with fabric in tension as a substitute for thick upholstery. I wanted a frame that would be resilient and elastic. I also wanted to achieve transparency of forms to attain both visual and physical lightness. Mass production and standardization had already made me interested in polished metal, in shiny and impeccable lines in space as new components for our interiors. I considered such polished and curved lines not only symbolic of our modern technology, but actually technology itself.

This chair is now being reproduced by Knoll International Furniture Company, and it is through their generosity that these quotes were made available.

Figure 9-4: Marcel Breuer chair, made of tubular metal, with caned back and seat. (Knoll International.)

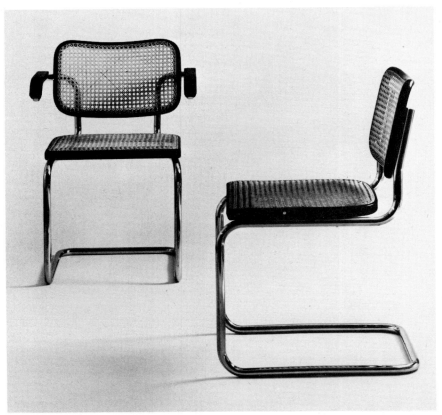

102

The International Style

LUDWIG MIES VAN DER ROHE (1886–1969). This innovative German architect and furniture designer succeeded Gropius as director of the Bauhaus from 1930 to 1933 then came to the United States. His work, which became known as the International Style, embodied his much-followed doctrine that "less is more." This principle was seen in his model house, shown in Berlin in 1931. As early as this, Mies van der Rohe used open space, low glass coffee tables, the Barcelona chair (1929), the Tugendhat chair (1929), and the Cantilever chair, accepted today as classic contemporary furnishings. He also further explored innovative uses of wood. The scale and proportion and the materials he used, which were so innovative then, were designed to be used appropriately in contemporary architecture; and we can now see the perfect blending of both. Knoll International is responsible for producing the chairs that were seen in the April 1977 Museum of Modern Art exhibit featuring Ludwig Mies van der Rohe's work.

In tribute to the genius of van der Rohe, Knoll continues to produce many of his well-known designs. Among the details that make Knoll's Barcelona and Tugendhat chairs special are the hand-sewn welts that join the leather panels of the cushions and the hand-turned screws through leather straps into the frames. These details require as much exacting craftsmanship as the finest eighteenth-century piece. (See Figure 9–5.)

ALVAR AALTO (1898–1976). Aalto was a Finnish architect and furniture designer well known for his "organic" style. He had continued the work of Breuer and Mies van der Rohe, using both solid and laminated woods. Aalto used white birch, in the molded and bent method, in design echoing the tubular steel chairs. This modern Scandinavian furniture enjoyed great popularity, and Aalto founded his own manufacturing plant, Artek, Ltd., in 1936.

Figure 9-5: The "Tugendhat chair" of Mies van der Rohe. (Knoll International.)

103

Figure 9-6: *A chaise longue designed by Le Corbusier. (Atelier International, Ltd.)*

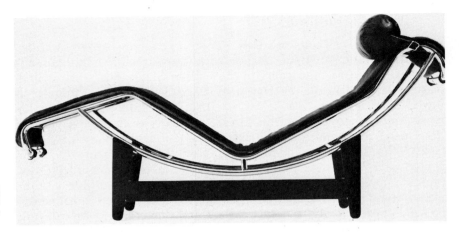

Figure 9-7: *Le Corbusier's glass-topped table, designed in 1928, which received the ASID design award in 1976. (Atelier International, Ltd.)*

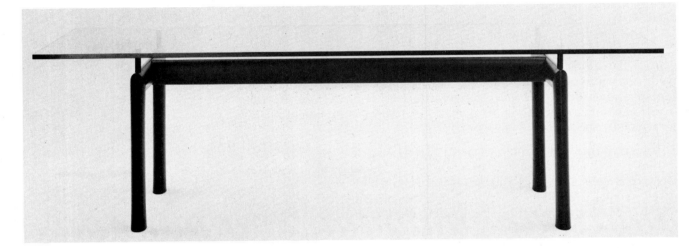

LE CORBUSIER (1887–1968). Charles Edouard Jeanneret-Gris, who became known as Le Corbusier, was born in Switzerland. Both architect and furniture designer, he is considered a French architect because of his extensive traveling. Le Corbusier brought an artist's eye for abstract form and sculpture, in combination with the philosophy of incorporating industrial technology, to his designs for functional houses. He believed that a house is a "machine to live in." He had a share in furthering the theories of the International Style, and was also influenced by the de Stijl school. His furniture is reproduced by Atelier International, Ltd. under license from his estate, with a stamp signature and serial number on each model.

Le Corbusier's pure classic designs in tubular steel add to the work of Breuer and Mies van der Rohe. This highly polished and angular steel tubing, used on chair frames even today, is hand-formed and bent with heat applied by use of special equipment to assume exact proportions. (See Figures 9–6 and 9–7.)

The closing of the Bauhaus in 1933 marked the end of the era of the International Style.

From the 1930s on, the dominant contributions to furniture design have been made primarily by Scandinavian, American, and Italian designers.

104

SCANDINAVIAN DESIGN

Scandinavian furniture design has centered in Copenhagen where the Danish Cabinetmakers' Guild was founded in 1941 by Johannes Hansen, master craftsman. His collaboration with the architect Hans Wegner, together with the prestige of Professor Kaare Klint and teacher Finn Juhl, brought acclaim to the Danish furniture industry. Hansen died in 1961, but the small workshop had grown to a flourishing enterprise. Paul Hansen, his son, a designer and engineer, is still carrying on furniture production there.

HANS WEGNER. A Danish architect and furniture craftsman, Wegner introduced a classic chair in 1969 which is a beautiful design because of the simplicity and harmony of the parts in relation to the whole chair. His sophisticated handling of the wood is as fine as that of any eighteenth-century craftsman. (The exclusive rights to this chair are held by Knoll International.) Furniture designs by Hans Wegner are a part of permanent collections in museums in Melbourne, New York, Goteberg, Oslo, Trandhjem, and Copenhagen. (See Figure 9–8.)

Figure 9-8: Chair by Hans Wegner. (Knoll International.)

AMERICAN DESIGN

EERO SAARINEN (1910–1961).

Saarinen was born in Finland, studied at Yale, and worked with his architect father at Cranbrook Academy, Michigan. Saarinen, with Charles Eames, won first prize in the functional furniture competition of the Museum of Modern Art in 1941. The prize-winning new designs were chairs consisting of plywood shells upholstered with foam rubber, whose legs were attached with electro-welded rubber connections. In the first of the four groups of furniture Saarinen designed was a lounge chair with an exposed molded plywood frame and an upholstered molded contour shell. The last group was dining furniture, made with cast plastic pedestals to create unity of line.

The first sketches for those pedestal pieces were made in the early 1950s. Saarinen's intent was clear: "The undercarriage of chairs and tables in a typical interior makes an ugly, confusing, unrestful world. I want to clear up the slum of legs. I want to make the chair all one thing again." He devoted endless hours to sketching, made scaled models of furniture, set up a scaled model room, and finally, with the help of the design development group of Knoll International,[1] created technology making possible his plastic forms and giving them a place in furniture design. The Pedestal Collection was introduced in 1956 and pieces are still being made today by Knoll International. (See Figure 9–9.)

Figure 9-9: *Eero Saarinen designed this chair to eliminate legs: "I want to make the chair all one thing again." (Knoll International.)*

[1] Designer Florence Knoll Bassett, once a student of Mies van der Rohe, is president of Knoll International Furniture Company. The Knoll design development group grew under her direction, with such designers as Pearson Petitt and Warren Platner. In 1949 she said, "An intelligent interior plan goes farther than furnishings, which fill the space. It strikes at the root of living requirements and changing habits. Planning involves technical efficiency, comfort, taste, and price."

CHARLES EAMES (1907–   ). A St. Louis architect, Eames worked with Saarinen at Cranbrook, designing molded plywood and metal furniture. He also used plastics, aluminum, and steel in his designs. The mass-produced Eames plastic chairs are as popular now as they were in 1946, and can be seen in the Museum of Modern Art.

American Furniture Manufacturers

Fine American furniture companies now employ numerous American designers as well as importing designs and finished pieces from abroad. I interviewed Mr. Irving Rosen of Pace Furniture for an in-depth study of the goals and methods of one leading American company; many others produce furniture of equally high quality.

Pace Furniture, a forerunner in the contemporary furniture scene since 1930, was formed by Irving and Leon Rosen, furniture designers, who both import and manufacture domestically. They continue to introduce the best examples of contemporary furniture.

The development of a new Pace design is approached from two points of view: marketing need and their own aesthetic creativity. Materials that inherently say quality are used in veneers, leather, acrylics, stainless steel, glass, and various fabrics.

Pace takes a great deal of time over each design at the very outset. Miniature models are built first; then full-scale ones; then a prototype product. During these three stages the design may undergo radical changes—or no changes at all. The initial designer's concept is the criterion, together with the material chosen for its aesthetic value. With design element foremost, construction is done in the most practical and long-lasting way. Many materials on the current scene in furniture had been used in the United States by domestic makers such as Pace before they appeared in imports. The beauty of these materials gives the piece its intrinsic physical appeal.

Contemporary Materials

Natural imperfections do not detract from the aesthetic value of materials used in today's American furniture. A sense of quality is the first consideration—but also a sense of frailty.

Glass, *of the right dimension, is reflective, transparent, light-looking. It encompasses its environment: it is practical yet delicate in its jewel-like quality. Scratches are natural and do not detract from its beauty.*

Leather *is also an "imperfect" material, with natural cracks or markings—yet its feel is superb, pleasing to the eye and the touch.*

Woods *such as burl, Japanese Tamo, elm, olive ash, burl ovankol wood, and pauferro wood, not to mention all the many veneers, also have natural imperfections and variations in thickness and graining. Small holes, plugged but still left showing after many coats of sealer and lacquer and hours upon hours of hand rubbing and polishing, do not detract from the wood's natural beauty.*

107

Figure 9-10: Contemporary desk by Leon Rosen of Pace Furniture. (Pace Furniture.)

Figure 9-11: Contemporary seating system consists of modular units upholstered in leather, suede, or (as here) imported fabrics: a visually exciting and extremely comfortable seating series. (Pace Furniture.)

Materials in combination are pleasing to the eye, too. Doors may be upholstered in suede or leather, combining well with hard materials such as marble tops. Legs made from clear acrylic may be combined with mohair fabrics, or steel with leather upholstery or the dark wood burls.

Elegant furniture designs are a blend of pure line and subtle use of quality material. Irving Rosen's statement to furniture designers is: "The most important thing for an interior designer to do is to be totally aware of what is available and the strength of each manufacturer; this is where the strength to his client lies." (See Figures 9–10, 9–11, 9–12, and 9–13.)

Figure 9-12: *Coffee table designed by I. M. Rosen for Pace Furniture: pure lines are visually as rewarding as a piece of fine sculpture. (Pace Furniture.)*

Figure 9-13: *Cylinder table designed by Janet Schwietzer can be used as an end table at various heights, or as a base for a glass-topped dining table. (Pace Furniture.)*

American Furniture of the 1960s and 1970s

Today the exquisite furniture designs of the 1930s by Breuer, Mies van der Rohe, and Corbusier, although they are still being produced, are being added to by new designers. The straight angular lines of the Bauhaus are being replaced by softer, more comfortable chairs. Philosophies change as fashions change: the emphasis is still on the human form, but new methods are used in creating comfort. Modular furniture has become important, and the technical breakthroughs of Italian designers, in particular, have made great changes in furniture design of the 1970s.

ITALIAN DESIGN

The philosophy of Italian design focuses on the pleasure of comfort more than on the pleasure of the eye. Italian designers are primarily concerned with the inner and lasting quality of furniture.

Modular Furniture

Since 1966, Italian designers have developed the art of modular furniture to a fine degree. Their constructions allow a variety of moods in a range of interior environments. The following pages exemplify the progress of Italian designers through products developed for Atelier International, Ltd. Furniture Company, a pacesetter in the contemporary scene. The seven stages of development shown mark the changes in modular furniture in the Atelier International line from 1966 to 1977.

MARIO BELLINI CHAIR, 1966. This chair was the first polyurethane piece produced in Italy for the commercial market. A group consisting of an armless chair, a single, right-arm chair and a single left-arm chair, an armchair, and an ottoman allows the designer to easily arrange any seating configuration desired. The individual units are locked together by concealed tabs. The construction of any one piece is the ultimate in simplicity: urethane slabs make up the back and arms, while a plywood box covered with urethane and overlying dacron provides the seat. These "building blocks" are individually upholstered with zippered covers and are belted together with leather straps, allowing flexible response to the pressure of the body. The key to the success of this design is the construction of the slabs and seats, in which different densities of urethane and dacron foam are employed. From the solid urethane core, there is a progression through lighter and lighter foams to the much lighter dacron cover. This method of construction produces a pleasing sense of softness and buoyancy in each seat cushion.

CIPREA, 1968. Designed by Afra and Tobia Scarpa. The advent of polyurethane led to more sophisticated one-piece constructions, such as this free-standing armchair with casters, and its armless counterpart. Unlike the modular units composed of slabs, this Scarpa creation is created by a single injection of polyurethane around a steel skeleton submerged in a mold. The entire chair is removed from the mold after the foam sets, and adorned with a slipcover. The soft dacron seat cushion is separate. (See Figures 9–14 and 9–15.)

110

Figure 9-14: "Ciprea," designed by Afra and Tobia Scarpa. This is a manufacturing photo of the unfinished molded polyurethane chair. (Atelier International, Ltd.)

Figure 9-15: "Ciprea," finished and upholstered in corduroy. (Atelier International, Ltd.)

111

SORIANA, 1970. Designed by Afra and Tobia Scarpa, this collection, winner of the coveted Compasso d'Oro in 1970, features an armless chair, two- or three-seat sofas, an ottoman, and a chaise longue. It represents a combination of the two earlier technologies, the composite and cast forms. The body of each piece consists first of varying densities of polyurethane foam which form the core. Dacron fiberfill is then placed around it. All is bound into a soft amorphous form by a blanket cover attached to a plywood base with disc feet and rear casters. The soft, shapeless piece is given proper anatomical form through application to its exterior of a high-carbon, spring-steel chrome-plated form. Tufting buttons are applied to further soften the construction. (See Figures 9–16 and 9–17.)

Figure 9-16: *Cross-section showing construction of "Soriana," designed by Afra and Tobia Scarpa. (Atelier International, Ltd.)*

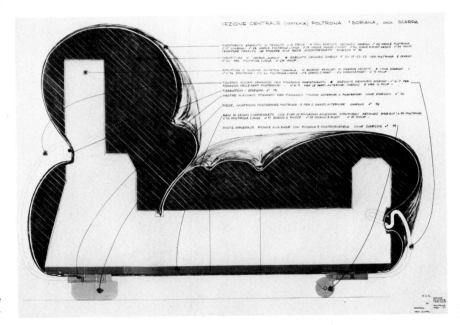

Figure 9-17: *Front and back views of the finished version of "Soriana." (Atelier International, Ltd.)*

MARALUNGA, 1973. Designed by Vico Magistretti. Offered as an armchair or two- and three-position sofa, each unit of this line has individual and independent headrests. Each piece is composed of panels constructed by injection of expanded polyurethane foam over a welded steel armature. The panels are padded with dacron fiberfill and bolted together to form the finished chair. Dacron fiberfill also makes up the loose seat cushions, folded arms and back. For ease of conversion from armchair to lounge, the armchair back cushion becomes a headrest simply by being turned lengthwise. The panels are handily unbolted for change of slipcover or other repair. (See Figure 9–18.)

Figure 9-18: "Maralunga," designed by Vico Magistretti. (Atelier International, Ltd.)

MARIO BELLINI SEATING SYSTEM, 1975. This later stage of development adds a new twist to the trend toward use of panels set with the introduction of Maralunga in 1973. It is a small-scale, very flexible modular seating system featuring ten panels that can be arranged into conventional armchairs and sofas, as well as nontraditional U-shaped and inner/outer corner configurations. Ganging devices link one unit to another. The construction consists of a steel armature and spring structure cast in polyurethane foam and covered with dacron fiberfill to supply softness, yet it maintains stability and support over time. These modular pieces also incorporate zippered slipcovers.

113

SOFTWARE SEATING SYSTEM, 1976. Designed by Mario Bellini, this concept in furniture design, says Stephen H. Kiviat of Atelier International, is a blueprint for the future. "It has a tremendous amount of latitude. You can make an incredibly large number of different pieces of seating with the same set of components," he says. Interior designers have unlimited possibilities for use in residential or contract interiors, because they can fashion any combination of armchairs, sofas, or nontraditional configurations for multiple settings and moods. The basic construction of very thin, yet strong panels is made by enclosing steel armatures and spring steel structures within cast polyurethane foam. Panel bolts and industrial zippers sewn into the panel covers are employed to fasten the units together. Cushions and pillows are dacron fiberfill, natural down feather, or both. Kiviat notes that the real art of making such furniture with urethane and dacron is understanding the "very tricky combination" of different densities of the materials. In the planning stage, prototype after prototype is fabricated until the proper combination of support and softness is reached. (See Figure 9–19.)

Figure 9-19: A single unit from Mario Bellini's "Software seating system," the latest conception in Italian furniture design. (Atelier International, Ltd.)

MOLDED PLASTIC, 1977. These pieces, comprising sixty-five different subassembly parts, are designed for flexibility of seating configurations. The shell is an injection-molded polyamide (nylon) chosen for durability and suitable for a variety of color finishes, creating a smooth finish on both sides. The bases are constructed of stainless, die-cast, brushed aluminum, chosen because of its light weight and its suitability to mass production. (See Figures 9–20 and 9–21.)

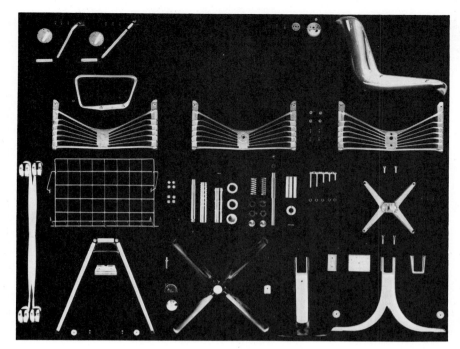

Figure 9-20: Parts used in molded plastic seating system: 65 components are used for flexibility of seating configurations. (Atelier International, Ltd.)

Figure 9-21: Molded plastic seating shown in one type of interior well suited to its use. (Atelier International, Ltd.)

The Cost of Quality

The basic expense of one of these pieces is considerably greater than that of other pieces on the market; the designer or client must realize, however, that because of its superior construction and quality, it will last many more years and amortize the cost. The leathers will mellow, soften, and improve with age; the cushions will soften and become even more comfortable with time. The style or design that is a work of art will never be dated. Instead of needing to be reupholstered or replaced, such furniture will increase in value and continue to be enjoyed. This is the lesson to keep in mind when buying any quality piece.

UNIVERSAL STYLE

We have evolved ever so slowly through furniture history to the present period, in which aesthetic ideals and technical knowledge culminate in a blending not only of art and science but also of universal strength. Today's designs can be an assemblage of materials from one country, designs from another, and manufacturing in still another. The international furniture shows, where the work of current designers can be seen, are vital for companies engaged in importing and exporting, each searching with a discriminating eye to fulfill the current marketing needs. Because the name "International Style" has become connected with the Bauhaus era, for my own purposes, I refer to today's furniture as *universal*.

● ● ●

Companies such as these, who are willing to share their vast knowledge in interviews with me, make this information possible: Mr. Stephen Kiviat of Atelier International, Ltd. deals with the technical processes in the development of Italian contemporary furniture, as well as produces the finest signed pieces of the furniture design masters. Mr. Irving Rosen shared with me his sensitive and aesthetic approach to fine design, exemplified in his own furniture designs at Pace Furniture Company as well as in his very discriminating eye for the work of other designers, included in the collection. For many years, Knoll Furniture has produced the pure contemporary lines of our finest designers, past and present, and is a leader in the furniture design field.

● ● ●

In these chapters on traditional and contemporary furniture, one area that has not been discussed much concerns the finishing touch of upholstery materials. This is because this choice of fabrics and other materials for the furnishings in a house is inextricably connected with the overall plan for the handling of color in each room.

Therefore, color is our subject in the next part of the book. No aspect of the design for a room can be considered in isolation; but of all areas for which thoughtful planning is necessary, perhaps color is the most important. Your color scheme will affect every single thing in a room, from sofas to ceilings. And the possibilities for exciting design that exist in color are unlimited.

III Color: Unlimited Possibilities

The world is filled with the magic of color, endless and limitless color, but how much do we understand of the ways in which color affects us?

Color adds beauty and diversity to our lives. Imagine for a minute a world without this wondrous element, and you will envision a drab and monotonous existence. Instead we have a treat for our senses, a lift for our moods, in the virtually unlimited variety of colors.

Your room awaits your selection of colors, like the canvas awaiting the touch of exuberant and exhilarating color. You are the artist; the decision is yours. You have the freedom to create any feeling or mood you wish to convey. The very first impression of a room is its color, be it bright and vivid or subtly neutral, shades of one color or strongly contrasting colors.

To make color theory work for you, you need to understand the basic facts about how color works. The tools are here; use them, and your color sense will develop. You will begin to think color, feel color, and enjoy the full scale of its nuances.

The information in this chapter and in Chapter 11 will be beneficial in developing any interior color schemes. Color surrounds us with chromatic subtleties that defy count; and its endless variety is a magnificent resource for you when you decide on a color scheme. The selection is entirely an expression of individual taste.

To a professional interior designer, this is a complex but rewarding assignment. The success of your venture will depend upon your knowledge of the theories of color; this knowledge will enable you to choose the most attractive palette for the desired effect of the room, fulfilling all of your aesthetic, functional, and psychological requirements.

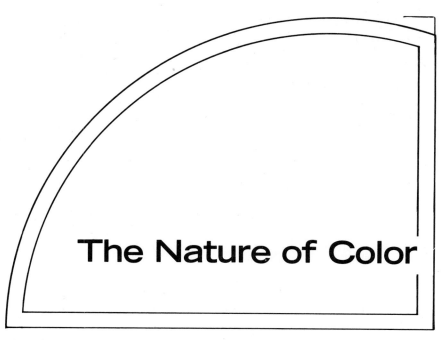
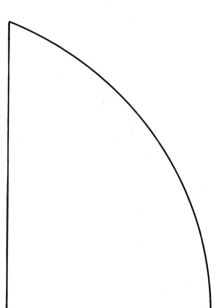

The Nature of Color

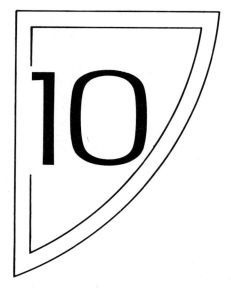

THE PHYSICS OF COLOR

Without light there would be no color: all the colors that exist are created by light.

The English scientist Sir Isaac Newton made a surprising discovery while he was trying to design a better telescope: he noted that a beam of sunlight shining through a prism separated itself into a band of color like a rainbow. His observation was the beginning of numerous scientific theories that are still revealing the wonders of color to us.

The white rays of sunlight, when subdivided either naturally or mechanically by a prismatic lens, give the color band called a *spectrum*. By holding a prism to sunlight you can see this radiant spectrum of colors: red, orange, yellow, green, blue, indigo, and violet. Each color consists of light waves of a particular length; a combination of waves of all lengths produces white light, and an absence of any light waves produces black.

The color of an object that we see is dependent upon the manner in which it absorbs and reflects light. When white light strikes an object, many of its hues are absorbed and others reflected. The rays that are reflected are the hues that the eye sees; they make up the "color" of the object.

Green grass, for example, absorbs the red and blue-violet rays of the sunlight and reflects only the green, thus creating the appearance of the color green. Orange-colored objects absorb almost all hues except orange, and this is the color that the human eye sees.

It is important to understand this today because of the many ways artificial light can affect color. For instance, warm light intensifies red, yellow, and orange and cool light intensifies blues and violets.

We have the ability to use light to our own best advantage to enhance whatever colors we have chosen.

119

PSYCHOLOGICAL EFFECTS OF COLOR

Color has a strong emotional effect on most people. Artists have long been aware of the emotional reactions that colors can induce in viewers. Interior designers, as well, are now recognizing the importance of color's psychological impact in their work.

The "temperature" of a color is one important element: there are warm hues and cool ones. Among light colors, cool colors such as blue, green, and turquoise suggest quiet and repose, and are logical choices for a room in a warm climate. The blood pressure and pulse rate are known to be reduced in the presence of cool colors. The coolness of the color has a calming effect: it acts as a sedative, and would be best used in any room where relaxation is important. In hospitals, operating rooms are usually painted a blue-green because it is easiest on the eyes.

The light warm colors, such as pale pink, yellows, melon, and cream colors, suggest warmth and congeniality. An ideal selection for a north room or a cold climate would be a warm-tone color scheme.

Stronger tones of warm colors give a sense of excitement and exhilaration; used in a family room, these colors make the room conducive to a happy atmosphere. Sunshine yellow would be suitable to an active, busy space.

The feeling or personality of the room, therefore, can actually be created through the use of color. Your individual choices in your home may be whatever colors best suit your tastes; but in a public space such as a school, theater, hotel or restaurant, it is important to use colors that will be attractive to the people who will be using the space, and that will create the mood appropriate for that space.

Human personalities are reflected in their chosen color schemes: an introverted person will be happiest in an environment of quiet restraint, while an extrovert will feel most at home in a vivid, dynamic color scheme. The younger the age, the stronger the preference for bright colors, including the pure primaries (red, yellow, and blue). Often, as people mature, their tastes become more subtle and sophisticated. Personal selections of color are usually made emotionally. To the average person a certain shade simply seems proper and pleasing, although the person may not have any idea why.

If you are an interior designer, however, you need to be familiar with the basic characteristics of any given color and the basic systems of color classification. These systems and characteristics have been developed as ways of describing or defining the virtually infinite variety of pigments that color our world.

PIGMENT THEORIES

Two different theories have been reviewed so far: the physicists' theory of light and the psychological theory of color/induced temperature sensation and emotion. This section is concerned with the use of color as it is available to us in pigments and dyes. The colors we deal with in interior design, as in art, are created by the use of pigments, mostly produced with chemicals.

The Three Major Color Characteristics

In describing any color, it is necessary to refer to its major characteristics. The three major characteristics of every color are defined as hue, value, and intensity.

Hue refers to the *name of the color* and its position in the color wheel. The hue is the same whether it is light or dark, dull or brilliant. It is what produces a color's *warmth or coolness:* red seems warm, blue seems cool.

Value describes the *lightness or darkness* of the color. Pink is a high (light) value of red; maroon is a low (dark) value; many values exist in between. The extreme value of white is the lightest white, while the darkest is black, and all the values in between are shades of gray.

Intensity or *"chroma"* indicates the *degree of strength* or saturation of a color, the purity of the hue. Scarlet red is a color of high chroma; rose is a softer color of weak chroma, because it has been grayed down or neutralized. One is an intense red, and the other is a less intense red, with many degrees of intensity between them.

The various ways of characterizing color have been organized into systems by three experts.

The Brewster System

Sir David Brewster developed the concept of the three primary colors: red, blue, and yellow. This pigment theory is the most familiar and by far the simplest, and leads to the understanding of the more complex systems of theories of Munsell and Ostwald (Figure 10–1).

The Munsell System

The system of color worked out by Albert Munsell is distinguished by the presence of five principal hues: red, yellow, green, blue, and violet—and five intermediate hues: yellow-red, green-yellow, blue-green, violet-blue, and red-violet. (See Figures 10–2 and 10–3.)

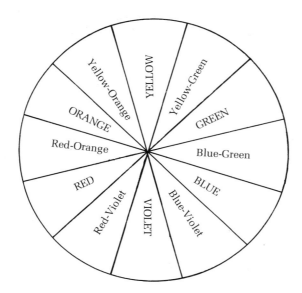

Figure 10-1: The Brewster color wheel, showing the familiar three primary colors: red, blue, and yellow. (Helene Levenson, ASID.)

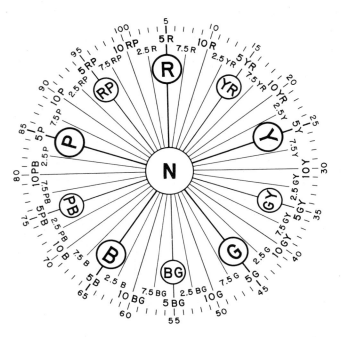

Figure 10-2: The Munsell system of denoting hues and their relation to one another. Five principal hues and five intermediate hues are encircled; a further breakdown into 100 hues is indicated by the outer circle of markings. Each color family is broken down into four parts (2.5, 5, 7.5, and 10). (Courtesy of Munsell Color, Baltimore, Md.)

The complete Munsell notation for any color is written as hue, value, and intensity (sometimes referred to as *chroma*). This is followed in more depth in Chapter 11.

The Ostwald System

The system formulated by Wilhelm Ostwald comprises three pairs of complementary (or opposite) colors: red and green, blue and yellow, and black and white. These six hues, plus five intermediates between each pair, are placed around a wheel or circle of hues. Value and intensity are not differentiated on the wheel: colors are lightened or darkened by the addition of more white or black.

Color charts have been standardized through the world, and colors are referred to by name, using a color wheel. In the color wheel illustrated, the various hues are arranged in a circle, each one shown in its most brilliant chroma (or intensity) at the outside of the wheel. The hues are then neutralized (grayed) in graded steps toward the center, until they approach the center, becoming neutral gray.

The strong intensities are more stimulating, the neutral ones are more restful. The best results in decorating can be obtained by combining a variety of different intensities and values. Values can seem to change under different kinds and different amounts of light. With paints, changes in value can be made by adding white to lighten a color of black to darken it. More neutral colors (colors of lower intensity) are made by mixing hues that are complementary or opposite on the color wheel.

Set against a contrasting value, the effect of a color changes. Gray set against black will appear lighter than the same gray set against white. This is also true with the values of all other colors.

The scales of intensity can be as varied as one wishes; the full intensity is the pure strength of a color, and it can be grayed down.

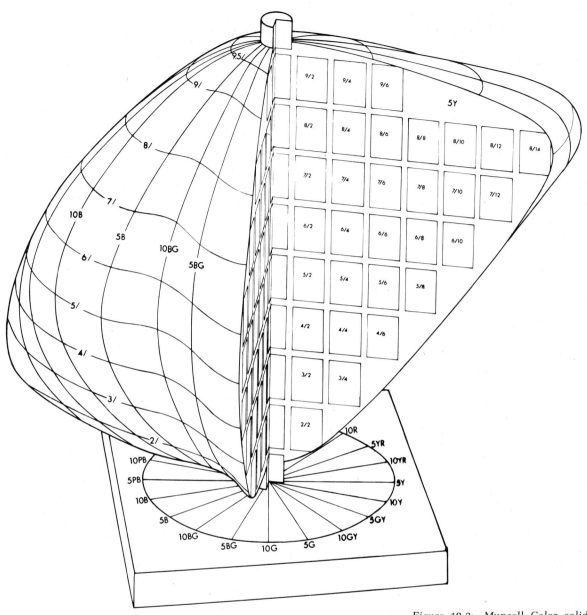

Figure 10-3: Munsell Color solid cuta-
way diagram to show constant hue 5Y.
(Courtesy of Munsell Color, Baltimore,
Md.)

You can also heighten the apparent intensity of a color simply by
placing it next to the color that is opposite it on the color wheel.
Thus, red will appear to be more intense if it is placed next to green.

We also are able to create optical illusions and camouflage
through use of color. Colors can affect the apparent size of a room or
its furniture. Warm hues of strong intensities tend to make an object
appear larger and seem to come forward in space. Cool colors, on the
other hand, make an object appear smaller and seem to recede in
space.

This can work to your advantage. For instance, if a sofa appears
too large for a room, it may be because of the fact that the upholstery
fabric is a warm color: covering it in a cool or neutral color will
make it appear smaller.

123

The apparent size of a room can be affected the same way. If a room has walls painted in a warm, intense color, the walls seem to advance and make the room feel much smaller. If the same room is painted in a light, cool color, the walls seem to recede and, therefore, give the illusion of much more space.

An all-white room will appear larger, a dark-paneled room smaller. The outlines of any object will stand out more clearly when it is placed against a background of contrasting color.

These theories can be used well in designing a room in which

Figure 10-4: Munsell hue, value, and chroma (intensity) scales in "color space." The value scale is graded in equal visual steps from black (bottom) to white (top). The circular hue scale is positioned in equal visual steps around this axis. Chroma, or intensity, scales radiate in equal visual steps from the neutral axis outward to the periphery of the color space. (Courtesy of Munsell Color, Baltimore, Md.)

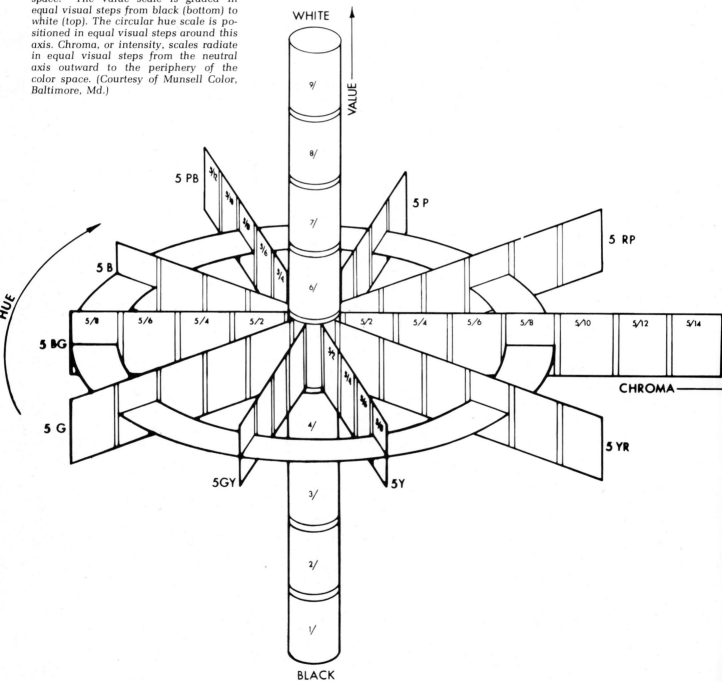

the proportions are not perfect. Color is a designer's most effective tool.

When you move from a consideration of characteristics and classification to the question of what colors to employ in an actual room, two things will guide you. Your own "eye" for what is pleasing and effective in a given space is most important. But your eye can be aided by a working knowledge of proven types of color schemes. There are innumerable color schemes—but a vast number of successful ones fall into the seven basic categories (Chapter 11).

Figure 10-5: *Contrasts of dark and light make this interior effective. Dark-matted paintings and dark wood table at rear stand out against light, airy wallpaper; light sofa and dark chairs each create contrast with their backgrounds. (Wallcovering Information Bureau)*

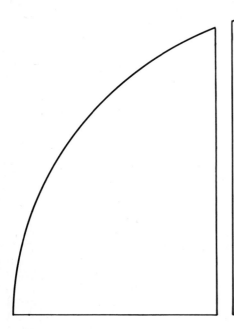

Color Schemes

Choosing your color scheme is by far the most fascinating and rewarding step in interior design. Like an artist approaching a new canvas, the designer with a knowledge of the time-tested color schemes can interpret or expand upon them to achieve any desired effect.

With each new interior, a new personality is created through a variety of contrasts, through balances of proportions, through light and shadow—and through color used for strength, impact, or serenity. These basic color schemes have been used with skill and imagination for countless interiors. Now you can identify them.

Color schemes fall into two general categories. All schemes using neighboring hues on the color wheel, and all monochromatic (or one-color) schemes, are called *related*. Schemes using opposite colors—complementary, double-complementary, split-complementary, triad, or tetrad—are called *contrasting*.

RELATED COLOR SCHEMES

Monochromatic Color Scheme

The monochromatic color scheme is derived from a single color (*mono* means one, *chroma* means color). This is one of the most often-used and effective types of color scheme. The single color can vary among all shades from high light to low dark, and from full intensity to almost neutral.

Green, for instance, can run the range of many hues, from the palest watery green to emerald green, through forest green, gray-green, and natural leaf-green tones. The colors can seem even more varied through the use of textures. The soft texture of emerald-green velvet on a sofa, near the hard texture of a gray-green flagstone floor, heightens the visual interest. Any color used alone with white is very effective—for example, an all-white room with accents of deep emerald-green used with plants and foliage.

126

Any one color, in its own range, creates a feeling of unity and harmony. The tried and true monochromatic scheme is a safe and effective one.

Analogous Color Schemes

The analogous color scheme includes three or more neighboring colors on the color wheel. This selection, too, is always harmonious and very successful.

Each of the colors can be used in its brightest hue and with its contrasting shades from lights to darks, thus obtaining a large variety within the three or more colors. Take for example a yellow, yellow-orange, orange, and red-orange combination. The range can include many tones from pale to deep yellow, blending gently into the various shades of orange, terracotta, red-orange, or russet. The depth and diversity obtained by these variations of each color, and their contrasts one against the other, combined with the use of textures and patterns throughout, have almost unlimited possibilities.

CONTRASTING COLOR SCHEMES

Complementary Color Schemes

The complementary color scheme is made up of any two opposite colors on the color wheel. Examples would be orange and blue, yellow and violet, or red and green.

This can be an extremely successful type of color scheme if it is used carefully. Contrasting colors can be very startling to the eye, if the same intensity is used for each hue. Red and green, as a color scheme for Christmas, is very effective in small doses—but it would be difficult to live with all year. However, the most beautiful interiors can be made up of pastel shades of dusty pink ranging to rose, contrasted with pale grayed greens. Another example would be a white room, a neutral background setting off many plants of various shades of green and green slate floors, with a contrasting brick-red wall and small amounts of accent color in deep brick-red. Navy with vivid copper color or even terracotta can be just as effective. (See Figure 11–1.)

An important rule to remember when you are using a complementary color scheme is not to use equal values and intensities of each color. If one color is vivid, use its opposite in a paler or grayed tone. This color scheme can give wonderfully dramatic effects. It is also just the right way to add a small amount of color to an interior that is too bland or too harmonious. This color scheme can bring out whatever it is in the room that you choose to accentuate—such as a painting or a collection of some sort.

Double-Complementary Color Schemes

The double-complementary color scheme is simply a further development of the complementary scheme, using two complementary sets of neighboring colors: for example, orange and red-orange used with blue and blue-green. This gives a little more variety to the range of hues and gives the harmonious effect of an analogous color scheme with accents in the complementary colors. (See Figure 11–2.)

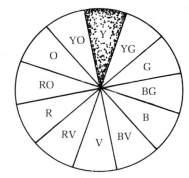

Figure 11-1: Color schemes based on the Brewster color wheel. Top to bottom: monochromatic, analogous, and complementary. (Helene Levenson, ASID.)

MONOCHROMATIC COLOR SCHEME

ANALOGOUS COLOR SCHEME

COMPLEMENTARY COLOR SCHEME

127

Figure 11-2: Color schemes based on the Brewster color wheel. Top to bottom: double-complementary, split-complementary, and triad. (Helene Levenson, ASID.)

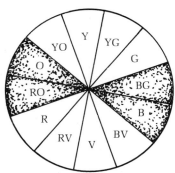

DOUBLE COMPLEMENTARY
COLOR SCHEME

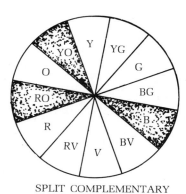

SPLIT COMPLEMENTARY
COLOR SCHEME

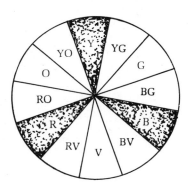

TRIAD COLOR SCHEME

Split-Complementary Color Schemes

The split-complementary color scheme is another variation on the complementary theme. It is made up of one hue and the two hues on either side of its opposite color. For blue, the opposite color is orange; the two hues on either side of orange on the wheel are yellow-orange and red-orange. Thus a blue and white interior with color accents in yellow-orange or harvest gold, with a rust brick floor, would be an effective split-complementary. This color scheme plan is also a good way to warm up an otherwise cool color scheme.

Triad Color Scheme

A triad color scheme consists of any three hues that are an equal distance from one another on the color wheel.

This can be an intensive color scheme; the answer to its successful use is, again, to use various shades of each color, not just the most brilliant hue of all three. If the colors chosen were blue, yellow, and red, an example of an effective triad color scheme could place navy or Williamsburg blue (grayed blue) against a mustard color with brighter red or darker red for accents. The possibilities in this scheme, as for the others, are limitless and intriguing.

Tetrad Color Scheme

The tetrad color scheme is composed of any four hues that are on equal distance from one another on the color wheel. This is actually a type of split-complementary color scheme, but does not use neighboring colors. It can lead to marvelous combinations of colors, all of which, with their tonal values, could possibly be found in one beautiful print fabric, with accents of each color used in small amounts throughout the room. A tetrad might, for instance, consist of blue, yellow-green, orange, and red-violet. This is a more intricate and very challenging color scheme.

In your final selection of colors, keep in mind that the color unity of the entire house or apartment is maintained by using one basic color scheme throughout, with variations in each room. If you were to jump from one set of split-complementaries to another, the effect would be much too jarring.

Let us take as an example a country home using the split-complementary color scheme of blue, yellow-orange, and orange-red, and follow the color scheme from room to room.

The front hall might have walls and ceiling papered in a navy blue and white pattern print, with bright yellow-orange flowers in a white bowl set against a mirror. The floor is white flat ceramic.

In the living room is a pale and subtle harvest-gold rug; a chair is covered in a tree-of-life print in bright harvest gold, various shades of blues to navy, and white. Placed on a navy and white sofa are many pillows, some in blues, and some in various shades of the harvest gold. The slightest touches of red-orange are introduced in minor accents. All is set against white walls.

128

Coming into the kitchen, the same colors are visible, but treated in an entirely different manner. The white walls are used again, but red-orange is now the main hue, in a toned-down earthy color, perhaps in a herringbone-patterned brick floor, used with shiny dark wood paneling on the cabinets. Gleams of copper light the room, and the deeper-color print at the windows is again the brick color (a shade of red-orange) with bright cobalt blue accents. Blue might also be used on painted finished chair frames. The vivid blue is now being used as the minor color, and an area rug in this blue might heighten the contrast.

This brick or red-orange color now leads by rug and brick floor to the family room. The color makes a slight transition from brick color to red, without jarring the eye. Red is the dominant color in the family room.

The entire color scheme flows, with many variations, from room to room.

TEXTURES AND PATTERNS IN COLORS

A variety of textures and surfaces will give your room even greater interest. Consider them in your overall scheme. Shiny surfaces can be chrome and steel, mirrors, lacquered furniture and walls, wet-look paper and fabrics, marble, satin, bright brass, and copper. Play up the impact with reflected light. Contrast a shiny surface with mellowed, hand-rubbed wood graining, soft wools, leather, suede, or a deep pile rug. Use straw, ceramics, foliage, bamboo, tiles, weavings—anything that will add interest to the textures in your room.

The use of patterns in various ways has become an important aspect of a successful color scheme. The mode may be anything from no patterns in a room to the extreme of countless patterns. In a no-pattern room, the interest is created entirely through the use of various textures; this can be extremely effective in a contemporary setting. Or one strong pattern in such a room, like an Oriental rug or an abstract-designed area rug, is sometimes a plus.

In a more traditional room, more patterns are usually the rule. These can appear in wallpaper, printed fabrics for upholstery and drapery, floor coverings, and accessories. The amount of pattern used is a personal choice. For a multipatterned room, some basic rules govern mixing and matching. Variations of designs can complement each other if done properly—or fight each other if done incorrectly. The size of the patterns should vary. For example, if you are using a large all-over print fabric, an accent fabric in a check, plaid, or stripe will relate, if the size is smaller or of a medium size. A third pattern, possibly a tiny repeat print, or small check or dot, would complete the size variations.

The colors in all these patterns must relate to one another for unity. The use of many patterns varies with changing trends in design. Our eye sometimes has to become accustomed to each new trend.

129

BREAKING THE RULES

The main concern in this chapter has been to stimulate and cultivate your interest in the magic of color. Use these rules as source material, along with the color schemes you will find in paintings, fabrics, rugs, and plants. Build on them, continue to develop your own color appreciation, and inevitably your flair for color will become more daring, more innovative.

There are always rules and styles that are "in." Following fashions in color is unnecessary; experiment, try new combinations, and follow your fancy. Today, more than ever in the history of interior design, there are infinite varieties of color for you to choose from. This, along with all your own sources of inspiration, should help you to achieve greater and more creative use of color.

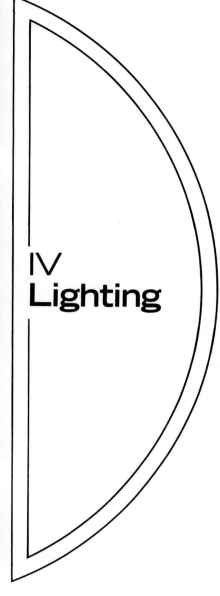

IV
Lighting

There is nothing in interior design more intriguing, more exciting, more filled with possibilities for creative effects than lighting. The opportunities for self-expression through the proper use of lighting are great; but so are its mysteries. How can the interior designer capture these desired effects—or even think in these terms—without the knowledge of how to achieve them?

The importance of good lighting is now gaining rapidly in interior design. Whereas for the past two hundred years the progress of knowledge about lighting was exceedingly slow, informative material is now becoming more readily available, and future progress is up to you, the designer.

131

Stage lighting has always been used to center attention on the main subject or focal point—highlighting or changing colors, creating moods and special effects, even stimulating psychological responses in audiences. In the hands of experts, stage lighting can beautify an area or create ugly shadows; it can compliment the actors or be very unflattering. Why, then, in our interior settings, should we leave these effects to chance instead of controlling them? Now with expertise and advanced equipment, we can do amazing things. Architects have very successfully planned buildings employing natural sunlight as part of their creation, casting the most interesting or useful shadows and creating the most efficient natural light source.

A few designers and architects today are expert in the technical intricacies of circuitry that lie behind every lighting plan—from a simple residential interior to a big commercial installation. Far more often, however, a designer (or a homeowner) works with a professional lighting expert at the detailed planning phase. The intent of this part of the book is not to turn you into an instant lighting expert; it is to acquaint you with the vocabulary of lighting, to provide a basic reference for terms and concepts in lighting, and to introduce to you some areas you may wish to study in further depth.

Chapter 12 deals with sources of light and the ways in which light is measured and controlled. Chapter 13 discusses applications of light— the many types of lighting systems that exist, ways they are classified, and ways to go about using them.

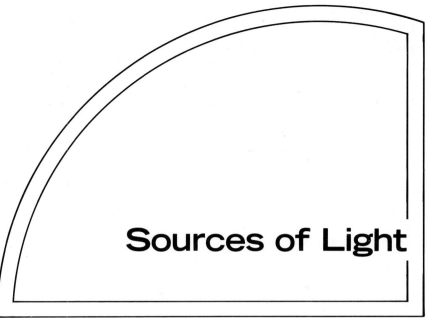

Sources of Light

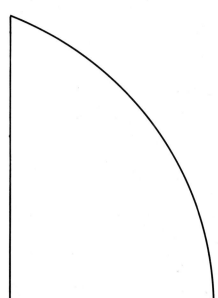

The sun is, directly or indirectly, the source of all our light. In the earliest times, people obtained light from flame—releasing the energy stored in organic matter by the sun. In order to prevent smoke and improve the light, the oil lamp was invented; during the Middle Ages, wax candles were burned. When gas lights later appeared, their flame provided still brighter light; then came gas mantles heated by this flame. Kerosene or whale-oil lamps were also used.

The first appearance of electric light came in the form of arc lights whose illumination was produced by a flaming arc of electricity between two carbon rods. Later, incandescent lamps had a filament of metal heated to a glowing point. Materials tried for these filaments were platinum, carbon, tantalum, and others. Tungsten wire has been used since 1910.

The newest form of lighting is produced by electricity passing through a gas. Mercury lamps and high-pressure sodium lamps, for instance, have an electric current passing through a mercury or sodium vapor. Fluorescent lights are also in this category. In them, the electricity passes through a mercury vapor producing ultraviolet rays which strike materials called phosphors; these in turn give off visible light. With the advancements of our present age, we have learned to control the various forms of energy and convert them to better and better light sources.

DAYLIGHT

The sun's direct light has subtle differences that defy count. The term *daylight*, for instance—does it apply to sunrise, 10 o'clock in the morning, noon, 4 o'clock in the afternoon, or sunset? How will it be different on a cloudy day, a sunny day, winter, or summer, at the same time? Will the same daylight, under exactly the same conditions, differ as seen on the north side from that seen on the south

133

side? Will it appear differently in a room with warm colors as opposed to one with cool colors? Will the climate of the area change the effect of the light? What *is* daylight?

Obviously, the sun is itself our most important light source. At an optimum time—a sunny, clear summer's day at noon—the light intensity on the earth's surface could reach a degree of 10,000 footcandles (see definitions under "Measurement of Light," p. 138). This is the equivalent of the light cast on a surface one foot away by 10,000 candles. But the sun is more than 93 million miles away from the earth; thus the sun, as a light source, is equal to 2.5 billion, billion, billion candles.

The optimum use and control of this tremendous light source, as well as the use and control of artificial light sources, is necessary in our interior environments.

ARTIFICIAL LIGHT

Our primary concern, in lighting an interior, is to get the utmost use and effect from electric light sources. These, unlike daylight, can be altered and completely controlled to provide us with light that is efficient for our work and aesthetically pleasing for our leisure moments.

Incandescent Lamps

The light source most familiar to the interior designer, and most widely used in general nonindustrial environments is the incandescent lamp. It is easily screwed into the familiar socket placed in walls, ceilings, or fixtures specially created by the designer for his or her interiors. The 60-watt bulb, operated at 115 volts, is of this type.

In most cases, these lamps consist of a filament of tungsten wire which resists the electricity flowing from the socket. This resistance produces a bright glow—and the characteristic heat that you feel when you come close to the lamp.

In most lamps above 40 watts, the filament is surrounded by an inert gas. This lessens evaporation of the tungsten in normal use and also serves to remove some heat from the filament.

The bulb surrounds the filament and encloses the inert gas. It is normally made of soft glass, although harder glasses are used for special applications such as outdoor lamps and high-intensity lighting. Bulbs come in a number of sizes and shapes—from the familiar pear shape of the type "A" lamp to parabolic configurations.

Bulbs can be coated on the inside or can be left uncoated to allow the full intensity of the filament source to illuminate an area. Those bulbs with finishes on the interior spread the rays of the filament source and produce the softer, more pleasing effect needed in interior design. Finishes include acid etching or white silica; translucent white coatings or silvery substances are sometimes used. The base of the lamp connects it to a socket. In incandescent lamps, this base is most often of a screw type, although prongs and pins are used for certain applications.

COLOR. Colored light is produced through the use of various finishes applied to the inside or to the exterior of a bulb; it is also created by use of colored glass in the bulb itself. The variety of colors available is suited to a range of interior design needs.

CLASSIFICATION. Lamps may be classified as one of five types: general-use, reflectorized, halogen, showcase, or decorative. The general-use lamps are the type A bulbs which radiate light in all directions; they require shielding by a shade for most uses. Reflector lamps (types R and PAR) consist of a single unit with light source (filament) and a reflector of aluminum or silver on the inside of the bulb. Halogen lamps employ quartz bulbs with iodine or bromine inside to keep the bulb clean. These are especially compact, heat-resistant, efficient lamps. Showcase lamps are tubular and are used in areas where narrow, longer lights are needed. Decorative lamps come in special shapes—such as Christmas tree lights. They are designed with appearance more than intensity in mind. (See Figure 12–1.)

VOLTAGE. When a designer considers the use of lamps for interior decorating, it is important that the voltage of the power supply be matched with that of the lamps. A lamp designed for lower voltage but used in a higher-voltage circuit will have a shorter lifespan than

Figure 12-1: Incandescent filament lamp types, showing wattages, lumens per watt, and lamp life in hours of each type. (From IES Lighting Handbook, 5th Edition, courtesy of Illuminating Engineering Society, New York.)

Type	Watts	Efficacy in Lumens/ Watt	Lamp Life In Hours	General Comments
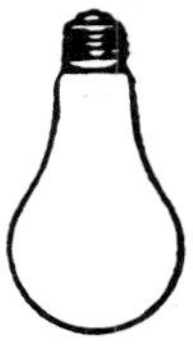 A, PS	40 to 300	12 to 20	750 to 1,000	Most wattages are available in more than one bulb size.
 R	30 to 300	—	2,000	Bulb Sizes R020 30 and 50 watt R-30 75 watt R-40 150 and 300 watt
 PAR	75 to 150	—	2,000	PAR-38 75 and 150 watt
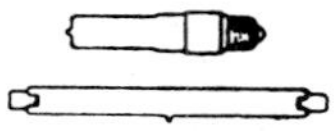 Tungsten Halogen	250 to 500	13 to 20	2,000	Single contact and two contact lamps plus a change of bulb size with wattage makes it important to select the specific lamp for which the luminaire was designed.

it is designed to have. When using a manufacturer's catalogue to order lamps, the designer should also have a clear idea of the characteristics he or she wants in the lamp—such as bulb shape, wattage, and classification.

Fluorescent Lamps

Another widely used item in interior design is the fluorescent lamp first introduced into commercial use in the late 1930s. This lighting source has qualities that can make it more desirable than incandescent lighting for closed spaces, especially if economy is desired and "natural" color (that is, resembling color seen by daylight) is required. The characteristic fluorescent tube may last ten times longer than an incandescent bulb and produce three to four times more light; it is designed to give light of daylight white or a variety of other natural colors without loss of light intensity.

Fluorescent lamps operate on electrical and physical principles slightly more complex than the incandescent bulb. Inside the fluorescent tube are two wires, or cathodes, which are connected to an outside electrical circuit of alternating current through a special lampholder. Pins on the outside of the fluorescent tube plug into the special holder.

Within the tube is a minute amount of inert gas or gases (argon, neon, krypton) which allow the electrical current to begin to flow between the cathodes when the lamp is activated. Also present is a small amount of mercury which, when it is vaporized by the current, emits invisible ultraviolet rays. These rays are converted to visible white light or light of different colors by phosphor materials which coat the inside of the tube.

BALLAST. Because the current passing between the cathodes would eventually be too high for the lamp and would destroy it, a fluorescent lamp also contains a ballast. The main function of the ballast is to control the voltage of the current inside to a safe level.

Fluorescent lamps used in interiors are available in a much smaller variety of shapes than are incandescent lamps. The most familiar and widely used is the simple, longitudinal tube which can be especially appropriate for indirect lighting in the home or office. Other shapes include circular tubes, U-shaped tubes, and tubes with twisted surfaces.

A common type of fluorescent light is the 40-watt lamp that draws 110 to 125 volts and an initial current flow of 430 milliamperes. There are, however, other types of lamps that require 800 or 1,500 milliamperes of current should the designer need a more powerful source.

Some lamps may have a reflector on the inner surface of one-half of the length of the tube. It serves to direct light out through the unshielded half to produce more light in one direction. Others have a line of clear glass, uncoated by phosphor, along the length of the tube. This design produces a very strong directional beam when the lamp is activated.

COLOR. Fluorescent tubes come in several white color values; it is best not to mix these in one room.

Deluxe Warm White is a new, improved color rendition and is not as bright as the standard warm white. It blends well with incandescent lighting and can be used in areas where both decorative light and coloring are of prime importance. Another improved color rendition, Deluxe Cool White, does not mix well with incandescent light but enhances cool decorative color schemes.

Warm White Standard tubes, used before the newer, improved types appeared, are about 25 percent brighter than the "Deluxe" varieties and provide a good work-light for utility areas. Other colors include: Cool White Standard, which intensifies cool colors and grays warm ones; White, which slightly dulls the appearance of warm colors; and Soft White, which gives off a pink light and so emphasizes the warm reds and pinks but grays the cool colors. Daylight Color tubes, seldom used in residential or restaurant design, tend to gray human complexions.

For decorative displays or theatrical effects, fluorescent lights are also available in pink, red, blue, and gold.

High-Intensity Discharge Lamps[1]

Although they are generally used outdoors, high-intensity discharge lamps (HIDs) may provide large amounts of light from a relatively small source in an interior setting. In the same family as fluorescent lamps, they employ a similar electrical and physical design. An arc of current is passed through a gaseous medium in a tube to produce light, and a ballast is provided to control the current. Unlike the fluorescent light, however, the tube is very small and is surrounded by a bulb. HIDs have a screw-in base, also, which requires the designer to exercise caution in their use: an HID may not be placed directly into a standard incandescent light socket.

High-intensity discharge lamps are available in three types. The mercury vapor lamp is a common HID, recognized by the blue-green color it emits—especially in street lights. Like the fluorescent lamp, the tube of a mercury lamp contains an inert gas and mercury, and when it is activated, electrical current initially flows through the gas to vaporize the mercury which then gives off light. But because the vapor is more highly pressurized than in a fluorescent lamp, it gives off more visible light than ultraviolet and requires little phosphor coating.

Two advantages of mercury HIDs, as compared to incandescent bulbs, are efficiency and long life. For instance, a 100-watt Deluxe White mercury lamp has an 18,000-hour average life, while a 100-watt inside frost standard incandescent household lamp has a 750-hour average life. As for the light output of these same two lamps, the mercury lamp is rated at 4,000 lumens and the incandescent lamp is rated at 1,750 lumens.[2]

Other types of HIDs include metal-halide lamps and high-pressure sodium lamps. The metal-halide lamp operates on the same principle as a mercury lamp, but the vapor contains other metals in

[1]Information on HIDs condensed from General Electric's book, *High-Intensity Discharge Lamps*, by permission of General Electric Co., Lamp Business Division.
[2]Information provided by General Electric Co., Lamp Business Division, and reprinted by permission.

addition to mercury, which cause its light to tend toward the blue-white end of the spectrum. The sodium lamp, which utilizes sodium and metals to produce current flow, is the most efficient of the three and produces a warmer light than the others.

MEASUREMENT OF LIGHT

Any lighting catalogue available for use by interior designers will contain numerical information on the characteristics of lamps. For this reason, it is important to know basic terminology describing lamp intensity, efficiency, and effect on an object.

Candlepower (I) and Candela (cd)

The *candlepower* (I) of a lamp is expressed in *candelas* (cd). A candela is the unit of measure of a standard candle *in a specified direction*, as opposed to light thrown in all directions or light reflected from an object. A wax candle, which casts the brightness of one candela in a horizontal direction, is the international standard by which all light source brightness is measured.

Lumen (Lm)

The lumen (Lm) is the unit of measurement of the total light output of a light source. It refers to light thrown on a one-square-foot area surface, all points of which are one foot away from a one-candela source. All light sources are rated by their manufacturers in lumens. A few examples:

- ○ 25 w. incandescent: 235 lumens
- ○ 60 w. incandescent: 870 lumens
- ○ 100 w. incandescent: 1750 lumens
- ○ 20 w. fluorescent: 820 lumens (Deluxe Warm White)
- ○ 40 w. fluorescent: 2150 lumens (Deluxe Warm White)

The light-producing ability of light sources is expressed in "lumens per watt." The performance of the above sources would be as follows:

- ○ 25 w. incandescent: 9 lumens per watt
- ○ 60 w. incandescent: 14 lumens per watt
- ○ 100 w. incandescent: 17.5 lumens per watt
- ○ 20 w. fluorescent: 41 lumens per watt
- ○ 40 w. fluorescent: 54 lumens per watt

Note that fluorescent lamps give more lumens per watt than incandescent, and that both sources have higher efficiencies in the higher wattages.

Footcandle (fc)

The footcandle (fc) denotes density of light on a surface. It is the illumination at a point on a surface that is one foot from a standard candle—or, expressed another way, one lumen per square foot of surface. Although this definition appears similar to that for a lumen, it concerns the illumination on an object removed from a source, not the flow of light from the source itself. Recommended illumination levels for various visual tastes are expressed in footcandles.

Footlambert (fL)

The footlambert (fL) is the unit of photometric brightness, or luminance, of an object. It is used to express the amount of light transmitted through or reflected from an object's surface. A surface that reflects or transmits perfectly diffuse light at the rate of one lumen per square foot of area has a photometric brightness of one footlambert. The footlamberts of a reflecting or transmitting surface are always less than the footcandles of original lumination, because no medium reflects or transmits 100 percent of the light that strikes it.

Dark colors reflect less than light colors, and so have lower luminance (fewer footlamberts), even though the amount of light falling on them is the same. To achieve equal visibility, higher footcandle levels are needed for working with dark materials than with light ones, because of the lower reflecting power (footlamberts) of the dark materials. Visibility is affected by *footlamberts*. We *see* luminance; we do *not* see footcandles.[3]

Reflectance, transmission, and absorption are terms used to describe three important characteristics of illuminated objects. For example, if 200 lumens are thrown on the inside of a one-square-foot spherical surface, the illumination of the surface is 200 footcandles. If 120 lumens are reflected from one side of that same surface, the photometric brightness is 120 footlamberts. Because 120 footlamberts is 60 percent of 200 footcandles, the *reflectance* factor of that surface is said to be point 6 (.6), or 60 percent. If 60 lumens are passed through the reflecting surface and observed from the other side, the brightness on that side is 60 footlamberts. Therefore, the *transmission* factor is point 3 (.3), or 30 percent. Because 120 lumens are reflected and 60 lumens are transmitted, 20 of the original 200 lumens are absorbed by the surface of the object in question; so the *absorption* factor is point 1 (.1), or 10 percent.[4]

The Light Meter

A useful instrument for measuring light in interiors is the simple pocket light meter. It consists of a photocell that converts light into a tiny electric current that is measured by an ammeter. The ammeter records on an easy-to-read dial the footcandles of light emitted from a surface. The instrument is unlike the human eye, however, because it must be corrected to read colors as we do—and to sense light as if it were coming from a surface directly perpendicular to it. The use of color filters and special materials accomplish these corrections. To be sure that the meter is corrected, look for the words "color corrected" and "cosine corrected" on the device.

[3] Ibid.
[4] Adapted from General Electric's book, *Light Measurement and Control,* by permission of General Electric Co., Lamp Business Division.

The simple light meter directly measures footcandles, and the advice of an experienced engineer or designer will help you to perfect its use in practical situations.

In order to measure reflectance, however, it is necessary to use a special procedure. Hold the meter directly perpendicular to the surface and approximately 5 to 6 inches away from it. The reading (in footcandles) will represent footlamberts, or photometric brightness. Divide the number of footlamberts by the number of footcandles of illumination in order to obtain the percent reflectance.[5]

Control of Light

The emissions of lamps themselves are controlled through the use in them of materials that reflect, transmit, refract, absorb, diffuse, or polarize light rays. The interior designer must become adept at using any one or a combination of these materials to create a pleasing environment.

Typical reflecting materials are aluminum, silver, or very white finishes. Transmitting materials include glass and plastics. Diffusion is accomplished by substances that scatter light evenly to produce a softened light and fuzzy-edged shadows—such as opalescent glass, cloudy plastic, or enameled glass. Refraction (bending or angling of light waves) occurs when light passes through prisms or lenses. Absorption is accomplished by colored substances. Polarized light, produced when the rays pass through a crystalline material, can be used to control undue reflection from a mirrorlike surface.[6]

GLARE. The contrasting of light values in interior design is important, but too much contrast can create an effect that is restless and tiring to the human eye. Excessive contrasts in light values, when some light is too bright, constitute glare; and control is necessary.

The most obvious type of glare is the direct glare caused by harsh reflection such as from a window or mirror. More difficult to correct is the diffused light that is not quite as obvious. Sometimes, too many lighting sources can conflict and cause a glare. Obvious solutions include moving light sources forward or backward, reducing the wattage of a bulb in a portable fixture, or using larger shades to cover exposed bulbs.

The basic terminology and background information presented in this chapter will help you plan the most effective use of lighting—both natural and artificial—in any given room. With an awareness of the various *sources* of light, and a familiarity with the ways in which light is *measured*, you can now proceed to the practical steps involved in the application of light. That will be the subject of Chapter 13.

[5] Adapted from General Electric's *Manual* by permission of General Electric Co., Lamp Business Division.

[6] Based on information in General Electric's pamphlet, *Control of Light*, and used by permission of General Electric Co., Lamp Business Division.

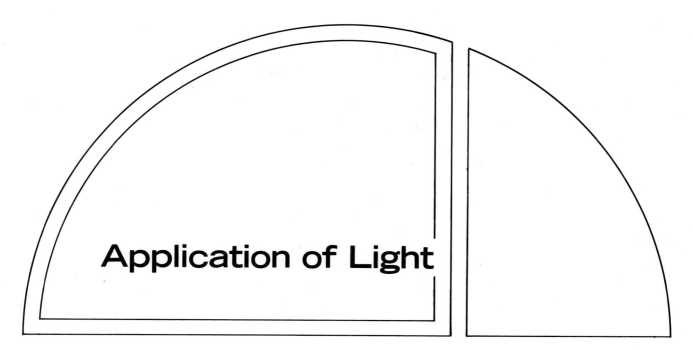

Application of Light

In this chapter we will look at the kinds of information you should have when you go about applying the abstract data about footcandles, lumens, luminance, reflectance, and so on, to an actual room lighting situation. At the outset, consider ways of classifying light sources: classifications that are used in catalogues and showrooms as well as in architectural plans and builders' specifications.

LIGHTING CLASSIFICATIONS

There are two general ways in which lighting systems are classified, according to the Illuminating Engineering Society. First: artificial light sources are classified in accordance with the *layout or location* relative to the visual task or object lighted. In this classification are general lighting, localized general lighting, and local (supplementary) lighting. Second: light sources are also classified in accordance with the CIE (International Commission on Illumination) luminaire types. Types of luminaire used are: direct, semi-direct, general diffuse (direct-indirect), semi-indirect, and indirect.

Classification by Layout and Location

GENERAL LIGHTING. This lighting system is used to determine a standard level of illumination on work planes throughout an entire area. (This allows flexibility for the later choice of individual task-area lighting.) For general lighting in conversation and relaxation areas and in passage areas, the recommended available light should be at least 10 footcandles—or about 11 dekalux (a dekalux is equal to .929 footcandles). For visual task areas, however, the recommendation is for 30 footcandles: about 32 dekalux. These are standards of the Illuminating Engineering Society.

141

LOCALIZED GENERAL LIGHTING. This form of lighting takes into consideration the requirements of visual task or work areas, while also providing illumination for the entire room area.

LOCAL LIGHTING. Designed strictly to provide light on and closely around the task area, this system usually is supplementary to the general lighting, for it is inadequate by itself.

Classification by CIE Luminaire Type

DIRECT LIGHTING. A direct lighting system is formed when luminaires direct 90 to 100 percent of their output directly down, whether to cover a small concentrated area or a more widespread one.

SEMI-DIRECT LIGHTING. The lighting distribution from the semi-direct luminaire is predominantly (60 to 90 percent downward, but with some upward component illuminating the ceiling and upper walls. Upward light, therefore, equals 10 to 40 percent.

GENERAL DIFFUSE LIGHTING. When the downward and upward portions of the light from luminaires are about equal, the luminaires fall into the general diffuse classification. Within this type are three subdivisions:

In the *direct-indirect* category, light distribution is up and down; the luminaires emit very little light at angles near the horizontal.

In the *semi-direct* classification, the lighting emits 60 to 90 percent of its output upward, and 10 to 40 percent downward.

Indirect lighting systems direct 90 to 100 percent of the light upward to the ceiling and upper side walls; therefore, the ceiling becomes the prime source of illumination. Reflected light from the ceiling and upper walls falls on the work plane. Care must be taken, therefore, that these surfaces have high reflectances.

TYPES OF FIXTURES

There is not a uniform lighting system for residential lighting practice, because each interior must be handled in an individual way. Before you begin to study the many kinds of fixtures that can be used to achieve the desired level of light for a given area, look at Figure 13–1. This chart shows the symbols used for luminaires affording various types of illumination. Together with the symbols are diagrammatic representations of incandescent and fluorescent fixtures, with indications of what type of illumination each provides.

Task Lighting

Task lighting is considered first in its relationship to the general lighting system. Thought must be given to the blending of three major zones: first, the task area itself; then the immediate area surrounding the task; and finally, the entire room area.

Figure 13-1: Lighting symbols and lighting fixtures, showing the type of illumination provided by each type of incandescent or fluorescent fixture. Reproduced from Graphic Guide to Interior Design by Forrest Wilson, Copyright 1977 by Litton Education Publishing, Inc., by permission of Van Nostrand Reinhold Company.)

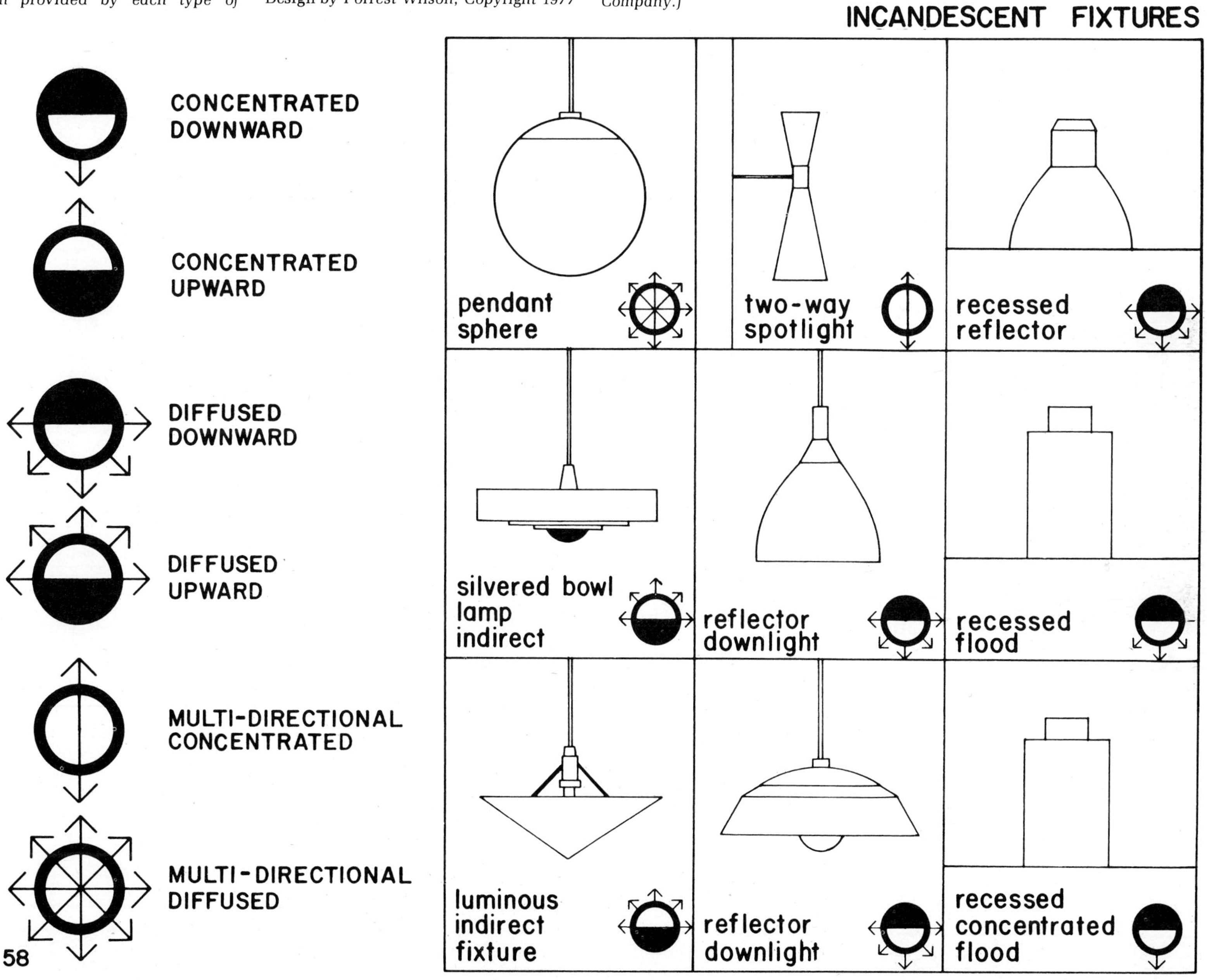

INCANDESCENT FIXTURES

pendant sphere

two-way spotlight

recessed reflector

silvered bowl lamp indirect

reflector downlight

recessed flood

luminous indirect fixture

reflector downlight

recessed concentrated flood

CONCENTRATED DOWNWARD

CONCENTRATED UPWARD

DIFFUSED DOWNWARD

DIFFUSED UPWARD

MULTI-DIRECTIONAL CONCENTRATED

MULTI-DIRECTIONAL DIFFUSED

58

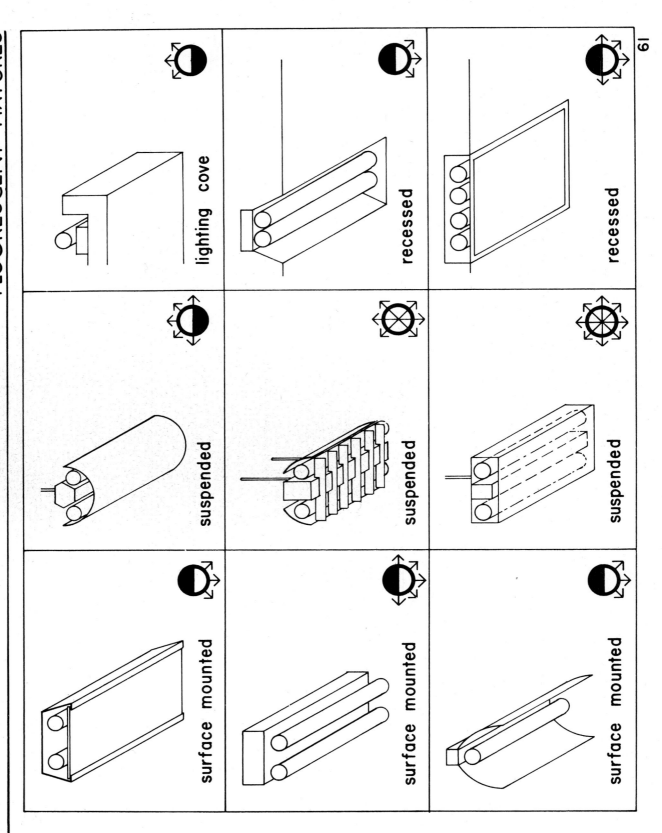

FLUORESCENT FIXTURES

lighting cove

recessed

recessed

suspended

suspended

suspended

surface mounted

surface mounted

surface mounted

Figure 13-1 (cont.)

19

Plate 3
Helene Levenson, A.S.I.D., NHFL: A monochromatic
color scheme evolved from a single hue of blue.
(Photo © Peter Vanderwarker)

Plate 4
Helene Levenson, A.S.I.D., NHFL: An analogous color
scheme employs three or more neighboring hues.
Shown here: yellow through orange to red.
(Photo © Peter Vanderwarker)

Plate 5
Helene Levenson, A.S.I.D., NHFL: A complementary
color scheme is built on any two hues directly
opposite each other on the color wheel—which
always creates a drama of color. Blue and orange
were chosen here. (Photo © Peter Vanderwarker)

Plate 6
Helene Levenson, A.S.I.D.,
NHFL: An all-neutral color
scheme is seen here, with gray
as its dominant color. (Photo
© Peter Vanderwarker)

Plate 7 (below)
Hortense Davis, F.A.S.I.D.:
Imaginative uses of fabric and
patterns in a beautifully designed
bedroom. (Photo by Louis Reens)

Plate 8
R. Michael Brown, A.S.I.D.:
Contemporary design at its best,
this den is a study in contrasts.
(Photo by Louis Reens)

Plate 9
Leon Barmache, A.S.I.D.: This
room, planned as a den/guest
room, contains all the elements
one could want for relaxation.
(Photo by Louis Reens)

Plate 10
Helene Levenson, A.S.I.D., NHFL: This country setting was transformed from a once-formal room by designing architectural changes. (Photo © Edward Jacoby)

Plate 11 (left)
Dana Noble, A.S.I.D.: This sitting room creates a peaceful atmosphere in muted colors. Fortuny fabric is used on the walls and Roman shades. (Photo © Peter Vanderwarker)

Plate 12 (opposite page)
William C. Elinoff, A.S.I.D. Assoc., of Martin Elinoff Associates: Yards and yards of muslin cover everything. In this chic, dramatic room, the color of muslin is then echoed in carpet, pillows, and draperies. (Courtesy of Lees Carpets; photo by Darwin K. Davidson)

Plate 13 (previous page)
Richard Fitz Gerald, interior designer: In the tradition of great decorating, the artifacts assembled here include rare Chinese porcelains, Tibetan figures, and an Indian *hare krishna* wall hanging. (Photo © Peter Vanderwarker)

Plate 14 (below)
Michael Robert Campbell, A.S.I.D. Assoc., of Campbell-Moreau Associates. This dramatic dining area is for the young at heart. (Photo © Peter Vanderwarker)

Plate 15 (above)
Michael deSantis, A.S.I.D.: To create a spacious feeling in a small area, furnishings with an airy outdoor look were selected. (Photo by Louis Reens)

Plate 16 (left)
Pat Payne, A.S.I.D.: Billows of luscious fabric, in a tent-like design, lower the ceiling and create an intimate air—an inviting corner for any room. (Photo © Edward Jacoby)

Plate 17 (above left)
Richard Fitz Gerald, interior designer: Sophisticated yet informal, 16th century combined with 20th century, this room is a marvelous mixture of styles, each complementing the other. (Photo © Peter Vanderwarker)

Plate 18 (left)
Helene Levenson, A.S.I.D., NHFL: An elegant contemporary dining room, created through the use of mirror and glass, is the framework for designs of today. (Photo © Peter Vanderwarker; wall photographs by Jean Weinstein)

Plate 19 (below left)
Elaine Newman, A.S.I.D., NHFL; Elaine Hillson Federman, A.S.I.D., NHFL: and Al Federman, A.S.I.D. (Hillson Interiors). In the sophisticated apartment of a woman executive, an all-white living room is the background for bright touches of color. (Photo © Edward Jacoby)

Plate 20 (lower right)
Helene Levenson, A.S.I.D., NHFL: Cheerful and charming, the deep blue of the balloon curtains is set off by crisp white accents and neutral straw wallcoverings and chairs. (Photo © Peter Vanderwarker)

Plate 21 (opposite page)
Ellen L. McCluskey, A.S.I.D.: This bedroom and enclosed terrace are a beautiful but practical world for a client who functions from a wheelchair. (Photo by Jaimé Ardiles-Arce)

Plate 22 (opposite page) Warren Platner: architect, interior designer, and designer of furniture, artwork, and decoration. In the West Parlor of Windows on the World, brass ceiling chandeliers are reflected in two triptych mirrors, one above the other, for added light and interestingly multiplied images. (Photo by Alexander Georges)

Plate 23 (top left) Warren Platner: architect, interior designer, and designer of furniture, artwork, and decoration. In the designer's own country home, the raised and indented window seat creates a special seating place. The painted shade opens by day to a river view and, when pulled down by night, becomes an important painting. (Photo by Ezra Stoller © ESTO)

Plate 24 (top right) Terry Cabot, A.S.I.D. Assoc.: An atmosphere of elegant informality welcomes the visitor to this cozy sitting area at the end of the front hall. (Photo © Edward Jacoby)

Plate 25 (right) David Barrett, F.A.S.I.D.: This city apartment entrance foyer was imaginatively converted to accommodate a dining area.

Plate 26

David Barrett, F.A.S.I.D.: A contemporary living and dining room in a city apartment has hand-painted fabric on a modular sofa and a macramé room divider and window treatment.

Plate 27
Warren Platner: architect, interior designer, and designer of
furniture, artwork, and decoration. Warren Platner's house was
conceived as a blend of inner and outer spaces, with a lively
interaction between living area and landscape. Furniture
designed by Mr. Platner and set in a great bay window
gives the sense of being in a sheltered balcony.
(Photo by Ezra Stoller © ESTO)

Plate 28
Ellen L. McCluskey, A.S.I.D.: This lady's bedroom—formal and
glamorous, yet comfortable—was created in the most elegant
manner by an internationally known designer. (Photo by Jaimé
Ardiles-Arce)

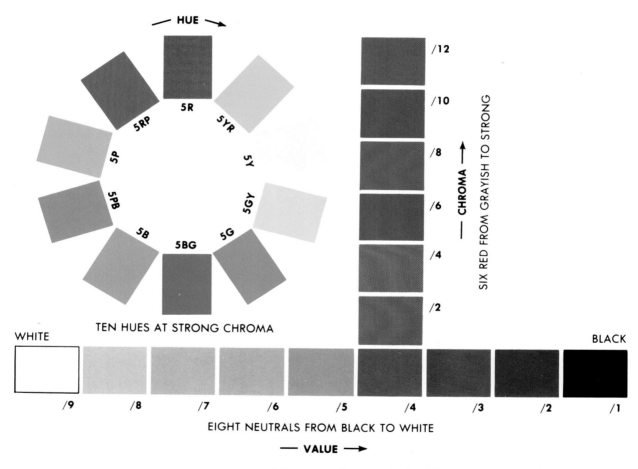

MUNSELL HUE VALUE / CHROMA CHART

HUE →

5RP
5R
5YR
5P
5Y
5PB
5GY
5B
5BG
5G

TEN HUES AT STRONG CHROMA

CHROMA ↑

SIX RED FROM GRAYISH TO STRONG

/12
/10
/8
/6
/4
/2

WHITE

/9 /8 /7 /6 /5 /4 /3 /2 /1

BLACK

EIGHT NEUTRALS FROM BLACK TO WHITE

→ VALUE →

Representative samples for N1/ are not achievable in matte finish.

Plate 29

The Munsell system identifies color in terms of three attributes—
hue, value, and intensity. (Courtesy of Munsell Color, Baltimore,
Md. 21218)

	Footcandles on Tasks
SPECIFIC VISUAL TASKS	
Dining	15
Grooming, shaving, make-up	50
Handcraft	
Ordinay seeing tasks	70
Difficult seeing tasks	100
Very difficult seeing tasks	150
Critical seeing tasks	200
Ironing (hand and machine)	50
Kitchen duties	
Food preparation and cleaning	150
Serving and other non-critical tasks	50
Laundry	
Preparation, sorting, inspection	50
Tub area-soaking, tinting	50
Washer and dryer areas	30
Reading and writing	
Handwriting, reproductions, and poor copies	70
Books, magazines, newspapers	30
Reading piano or organ scores	
Advanced (substandard size)	150
Advanced	70
Simple	30
Sewing (hand and machine)	
Dark fabrics	200
Medium fabrics	100
Light fabrics	50
Occasional-high contrast	30
Study	70
Table games	30
GENERAL LIGHTING	
Conversation, relaxation, entertainment	10
Passage areas, for safety	10
Areas involving visual tasks, other than kitchen	30
Kitchen	50

Reprinted from the *IES Lighting Handbook*, 5th ed., by permission of the Illuminating Engineering Society, New York. For proper application of these levels of illumination, refer to Section 15 of the *Handbook*.

In task lighting, besides the general considerations, the designer must keep in mind the specific characteristics of the individuals for whom the task lighting is planned. These include reduced vision problems (as in the case of the elderly) and consideration of whether the task is mainly performed during daylight or night-time hours. In all task lighting, the designer must determine what activities are to be performed in order to recommend luminance ratios in the field of view. Study the following table, which gives illumination requirements for all sorts of household tasks. Then examine the diagrams (Figures 13–2, 13–3, and 13–4) and their explanations; they will give you an idea of some of the many considerations and possible choices of lighting fixtures in typical task lighting situations.

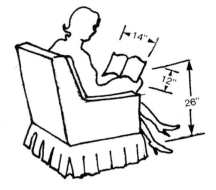

Figure 13-2: Reading in a chair. (From IES Lighting Handbook, 5th Edition, courtesy of Illuminating Engineering Society, New York.)

READING IN A CHAIR (SEE FIGURE 13–2)[1]

1. *The Task:* Typical reading tasks in a home encompass a wide range of seeing difficulty, from short-time casual reading of material with good visibility (large print on white paper) to prolonged reading of poor material (small type on low-contrast paper).

2. *Description of the Task Plane:* The task plane measures 14 inches (36 centimeters) wide by 12 inches (31 centimeters) high with the center of the plane approximately 26 inches (66 centimeters) above the floor. The plane is tilted at 45 degrees from the vertical. The reader's eyes are approximately 40 inches (102 centimeters) above the floor.

3. *Illumination Recommendations (Minimum on the Task Plane at Any Time:*
   a) Normal reading of books, magazines, papers—30 footcandles (32 dekalux).
   b) Prolonged difficult reading of handwriting, reproductions, poor copies—70 footcandles (75 dekalux).

4. *Special Design Considerations:* Normal seated eye level (38 to 42 inches [97 to 107 centimeters] above the floor) is a critical consideration when the light source is to be positioned beside the user. The lower edge of the shielding device should not be materially above or below eye height. This will prevent discomfort from bright sources in the periphery of the visual field and yet permit adequate distribution of light over the task area. Variations in chair and table heights necessitate selection and placement of equipment to achieve this relationship for each individual case.

5. *Typical Equipment Locations:*
   Table-mounted alongside or behind the user.
   Floor-mounted alongside or behind the user.
   Wall-mounted alongside or behind the user.
   Ceiling-mounted
   a) Suspended beside or behind the user
   b) Surface—large-area
   c) Recessed—large-area
   d) Large luminous element or luminous ceiling.
      Directional small-area luminaires may be used (wall, ceiling, pole-mounted) in combination with other larger-area diffusing luminaires.

Figure 13-3: Study desk. (From IES Lighting Handbook, 5th Edition, courtesy of Illuminating Engineering Society, New York.)

WORKING AT A STUDY DESK (SEE FIGURE 13–3)[2]

1. *The Task:* The task is prolonged, including difficult reading, handwriting, typing and drawing. It involves fine print and close detail.

2. *Description of the Task Planes:* The primary task is a plane 14 by 12 inches (36 by 31 centimeters) parallel with the desk top. The bottom edge of the task plane is 3 inches (7.6 centimeters) from the front edge of the desk. A secondary task plane for reference books, large drawings, etc., measures 24 inches (61 centimeters) deep by 36 inches (91 centimeters) wide with the front edge at the front of the desk top.

3. *Illumination Recommendations (Minimum on the Task Plane at Any Time):*
   a) Primary task plane—70 footcandles (75 dekalux).

[1] Reprinted from the *IES Lighting Handbook*, 5th ed., by permission of the Illuminating Engineering Society, New York.
[2] *IES Lighting Handbook.*

b) Maximum illumination on the primary plane should not exceed the minimum by more than 3 to 1.

c) Secondary task plane—30 footcandles (32 dekalux).

4. *Special Design Considerations:* The lighting equipment should be located so that shadows are not cast on the task area by the user's hand. The surface of the desk top should be nonglossy and light in color (30 to 50 percent reflectance). The luminance of any luminaire visible from a normal seated position should be no more than 150 footlamberts (510 candelas per square meter), no less than 50 (170).

5. *Typical Equipment Locations:*
Desk-mounted (1 or more luminaires).
Wall-mounted (1 or more luminaires).
Ceiling-mounted (1 or more luminaires).
Floor mounted.

READING IN BED (SEE FIGURE 13–4)[3]

1. *The Task:* The majority of people who read in bed are only casual readers, perhaps reading for a few minutes before going to sleep. They are often interested in closely confining the light distribution so as not to disturb another occupant of the room. Such lighting arrangements are not satisfactory for comfortable reading over a long period. The following recommendations are for the individual who reads for a more extended period, or for the person who performs very critical eye tasks while confined to bed. The normal materials vary from books and magazines to pocket editions and to newspaper print. Occasionally other eye work is performed in bed (usually by people confined to bed) including hobbies, crafts, sewing, embroidery, etc.

2. *Description of the Task Plane:* The task plane is 12 by 14 inches (31 by 36 centimeters) tilted at an angle of 45 degrees from the vertical. The center of the task plane is 24 inches (61 centimeters) out from the headboard or wall and 12 inches (31 centimeters) above the mattress top. There are no customary reading positions or habits. These recommendations are based on the assumption that the reader is in an upright or semireclined position.

3. *Illumination Recommendations (Minimum on the Task Plane at Any Time):* Normal reading—30 footcandles (32 dekalux). Serious prolonged reading or critical eye work—70 footcandles (75 dekalux).

4. *Special Design Considerations:* Equipment should be located so that no shadows are cast on the reading plane by the head or body, and so that the luminaire does not interfere with a comfortable position for the reader.

5. *Typical Equipment Locations:* Wall-mounted directly in back of or to one side of the user (both linear and nonlinear designs).
Luminaire on bedside table or storage headboard.
Pole-type luminaires (floor-to-ceiling or table-to-ceiling).
Ceiling-mounted
   a) Suspended: adjustable or stationary
   b) Surface-mounted: directional or nondirectional
   c) Luminous-area panel: surface mounted or recessed
   d) Recessed: directional or nondirectional Luminaire incorporated into furniture design.

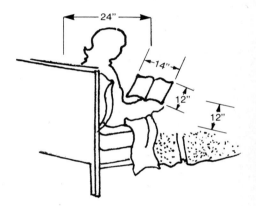

Figure 13-4: Reading in bed. (From IES Lighting Handbook, 5th Edition, courtesy of Illuminating Engineering Society, New York. For similar data for eleven other tasks, see section 15 of the Handbook.)

[3]*IES Lighting Handbook.*

Portable Lamps

This functional form of lighting can make major contributions to the general illumination as well as to the specific task. Choice of portable lamps should be determined by these factors:

UNDER-THE-SHADE COMPONENTS. Under the shade, a white bulb will provide a reasonable amount of diffusion. Other components that help to diffuse, reflect, refract, or shield the light—such as bowls, shields, and dishes—can improve lighting quality further.

VARYING LIGHT OUTPUT. A full-range dimmer, to lower lights for activities where a lower light level is preferred, provides flexibility. High-low and three-way switches for three-way lightbulbs are another suitable means of achieving flexibility—so that, again, a single fixture may afford both general and task illumination, as needed.

POSITION OF LIGHT SOURCE. The light source should be as low within the shade as possible, if maximum illumination on a reading or work plane is desired.

SHADE VARIATIONS. When useful illumination is necessary, keep in mind the spread of both the downward and the upward light. Deep, narrow shades are undesirable because they restrict both. The degree of translucence of the shade is vital to visual comfort; shades range from opaque to highly translucent.

LAMP PLACEMENT. There must be a correlation between the height of the table and the height of the lamp used in reading. (See Figure 13–5.)

Figure 13-5: Lamp placement. Average seated eye level is 38 to 42 inches above the floor. Lower edge of floor or table lamp shades should be at eye level when lamp is beside user. This is the correct placement for most table lamps, and for floor lamps serving furniture placed against a wall. Floor lamps with built-in tables should have shades no higher than eye level. For user comfort, when floor-lamp height to lower edge of shade or lamp-base-plus table height is above eye level (42 to 49 inches), placement should be close to right or left rear corner of chair. This placement is possible only when chairs or sofas are at least 10 to 20 inches from wall. (From IES Lighting Handbook, 5th Edition, courtesy of Illuminating Engineering Society, New York.)

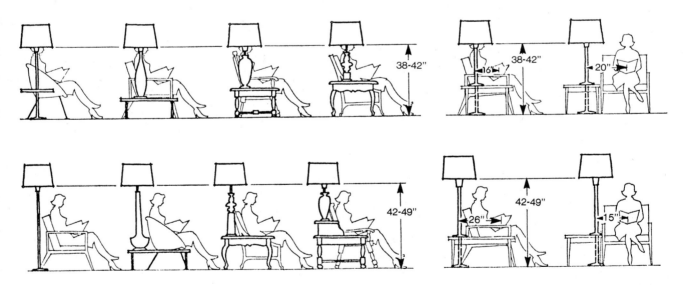

Immediate Area Lighting

It is necessary to use units that will direct light to walls and other vertical surfaces, when your goal is an appropriate amount of illumination on the area *surrounding* a specific task area. Some useful types of fixture for immediate area lighting are:

148

WALL WASHERS. Wall washers direct a broad spread of light downward onto a wall, providing shadowless coverage and coating a vertical surface with an even light to enhance the surface patterns such as those of wood, stone, or brick. They are mounted in or on the ceiling along lines precisely parallel to the wall surface, at intervals, so that the light covers the entire vertical plane. Placed at a distance of 3 to 4 feet from any surface, they illuminate well.

RECESSED LUMINAIRES. These are usually fluorescent. They are installed in the ceiling and are shielded with lenses, diffusers, or open louvers which may either direct or diffuse light output while concealing the lamp itself from view. Recessed luminaires can be made a part of the room's architecture—as in cornices, luminous wall panels and ceilings, wall brackets, and lighted soffits. Since all their light falls essentially in one direction, they have what is called a "direct distribution."

UPLIGHTS. Small "cans"—so called because of their cylindrical shape—with reflectorized lamps inside, uplights can be placed on a floor to illuminate the ceiling; and they are particularly effective from a design standpoint when they are used directed upward through trees and plants. (Uplights do not contribute to plant growth, however.)

DOWNLIGHTS. Incandescent downlights can be very effective to control highlights. They can be used to provide complete illumination for an area, or, better, can be supplemented with other types of lighting. Open reflector downlights are used in low-ceiling areas to control shadow value on objects.

REFLECTORS. Reflectors, with the lens type of downlight, provide additional directional control of light and also soften the shadow value.

DOWNLIGHTS WITHOUT REFLECTORS. Downlights without reflectors or lenses, usually "cans," may be placed in high ceilings and may use high-wattage PAR or R lamps to provide efficient point illumination.

SPOTLIGHTS. The accent light or spotlight has a lamp set in an adjustable fixture such as a ceiling-mounted "bullet," which enables the beam to be aimed at objects rather than straight at the floor. Some uses of spotlight are for accent-lighting statues, paintings, plants, or architectural features.

TRACK LIGHTING. Track lighting can be advantageous when permanent installation is not possible. Ceiling-mounted metal strips come in various lengths and have outlets every few inches; and they accommodate bulbs of many sizes and shapes—even pendant fixtures.

Entire Room Area

Ceiling-mounted or pendant luminaires, when used for general illumination of walls and ceilings, are used to direct light in a very wide pattern. Their luminance should be considered in relation to room reflectances. The light source, whether it be incandescent or fluorescent, should not be visible and should be shielded from direct view.

149

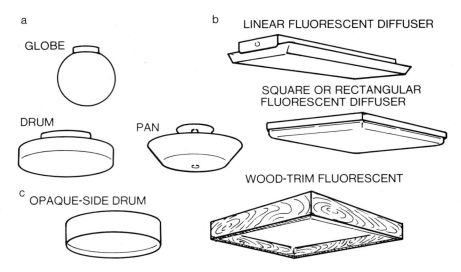

Figure 13-6: Ceiling-mounted luminaires for entire room area illumination. (From IES Lighting Handbook, 5th Edition, courtesy of Illuminating Engineering Society, New York.)

The designer in search of a workable lighting system for an entire room may start with either pendant or ceiling-mounted general diffusing luminaires; occasionally, downlighting or direct-indirect luminaires can contribute substantially to entire room lighting. (Figures 13–6 and 13–7 show samples of fixtures used for entire room lighting.) Note that diffuse downlighting luminaires (Figures 13–6c) cast light in more limited and specific directions than general diffusing ones, so that both their location and the size and brightness of colors in the room must be considered carefully. Direct-indirect pendant luminaires provide generous upward light, which contributes to room lighting, as well as functional downlighting.

Figure 13-7: Pendant luminaires for entire room area lighting. (From IES Lighting Handbook, 5th Edition, courtesy of Illuminating Engineering Society, New York.)

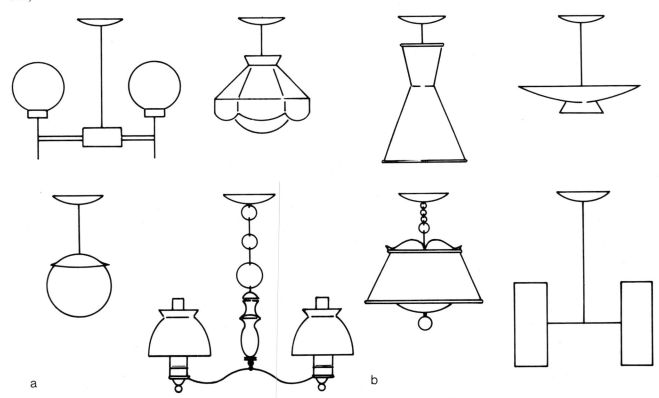

A combination of some of the many types of fixtures on the market today often gives the most satisfactory illumination for the entire room in a residential plan. For commercial installations, on the other hand, the *grid* system with lights within the grid is often the most suitable. Other classifications of commercial hung-ceiling construction are flange, hook, and metal pan; and they must be taken into consideration when you are planning recessed or semi-recessed luminance. Planning the right ceiling system can be a complex process.

SPECIAL EFFECTS

The designer has such access to a wide range of special effects—including lamps, wall lights, spots, uplights, downlights, floods, accent lights, luminous walls, ceiling lights, skylights, architectural lighting—that the choices and the interrelating of many can be a challenge. The tables on the following pages itemize some design considerations and typical techniques in accent lighting.

Decorative Accent Lighting Design Considerations and Techniques

Design Considerations	*Typical Techniques*
PAINTINGS, TAPESTRIES, AND MURALS	

Avoid
1. Shadows of frames.
2. Specular reflections from picture, frame, or glass.
3. Excessive differences between lighted object and surrounding areas.
4. Higher levels for extended periods may cause deterioration of the paint surface.

Consider
1. Sight-lines of people seated and standing.
2. Above all, the artist's intent.
3. Lighting equipment placement—should be placed so that light rays reach the center of the painting at an angle of 30 degrees to avoid surface reflection of the light source and any disturbing shadows of frame, heavy paint texture, etc.

1. Entire picture wall lighted by cornice or wall-wash equipment.
2. Individual frame-mounted luminaires.
3. Individual framing spots.
4. Individual spot or flood lamps not confined to picture area.
5. Lighting from below by luminaires concealed in decorative urns, planters, mantels, etc.

SCULPTURE

1. A sculpture is a three-dimensional object in space—to obtain a good three-dimensional effect with transparent shadows, use a luminance ratio between 2 and 6. If the modeling ratio is reduced below 2, the lighting becomes too "flat" and solid objects appear two-dimensional. If the ratio is above approximately 6, the contrast tends to become unpleasant, with loss of detail in the shadows or in the highlights.

Adjustable spots, floods, individual framing spots, back lighting.

151

Design Considerations   *Typical Techniques*

2. Amounts of pleasurable specular reflection.
3. Experimentation with diffused and/or a directional source or sources—will help to determine the most acceptable solution.

PLANTERS

1. Lighting that provides for plant enhancement may not necessarily be suitable for plant growth. Plants may have to be rotated to a plant-growth area from time to time to keep their beauty.
2. Plants tend to grow toward the light. This should be kept in mind when locating equipment.
3. Light sources, particularly incandescent, should not be located too close to plant material because the heat may be detrimental.
4. Backlighting of translucent leaves often will reveal leaf structure, color, and texture.
5. Front lighting of opaque leaves often will reveal leaf structure, color, and texture.
6. Front lighting of opaque leaves often will add sheen, texture, and accentuate form.
7. Silhouetting of foliage can be an additional dimension.
8. Take the necessary fire safety precautions if artificial plants are used.
9. Bear in mind, live plants are not static; they change in height and bulk.

1. Incandescent downlights, recessed, surface mounted, or suspended above planting area.
2. Luminous panel or soffit using fluorescent and/or incandescent sources.
3. Silhouette lighting with luminous wall panel, lighted walls, concealed uplights.
4. Low-level incandescent stake units.
5. Special planting racks containing fluorescent and/or incandescent lamps especially selected for plant growth.
6. Luminaires recessed in earth to provide uplight.

NICHES

1. Lighting method is determined by what is to be displayed in the niche.
2. Brightness of shielding media and interior niche surfaces should be carefully controlled to avoid extreme difference to surrounding areas.

1. Incandescent spotlights from one or more directions.
2. Incandescent or fluorescent sources concealed vertically or horizontally at edges.
3. Luminous sides, bottom, top, back, or combinations.
4. Lamps concealed in back of object to create silhouette effect.

BOOKCASES

1. Distribution of equipment to light faces of book covers and other objects on all shelves.
2. Luminance ratios of bookcase area and surrounding wall surfaces.

1. Adjustable spot or flood lamps or wall washers aimed into shelves from ceiling in front of bookcase.
2. Lighted bracket, cornice, or soffit extending in front of shelves.

152

Design Considerations   *Typical Techniques*

3. Tubular sources concealed vertically at sides of bookcase or horizontally at front edge of individual shelves.
4. Lighting concealed at back of bookcase for silhouette effects.
5. Some bookshelves may require modification to allow ample spread of light over entire bookcase. For example: cut shelves back, or use plastic or glass shelves.

FIREPLACES

1. Brightness relations of surrounding area to facing of brick, stone, wood, etc.
2. The mantel as a decorative wall treatment and as the focal point of interest.
3. Orientation in the room.

1. Cornice and wall brackets.
2. Recessed or surface-mounted downlights close to fireplace surface for grazing light.
3. Adjustable spots or floods (ceiling mounted) aimed at decorative objects, mantel—or grouped together to light entire fireplace wall.
4. Recessed or surface-mounted wall washers for even distribution of light over entire fireplace surface.
5. Lighting equipment concealed in mantel to light picture or objects above and/cr surfaces below.

TEXTURED WALLS AND DRAPERIES

1. Grazing light to emphasize textured surfaces.
2. Light pattern created by luminaires close to walls.

1. Recessed or surface-mounted downlights located close to the vertical surface to direct grazing light over the surface.
2. Cornice, valance, wall brackets, or wall washers.
3. Individual adjustable incandescent luminaires.
4. Concealed up-lighting equipment.

LUMINOUS PANELS AND WALLS

1. Luminous elements larger than about 16 square feet should not exceed 50 footlamberts average luminance when they will be viewed by people seated in a room.
2. Luminous elements of smaller size (or larger elements seen only in passing) may approach 200 footlamberts average luminance.
3. Variable controls are valuable in adjusting luminance of panel to desired level for room activities.
4. Uniform luminance of a luminous surface may or may not be desirable and is dependent on spacing of the light source.

1. Fluorescent lamps uniformly spaced vertically or horizontally in a white cavity.
2. Fluorescent lamps placed top and bottom or on each side of a white cavity.
3. Random placement of incandescent lamps (perhaps with color) in a white cavity.
4. Uniform pattern of incandescent lamps in a white cavity.
5. Incandescent reflectorized lamps concealed at top or bottom of a white cavity to reflect light from back surface of cavity.
6. For outdoor luminous walls, floodlamps directing light to diffusing screen from behind.

153

Design Considerations   *Typical Techniques*

5. Overall pattern, shielding devices, structural members, or other design techniques to add interest and relieve over dominance and monotony of large, evenly illuminated panels.

OTHER ARCHITECTURAL ELEMENTS

Many residences have especially distinctive architectural features that require special lighting. Because of the variety of problems it is difficult to list design considerations that apply to all. In general, however, the following guides apply to all:

a. Conceal the light source from normal view.
b. Avoid "unnatural" lighting effects.
c. Do not introduce lighting patterns that conflict or distract from architectural appearance of the element being lighted.

LUMINAIRES AS DECORATIVE ACCENTS

1. Luminance of luminous parts of luminaires can be critical.
2. Luminaires should not introduce distracting or annoying light patterns.
3. Where exposed lamps are used for a desired decorative effect, dimmer controls to provide higher or lower luminance should be considered.

1. Decorative crystal chandeliers, wall sconces, lanterns, and brackets.
2. Decorative portable lamps.
3. Pendant luminaires.

DINING AREAS

1. Type of illumination for a formal dining area is largely a matter of personal taste. The desired mood or atmosphere, choice of luminaire, and brightness in the room are all to be considered.
2. Footcandle level is also a matter of personal preference; 15 footcandles or more is generally desirable. Variable controls provide flexibility to adapt a level of illumination to fit the particular occasion.
3. Strong downward component will accent the table setting, creating attractive focal highlights; but if unbalanced, will render faces poorly and create harsh shadows.
4. Unshielded sources in low wattage can often be tolerated, especially if some general lighting is present and the background is not too dark.
5. In situations where the dining table is moved from time to time, a flexible means of mounting the luminaire or luminaires is desirable.

1. Decorative chandelier or pendant cluster suspended over center of table and supplemented by two or more recessed louvered ceiling downlights. Both chandelier and downlights on dimmer control.
2. Same as above, but augmented by some form of structural or built-in lighting (valance, cornice, luminous panel, etc.) to enhance and bring out character of rest of the room.
3. Pattern of dimmer-controlled ceiling downlights, designed to accent the table settings, but to avoid harsh downlighting directly on people at table. Carefully used tinted lighting can be employed here.
4. Pull-down pendant luminaire with strong downward component plus generous upward light located over center of table. Best supplemented by other structural room lighting.

 Reprinted from the *IES Lighting Handbook*, 5th ed., by permission of the Illuminating Engineering Society, New York.

Lighting Control

Dimming and switching are two types of light control. For incandescent lighting dimming is often very desirable; fluorescent dimming requires greater knowledge. HID dimming is also available. Electrical outlets, usually duplex, should be supplied along a wall at intervals of no less than 6 feet. All outlets should be controlled by switches, with care not to overload.

LIGHTING PLANS

When a house is being built, a lighting consultant can work with the architect or designer on the diagrammatic planning of types and placement of luminaires. This is the ideal situation. Far more common, however, is the situation in which the designer must work with—or around—existing natural light and artificial lighting fixtures.

Either way, it is important for the designer to know how to make a lighting plan.

Lighting Design[4]

A working method of designing lighting is to first determine the light levels required for each seeing task in the space and then simplify without loss of convenience. Determine the reflecting qualities of floors and ceiling. The level of reflected light should be just below the working level.

After planning working lights and making certain that the walls and ceilings reflect enough light to avoid gloom, the scheme is complete. To check yourself, move around the space and consider whether the lights in distance parts of the room will be in the line of vision and thus produce glare.

Consider the plan of the light source. What pattern do they make in isolation? Lighting accents should coincide with accents of the total plan.

Artificial light is designed and calculated as an integral element of the total design. There are essentially three primary factors to consider: the fixture, its relation to the working surfaces, and its relation to the reflecting surfaces of the space. Light room surfaces reflect light; therefore less illumination is needed and glare is reduced by lighting sources.

Lighting must be designed for seeing tasks. Uniform lighting is used for uniform activities such as factory or office work. In the home the tasks differ as in schoolwork, hobbies, reading, cooking, and watching television; therefore, lighting must be varied. [See Figures 13–8 and 13–9.]

[4]Reprinted from *Graphic Guide to Interior Design* by Forrest Wilson, © 1977 by Litton Educational Publishing, Inc., by permission of Van Nostrand Reinhold Company.

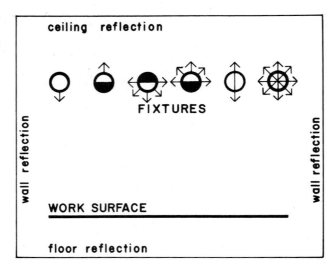

Figure 13-8: Lighting plans: diagram of reflective surfaces (ceiling, walls, floor, work surface). (Reproduced from Graphic Guide to Interior Design by Forrest Wilson, Copyright 1977 by Litton Education Publishing, Inc., by permission of Van Nostrand Reinhold Company.)

Figure 13-9: Lighting plans: plan for a dining room; plan for a factory workroom, showing positions and types of fixtures to be used. (Reproduced from Graphic Guide to Interior Design by Forrest Wilson, Copyright 1977 by Litton Education Publishing, Inc., by permission of Van Nostrand Reinhold Company.)

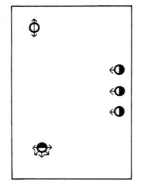

PLAN
DINING ROOM

PLAN
FACTORY WORKROOM

An architect's electrical plan shows the location of the convenience outlets, special outlets, floor outlets, wall outlets, and ceiling outlets. On this plan is usually the lighting plan, showing location of fixtures that are built in. This is submitted by the architect to the designer, who can change this basic electrical plan to suit the particular needs of the interior space; e.g., allowing for furniture placement, plants, and so forth. The designer then adds the *lighting plan* to this. In a residence, a reflective ceiling plan—showing the grid system—would *not* be used.

Lighting Plan

A lighting plan is then drawn up to specifications, locating individual lights in relationship to each other and in accordance with the rooms' dimensions. This shows where switches and connectors are. This plan is basically used in a fixed ceiling; it shows where sockets have to be plugged into a ceiling to allow for wiring to go through that ceiling.

Reflective Ceiling Plan

This is different: a reflective ceiling plan places a grid system, just locating the lights within that grid system. A grid system shows the grid structure of lines that separate the lights. An X marks each place where a light is to go; each light can be lifted out and moved. A grid system, in essence, uses the ceiling to reflect the light downward.

FIXTURE LAYOUT. When using incandescent or HID fixtures in a grid plan, locate them the same distance apart both lengthwise and crosswise in a room. As for the relationship of the grid to walls, the conventional layout for incandescent lamps in an office or large working space places fixtures 2½ feet from each wall. If obstructions such as beams prevent a straight-line layout, sometimes more lamps of lower wattage can be used to create rows spaced around the obstructions.

Fluorescent fixtures in rooms call for continuous connections to prevent the use of more than one electrical fixture per row. When obstructions are present, lamps may at least be connected continuously until they reach an obstruction. The bank on the other side of it requires another connection.

Zonal Cavity Method

To determine the number of incandescent or fluorescent fixtures needed in a square or rectangular room, apply the formula to establish the average maintained illumination level for a horizontal plane:

$$\frac{fc \times width \times length \text{ (or ceiling area)}}{\text{lamps per fixture} \times \text{lumens per lamp} \times C.U. \times L.L.F.}$$

where:

○ fc = the desired minimum level of illumination in footcandles
○ width = width of room
○ length = length of room
○ lamps per fixture = number of sources of light for each fixture
○ lumens per lamp = light output of a single lamp
○ C.U., L.L.F. = special factors available on fixture catalogue sheets, which can be explained by your maintenance or illumination engineer

When determining the number of fixtures needed in an L-shaped room, however, remember to calculate the number for each leg of the "L" separately.

Remember also that this formula and calculation will give the number of fixtures needed to produce a desired illumination in footcandles in a horizontal, not vertical plane. The calculation normally concerns light thrown horizontally on a desk for reading of a piece of paper resting flat upon it. It does not determine footcandles available in a vertical plane, such as light striking the front of a vertical file or a painting on a wall, for example.

In a typical layout, vertical footcandles turn out to be about one-half the horizontal footcandles. This difference must be taken into account if the designer is involved in a working or living space in which illumination in the vertical plane is important.

Symbols and Abbreviations

Familiarity with the following symbols and abbreviations is important for communication with design engineers and understanding of literature connected with lighting plans.

157

INSTITUTIONAL COMMERCIAL & INDUSTRIAL OCCUPANCIES

⊢○	NURSES CALL SYSTEM DEVICES (ANY TYPE)
⊢◇	PAGING SYSTEM DEVICES (ANY TYPE)
⊢□	FIRE ALARM SYSTEM DEVICES (ANY TYPE)
⊢◇	STAFF REGISTER SYSTEM (ANY TYPE)
⊢⬠	ELECTRICAL CLOCK SYSTEM DEVICES (ANY TYPE)
⊢◀	PUBLIC TELEPHONE SYSTEM DEVICES
⊢◁	PRIVATE TELEPHONE SYSTEM DEVICES
⊢⌂	WATCHMAN SYSTEM DEVICES
⊢◁	SOUND SYSTEM
⊢◎	OTHER SIGNAL SYSTEM DEVICES
[●C]	SIGNAL CENTRAL STATION
▭	INTERCONNECTION BOX
– – – –	AUXILIARY SYSTEM CIRCUITS

Any line without further designation indicates two-wire system. For a greater number of wires designate with numerals in manner similar to 12- no. 18W - $3/4$" C. Designate by numbers corresponding to listing in schedule.

▭A,B,C, ETC.	SPECIAL AUXILIARY OUTLETS

Subscript lettering refers to notes on drawings or detailed description in specifications.

PANELBOARDS

▭	FLUSH MOUNTED PANELBOARD & CABINET
▭	SURFACE MOUNTED PANELBOARD & CABINET

BUSDUCTS & WIREWAYS

T T T	TROLLEY DUCT
B B B	BUSWAY (SERVICE, FEEDER OR PLUG-IN)
C C C	CABLE THROUGH LADDER OR CHANNEL
W W W	WIREWAY

SIGNALING SYSTEM OUTLETS RESIDENTIAL OCCUPANCIES

▫●	PUSH BUTTON
◻	BUZZER
◖	BELL
◖	BELL & BUZZER COMBINATION
◇	ANNUNCIATOR
◀	OUTSIDE TELEPHONE
◁	INTERCONNECTING TELEPHONE
◀	TELEPHONE SWITCHBOARD
BT	BELL RINGING TRANSFORMER
D	ELECTRIC DOOR OPENER
M	MAID'S SIGNAL PLUG
R	RADIO OUTLET
CH	CHIME
TV	TELEVISION OUTLET
T	THERMOSTAT

ELECTRICAL DISTRIBUTION OR LIGHTING SYSTEM, UNDERGROUND

M	MANHOLE
H	HANDHOLE
TM	TRANSFORMER- MANHOLE OR VAULT
TP	TRANSFORMER PAD
– – – –	UNDERGROUND DIRECT BURIAL CABLE
–⊏–	UNDERGROUND DUCT LINE
⊗	STREET LIGHT STANDARD FED FROM UNDERGROUND CIRCUIT

ELECTRICAL DISTRIBUTION OR LIGHTING SYSTEM, AERIAL

○	POLE
⊙	STREET LIGHT & BRACKET
△	TRANSFORMER
———	PRIMARY CIRCUIT
– – –	SECONDARY CIRCUIT
→	DOWN GUY
•—	HEAD GUY
○—→	SIDEWALK GUY
⊣	SERVICE WEATHER

PANELS CIRCUITS & MISCELLANEOUS

▬	LIGHTING PANEL
▨	POWER PANEL
———	WIRING, CONCEALED IN CEILING OR WALL
– – –	WIRING, CONCEALED IN FLOOR
- - - -	WIRING EXPOSED
——→	HOME RUN TO PANEL BOARD.

Indicate number of circuits by number of arrows. Any circuit without such designation indicates a two-wire circuit. For a greater number of wires indicate as follows: ⧟ (3 wires) ⧟ (4 wires), etc.

———	FEEDERS

Use heavy lines and designate by number corresponding to listing in feeder schedule.

——○	WIRING TURNED UP
——●	WIRING TURNED DOWN
Ⓖ	GENERATOR
Ⓜ	MOTOR
Ⓘ	INSTRUMENT (SPECIFY)
T	TRANSFORMER (OR DRAW TO SCALE)
⊠	CONTROLLER
▭	EXTERNALLY OPERATED DISCONNECT SWITCH

[5]Table reprinted from *Architectural Graphic Standards*, 6th edition, by Ramsey and Sleeper, by permission of John Wiley & Sons, Inc.

Any standard symbol as given above, with the addition of lower case subscript letter, may be used to designate some special version of standard equipment of particular interest in specific set of architectural plans. When used they must be listed in the schedule of symbols on each drawing and if necessary further described in the specifications.

LIGHTING OUTLETS	RECEPTACLE OUTLETS	SWITCH OUTLETS

CEILING, WALL

○ —○	SURFACE INCANDESCENT
® —®	RECESS INCANDESCENT
® —®	BLANKED OUTLET
®	DROP CORD
® —®	ELECTRICAL OUTLET
® —®	FAN OUTLET
® —®	JUNCTION BOX
Ⓛ —Ⓛ	LAMP HOLDER WITH PULL SWITCH
® —®	OUTLET FOR VAPOR DISCHARGE LAMP
⊗ —⊗	EXIT LIGHT OUTLET
⊗ᴿ —⊗ᴿ	RECESSED EXIT LIGHT OUTLET
Ⓛ —Ⓛ	OUTLET CONTROLLED BY LOW VOLTAGE SWITCHING WHEN RELAY IS INSTALLED IN OUTLET BOX
◻	SURFACE OR PENDANT INDIVIDUAL FLUORESCENT FIXTURE
◻ᴿ	RECESSED INDIVIDUAL FLUORESCENT FIXTURE
◻▭	SURFACE OR PENDANT CONTINUOUS ROW FLUORESCENT FIXTURE
◻ᴿ▭	RECESSED CONTINUOUS ROW FLUORESCENT FIXTURE

RECEPTACLE OUTLETS

—⊖	SINGLE RECEPTACLE OUTLET
⊜	DUPLEX RECEPTACLE OUTLET
⊕	TRIPLEX RECEPTACLE OUTLET
⊕	QUADRUPLEX RECEPTACLE OUTLET
◒	DUPLEX RECEPTACLE OUTLET-SPLIT WIRED
◒	TRIPLEX RECEPTACLE OUTLET-SPLIT WIRED
▽	SINGLE SPECIAL-PURPOSE RECEPTACLE OUTLET
▽	DUPLEX SPECIAL-PURPOSE RECEPTACLE OUTLET
⊜ R	RANGE OUTLET
▲ DW	SPECIAL PURPOSE CONNECTION
⊜ X"	MULTI-OUTLET ASSEMBLY
Ⓒ	CLOCK HANGER RECEPTACLE
Ⓕ	FAN HANGER RECEPTACLE
⊟	FLOOR SINGLE RECEPTACLE OUTLET
⊟	FLOOR DUPLEX RECEPTACLE OUTLET
△	FLOOR SPECIAL PURPOSE OUTLET
◼	FLOOR TELEPHONE OUTLET-PUBLIC
◩	FLOOR TELEPHONE OUTLET-PRIVATE
⊞	UNDERFLOOR DUCT AND JUNCTION BOX FOR TRIPLE, DOUBLE OR SINGLE DUCT SYSTEM AS INDICATED BY NUMBER OF PARALLEL LINES
⌗	CELLULAR FLOOR HEADER DUCT

SWITCH OUTLETS

S	SINGLE POLE SWITCH
S₂	DOUBLE POLE SWITCH
S₃	THREE WAY SWITCH
S₄	FOUR WAY SWITCH
Sᴅ	AUTOMATIC DOOR SWITCH
Sₖ	KEY OPERATED SWITCH
Sᴘ	SWITCH AND PILOT LAMP
Sᴄʙ	CIRCUIT BREAKER
Sᴡᴄʙ	WEATHERPROOF CIRCUIT BREAKER
Sᴍᴄ	MOMENTARY CONTACT SWITCH
Sᴿᴄ	REMOTE CONTROL SWITCH
Sᴡᴘ	WEATHERPROOF SWITCH
Sꜰ	FUSED SWITCH
Sᴡꜰ	WEATHERPROOF FUSED SWITCH
Sʟ	SWITCH FOR LOW VOLTAGE SWITCHING SYSTEM
Sʟᴍ	MASTER SWITCH FOR LOW VOLTAGE SWITCHING SYSTEM
Sᴛ	TIME SWITCH
Ⓢ	CEILING PULL SWITCH
⊖ₛ	SWITCH AND SINGLE RECEPTACLE
⊜ₛ	SWITCH AND DOUBLE RECEPTACLE

| ○ A,B,C ETC. |
| ⊜ A,B,C ETC. | } SPECIAL OUTLETS |
| S A,B,C ETC. |

V Fabrics, Wall Coverings, Window Treatments

The preceding chapters of this book have dealt with the major steps that are taken in designing a space. The basis for everything is the overall plan: it defines the architectural framework, the individual tastes, and the functional requirements that must be considered. The next step is learning to recognize and choose from period and contemporary styles, followed by the planning and selection of furniture, then the choice of colors and the planning of lighting arrangements.

In Part V we will advance into three closely related areas, all of which depend on the discoveries and decisions that have been made earlier. Before you consider fabrics, wallcoverings, or window treatments you must already have a clear picture of the style, color, lighting

161

scheme, and so on in the room in which you are working. Then you can focus on the surface textures and patterns that will be provided by upholstery fabrics; by wallcoverings of paper, fabric, or any of countless other materials; and by draperies, screens, shades, shutters, and other window treatments.

We will explore fabrics in general in Chapter 14, then go into the two connecting areas of wallcoverings and window treatments in Chapters 15 and 16.

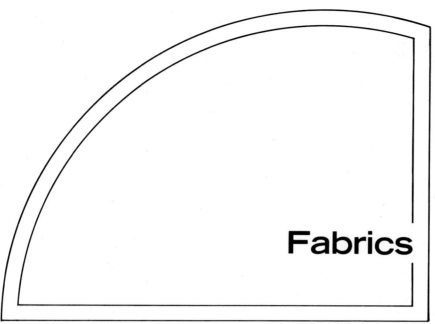

Fabrics

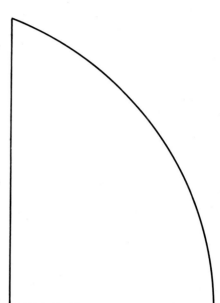

14

Fabric can be used on walls—upholstered, draped, or paper-backed; it can be used on ceilings in many forms. It is used for pillows, bedspreads, lampshades, upholstery, picture frames, trims, tables, drapery, and window treatments of all types. Fabric can even be laminated into floor tiles or formica for furniture or counter-tops. It can be vinylized for outdoor use, or fire-proofed, water-proofed, Scotchgarded, and even given insulation qualities.

Fabric alone can transform any interior space into an ambiance of color, texture, and pattern to suit every design and scheme. The designer can choose from different styles ranging from traditional to contemporary; can blend varying shades of every conceivable color; and can harmonize combinations of textures to appeal to the sense of touch as well as that of sight.

Through textural effects the designer can create variations within the interior, because each texture reflects light in its own way. Velvets, soft wools, and satins can be used in alliance with harder materials such as rep files or metal fibers. With so many types of fabric—including polished cotton, tweeds, crewel brocades, linens, Fortuny silks—to choose from, the possibilities are almost endless. Each type can be treated differently—smooth or draped, gathered, shirred, quilted; it can make use of trapunto, or be stitched to enhance the particular surface it's placed upon.

The possibilities for coordination of patterns, too, are limitless. Stripes, florals, and geometric designs can be placed to contrast with and enhance one another. The various sizes within these combinations of patterns also create interest.

Any piece of furniture will take on a new life with the addition of fabric alone. The same sofa will look entirely different upholstered in a navy velvet than in a white brocade or a colorful garden print. Fabrics also have the ability to minimize or expand the apparent size of a piece. Soft green fabric on a chair will make it appear much smaller than a bold red print would. Two rooms with identical floor 163

Figure 14-1: *Spinning wool as it was spun in American homes before the Industrial Revolution. At right is a clock reel, which both holds and measures the spun wool yarn. (Old Sturbridge Village Photo by Donald F. Eaton.)*

plans and furniture, but with different groups of fabrics, will appear totally different from each other.

The designer can use fabrics in so many ways that there is always a new challenge to pursue. Manufacturers add new and exciting editions every year, each one with many possibilities; many fabric companies even offer the option of custom coloring for further individuality.

Basic information as to the properties of these design fabrics is necessary in order to obtain the most satisfactory results. It takes time and practice to utilize fabrics properly, because each one has its advantages and disadvantages.

INTRODUCTION TO STORY

After viewing an extremely informative film shown by Arthur H. Lee and Jofa, Inc. entitled "Limited Editions," which is a story on how fabric is made, my enthusiasm for its content prompted me to work directly from it and the script. Produced by G. P. and J. Baker in England, it is based on the processes involved in textile printing, an enlightening story relating the techniques of manufacturing fabric imparts to you an appreciation of the skill necessary for the development of this product; and it gives insight into the complexity of printing exclusive textile designs.[1]

[1]The film *Limited Editions*, produced in England by G.P. & J. Baker, was made available through the generosity of Derek A. Lee, C.B.E., President and Chairman of Arthur H. Lee and Jofa, Inc., textile manufacturers and importers. Information from the script and the film is adapted here by permission. For Mr. Lee's continued interest and assistance to the field of textile education, we are grateful.

HOW A FABRIC IS MADE:
THE STORY OF FABRIC

Showroom

In a typical fabric showroom, an interior designer browses through racks of colorful fabrics. She hesitates, looking closely at the surface of a piece of cloth printed with a complex design of flowers and branches, noticing at least ten colorways, and marveling at its unique quality. What sets this fabric apart from the others?

One of the first things, of course, is design and color. Consider for a moment the fact that every leaf and flower has to be planned and drawn, every color and shade chosen, all on paper, long before the design is printed on cloth. An artist might adapt designs from the past: perhaps a fourteenth-century Peruvian shawl, a hand-painted wallpaper, or a seventeenth-century Chinese design. Designs might come from collections of wallpapers and fabrics assembled over many years—not to be reproduced but to be adapted for use with modern textile printing machinery. The fabric design artist has to know the limitations of this machinery and also the characteristics of the different cloths on which the pattern is to be printed.

Figure 14-2: A charming bedroom design incorporates fabrics in many ways: quilted bedspread with fabric-covered buttons, pillow shams, ruffled tie-back draperies, fabric-laminated window shades, picture frames made of fabric, and a wall upholstered in fabric over layers of dacron. (Helene Levenson, ASID. Photo © Peter Vanderwarker.)

Scotland

Familiarity with a cloth begins with finding out where it comes from. Let us take one example: a piece of printed linen from Great Britain. In Dundee, Scotland, for hundreds of years, the most important export was linen cloth. The east coast of Scotland imported raw flax from Belgium and the Netherlands, where it had been grown, then produced and exported the finished cloth.

Flax

A Belgian ship docks at Dundee and flax is swung out of the hold. There is great activity on the quay as the bales are wheeled away into the warehouse. The flax is loaded onto an open lorry which drives through an arch in a ruined castle—a remnant of the Middle Ages, when this small town was the capital of Scotland. The lorry arrives at the factory, and the flax is unloaded by forklift truck.

This is where a large proportion of the yarn for pure linen or for linen and cotton union starts its life. Flax in its raw state is a tangled mass of long and short fibers. The first job is to straighten the fibers and separate the long from the short. This process is called "hackling."

Hackling

The hackling machine combs the fibers mechanically, rather than by hand, as was done until the early years of this century. The long staple or "line" emerges from the hackling machine as a continuous sliver. The short fibers are discarded.

Line Preparing

This is the process of mixing and blending many long strands of flax of different origin, quality, and color to produce a strong and even mixture. The skill of producing fine linen thread lies first in buying the right raw materials, then in blending them in the best way at the line-preparing stage.

Spinning Shed

The long fibers have now been prepared so they can be spun into thread for making fine linen. In the spinning sheds are frames where the threads are put onto spools. The truck, now loaded with spools, leaves to travel a hundred miles south to the town of Kirkcaldy, where the cloth will be woven.

Bobbins

The thread is wound from the spools onto bobbins designed to fit into the shuttles of the looms to provide the weft (thread running across the width) in the finished cloth. (In a linen-cotton mixture, the cotton thread is used for the warp—that is, the cotton threads run lengthwise in the cloth.) Each spool holds about 12,000 yards of yarn. The warp threads, having been sized for strength, are fed into beam winding machines and are ready for the looms. The bobbins are fed automatically into the shuttle as the yarns are used up.

Weaving

Weaving is a craft here, developed by many generations of people working in the same place, all understanding the qualities of fine linen. Various cloths are woven and pass inspection before beginning another journey south. The cloths cross the border to Lancashire—another traditional center of the textile industry in Britain—and arrive at a small mill for printing.

Block-Printing

This is one of the few places in the world where wood block-printing of textiles still goes on; where exclusive designs are printed using methods practised and virtually unchanged for almost 4,000 years. In one of the more complex designs, there may be as many as 30 colors involving the use of up to 150 differently shaped blocks.

The design of the fabric is carved on a series of blocks; each block is pressed onto a felt pad impregnated with the color, then placed on the fabric. The pattern is built up gradually by the successive use of individual blocks. Each block is lowered onto the cloth, hammered with a wooden mallet, and lifted, leaving an impression with each color contributing to the finished design.

The blocks themselves are works of art, sometimes over 250 years old. There are copper-faced blocks, wood-carved blocks, and areas where felt has been inserted to carry the "weight" of color. Reproducing such blocks today is not economically feasible.

Because highly skilled people are needed to do this block-printing, and production rate is slow, a method called screen-printing is used today to produce at a more acceptable price.

Figure 14-3: Block printing a fabric by hand. (Arthur H. Lee & Jofa, Inc.)

Screen-Printing

HAND METHOD. Hand screen-printing is ideal when used with limited screens and a self-contained repeat size. The screen has a fine mesh of holes in it; where it is required to print, these holes are left open. Where a blank is needed so that another color can be applied later, the screen is coated with an impervious substance. Then the dye is carefully hand-squeezed through carefully by hand by highly trained workers. Mechanization is the logical next step, and automatic screen-printers do a great deal of modern fabric printing.

MECHANIZED METHOD. The squeegee advances up the table automatically in this method, then speeds back down the table to start another run. Mechanized screen-printing still produces quality textiles, but at an acceptable price.

As our survey of printing techniques advances, we find ourselves on the edge of the City of Carlisle, in a modern textile mill that produces quality printed fabrics suitable for today's market. The raw ingredient once more is cloth from the mills of Scotland and Lancashire. But at this modern mill an ancient craft now meets the twentieth century.

Preparing Cloth for Printing

The techniques used here are extensions of the silk-screen principle; but first the cloth has to receive extra preparation. A huge roll of gray cloth is slowly unrolled, then singed so that surface hairs will be removed. Next it is put into a bleach bath, then run over heated rollers to be dried so it will have just the right moisture content for the next stage; finally it is rolled up. Next, it is put into a "stentering" machine and straightened to ensure that the weft threads run truly and squarely across it; if necessary, it is stretched. Now it is ready for printing.

Figure 14-4: A traditional printed fabric: "Jacobean Tree." (Arthur H. Lee & Jofa, Inc.)

Flat-Bed Screen-Printing

A gumming roller, sticking the cloth onto an endless moving belt called a blanket, keeps the cloth from shifting during printing. Now the automatic *flat-bed printing machine* comes into play, as each screen applies a different color while the cloth advances automatically. The first screens apply the outline, then successive screens apply the head colors and finally the background. Repeat after repeat, the cloth advances to the end of the bed, where it is rolled up.

SCREEN-MAKING. To make these screens, the artist has to break down the design into different colors and trace each color into a tracing foil for a separate stencil, each stencil becoming a separate screen. Some fabrics have over a dozen various colorways to a single design. Screens are no longer made of silk; polyester is much stronger. The screen fabric is stretched over a frame and the image transferred onto it photographically. A light-sensitive emulsion coats the screen, which is placed section by section over the stencil and exposed to light. The process is repeated until the whole area of the screen is exposed.

A complete screen is then fitted into the printing machine, where an exact amount of dye or color is poured into the troughs. The design is then transferred onto the cloth.

COLORS. Chosen carefully to suit each design, fabric dyes are mixed with a form of gum to give them the right consistency for printing. The mixtures are tested for printing, with the knowledge that the colors can change in later stages of fixing and drying. The dye then is metered out by a computer and buckets fill with color. A wide range of good, fast colors has been an important achievement of the industry in the last fifty years.

Rotary Screen-Printing

A revolution in screen-printing has been brought about by the introduction of the *rotary screen printer*. This is a cylinder made of perforated nickel. The color is fed inside the cylinders, where its depth is controlled electronically. The squeegee remains, still pressing the dye through the revolving screen downward into the cloth beneath.

In a dark room, under yellow light, the image has been photographed onto these cylindrical screens in the same way as for the flat screens, except that the tracing is wrapped around the cylinder before it is exposed. The cylinders are then fitted into the machine, ready for printing.

Aging

Now the fabric, completely printed, is passed through a "padding" liquor which reduces the colors and allows them to penetrate into the fiber of the cloth. Next, it goes through the oxidizing and fixing baths, changing color as it passes through each successive bath. Now it is ready for finishing.

Finishing

The finishing department can give designs printed on cotton a glazed effect by putting the fabric through the chintzing machine, passing it between rollers running at different speeds.

A similar effect is achieved by a "shinering" machine, where the cloth passes under an engraved roller which lays all the fibers on the surface in one direction. The shinering machine is often used on satin. This finish stabilizes the cotton and achieves crease-resistance and permanency in the finish.

Off into the World

After the cloth passes the inspection tables, a roller measuring gauge runs over it. Then it is off on another trip south, to warehouses at High Wycombe, where labels stamped with the names of countries in Europe and farther afield are fastened to the rolls of fabric. Modern technology is the servant of craftsmanship.

Samples are then shipped to the showrooms around the world—showrooms where interior designers bustle about, looking through racks for just the right fabric for that particular client. This is the point at which our story began, and we leave the designer to complete her choices, with a new understanding and appreciation for the skill and technology involved in creating these decorative fabrics.

FIBERS

The selection of a fabric to suit a particular need requires knowledge of the strengths and weaknesses of the fiber content. Many textiles blend two or more fibers in order to combine the best features of each. A basic understanding of the nature of fibers is, therefore, essential.

The tables on the following pages list the generic names of the fibers, along with trade names, where they are applicable. Also listed are the basic characteristics of each fiber along with its common uses. Fibers are classified as either natural or synthetic (man-made).

WEAVES

Weaving is the process of interlacing two systems of yarn at right angles to each other to produce fabric. The lengthwise threads are called the warp; individually they are known as ends. The crosswise threads are called the *filling* or weft; individually, they are called picks. Weaving is done on a loom that interlaces the warp and filling threads according to a prearranged plan.

Three weaves are basic to all woven fabrics. These are the plain weave, the twill weave, and the satin weave. Every woven textile is one of these weaves or a variation thereof. The three types of weave are shown in the diagrams (Figures 14–5, 14–6, and 14–7). The dark lines represent the warp, and the light lines the filling.[2]

[2]The following information on weaves is reprinted by permission of Payne and Company.

Figure 14-5: *Plain weave: the most common and the strongest of all weaves. (Payne and Company.)*

Figure 14-6: *Twill weave: the number of yarns passed over and under in both warp and filling are varied. (Payne and Company.)*

Figure 14-7: *Satin weave: the weakest of the three basic types. (Payne and Company.)*

Fibers

NATURAL FIBERS

Generic Name	Trademarks	Characteristics	Common Uses	Care
Cotton		Medium strong, durable, absorbent, easily dyed, excellent launderability. Wrinkles readily, unless protected by finish; can be damaged by mildew.	Most widely used fiber alone or in blends with man-made fibers for household fabrics; all weights from sheer to heavy duty.	Usually washable. Launder or dry clean according to instructions. Iron damp or on wrong side with hot iron.
Linen (flax)		Same as cotton except has superior strength, especially when wet; very absorbent.	Blends with other fibers.	Usually washable. Launder or dry clean according to instructions. Iron same as cotton.
Wool & (other animal hair fibers) Angora, Camel, Alpaca, Cashmere, Vicuna, Mohair.		Warmth, resilience, medium strength, absorbent, dyes well, flame resistant, dries slowly, felts in hot water with agitation.	Woven and knitted cloth of all weights; carpets, blankets, etc. Also important in blends with man-made fibers.	Dry clean, unless labeled or known to be washable.
Silk		Fine, delicate strong fiber with lustrous finish, drapes well, absorbent, dyes readily; damaged by chlorine, bleaches, and sunlight.	Fine fabrics, both woven and knitted, for many types of household uses. Often blended with other fibers.	Dry clean, unless labeled or known to be washable. Iron on wrong side or with press cloth; moderate hot iron.

MAN-MADE FIBERS

Generic Name	Trademarks	Characteristics	Common Uses	Care
Rayon (Cupra) (Viscose)	Bemberg Coloray Darelle Durafil Avril Vincel	Absorbent, dyes readily, moth resistant; special finishes will give properties of crease resistance and water repellency. Yarns can be medium or high strength.	Used alone or in blends with natural or other man-made fibers for all kinds of woven or knitted fabrics for all household uses.	Dry clean, unless labeled washable. When laundered—can be ironed as for cotton; iron damp on wrong side.
Acetate	Celacloud Celara Chromspun Quilticel	Adequate strength, moderate absorbency, good drape, little or no shrinkage, moth resistant; can be solution-dyed; melts at high temperature.	Used alone or in blends with natural or other man-made fibers for all kinds of household uses. Acetate tricot is also used for bonding to other fabrics.	If washable, launder by hand, do not wring; iron damp on wrong side at low temperature. Dry cleans readily.
Triacetate	Arnel Trilan	Higher wet strength than regular acetate (diacetate), withstands higher temperatures, dyes well; resists shrinkage, moths, takes durable pleats.	Used alone or in blends with natural or other man-made fibers, for all kinds of woven or knitted fabrics for all manner of household uses.	Launder by hand or machine in warm water, not hot; easily ironed (some fabrics need very little). Readily dry cleaned.
Metallic	Lamé Lurex Mylar	Nontarnishable, washable when protected by film. Can be produced in colors as well as silver, gold.	Decorative fabrics and trimmings; solid lamé or glitter effects added to other fabrics.	When used in fabrics that are washable, these yarns need no special care. Also dry cleanable.
Acrylic	Orlon Acrilan Courtelle Creslan Zefran	Also thermoplastic with all quick drying, easy care properties. In addition has great bulking power for soft, warm, and lightweight fabrics, takes brilliant, fast colors.	Knits of all types; also wool-like woven fabrics, deep pile fabrics and carpets.	Same washability as above, except for deep pile fabrics or artificial fur fabrics which should be cleaned by fur cleaning processes, unless labeled washable.

MAN-MADE FIBERS

Generic Name	Trademarks	Characteristics	Common Uses	Care
Nylon	Antron Cadon Cantrece Courtauld's nylon Cumuloft 501/N Union Carbide nylon	Superior strength and abrasion resistance. Lightweight and thermoplastic (yarns can be heat-set for stretch or texture—fabrics for smooth finish resistant to shrinkage). Quick drying fabrics.	Most widely used man-made fiber suitable for either sheer hosiery or strongest rope; in fabrics for all kinds of household use. Textured yarns in stretch fabrics, carpets; high strength yarn in fish nets, industrial fabrics and tire cord.	Washable by hand or machine in soap or detergent. Drip dry when hand washing. In automatic dryer, keep temperature low. Little or no ironing needed. Iron also at low temperature. Wash white items alone and turn knitted fabrics inside out when laundering.
Vinyon	Rhovyl	High resistance to chemicals; flame proof but melts at low temperature.	Draperies, pile fabrics and industrial uses.	Wash in lukewarm water, drip dry. Cool iron. Deep pile fabrics should be dry cleaned.
Polyester	Terylene Trevira Dacron Kodel, Tergal Tetoron Crimplene	Shares strength, lightweight and abrasion resistance with other thermoplastic fibers. Resilient and versatile for blending with natural and other man-made fibers.	Widely used in blends with natural fibers for all kinds of fabrics, particularly those given durable press finishes. Also used alone in variety of household fabric such as curtains, drapes, or carpets.	Washable by hand or machine in soap or detergent. Drip dry when hand washing. If automatic dryer is used, keep temperature low. Little or no ironing needed. Iron at low temperature. Wash white items alone.
Modacrylic	Dynel Verel Kanekalon Teklon	Resilient and resistant to chemicals. Light weight soft and wrinkle resistant.	Mainly used in carpets, synthetic furs.	Same easy care washability as above. Use cool iron. Deep pile fabrics or artificial fur should be cleaned by fur processes, unless labeled washable.
Chlorofibers (Saran)	Rovana Velon	Naturally water repellent, abrasion resistant, strong. Resists sunlight, moths and mildew. Color fast.	Auto seat covers, outdoor furniture upholstery, webbing.	Wash off with soap and water. Do not iron.
Olefin (Polypropylene)	Celaspun Protel Herculon	Lightweight, strong, thermoplastic and resilient. Resists sunlight and chemical deterioration. Can be solution dyed.	Carpeting, cordage and upholstery.	Care instructions as for other thermoplastic wash and wear fibers. Should not be dry cleaned. If ironing needed—keep temperature low.
Nytril	Darvan	Soft, resilient but melts at low temperatures. Good wrinkle resistance.	Used in blends with wool in pile fabrics.	Washable by hand in warm, not hot water. If ironing is needed—keep temperature low.
Glass	Fiberglas Vitron	Good tensile strength. Unaffected by moisture and sunlight. Excellent chemical resistance and insulating properties. Non-flammable.	Draperies, sheer curtains and industrial fabrics.	Launder in warm water with mild soap or detergent. Drip dry without wringing or flexing. No ironing needed.

Reprinted by permission of Payne and Company.

Plain Weave

The plain weave is the most common and the strongest of all weaves. This is the simplest form of interlacing the warp and the filling—and the form in which the threads can be woven the tightest. Note that each filling yarn passes successively over and under each warp yarn, alternating in each row.

Twill Weave

The twill weave accounts for about 12 percent of all woven goods. Its strength is almost as great as that of a plain weave, although the interlacing of threads is not as tight. The twill weave is formed by varying and alternating the number of yarns passed over and under in both the warp and the filling, so that diagonal lines show on the face of the fabric.

Satin Weave

The satin weave is the weakest of the three basic types, since its threads are more widely spaced. This weave consists of threads that are not raised consecutively, as in the twill weave, but with long floats in either the warp or the filling.

Jacquard Weave

As we mentioned earlier, there are three basic weaves, and variations on them. One important variation is the Jacquard weave, a type that makes most intricate patterns. The patterns are woven by means of cards similar to player-piano cards. The original design is sketched and then charted on pattern paper. From the pattern, holes are punched in the Jacquard cards, which are laced together to form a continuous chain. The Jacquard loom is so constructed that each warp thread can be raised or lowered to make the patterns. In the weaving process, needles pass through the holes in the cards and control the warp threads to create the design.

PATTERNS

Now that we have looked at two of the basic aspects of textiles, fiber content and weave, we are ready to discuss a third—*pattern*. With an endless array of "documentary" patterns (that is, adaptations or exact copies of old designs) being reproduced today, in addition to contemporary offerings, the selection of plain and patterned fabrics reaches gigantic proportions. A designer's proficiency can be measured by his or her ability to use these patterns to their best advantage.

A designer may use a single pattern for an entire room setting, or mix many patterns together, keeping in mind of course that the scales of the patterns must differ and that they must have a color combination in common.

Pattern mixing can lend a great deal of interest to a room, and a competent and imaginative professional designer can achieve distinctive results.

Shown here is a photographic sampling of popular patterns, each one having its own particular characteristics. Many are from Brunschwig & Fils, Inc., internationally known among designers and architects as leading textile manufacturers. Founded in Paris in 1880, this company is still noted for its imported and domestic decorative fabrics, trimmings, and wallpaper. In contrast to this old established firm is a newer and fast-growing firm called China Seas Inc. This company is responsible for the revival of batik in the U.S.A. and Europe. It distributes internationally and has factories in Indonesian and Indian villages. China Seas fabrics are designed to offer a great range of possibilities for combining and interrelating textures, shapes, and styles. (See Figures 14–8 through 14–16.)

Figure 14-8: An 18th-century toile de Jouy design, originally printed by Oberhampf and reproduced in honor of America's bicentennial, depicts idealized scenes of the young republic. This toile de Jouy has been printed in France since 1786. "(Brunschwig & Fils, Inc., available exclusively through decorators and fine stores.")

Figure 14-9: An Indian-inspired cotton printed fabric with a large, leafy paisley design, found by Zelina Brunschwig in Paris and reproduced by a fine Alsatian printer to give the look of the original block print from which it was taken. (Brunschwig & Fils, Inc.)

Figure 14-10: "Rose Damask" is a faithful adaptation of a Victorian pattern which has been updated in color only. (Brunschwig & Fils, Inc.)

Figure 14-11: "Hatvan" Hungarian flamestitch in a shell motif. (Brunschwig & Fils, Inc.)

Figure 14-12: Patterned glazed chintz adapted from a Victorian design of about 1840, when roller-printing still used artist-engravers. (Brunschwig & Fils, Inc.)

Figure 14-13: Glazed chintz in a traditional English block print with a botanical look in its exquisite study of flowers from an English garden. (Brunschwig & Fils, Inc.)

177

Figure 14-14: Decorative fabric trimmings: braids, fringes, and tie-backs. (Brunschwig & Fils, Inc.)

Figure 14-15: An all-over repeat pattern called "Java," available in many color combinations and with matching wallcovering. (China Seas, Inc.)

Figure 14-16: Exotic bird pattern, "Bali," comes in many colors with matching wallcovering available. (China Seas, Inc.)

FLAME-RETARDANT FIBERS

Because of the ever-increasing demand for flame-retardant fabrics, in both commercial and residential use, new synthetic fibers are being developed which will neither burn nor melt. Especially noteworthy are two new fibers; others will continue to be introduced to the market.

Sef Modacrylic

This is a fiber produced by Monsanto, with the following characteristics: it has superior flame retardancy; processes extremely well in yarn and fabric manufacture; dyes very well; has superior draping potential; has outstanding resistance to sunlight degradation; possesses outstanding soil- and stain-release characteristics.

Kohjin Cordelan

This new synthetic fiber produced by Kohjin Co., Ltd. in Japan has superior whiteness compared with modacrylics; has less static electricity than any other synthetic fiber; has high flame resistance and

179

will not melt; resists chemicals well; does not absorb oil-borne stains; and possesses a softness or "hand" that can be compared with cashmere.

FINISHING PROCESSES

When fabric has been made in one of the many weaving processes, it is in a rough state known as gray goods or greige goods. Before any printing or dyeing of the cloth, it must be "finished"—that is, cleaned, most often bleached and stretched to the proper width. Other preliminary treatments of cloth vary according to the type of fibers used, but all cloth must be treated in some manner to be brought to a usable state. Such finishing processes, some of which are done before dyeing or printing and some after, are listed below.[3]

Flameproof Finishes

There are two basic types of flameproof finish available: the durable and the renewable. The durable treatment allows the fabric to be washed or dry-cleaned repeatedly and still retain its flameproof quality. Fabric that has had the renewable, or nondurable, treatment will not undergo washing or dry-cleaning without losing its flame-resistant character. Some fabrics of man-made fibers, such as *Sef Modacrylic* and *Kohjin Cordelan*, are inherently flameproof and require no additional treatment.

Resin Textures

Resin treatment is applied to dyed or printed cloth to create many textural effects. Cotton can be made to look like satin; plain cloths can be made to look like seersucker; and embossed effects of all types can be achieved. The resin treatment adds dimensional stability, crispness, and resistance to wrinkles and stains. After the resin treatment has been applied and dried, the fabric can be put through rollers to achieve a polished, glossy effect such as with chintz.

Insulating Finishes

An insulation quality can be achieved by applying a milium finish to the cloth. This application makes the cloth retain either heat or cold, and the effectiveness of the finish does not diminish in use or in the laundering process.

Wash-and-Wear Treatment

This term applies to fabrics that can be washed, drip-dried or machine-dried, and used again with little or no ironing. This quality is achieved by chemically impregnating the fibers with resin as well as by combining man-made fibers with natural fibers.

[3] The information on finishing processes is based on data provided by Payne and Company and is used by permission.

Scotchgard and ZePel Finishes

These are trade names for chemical stain repellers which form a shield around each fiber in a fabric so that it will repel both water-borne and oil-borne stains and resist absorption of household dust and dirt. These treatments are not affected by dry-cleaning.

Shrinkage Control

Shrinkage control essentially removes the stretch from cloth. It is accomplished by a patented process called compressive shrinking; one of the leading trademarks in this field is *Sanforized*.™

Water-Repellent Finishes

There are two basic types of water-repellent finish: durable (that is, permanent) and renewable. The permanent finish is achieved by impregnating fibers with a resin or other chemical. The fabric is not coated, so that the cloth can "breathe." *Sylmer* is a trade name for this process.

Renewable finishes are wax applications. In one form or another they partially coat the fabric, and reprocessing can be done by laundries or dry-cleaning firms. By-products of water-repellent finishing processes are spot and stain resistance: a water-repellent fabric also repels waterborne spots and stains, though not oil stains.

Waterproof Finishes

Waterproof finishes differ from water-repellent types in that the fabric is completely coated with vinyl, rubber, or some other waterproof substance, and becomes nonporous.

Mildew-Resistant Finishes

Mildew, mold, and fungus are formed on fabrics by exposure to warm, moist conditions. The growth of these organisms can be controlled if the fabric is treated with toxic compounds that destroy them. A fabric that is waterproofed is also generally mildew-proof.

This survey of special finishing processes completes our study of fabrics. You will find on the following pages a listing of specialized terminology used in the fabric industry and in interior design; study these terms.

With a knowledge of fibers and their characteristics, a familiarity with weaves and finishes, and the ability to describe the item you want accurately through correct terminology, you can begin to choose your fabrics with more authority. You will find that certain textures and colors and patterns delight you, while others do not. Taste is always a first consideration in the choice of fabrics. But the purpose of this chapter has been to equip you with knowledge that will enable you to choose the fabric that will not only suit individual taste but also serve its function efficiently and contribute to the overall design of whatever room it graces.

In the next chapter, we will discuss fabrics in some of their many specific uses.

FABRIC TERMINOLOGY[4]

Armure: A raised satin motif on a plain rib construction.

Barathea: A rib weave usually done in a minute brick fashion giving a pebbly appearance.

Batik: A method of resist dyeing which employs wax as the resist. The pattern is covered with wax, and the fabric is then dyed, producing a white design on a dyed ground. The waxed patterns will not take the dye, and the wax is removed after dyeing. The process is repeated to obtain multicolored designs. The effect is sometimes imitated in machine prints.

Boucle: Plain weave using plied or uneven yarns with loop surface, giving a rough appearance to the face of the cloth.

Bourette: Originated in France. A twill or plain weave. The yarns are interspersed with nubs, giving the material a dull nubbed surface effect.

Brocade: Multicolored jacquard woven fabric with floral or figured pattern emphasized by contrasting colors. The color is introduced through the filler yarns. The background may be either satin or twill weave.

Brocatelle: A tightly woven jacquard fabric with a warp effect in the figure which is raised to give a puffed appearance. The puff effect is created by several kinds of fillings; tension weaving of a linen; or nylon which shrinks after a heat process.

Broche: A fabric decorated with special threads introduced usually in the filling which are not necessarily part of the face fabric. Generally these yarns are clipped on the reverse side and appear only where the motif is present.

Chenille Fabric: A fabric woven with chenille yarns which have a pile effect similar to velvet, and when woven through various warps can create a pile-like velvet, or, if woven on a jacquard loom, can look similar to a cut velvet.

Chevron: Broken twill or herringbone weave giving a chevron effect, creating a design of wide "V's" across the width of the fabric. See "Herringbone."

Chintz: A plain tightly woven cotton fabric with fine yarns and processed with a glazed finish. Used as a plain dyed fabric or a printed fabric. The term is sometimes used for unglazed fine count cottons.

Color Line: Refers to the complete color range of a given series.

Color Flag: The series of clippings attached to a purchase sample to show the color line.

Colorway: An individual color of a particular style or pattern.

Converter: Company who issues instructions to dyers and finishers to process their own greige goods into finished goods.

Converting: The processes by which greige goods are made into finished salable goods.

Crewel: Chainstitch embroidery made with a fine, loosely twisted, two-ply worsted yarn on a plain weave fabric. Done by hand, for the most part, in the Kashmir Province of India and in England.

Crocking: Rubbing off of color from woven or printed fabrics.

---

[4]The terminology of fabrics is reproduced by permission of the ASID Industry Foundation Bulletin, prepared by Courtesy of Stroheim and Romann.

Damask: A jacquard woven fabric with floral or geometric patterns created with different weave effects. Can be woven self-tone; one color warp; different color filling. Distinguished from brocade because face of fabric is flatter.

Decorative Fabric Wholesaler: A firm that creates, styles and colors decorative fabrics and provides service for merchandise sold at wholesale to interior designers, architects, furniture manufacturers, etc.

Douppioni: Also spelled doupioni, doppione, douppione and referred to as doupion silk. An irregular rough silk reeled from double cocoons that have grown together, resulting in a slubby, interrupted texture. Irregularity in sheerness or weight, referred to as cross bands or shadings, are common. Black specks sometimes appearing in douppioni silk fabrics are part of the original cocoon and cannot be removed without weakening the fiber. Their inherent properties are not to be considered flaws or defects in the fabric.

Dyeing: The coloring of greige goods or fibers with either natural or synthetic dyes. This may be done in many different ways depending on the type of fabric (or fiber), the type of dye and the desired result. Some of the more common methods are:

1. Piece Dyeing: Fabric is passed through the dye solution for a specified length of time.
2. Vat Dyeing: An insoluble dye that has been made soluble is put on the fiber and then oxydized to the original insoluble form.
3. Solution Dyeing: A solution of dye is added to the liquid synthetic before spinning it into a yarn.
4. Yarn Dyeing: Yarn is dyed before it is woven into fabric.

Dyer: A term used to refer to a finishing plant which dyes greige goods or fibers.

Faille: A flat, ribbed fabric woven with fine yarns in the warp, with heavier yarns in the filling, using a plain weave. The ribbed effect is flatter than grosgrain and smaller than a repp. The fabric is the base cloth used for Moire.

Fibers—Natural Fibers: Cotton • Wool • Silk • Linen • Hemp.

Man-Made Fibers—Generic Classification: Acetate • Acrylic • Glass • Modacrylic • Nylon • Olefin • Polyester • Rayon • Saran • Spandex • Vinyl.

Fiber Content: The make-up of the yarn content of any given fabric. (i.e. 60% cotton and 40% rayon.) By regulation of the Federal Trade Commission, this information must be provided in all price lists.

Fiberglass: Fibers and yarns produced from glass and woven into flexible fabrics. Noted for its fireproof qualities. Beta fiberglas is a trademarked glass fiber.

Fill or Filling: The threads running widthwise across a piece of fabric.

Finished Goods: Fabric that has been processed by dyeing, printing, applying of special resins and finishes, etc.

Finishing: The process of dyeing, printing, etc., of greige goods.

Finishing Plant: A place that dyes, prints, etc., greige goods.

Frieze: A very strong plain fabric with a fine low loop surface woven on a wire loom to maintain an even size to the loops. Usually made with wool warp, cotton filling, but can be of other fibers.

183

Gauze: A thin sheer fabric constructed with either a plain, leno or dobby weave. Specifically for use as curtains against glass windows to diffuse light.

Greige Goods: The raw or unfinished goods which have been woven but are otherwise unprocessed (dyed, printed, etc.).

Haircloth: A very stiff wiry cloth made with a single horsehair filling, usually on a cotton warp. The width of the fabric is determined by the length of the horsehair in the filling. A plain, satin, leno or dobby weave. No more than 26″ wide, as width is determined by length of horse's tail.

Herringbone: A broken twill weave composed of vertical sections which are alternately right hand and left hand in direction. Also called chevron weave, especially when arranged in wide stripes.

Imberline: A jacquard fabric, usually a damask design with a stripe woven in the ground or as a satin overlay centered on the design. Usually three or four stripes to a 50-inch width.

Jacquard Design: A woven design made with the aid of a jacquard head (this constitutes a jacquard loom) and may vary from simple, self-colored, spot effects to elaborate, multicolored, all-over effects.

Lampas: A term describing a jacquard fabric; a term interchangeable with a brocade or damask. Can be two-tone or multicolor, the difference being that the design has a greater raised effect on the face of the fabric.

Leather: The skin of an animal tanned or otherwise dressed for use. Full Top Grain, indicating the very best hides available on the world market today. Only the finest hides, those which do not require sanding or buffing to remove defects or imperfections, can be classified as Full Top Grain. These premium hides in their natural, unadulterated state retain the superior characteristics of suppleness and tuftability found only in genuine Full Top Grain leather.

Lisere: A jacquard fabric usually made with a taffeta or faille ground. The design is created by colored warp threads brought up on the face of the fabric, leaving loose yarns on the back. These threads are sometimes clipped.

Loom: A machine on which the weaving is done. The warp (lengthwise) threads are secured on the loom through the eyes of beddles and attached to the loom beam at the front of the loom. The filling (crosswise) thread darts between the warp threads as they are alternately lifted and lowered sometimes carried by a shuttle, sometimes propelled by air pressure, or other methods, in shuttleless looms.

1. The PLAIN WEAVE consists of one thread over and one thread under. This type is found in sheeting.

2. The TWILL WEAVE has each warp thread passing over two or more filling threads, with the interlacing advancing one thread on successive warps. This type, with its "diagonal line," is found in denims.

3. The SATIN WEAVE has few interlacings widely but regularly spaced, resulting in a lustrous "right" side and dull back. This type is found in dress goods.

Matelasse: A jacquard fabric woven with heavy "stuffer" filling yarns to create a puffed quilted effect.

Mill: The place where fabric is woven.

Moire: Base cloth must be a faille. A finish achieved with engraved rollers which press the design into the fabric, causing the crushed and uncrushed parts to reflect light differently (called "Water-Marked"). Sometimes it is done with the fabric folded the length of the goods—leaving a center crease—more often folded with crease on the width of the goods and fabric cut at this fold eliminating a center crease.

Natural Fibers: Those fibers which come from cotton, wool, silk, and flax (linen).

Ninon: A smooth lightweight fabric made in a plain weave giving the effect of a very fine mesh.

Ombre: A fabric woven with shades of one color from light to dark in the warp, usually creating a striped effect.

Ottoman: A firm lustrous plain weave fabric with horizontal cords which are larger or rounder than those of a faille. The fine warp totally covers the heavier filling.

Pattern: Descriptive name used for the design on finished goods.

Piece Goods: Finished goods in a salable state. Pieces generally run 50 to 65 yards.

Pilling: Formation of fiber fuzz balls on fabric surface by wear or friction, encountered in spun nylon, polyester, acrylic, cashmere, or soft woolen yarns.

Plisse: A fabric with a crinkled or puckered effect, generally in the direction of the warp, which is created either by tension weaving or through the application of a caustic soda solution which shrinks part of the yarns on the back of the cloth.

Pocket Weave: A jacquard double-layered fabric with several warps. The design is created with both warps and fillings.

Polished Cotton: A plain weave cotton cloth characterized by a sheen ranging from dull to bright. Polish can be achieved either through the weave or the addition of a resin finish. Can be a solid color, usually piece dyed or printed.

Printing: A term referring to methods of applying designs to greige goods. Some types of printing are: roller printing, screen printing, and handblocked printing.

Quilting: Process of applying stitching (usually in a decorative design) to two pieces of fabric with a filling (such as cotton batting) between them.

Remnant: A piece of fabric usually less than three yards.

Repp: Plain weave fabric with narrow ribs running the width of the fabric. Usually a fine warp and heavier filling yarns.

Sateen: A highly lustrous fabric usually made of mercerized cotton with a satin weave.

Selvage: Narrow edge of woven fabric (warp direction) usually of stronger yarns or denser construction than body of cloth.

Series: Those numbers indicating a pattern and its various colorways, i.e., 15807-16.

Strike Off: The term used to refer to the first run of a new pattern or style.

Suede: A tanned animal skin, with the flesh side rubbed into a nap.

Swatch: A small sample of a piece of fabric.

Synthetics: Man-made, scientifically produced fibers used in many fabrics. Some types of synthetics are: rayon, nylon, polyester, and fiberglass.

Taffeta: A fine, plain tabby weave fabric, usually with a sheen on its surface.

Antique: Plain warp with a thick and thin filling (i.e., silk douppioni).

Plain: Warp and filling usually the same size yarns.

Tapestry: A heavy jacquard fabric usually multicolored. Warps and filling very tightly woven. The designs vary from traditional to contemporary. Used for upholstery only.

Toile de Jouy: A floral or scenic design usually printed on cotton or linen. Originally printed in Jouy, France, the fabrics were printed in single colors from engraved copper plates, the designs were characterized by classic motifs beautifully engraved and finely colored. Today, some are multicolored.

Tussah: Sometimes called "Wild Silk." It is the product of the uncultivated silkworm—more uneven, coarser and stronger than true or cultivated silk. Tussah takes dye poorly and is therefore often woven in its natural color, which ranges from ecru to dark brown. Considerable color variance within each length is not unusual and is considered an intrinsic characteristic of the fabric.

Union Cloth: A plain weave fabric made from two or more different fibers, most often a cotton warp and a linen filling.

Urethane Upholstery: A name for a group of organic chemical compounds or resins such as polyesters and polyethers. These compounds make up the skin which is bonded to a cotton backing.

Velvet: A closely woven pile fabric, it can be made of many fibers: silk, cotton, rayon, dralon, etc.

○ *Crushed Velvet:* Most often the fabric is pulled through a narrow cylinder to create the crush. Sometimes, as with linen velvet, a roller is used to give a repeat to the design.

○ *Cut Velvet:* A jacquard design, usually cut and uncut pile on a plain ground. Sometimes the design is a solid color and sometimes multicolor.

Velour: A term loosely applied to all types of fabrics with a nap or cut pile on one side. Specifically, it is a cut pile fabric similar to regular velvet but with a higher pile.

Vinyl Upholstery: A polyvinyl chloride film with a fabric backing.

Warp: The threads running through the length of a piece of cloth.

Yarn Dyed: Goods made from yarns that are dyed before they are woven or knitted into a fabric.

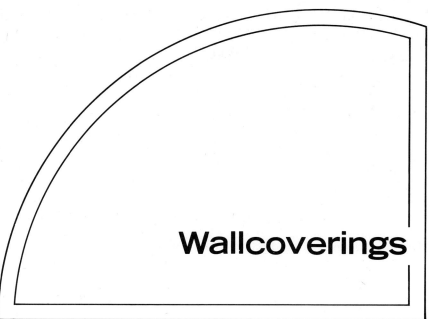
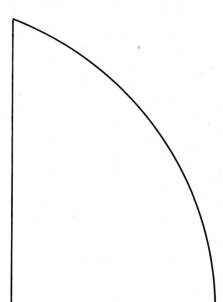

Wallcoverings

Ever since people lived in caves, they have decorated their walls, either in a realistic fashion or with ornamental designs. There are two ways to decorate a wall (or ceiling): the decorative motif can be drawn, painted, stencilled, appliquéd, or frescoed directly onto the wall; or an ornamental covering material can be placed over the wall, covering it and adding interest and beauty to the room.

In this chapter we will deal with wallcoverings, which have become by far the most practical and widely used way to decorate the walls of a room. We will look first at the development of wallpaper through history, then at the way wallpaper is made and printed today and at some of its specialized uses. Finally, other wallcoverings, including fabric, will be considered.

WALLPAPER IN HISTORY

The story of wallpaper began in ancient China, where paper itself was invented (and remained a well-guarded secret for hundreds of years). There, rice paper was used on walls as early as 200 B.C. In Europe, woven materials and tapestries were hung on the walls to keep out the cold, starting as early as the Middle Ages.

In about 1586, the "Corporation of Domino Makers, Tapestry Makers, and Picture Makers" was founded in France. These craftsmen started out by imitating the marbled papers of the Near East—which had swirling patterns made by floating pigment, not a printing process—but later developed block-printed paper suitable for wall application. This was so successful that by 1599 the charter for the "Guild of Paper Hangers" was established.

The Dutch used embossed and painted leather wallcoverings in the seventeenth century; meanwhile, however, the use of wallpaper proper increased steadily in popularity throughout Europe.

187

In England, the oldest surviving wallpaper "document" was made in 1509, using a stencilled pomegranate pattern. In 1558, during the reign of Queen Elizabeth I, English artisans printed papers by letterpress. Also popular were flocked papers, whose surface was given a brushed or fuzzy texture by the gluing of various fibers onto parts of the paper to create a design.

Originally printed mostly by hand, English wallpapers began to be produced with copper plates in the Gothic Revival period of the nineteenth century. William Morris and his followers reacted by returning to hand-printing by the wood-block method—creating designs that influenced the development of Art Nouveau.

In America's early years many papers were imported, but Americans began manufacturing tasteful copies by 1740. During the second half of the nineteenth century, machine-made papers suffered the same decline in quality in the United States as they did in Europe; but the design and production of wallpapers picked up in status under the influence of the Bauhaus designers in the 1920s and 1930s.[1]

WALLPAPER TODAY

Wallpaper today is more popular than ever, and walls have a new importance in the decorating scene. Positive statements are now being made with wallpaper: there is no easier way to achieve individuality than through wallcovering design. The right pattern can give a city apartment the air of a country cottage or create a contemporary feeling in an old house. Old rules are being broken; new innovative ideas are now offered. Wallpaper sets the mood, creates the scene, blends your color scheme, and ties your room together. Equally important, harmonizing wallpapers can be used to create a thematic tie between one room and another.

Thanks to technical advances, modern printed wallcoverings can be produced in large volume without sacrificing the highest quality. Modern methods of wallpaper printing fall into three main categories: surface printing, rotogravure printing, and silk-screen printing.

Surface Printing

Surface printing accounts for the largest volume of printed papers. Originally wooden rollers were used for surface printing; today, this process is done with engraved metal rollers, and each roller prints just one color. Many rollers can be used for a multicolored pattern.

Rotogravure Printing

The newest method used today, rotogravure printing uses copper-covered steel rollers, photographically engraved to produce rotogravure patterns. The pattern is cut into the roller by an intaglio process, and the depth of each incision determines the value of the color. Each roller still carries just one color, but may print varying shades of that color.

[1]Information on wallpaper in history provided by Lis King of the Wallcovering Industry Bureau and used by permission.

Figure 15-1: Pattern power in an oversized, stylized printed design called "Victoria," by Walls Today, Inc., gives interest to plain modern architecture and unifies a mixture of contemporary furnishings and Oriental accent pieces. (Wallcovering Industry Bureau)

Figure 15-2: Two color-coordinated wallcoverings, York's "Heirloom" (left) and "Gingham," provide country appeal in a standard dining ell of a development home. (Wallcovering Industry Bureau)

Silk-Screen Printing

Silk-screen-printed wallpaper can be made by one of two processes: either entirely by hand, or partly by hand and partly by machine. Designs are applied with individual screens. One screen is used for each color in the design, and the color is squeezed or brushed through the cutout portion of the screen onto the wallpaper—as in the screen-printing of fabrics.

There is an abundance of wallpaper patterns, including paisleys, patchworks, geometrics, florals, toiles, damasks, lattice designs, animal prints, scenics, borders, contemporary designs, basket weaves, stripes, polka-dots, crewels, marbles, chinoiseries, architectural designs, country prints, stencils, frieze patterns, and more. (See Figures 15–3, 15–4, and 15–5 for some examples.)

Textures include moiré, sculptured, flocked, tea chest, vinyl, woven, grasscloth, embossed, stippled, shiki silk, and mylar papers.

Figure 15-3: Traditional setting using two York wallcoverings, "Rouen" (in dining room) and "Brittany" (in hallway and on door leading to the dining room). (Wallcovering Industry Bureau)

190

Figure 15-4: Three designs from Karl Mann Associates' "Art Bizarre" collection: top, "Kashmir"; lower left, "Madras"; lower right, "Mother Nature." (Karl Mann Associates.)

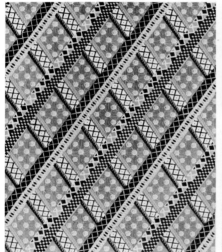

Figure 15-5: "Barcelona" wallcovering. (William Skilling for Karl Mann Associates.)

Special Uses of Wallcoverings

The right wallcovering, used properly, can alter the apparent shape of a room and camouflage architectural flaws. There are a few tricks to achieving these aims:

LOW CEILING. A wallcovering pattern can lead the eye upward. Use pale colors, in textures or small patterns or a vertical stripe, to give the illusion of greater height.

HIGH CEILING. To accomplish an apparent reduction in the height of the ceilings seen in many older houses, use papers with a horizontal pattern or wide border pattern on the walls; or add strong patterned paper or dark color to the ceiling treatment. (Another possibility is to add deep beams.)

TOO-SMALL ROOM. To make a small room appear larger, use cool colors on the walls—this will make them seem to recede. Or try an allover, open pattern on a light ground.

TOO-LARGE ROOM. To make an overscale room appear cozier, use warm colors on walls; this will make them seem to advance or come forward. Papers with dark grounds can be used, as can architectural trim or panel papers, to break up the expanse of wall area.

Figure 15-6: A fabric-backed vinyl wallcovering for an all-American little girl's room: "Sunshine" from Stauffer's "Children of All Ages" collection. (Wallcovering Industry Bureau.)

TOO-NARROW ROOM. A narrow space can be "opened up" by the use of strong color or design on the two shorter walls. The longer walls should have either a reflective surface—such as mylar, mirror, or foil paper—or a paper creating the illusion of perspective or depth.

BROKEN-UP WALL SPACE. The use of an all-over pattern on wallpaper will camouflage displeasing interruptions to a wall. (Such a pattern can also be used to cover doors, woodwork, or even furniture.)

COOL ROOMS. The obvious use of a warm color such as red, pink, or terra cotta will help to make a chilly room feel cozier.

WARM ROOMS. Cool colors such as blue or green will give a cooling effect in a room in a hot climate—or where the afternoon sun "heats up" the space.

OTHER WALLCOVERINGS

Rich though the choice of wallpaper today may be, this is only part of the overall range of wallcoverings available.

Fabric, perhaps the most important wallcovering other than paper, can be used in many ways. One method is to paperback the fabric and then install it in the same manner as wallpaper—using a line paper first.

Figure 15-7: Vinyl acrylic wallcoverings in an Oriental mood: "Dynasty Toile" (above the chair rail) and "Macao" (below), both from Christopher Prints. (Wallcovering Industry Bureau)

193

Figure 15-8: *Cane-patterned ceramic tile in green and white by Mid-State turns awkward architectural features, so common in remodeled older houses, into an asset in this bathroom with dormer window. (Photo: Tile Council of America)*

Figure 15-9: *An imaginative use of glazed ceramic tile adds special flair to a fairly standard dining set. The shining wall of tile reflects the pool beautifully. (Photo: Tile Council of America)*

Or the walls can be prepared with a layer of dacron, then upholstered, using cord or welt at seams and edges to conceal tacks. For a large wall area, the fabric can be seamed first and then installed: this is how wallcovering originally looked when fabric was used to keep out the cold. It is still a very beautiful finish to any interior.

The fabric can also be gathered, box-pleated, or softly draped on the walls for a striking effect. Fabric can be paperbacked or gathered for the ceiling treatment as well.

The term *wallcovering* encompasses all the materials other than paper used on walls. This partial listing can give you ideas for further study: wood paneling, mirrors, murals, silk, cork, bamboo, grasscloth, tile, felt, metallics, mylar, vinyl, rugs, collage, stucco, plaster, brick, stone, ceramics, trellises, moldings, leather (plain or embossed or patent), frescoes, marble, lucite panels, screens, chrome, steel, and copper.

The most familiar wallcovering of all is, of course, paint. Paint can be applied either plain—in a flat, high-gloss or semi-gloss finish—or in a more decorative manner, such as stippled, glazed, antiqued, lacquered, grained, or marbled, or with surfaces of silver or gold leaf.[2]

The choice of wallcovering materials is a step that cannot be taken in isolation. It depends on your comprehensive plan for a room, and on the furniture style, color scheme, lighting plan, and upholstery materials that you have selected. (Some of your thinking about upholstery materials depends partly on your ideas about wallcovering, too.) Once you have your wallcovering plan worked out, however, you are ready to decide upon another exciting and important element of your room: window treatment. We will look at a variety of window treatments in the next chapter.

[2]Wallcovering information provided by Lis King of the Wallcovering Industry Bureau and used by permission.

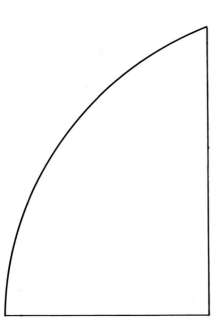
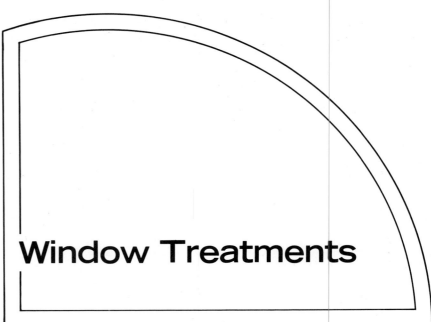

Window Treatments

Windows have always served two contrasting functions: first, to let in light and air; and second, to protect the inhabitants of a building from wind, weather, and hostile visitors. Thus, in medieval European castles, the windows were narrow and located high in the walls to protect against attack. In Gothic England, windows were either glazed or covered with oiled paper or cloth. During the Tudor period, glass became widely used, and window treatments changed from being merely functional to being decorative. Draperies were originally used to keep out the cold—first simply as leather or cloth hung in front of the window, and later constructed so that they could be drawn aside. Drapery fabric began to be a reflection of the prevailing fashions, and wool decorated with crewel work, as well as linens, silks, damasks, and velvets, were utilized. From the sixteenth century to the present, a variety of elaborate window treatments have been tried. Window treatments are still changing and continuing to develop, and current styles incorporate many fabrics and materials that were never known or used before.

Window treatments have changed—and so have windows themselves. From a hole in a wall, to a small and foggy mullioned rectangle, to a tall Victorian bay, to a broad wall of solid glass: the shapes, sizes, and uses of windows have been transformed over the centuries. In twentieth-century America the designer will encounter shapes as old as the seventeenth century, and as new as tomorrow. What is the best way to approach window treatments so that both protective and decorative elements will be best served?

Once again, we find that all preceding areas of study come into play as we consider this newest one. Window treatments will depend on the style, colors, and lighting arrangements in a room; they will relate closely to decorative fabrics and wallcoverings. With the central plan always in the picture, the designer needs to become acquainted with some traditional and some brand-new ways of drap-

196

ing, shading, covering, and framing windows. In this chapter we will look at a sampling of window treatments, beginning with the most widely used of all: fabric drapery.

DRAPERY STYLES

Today's window styles follow the architecture, rather than concealing it, as the "wall-to-wall" drapery of earlier years did. Your choices of fibers, colors, patterns, and textures must all be suited to the room's decorating scheme. Generally, fabrics on windows should be amply full (see the definition of *fullness*, in the "Terminology" section). I recommended two-and-one-half times fullness, with deep double 10-inch hems, and triple fullness for sheer fabrics. Floor to ceiling drapery is usually preferable, unless there's a good reason for using short drapes—such as radiator interference.

Figure 16-1: Window treatment, early 18th century (1709-1769). (From "Window Treatments through the Ages," courtesy of Kirsch Company.)

197

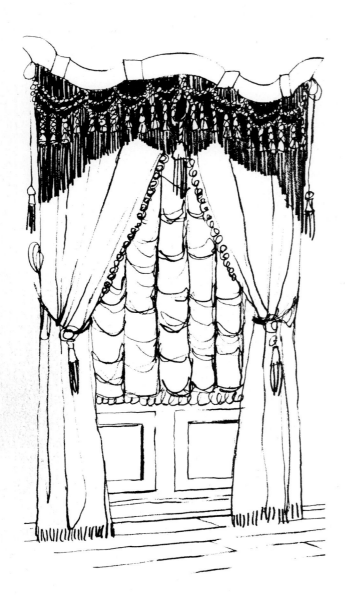

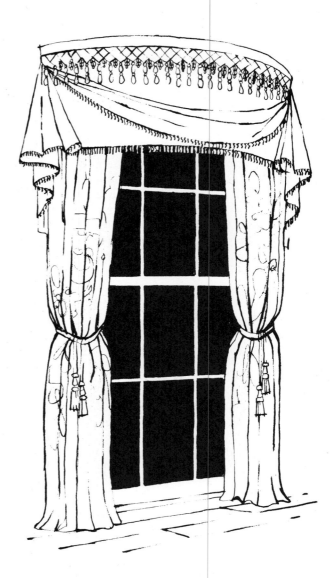

Figure 16-2: Left: Window treatment, early 18th century (1709-1769). (From "Window Treatments through the Ages," courtesy of Kirsch Company.)

Figure 16-3: Right: Window treatment, late 18th century (1770-1820). (From "Window Treatments through the Ages," courtesy of Kirsch Company.)

Pleats

There are a great number of drapery headings that you may use to form a variety of pleats:

Pinch pleats are made by dividing large pleats into three smaller creased ones.

Box pleats are large pleats pressed flat so that each fold is an equal distance from the center line of the pleat. The spaces in between are the same width as the finished pleat.

Cartridge pleats are round, 2- to 2½-inch pleats, filled in with cotton or paper to hold the shape. They are generally spaced 2 to 3 inches apart.

French pleats have three folds; they are most often used in standard draperies. They are made by dividing one large pleat into three smaller ones, but not creasing them.

198

Smocking is another type of heading. It is made as in smocked trim on dresses: with double or triple rows of puckers created by a line of stitching through the fabric according to a set pattern.

Shirring is created by a row of gathering on a pole or rod. In this case, there should be three times as much fabric as the length of the rod.

Accordion pleats can be made easily with patented devices that allow the creation of neat, even folds that snap on and off a traverse track without hooks. These units can be stacked in a minimum amount of space.

Ripplefold pleats, made with Kirsch's Ripple Fold heading system, are soft and rounded vertical pleats. These also snap on and off, and they are also the same front and back.

Flat-top draperies are usually made with *Velcro* tape and can be used in areas where there is not enough room for the 3½ or 4 inches of projecting pleat fullness.

199

Top Treatments

Just as draperies themselves come in many styles and forms, so do top treatments—the handling of the area which includes the top edge of the window frame, the wall above the window, and the top edge of whatever drapery (or other decorative element) is chosen. Your selection of top treatments must always be made in relation to the height, size, and style of your room. With experience and research you will soon form your own ideas about top treatments. Here are several popular and effective ones:

Pole treatments lend a nice airy feeling to a room, either with drapery hanging just below the pole (attached by invisible means or with rings), or with drapery fabric fully gathered onto the pole. Large poles can be brass, or painted or stained wood, or upholstered, shirred with fabric, or even wallpapered.

Valances are horizontal pieces across the top of the window, and are always made of fabric—often the same as that of the main draperies. They can be short and pinch-pleated, box-pleated, scalloped or shaped, flat, swagged, cut into jabots, shirred, or gathered. They can also be gathered on a wooden, brass, or fabric-covered pole.

Figure 16-6: Pole treatment, the curtains suspended from a print-covered rod and primly tied back to show off the shade. (Window Shade Manufacturers Association, Hilda D. Sachs.)

Figure 16-7: Valance treatment in interior designed by Constance Mercer. (Constance Mercer, ASID, of S. D. Jeffery Assoc. Photo courtesy ASID Public Relation Chairman, Ola Pfeifer.)

Cornices make an interesting and attractive top treatment. Cornice boards are always made of wood, with edges cut either straight or curved. A cornice may be beautifully finished natural wood, or it may be painted, or padded and covered with fabric. A cornice treatment gives you the option of any size or shape desired, and may even extend down deep on both sides. You can use this technique in conjunction with draw draperies by fastening the traverse rods onto the cornice board. You can also face cornices with other materials, such as mirror, bamboo, straw, or wallpaper to blend with the decor.

Lambrequins are usually made of plywood and covered with fabric or sometimes wallpaper or other materials. They extend all the way down either side of the window as well as across the top, framing the window on three sides.

Drapery

Draw draperies are pinch-pleated panels that can be pulled across a window. These use a traverse rod, master carrier, and pull cord(s); they can be pulled two ways, or from either side, and can be used in conjunction with cafe curtains as well.

Overdrapes are stationary draperies used on either side of a window with other window treatments between them. In conjunction with overdrapes you can use regular drapery fabrics—or architectural sheers, Roman shades, laminated shades, Austrian shades, shutters, panels, or horizontal or vertical blinds. The overdrape can be left straight or can be tied back.

Tie-backs can be of the same fabric as the drapery itself, or in a contrasting fabric. Tie-backs can have a border, for accent; or they

201

Figure 16-8: Over drapes with laminated shades, in designer John Hayden's imaginative bedroom for a contemporary apartment. (Window Shade Manufacturers Association.)

can be shirred or shaped. They can be tied at different levels, from two-thirds of the way down, at sill height, to a very high one-third from the top. (In my opinion, a tie-back right in the middle of the length of the drapery or curtain is not as effective as either of the preceding choices.)

Considering the vast array of drapery styles, the above information is only a small representation. With imagination, you can translate these basic types into many individual creations.

OTHER WINDOW TREATMENTS

Among today's generation of interior designers, window treatments other than traditional fabric draperies have gained greater and greater popularity. Curtains, shades, and blinds, the basic old standbys, are finding attractive and functional new uses in both home and commercial installation.

Curtains

Curtains are simply flat fabric panels with a hem on the top that slips and shirrs onto a curtain rod. (Or fabric loops or rings, as for cafe curtains, can be used.) Bottom rods can be used for stationary curtains for doors or the inside glass panels of breakfronts.

202

Shades

Today window shades can make a decorative contribution as well as a functional one. They can make a room appear larger, or optically modify the shape and size of windows that need correction without actual architectural changes. They can complement the understated contemporary or blend with traditional styles, as well as serve functionally for light and heat control. Specialized shades in current use include the following:

Roman shades are fabric-covered shades of horizontal panels, folding up in accordion pleats from the bottom. These shades can be used with solid or patterned material, either alone or with over-drapes.

Laminated shades have a decorative fabric bonded permanently onto the shade-cloth with an adhesive. The laminated shade is installed and operated as any window shade.

Austrian shades are actually shirred curtains that are pulled up like ordinary shades, but with cords rather than by means of a roller. In the past, Austrian shades were made of sheer fabric; now they can be made with any lightweight fabric.

Balloon shades are made of soft fabric, with cords placed vertically along the shade to hold the fabric in place. When the cords are pulled, balloon shades billow in folds. They have fewer folds than the Austrian shade, but they are much deeper and fuller.

Wood shades come in many types. Some are made of narrow horizontal wooden strips connected with thread (sometimes colored) woven on both sides. Others are made of bamboo, tortoise-shell, or woven wood.

Fabric-woven shades are made with textured fabric used in conjunction with wood in many colors, patterns, and designs. A new addition to the decorating scene is the vertical woven blind made of

Figure 16-9: *Painted shades designed by Emily Malino for an elegantly austere townhouse living room. For painting, shades are laid flat and the areas to be done are marked with masking tape. When paint is dry, the tape is removed, and all edges are perfectly straight. (Window Shade Manufacturers Association, Hilda D. Sachs.)*

fabric in approximately 5-inch widths. When they are closed, these woven strips fold one in back of another, creating the look of a macramé panel on either side of the window. Top and bottom rods are required.

Figure 16-10: Left: See-through shades made of fiberglass (Joanna's "Comfort Shades"), together with classic fanlight-shaped headings and shutters, blend contemporary and traditional in a remodeled townhouse living room by Arthur Leaman, ASID. (Window Shade Manufacturers Association.)

Figure 16-11: Right: Balloon shades are chosen for a pretty country kitchen, to allow maximum morning sunlight. (Helene Levenson, ASID. Photo © Peter Vanderwarker.)

Blinds

Blinds have many functional and decorative uses. They can be either horizontal or vertical.

Venetian blinds are not a contemporary invention. The first idea of rotatable parallel louvers for window treatment was brought from the Far East to Venice by Marco Polo; thus they became known as Venetian blinds. They consist of horizontal panels that open and close at angles, depending on the privacy needed. They have been highly popular in the United States for many years, and are still much used, but vertical blinds are gaining a new popularity.

Vertical blinds are used by designers and architects in all parts of the world for residential as well as commercial developments. They are usually made of rigid vinyl, and they offer options of finishes such as natural wood, colors, opaque or translucent vinyl-impregnated fabric, solid colors used alone or together, and graphic patterns. Special louvers are also made for the application of wallpaper and fabric, as well as ones with mirror surfaces on both sides. All have a wide range of decorating possibilities.

For example, vertical blinds can be used as room dividers, for control of privacy or light, and will stack neatly against the wall when not in use. They can be used in window situations that present problems due to architectural angles, or for two-story windows. They

Figure 16-12: Vertical blinds, with wall-paper covering each vertical strip. (Courtesy of Louver Drape Company, Inc. Photo by Lee White Photography.)

Figure 16-13: Vertical blinds in a new mirror-like finish. (Courtesy of Louver Drape Company, Inc. Photo by Lee White Photography.)

205

Figure 16-14: Vertical blinds by Graber, made of Calypso shade cloth, are headed by a matching valance that frames the window and conceals the hardware, in this garden living room by designer Carol Weil. (Window Shade Manufacturers Association, Hilda D. Sachs.)

Figure 16-15: Cloth vertical blinds, made of Breneman's buckwheat "Spice," help establish the airy climate of architect and designer Paul Segal's cosmopolitan living room. (Window Shade Manufacturers Association, Hilda D. Sachs.)

also control exterior heat, glare, and direct light. In many new build-ings, particularly, the maximum use of glass areas plays an integral part in the overall design. Window coverings should enhance the light and view potential, but eliminate glare and excess heat; vertical louvers can be controlled to block sun and change hourly as the sun moves during the day.[1]

DRAPERY MEASURING

Accuracy in measuring is a requisite for successful drapery-making and installation. Measurements should be carefully taken with a quality tape measure, preferably not less than 10 feet long.

It is an excellent idea always to make a sketch of the window and to put the accurate, explicit measurements on your sketch. Re-viewing the sketch with your fabric dealer will eliminate any misun-derstanding as to exactly how the window is to be treated. Do you want the draperies to hang from the ceiling to the floor, or only from the top of the window frame to the window sill? Will there be a valance or a cornice? Will the floor be bare or carpeted? All these variations will make a difference in the finished length of the drap-eries.

Accurate measuring has several other important features. The measurements you take determine the amount of fabric required for the window treatment; thus exact measurement is important in deter-mining total decorating cost. The measurements will have to be used in filling out an accurate work order for the workroom to use in making the draperies. And the sketch you prepare may also be used by an installer who has not previously seen the area to be treated.

Drapery Terminology

There are a number of terms commonly used in work with draperies. It is important to understand these terms and use them correctly. Some of the most common terms are listed below.[2]

Width of Fabric: A width of fabric is the total width of the goods, meas-ured in inches, as it comes from the roll. Generally, the width is 36, 45, 48, or 54 inches. There are some fabrics produced in 72-inch widths or even as wide as 118 inches.

Panel: A panel is the name given to one-half of a pair of draperies. A panel may consist of one or many widths of fabric depending upon the width of the window and the drapery style being used.

Pattern Repeat: This term is used with printed drapery fabrics, to de-scribe the measured distance between one point of a pattern and the point where that same part of the pattern appears again. The length of the repeat is an important consideration in making drap-eries, because it has a bearing on the amount of fabric required to make the draperies; some fabric has to be wasted in order to match the pattern when one width is sewed next to another.

Cut Length: The length of fabric that must be cut from the piece to allow for enough fabric to provide for the heading and the bottom hem is referred to as the total cut length.

[1]Information provided by the Louver Drape Company, Inc., and used by permis-sion.

[2]Information provided by Payne Fabric Company and used by permission.

207

Fullness: This term is used to describe the amount of fabric used in the pleating or gathering process. Drapery can be pleated to double fullness (that is, using fabric twice as wide as the rod is long) although two-and-one-half times fullness is generally preferred for an amply full look. With a sheer fabric, triple fullness is desirable. Drapery should be lined and interlined to accentuate the fullness.

Overlap: The overlap is the measurement of the drapery affixed to the master carrier of a traverse rod, which overlaps with the opposite panel when the two panels of drapery meet in the center of the rod. A standard overlap is 3½ inches on each panel.

Return: That part of the drapery which extends around the rod to the wall surface from the face of the rod is called the return. You should always take the return measurement when you are considering the amount of fabric you need for a pair of draperies, because the return may vary, particularly in the case of a double-hung rod. A standard return is 3½ inches on each panel.

Heading: The heading is the top part of the drapery and is the area where the pleats are formed. The standard heading is 4 inches deep, and is usually interlined with some stiffening material.

Bottom Hem: At the bottom of the draperies a hem is formed to provide a finished appearance; a standard depth for a bottom hem is a double (folded over) 4 inches. (My preference is for a deep double 10-inch hem.)

Side Hem: The side hem is the hem at either side of a panel; it provides a finished appearance. A standard depth is double 1½ inches.

Weight: A piece of metal, usually lead, is often sewn into the bottom hem of a drapery to provide additional weight to help the fabric hang straight.

Mitered Corner: The folding of the bottom corner of the drapery with a 45-degree angle on the hem side is called a mitered corner. This allows the drapery to hang straight.

This chapter has provided a guide to the broad categories and specialized terminology of window treatments—from the most old-fashioned, such as ruffled curtains with tie-backs, to the newest vinyl products in shades and blinds. The next part of this book will also cover both the old and new—in floor coverings. Here again, the wealth of possibilities is great; and as with wallcoverings, it is vital that the designer consider this element as closely related to all other aspects of the total plan for the whole space.

VI
Floor Cover-ings

What happens to the floor of a room depends on those three essential parts of your overall plan: the architecture of the room, the personalities of its inhabitants, and the uses the room will fulfill. The floor must make sense, in terms of style, color, and texture, with all the other components of the design for the room. It can offer contrast or can provide an echo; it can enrich a room through pattern or afford a rest for the eye in an already detail-rich space. It can be shiny and full of light and reflections; it can be lush and soft with a shaggy texture that absorbs sound and adds warmth.

209

FLOOR COVERINGS IN HISTORY

History shows that floor coverings in the form of woven goods were in existence in Egypt as early as 3000 B.C. Patterned fabrics were placed before the thrones of the pharaohs. In pre-Christian Persia, fine wool from sheep was woven into rugs. In the Europe of the Middle Ages, floors were spread with rushes or dried grass until the thirteenth century, when the Moors who had settled in Spain brought the first rug looms to Aubusson, France. Woven rugs were imported from Turkey to England in the fifteenth century; and in 1608, Henry IV of France hired weavers for his looms in the Louvre. The rug factory at the Savonnerie ("soap works") outside Paris was founded in 1618. French weavers also immigrated to Brussels, a city that was already a center for tapestry-making and looped-pile floor coverings.

In the seventeenth century, too, rug-weaving guilds were established in England. The great British rug industry centered at Kidderminster, Axminster, and Wilton; and a peak of production was reached starting about 1740. Carpet-weaving of both the Brussels and the French Savonnerie types affected the British industry. Hand looms continued to be used until the first power loom adapted to rug-weaving—based on inventions of Cartwright, Arkwright, and Jacquard—appeared in 1839. The new power-loom method soon spread to other countries, including America.

At first, early colonists in America had been too involved in developing their new continent to bother about decorations such as rugs on floors. Sand was used in many homes in the eighteenth century and even into the nineteenth century: it absorbed moisture and, when swept up, helped clean the floor. In the eighteenth century straw matting was introduced as a floor covering in many different colors and designs. Because rugs of all types—except those that were home-made—were scarce, painted floors and floor oilcloths became popular in a great variety of designs, including block-printing and stenciling. These techniques emerged in England in the early eighteenth century. In America, rug substitutes were seen in various types and qualities, ranging from crude home-made clothes to costly professionally made linen or cotton canvas rugs in varying weights. Their status value depended on their cost. Because they could be repaired and refinished, this was a thriving business in the eighteenth century, until woven carpets became popular in the 1830s.

Folk rugs came into prominence in America in the nineteenth century, including rag, braid, Venetian, yarn-sewn, hooked, needlepoint, and shirred rugs. The designs of these were at first copies of English and European models, but native designs became more prominent in the second half of the century.

The progress of the rug industry in the United States has been rapid; since 1840, this country has dominated the world carpet industry. Power-loom carpet weaving in the United States got its start through the boundless energy of Erastus Bigelow, who was responsible for most of the important early inventions and whose basic devices were still intact and in use 100 years later. In 1846, the Jacquard power loom for Brussels carpeting and the development of multiple-shuttle boxes for wefting eventually led to mass production of two- and three-ply ingrains and many other weaves. [1]

This brings us to the present. In our time both machine-made and hand-made carpets are available to the designer; and it is important for you to have basic information about both. In Chapter 17 we will look at production methods and fibers used in machine carpet manufacture. Chapter 18 will introduce modern-day custom rug manufacture, as well as discussing the classical techniques used in the weaving of Oriental rugs and some of the many other hand-crafted area rugs. Chapter 19 explores some of the many other forms of floor covering equally important in contemporary life.

Figure VI-1: The antique carpet used in this library by designer Philip H. Smith, ASID Associate, of Boston, sets the theme for the much loved treasures seen here. The feeling of old world comfort is apparent. (Philip H. Smith, ASID Associate. Photo: William W. Owens, Jr.)

[1]Information provided by Anthony Landreau, Curator of the Carnegie Museum, Pittsburgh, Pennsylvania, and used by permission.

211

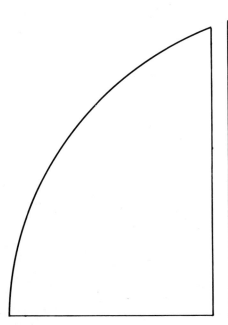
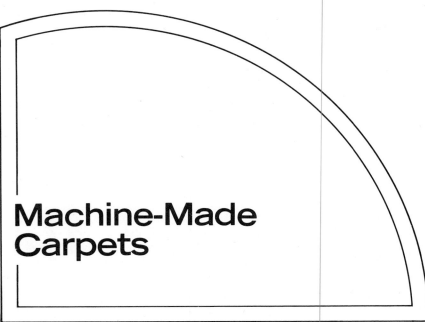

Machine-Made Carpets

For practical purposes, a large proportion of the rug or carpets the homeowner or designer selects today are machine-made products. But machine-made carpets embrace a variety wider now than ever before, as a visit to a single rug showroom will indicate. Because a carpet is usually a costly purchase, the ultimate choice must be determined by a careful evaluation of the properties of each type of rug and its suitability to a given area. For home use, a plush wall-to-wall carpet would be quite suitable; while for a public space, or an area with a lot of traffic, a tighter, more durable weave is desirable. You need to know how to compare qualities of durability, flame resistance, dirt retention, and textural varieties, as well as the more obvious aesthetic appeal. In order to do this, you should know how the various kinds of carpeting are made and what the characteristics of their fibers are. In choosing floor coverings, as is true of so many other areas of interior design, the best equipment you can start out with is the ability to ask the right questions.

MANUFACTURING TECHNIQUES

Early in the 1950s, the American carpet industry was thrust into a remarkable technological revolution.[1] It was then that the technique of making carpet on relatively low-cost, high-speed tufting machines was developed. Concurrently, domestic petrochemical companies were beginning to manufacture fibers in deniers (weights) suitable for carpet use. In rapid order, rayon, nylon, acrylics, modacrylics, olefins, and polyesters were introduced to a market that had been dominated almost completely by wool until the end of World War II. With the new pile fibers plentiful and carpet production accelerating at an enormous rate, new tufting and dyeing techniques were perfected and quality continued to improve.

[1] The information in this section is adapted from *The Carpet Specifier's Handbook*, 1974 ed., copyright © 1973 by The Carpet and Rug Institute. Used by permission.

The two most important techniques of machine carpet manufacture are tufting and weaving.

Tufted Carpet

A tufting machine is similar in principle to an ordinary sewing machine. The difference is that a sewing machine stitches only a single row at one time, but a tufting machine uses hundreds of needles which stitch simultaneously through a backing material as much as 15 feet wide. The rug or carpet is made by adding tufts to this previously produced backing.

A secondary back is usually adhered to the carpet for added strength, dimensional stability, and tuft bind. In some instances, a high-density foam rubber, sponge, or vinyl cushion may be used in lieu of the secondary back.

Tufted carpet is commonly made in 12- and 15-foot widths for wall-to-wall installation; or it can be cut into rugs of any size. Tufted carpet "tiles" with a variety of backings are also available. In the tufting process the machine can create many attractive styles, including tweeds, solids, and stripes. Pattern attachments on the machine can also produce high–low sculptured and embossed effects.

CUSTOM-TUFTED CARPET. Original designs, superdense faces, and textures that seem hand-made can be produced in custom-tufted carpet. This process employs two machines different from mass-production equipment in size and flexibility; otherwise, however, the manufacturing principles are exactly the same.

Figure 17-1: Wall-to-wall carpet. (The Carpet and Rug Institute.)

Figure 17-2: Axminster carpeting, in a variety of geometric patterns from the world's oldest and still prestigious carpet mills, manufactured by expert craftsmen in the Wilton Royal Carpet Factory, Wilton, England. (Wilton Royal, Inc., photo courtesy of N. H. Miller & Co.)

Woven Carpet

Weaving encompasses three basic machine techniques. Velvet, Wilton, and Axminster looms, and variations of these machines, each have their own singular capabilities. As you judge the relative quality of carpets, you must compare face weights, pile heights, and density factors. In general, the deeper, denser, and heavier the pile—all else being equal—the better the carpet.

VELVET. Velvet carpet employs the simplest of all carpet-weaving techniques. The warp and the weft are of linen (or some other sturdy fiber), and the pile—whether wool or one of the synthetics—is drawn through into loops that are later sheared off to produce the velvet texture. Velvet carpet is commonly available in solid colors; however, the range of color and texture variations possible on a velvet loom are almost limitless. Included in possible special texture effects are cut-pile plushes, cut-pile twist (known as frieze), pebbly uncut-loop pile, and multilevel sculptured effects. Pile yarns can also be selectively cut and uncut for another unusual surface texture.

214

Figure 17-3: A practical, long-wearing carpet. (The Carpet and Rug Institute.)

WILTON. Wilton carpet derives its name from the town in England where the Wilton loom was developed. The loom is distinguished by its specialized Jacquard system—a series of pattern cards, perforated like player-piano rolls. The cards regulate the feeding of different-colored yarns into the pile surface.

Though the number of colors possible on a Wilton loom is not unlimited, the Jacquard mechanism assures accurate reproduction of intricate patterns with great clarity and definition. As weaving proceeds, one color at a time is drawn into the pile, and the colors not required are buried beneath the surface. These buried yarns give additional body, resilience, and strength to Wilton carpet.

Wiltons come in a wide range of multicolor patterns as well as solids, and are also available in numerous textures, including modern carved effects. Carved Wilton rugs are particularly handsome.

AXMINSTER. Axminster carpet is also named for a town in England. Axminsters are distinguished by an almost limitless choice of designs and colors. Patterns can be stylized, geometric, classic, modern, or floral.

215

Figure 17-4: Close-up of Stark Carpet Corporation's "Helios," designed by Nadia Stark. "Helios" is of all-wool Wilton construction, in a natural color, and is made in Belgium with specially spun yarn to create a multi-level surface. (Stark Carpet Corporation.)

Axminster looms are nearly as versatile as hand-weaving. The machines make the pile loops one color at a time, interlocking the weft about them. The pile is cut, with few exceptions, and almost all the yarn appears on the surface. Another distinguishing feature of Axminsters is the heavily ribbed back: the carpet can be rolled lengthwise, but not the other way.

Changing patterns on the Axminster loom is a slow and demanding process requiring great skill. Separate lengths or ends of different-colored yarns must be set in with absolute accuracy to insure faithful pattern reproduction.

OTHER CARPET WEAVES. Loomed carpet produced on a modified upholstery machine is also manufactured for commercial use. Because of its rubber backing it is known as a sponge-bonded, high-density fabric; almost invariably, its pile yarns are nylon. Other machine-made carpet varieties include knitted carpet (usually available in solids or tweeds) and needle-punched carpet, which is made of synthetic fibers and is flat, dense, and abrasion-resistant.

216

CARPET YARNS AND FIBERS

Yarns

The final choice of face fiber may depend on the construction of pile yarns. In yarn construction, weight, plies, and twist are the critical quality factors.

Yarn weight is expressed as count, which indicates the fineness or coarseness of the finished yarn. In the United States two systems are used to define yarn count. The first, or "woolen" count (which can apply to any yarn, woolen or not), is the number of running yards in one ounce of finished yarn. Traditionally, this count includes the number of plies in the yarn as well. For example, a "2-ply 50" or "2/50" count indicates 50 yards of 2-ply yarn per ounce.

The second count system is **denier:** measurement of weight in grams of a standard 9,000-meter length of yarn. A 2,500-denier yarn, for instance, is a yarn of which 9,000 meters weighs 2,500 grams.

Ply affects three aesthetic values: color, surface texture, and feel underfoot. It is appearance, more than performance characteristics of finished carpet, that is affected by the number of plies in finished yarn. A deeper, denser, heavier carpet made from 2-ply yarns may

Figure 17-5: Synthetic yarns in a durable multi-colored shag carpet, ideal for a family room. (The Carpet and Rug Institute.)

Figure 17-6: Carpeting is on the walls in this practical study-workshop. (The Carpet and Rug Institute.)

outperform a carpet more loosely and lightly constructed of 4-ply yarns. Different-colored yarn plies (different "ends" of yarn) mixed together produce "moresque" yarns for multitoned tweed effects.

Twist is the number of turns about the axis per inch of yarn. It is what holds the yarn together.

Fibers

The pile fibers most commonly used in commercial carpet, in alphabetical order, include acrylic and acrylic/modacrylic blends, nylon, olefin (polypropylene), polyester, and wool.

The fiber that is best suited to a living room would be out of place in a bathroom; the fiber that adds restful charm to a bedroom would be unsuitable to an office foyer. It is essential that you learn the properties of each fiber—what each is made of; how much heat each can take without damage; how resistant to wear, fading, and staining each is. The table on the following pages provides this information.

218

Properties of Fibers Used in Carpet Manufacturing

GENERIC TERM	ACRYLIC	MODACRYLIC	NYLON	OLEFIN (Polypropylene)	POLYESTER	WOOL
DEFINITION	Fiber-forming substance is any long chain synthetic polymer composed of at least 85% by weight of acrylonitrile units.	Fiber in which fiber-forming substance is any long chain synthetic polymer composed of less than 85% but at least 35% by wt. of acrylonitrile units.	Fiber-forming substance is any long chain synthetic polyamide having recurring amide groups as an integral part of the polymer chain.	Fiber in which fiber-forming substance is any long chain synthetic polymer composed of at least 85% by wt. of ethylene, propylene, or other olefin units.	Fiber in which fiber-forming substance is any long chain synthetic polymer composed of at least 85% by wt. of an ester of a dihydric alcohol and terephthalic acid.	Fiber in which amino acids units are combined into peptide chains possessing multi dimensional stability resulting from hydrogen bonding and cross linking forces of cystine molecules through their sulfur bonds.
EFFECTS OF HEAT	420–490°F. sticking temperature	275–300°F. sticking temperature	Sticks 320–375°F. Melts 425°F.	Melts 250–333°F.	Sticks 445–455°F. Melts 482–554°F.	Scorches at 400°F., chars at 572°F.
EFFECTS OF ACIDS, ALKALIS, AND SOLVENTS	Generally good resistance to mineral acids. Fair to good resistance to weak cold alkalis. Good resistance to common solvents.	Excellent resistance to highly concentrated acids. Unaffected by alkalis. Soluble in warm acetone.	Resistant to weak acids but decomposes in strong mineral acids. Alkalis have little or no effect. Soluble in phenol and formic acid.	Excellent resistance to most acids and alkalis. Generally soluble above 160°F. in chorinated hydrocarbons.	Good to excellent resistance to mineral acids. Some affected by concentrated sulphuric acid. Decomposes in alkalis at the boil. Generally insoluble in common solvents but soluble in some phenolic compounds.	Uneffected by mineral acids. Generally good resistance to weak cold alkalis. Resistance to organic solvents.
DYESTUFFS USED	Acid, basic cationic, chrome, direct, disperse, napthol, neutral premetalized and sulphur. Some fibers are solution-dyed.	Basic, cationic, disperse, neutral premetalized and vat.	Acid, direct, disperse and premetalized. Some fibers are now solution-dyed.	Usually pigmented before extrusion. When modified can be dyed with selected dyestuffs.	Cationic, developed and disperse.	Acid, premetalized, fiber reactant, chrome vats and direct.
RESISTANCE TO MILDEW, AGING, SUNLIGHT AND ABRASION	Excellent resistance to mildew and aging and generally good resistance to sunlight and abrasion.	Not attacked by mildew. Good resistance to abrasion, sunlight and aging but some loss in tensile strength may be noted in the case of Dynel upon prolonged exposure to sunlight.	Excellent resistance to mildew, aging and abrasion. Some degradation may result from prolonged exposure to sunlight.	Not attacked by mildew. good resistance to aging, abrasion and indirect sunlight. Can be stabilized to give good resistance to direct sunlight.	Excellent resistance to mildew, aging, and abrasion. In some instance prolonged exposure to sunlight will result in some loss of strength.	Generally excellent resistance to aging and abrasion. Good fastness to sunlight and mildew.

Backing Materials

In woven and knitted carpet, backing yarns and pile yarns are woven or knitted together as the carpet takes shape. Fibers used in the back can be of linen, jute, kraftcord, polyester, polypropylene, cotton, or rayon, or combinations of these.

In tufted or needle-punched carpet, however, a preformed back is used, and pile yarns are stitched, imbedded, or bonded into it.

DYEING AND PRINTING

Dyeing

Dyeing textiles of any kind is a precise and demanding science—and this is especially true with carpet. The following list of definitions of dyeing techniques is meant to serve one overriding purpose: to strengthen the carpet buyer's resolve to seek the best advice possible from the carpet manufacturers.

STOCK DYEING. This is one of the earliest techniques: it consists of raw-stock dyeing and is used to color the carpet fibers before they are spun into yarn.

SKEIN DYEING. Very much the same in principle as stock dyeing, skein dyeing colors the fibers after they have been spun into yarn "singles" (single strands, unplied).

PACKAGE DYEING. In this technique, spun yarns are wound on large perforated forms. Under heat and pressure, dyes are forced through the perforations and onto the yarn. This "inside-out" soaking action distributes the color evenly. After drying and rewinding, preplied package-dyed yarns are ready for tufting or weaving without further processing.

SPACE DYEING. Space dyeing applies different colors side by side on the same piece of yarn. The effect in finished carpet is random-colored pile, usually composed of three or more tones.

SOLUTION DYEING. Solution-dyed (or producer-dyed) yarns are made of synthetic fibers that are precolored in their liquid state before drawing.

PIECE DYEING. The piece-dyeing process colors up to 150 running yards of carpet that has been tufted of undyed yarns (gray or greige goods). Before the back coating and secondary back are applied, carpet that is to be piece-dyed is put into a dye bath in a large stainless steel tank called a *dye beck*. Rollers or expander bars keep the carpet moving evenly, and pumps or impellers keep the dye liquid circulating freely. After dyeing, the carpet is washed and dried.

RANDOM MULTICOLOR DYEING. Multicolor dyeing can be achieved with a random dye applicator, or what is called a TAK random pattern machine. The machine disperses regulated amounts of dye on carpet already dyed in a single ground color or even on undyed goods. Several TAK dyers can apply several colors at intervals to achieve unusual pattern effects.

DIFFERENTIAL DYEING. As its name implies, differential dyeing produces two or more colors, or tones of a single color, in a single dye bath. This process uses variously modified or variously formulated yarns, so that some sections of the yarn accept certain dyestuffs more deeply than others.

Printing

An increasingly popular technique, the printing of tufted carpet with colorful, sometimes intricate designs allows tremendous styling flexibility. Original patterns of all kinds can be printed directly on the pile with good, crisp definition. (In woven carpet, the colored yarns forming the design are an integral part of the weaving process.)

Printed carpet is manufactured first, usually as totally uncolored greige goods, and the pattern is then applied. Because of the great flexibility and relative speed of the printing, the equipment and techniques have received a great deal of attention, and new and refined kinds of equipment continue to be developed at a regular pace. In principle, however, carpet is either roller-printed or screen-printed.

ROLLER PRINTING. Not unlike roller printing in the textile industry, this process employs embossed cylinders to deposit the design on the face of the carpet. Several of these cylinders in tandem, each printing a different color, produce the multi-colored effects characteristic of printed carpet.

SCREEN PRINTING. This technique employs flat templates, or screens, through which dyes are forced to form the finished pattern on the carpet pile. Each color in a multicolored pattern requires its own screen. Somewhat akin to screening is *deep-dye printing*, which puts down all the colors in the design at the same time. An electrostatic charge forces the premetallized dyes used in this process deep into the pile.

REMOVING STAIN FROM RUGS

The following table will be valuable for continuous reference. Be sure to *pretest* every stain remover on a concealed corner of your rug or carpet before you apply it to the stain; and always apply the cleaning materials *in the order shown on the table*. The stain-removal materials, listed here with their code letters, are identified by letter only in the table.

In this chapter on machine-made rugs it has become apparent that a wealth of diversity exists within the realm of mass-manufactured carpeting. Different fibers, different tufting, weaving, dyeing, and printing techniques can afford a huge choice to the shopper in search of the perfect rug. Yet there will always be times when no standardized product, however fine its quality, seems to meet the precise requirements of a certain space. In these instances a custom-made rug or other hand-crafted area rug can be the answer. In Chapter 18 we will look at some modern custom-made rugs—and at Oriental and other hand-made rugs, which, though they may not be made to the specifications of the individual buyer, are also examples of the finest materials and craftsmanship available in rugs today.

221

Key to stain removal techniques:

A: Detergent solution (one teaspoon of a neutral detergent such as Tide or All in one pint of warm water)

B: Stain remover with no oil in it

C: Dry-cleaning fluid (any common brand, used according to the manufacturer's directions)

D: Rust remover (any common brand)

E: Acetone (any common drugstore variety, or use nail polish remover that contains no lanolin)

F: alcohol (rubbing, denatured, or isopropyl type)

G: Water

H: Ammonia (a 3% solution)

I: Acetic acid or white vinegar

J: Dry ice or chemical freezing compound

If stain consists of type of stain on left, then apply the removal procedure in the order indicated by the key letters on the right—until the stain is removed.

Stain	Procedure	Stain	Procedure
Animal Glue	F-A-H-I	Grease, Car	C
Argyrol	A-G	Ice Cream	A-G
Beer	A	India Ink	B-C-A-G
Betadine Solution	A-C	Iodine Tincture 2%	A-C-I
Blood	A-H	Iron Rust	Vacuum, then D-G
Calamine Lotion	A-I	Latex Paint	B-C
Carbon Black	Vacuum, then A-G	Linseed Oil	C
Cascara Sagrada		Lipstick	B-C
Fluid Extract	A-H	Magnesia Magma	A-I
Catsup	A-H	Merthiolate	A-G
Chewing Gum	C, or ChemSpec	Milk	A-G-H
Clay	Vacuum, then A-G	Mustard	A-H-I
Cola	A-G	Nail Polish	E
Coffee	A-G	Oil, Car	C
Colored Paper	A-H	Oil Paint	B-F-A-G
Crayon	B-C	Peptol Bismol	A-H
Duco Cement	B-C	Permanent Ink	B-C-A-G-I
Egg	A-G	Rouge	C
Enamel	B-F-A-G	Rubber Cement	B-C
Ferrous Sulfide		Shoe Dye	B-C-H
Compounds	A-I	Shoe Polish (liquid)	B-C-A-G
Food Dye	A-G	Tar	B
Fruit Juice	A-G	Tea	A-G
Furniture Dye	B-C-F-A-G	Urine	A-G
Glyceryl Guaiacolate	A-H	Washable Ink	A-G-H
Grape Drink	A-G	Water Colors	A-G-H
Gravy	A-G	Wax (candles)	Steam, then C

Reprinted from *The Carpet Specifier's Handbook*, 1974 ed.; copyright © 1973 by The Carpet and Rug Institute. Used by permission.

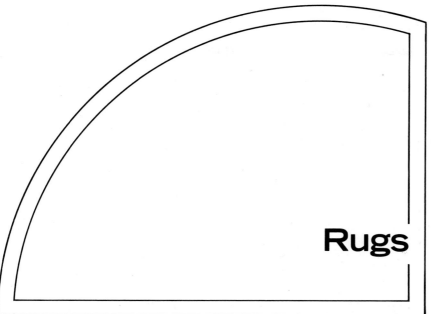

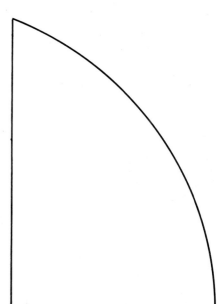

Rugs

A custom-made rug is truly a unique work of art, an opportunity to express the highest degree of artistic endeavor. For an interior designer or architect, the option of using any weave density, color, or pattern suitable to the requirements of the interior setting provides the vehicle for individual designs and suits his or her appreciation of fine materials and workmanship. Imagine the unlimited variety of patterns alone: geometrics, free-forms, abstracts, Oriental motifs, florals, traditional designs, or original ones—all created in different textures and densities and all custom-colored to suit the designer's needs.

There are many fine companies today working to make this possible. I have chosen one as an example: an impressive name that is synonymous with this kind of service—the prestigious V'soske Rug Co.

CUSTOM-MADE RUGS: THE V'SOSKE TECHNIQUE

A company of the highest caliber, V'soske is dedicated to the time-honored craft of rug-weaving. During the 1920s, when many significant changes were taking place in the arts and in crafts, a group of American brothers of Polish descent conceived a new idea for making rugs and carpets by hand. The idea was to tuft wool yarns through a strong cotton base, using a needle that could produce various densities and heights of pile. Years of experiments resulted in what is known today as the *V'soske technique*—a method of hand-tufting that has revolutionized the ancient art of rug-making.

Tufting machines made only one height; because V'soske was able to develop needles to produce different pile heights, this made it possible to shear and produce different depths of pile. Originally rugs were   223

Figure 18-1: A painting from the "Wanderers" series of Nicholas Orsini, interpreted in a hand-made wool rug by Stanislav V'Soske. (V'Soske, Inc., Frances Davison.)

Figure 18-2: Custom rugs offer unlimited options: this intricate pattern and weave can incorporate any number of colors. (V'Soske, Inc., Frances Davison. Photo: Bill Hedrich, Hedrich-Blessing.)

Figure 18-3: Above: A variety of the textures and patterns available in custom-tufted rugs. (V'Soske, Inc., Frances Davison.)

Figure 18-4: Below: Workers in the V'Soske plant. (V'Soske, Inc., Frances Davison.)

Figure 18-5: Left: Embroidering a floral pattern on a V'Soske rug. (V'Soske, Inc., Frances Davison.)

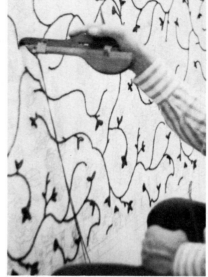

Figure 18-6: Right: Another hand-tooled pattern. (V'Soske, Inc., Frances Davison.)

Figure 18-7: The V'Soske rug is tufted vertically. (V'Soske, Inc., Frances Davison.)

hooked horizontally; the V'soske rug is done vertically, enabling many people to work at once, therefore saving a great deal of time.[1]

Besides the quality and appearance of the rug, the hand-tufting method had further objectives: "to release the designer from the restrictions necessarily imposed by the warp and weft of the traditional loom and to offer versatility in the interpretation of design."[2]

In custom-made designs, each rug is hand-tufted and individually hand-carved (now with electric tools) and hand-sheared with a small shears.

[1] Quote from Fran Davison, Boston representative of V'soske Rug; used by permission.
[2] Davison.

226

Figure 18-8: Contrasting colors and depths of tufting give this hand-carved rug its dramatic effect. (V'Soske, Inc., Frances Davison.)

In the creation of a custom rug, many individual talents are incorporated. Each rug goes through many stages: the designer's conception, the showroom representatives' advice and knowledge as to how to interpret the ideas, the artists' design and color renderings, the spinning of the yarns, the hand-tufting and hand-shearing, the dyeing processes, and finally completion.

Custom Rug Materials and Dyes

TUFTING. Although pure silk carpets are woven in Puerto Rico for some V'soske rugs, the main material used is virgin, skein-dyed wool, usually obtained in Ireland and Puerto Rico. There are thirty-five different yarns, from fine to coarse. The particular qualities of wool are many: durability, beauty, resilience, ease of maintenance, infinite variations (between breeds of sheep), affinity to dye, versatility in construction, and resistance to burn damage. Its qualities do not diminish with age.

BACKING. All V'soske rugs are tufted on cotton backing through minute holes to accommodate the fine yarns.

227

Figure 18-9: A Romanian Kelim rug (also spelled Kilim or Kelem), "Creatures of the Earth," designed by Nadia Stark in tapestry quality wool. (Stark Carpet Corporation.)

Figure 18-10: Inspired by a similar Oriental carpet in the Negresco Hotel on the French Riviera, this Nadia Stark carpet is pure wool and is called "Negresco." (Stark Carpet Corporation.)

DYES. In V'soske files there are over 100,000 color formulas used in their company's own dye plant—enough to match any custom sample.

The photos on these pages, showing rugs made by V'soske and Stark, suggest quality that can be obtained through custom work. Characteristic of all fine custom rug manufacturers is attention to color, durability, and excellence of design, and the use of fine natural materials.

ORIENTAL RUGS

It is outside the scope of the average person or even the professional interior designer to become an expert on the subject of Oriental rugs, for this requires intensive research, years of working with different rug types, and travel to various places in the world to see rugs made. The study of Oriental rugs can be fascinating; but from the point of view of interior design, the thing to do is to learn to appreciate the different kinds of colors and patterns that come from various parts of the rug-weaving world—and even to study the cultures that produced these rugs—and then decide how to integrate them with your own design concepts.

Figure 18-11: An Oriental rug in the dining room of Joyce Ballou Gregorian's country home is compatible with a 16th-17th century Italian chest and a clock dating from 1837. (Joyce Ballou Gregorian. Photo: Dennis Brearley.)

Figure 18-12: This Turkish Dosmealti rug in soft reds, white, brown, and blues is a practical and long-wearing addition to Joyce Ballou Gregorian's kitchen. (Joyce Ballou Gregorian. Photo: Dennis Brearley.)

An Oriental rug is a hand-crafted, individually made work of art, and has a pure and timeless beauty. It is also the most durable of floor coverings. Oriental rugs are at home in the most contemporary setting—especially in those which include bold geometric patterns, either in colors or in neutral shades. Their warmth is complemented by the pure lines of chrome or wood furniture, or by backgrounds such as glass or mirrored walls, or by contemporary wood, brick, or ceramic floors.

In traditional rooms, of course, the Oriental rug has always been the focal point—whether the setting is the delicacy of a formal French style or the mellow warmth of a library in a stately Federal home. The rug sets the theme, unifies the furnishings, and complements the accessories.

Country settings or antique farmhouses are in perfect union with bolder and coarser primitive Oriental rugs. The designs and bright, pure colors in such rugs set the pace for the "country" feeling; and the practicality of these sturdy rugs is particularly compatible with the casual way of life.

It is advisable now—as it has been for centuries—to purchase an Oriental rug as a work of art to be enjoyed for a lifetime as well as for generations to come. An Oriental rug, like any work of art, makes an artistic and historical statement, except that in the case of a rug we do not know the individual weaver, but only his ethnic and cultural background. Learning about the peoples who make these rugs is as fascinating as viewing the finished product, and this is also the key to real understanding of the rugs.

In his book, *Oriental Rugs and the Stories They Tell*, Arthur I. Gregorian, noted authority on Oriental rugs, says:

Each rug is the combination of the particular craftsmanship of one weaver or group of weavers, and the inherited traditions of a particular culture. From the culture of the weaver come the ethnic tastes, abilities, and limitations of material and vision which frame the weaver's personal artistry; and it is this cultural influence which is hardest for the educated Western mind to understand. There is a thread of tradition binding them together artistically while each shows, also by its liveliness and simplicity, the common humanity of the various weavers.

Oriental Rugs in History

Many books have been written on the rich historical background of Oriental rugs. Joyce Ballou Gregorian, another Oriental rug expert, has sketched their history in a brief summary:

Oriental Rugs are hand-woven textiles from Turkey, the Caucasus, Iran (Persia), Afghanistan, and to a much lesser extent, India and the Orient. The rugs first known in the West were those from the Ottoman Empire, for the most part Turkish and Caucasian pieces, brought back by merchants from the great port of Constantinople. Later traders ven-

Figure 18-13: *Persian girls working on Isfahan rugs. (Gregorian Rug Company.)*

231

tured into Persia, the true heartland of fine rugs, and finally during the late 1800s Russian activity in Central Asia made Turkoman Boukara carpets available to the West. Chinese pieces, always more of a rarity, were a part of the general China trade more than of rug trading per se.

Only recently have Oriental rugs been in common use as floor carpets. We have the evidence of the Dutch and Italian masters to show us how rugs were used on tables and sideboards in the late Renaissance: as late as our own Revolutionary era rugs were more often coverings for furniture than floor. But during the 1800s rugs from various parts of the world became more popular and more abundant, and paintings often show an Oriental rug on the parlor floor or before the fireplace. And now, of course, we have in this country an unparalleled selection of carpets from all over the world from which to choose.[3]

Classification of Oriental Rugs by Pattern Type

One helpful way to identify Oriental rugs is to use a simple cultural classification of all Persian Oriental rugs, according to their general pattern type. There are three broad categories:

GEOMETRIC RUGS. These are the rugs of the tribal and primitive village people of Persia who are making the rugs today under the same conditions as in the past. They have no possessions except their tents and their sheep.

Each tribe is distinguished by its own rug style: originally these were nomadic tribes, and thus isolated from one another, so each family evolved its own designs. These are simple, geometric designs in a series of medallions of coarse wool, with bright and bold colors.

Individual identification of geometric patterns, however, can be misleading—because people have married into a different tribe, or moved from one village to another, taking with them their own old family designs and incorporating them into the style of their new family. You will frequently see a rug that shows design characteristics from one tribe, but woven with the wool and the style of another tribe. As you examine a rug, you have to feel it, see what kind of wool it's made with, see how it's woven and what edgings are used. Even then, there can often be doubt: it is a complex field. Some leading geometric rugs are the *Kazak*, woven with sharp reds, blues, and off-whites; the *Bachtiari*, in which bright yellows, greens, and reds predominate; and the rugs from Afghanistan, where *Boukara* rugs are woven, which usually use some shade of red (or, more recently, ivory) for a dominant background color. The most primitive tribes in Persia and in the small countries adjoining Persia are those which live in the Caucasus in Belouchistan, and in Afghanistan, near Shiraz and Isfahan. Through their artistry many of their tribal names are familiar in American rug studios.

FLORAL RUGS. The weavers of floral-patterned Oriental rugs are educated urban people, sometimes philosophers and poets, leaders in Oriental art and handwork. For centuries the most magnificent works

[3] From *Oriental Rugs in the West*, by Joyce Ballou Gregorian of Gregorian Rug Company; used by permission.

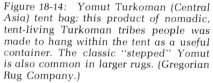

Figure 18-14: Yomut Turkoman (Central Asia) tent bag: this product of nomadic, tent-living Turkoman tribes people was made to hang within the tent as a useful container. The classic "stepped" Yomut is also common in larger rugs. (Gregorian Rug Company.)

Figure 18-15: A classic geometric Bergamo rug from the Aegean coast of Turkey (ancient Pergamum). The square proportions, wide striped selvage, and interestingly knotted fringe are typical of Turkish weaving. (Gregorian Rug Company, Joyce Ballou Gregorian. Photo: Roy F. Whitehouse.)

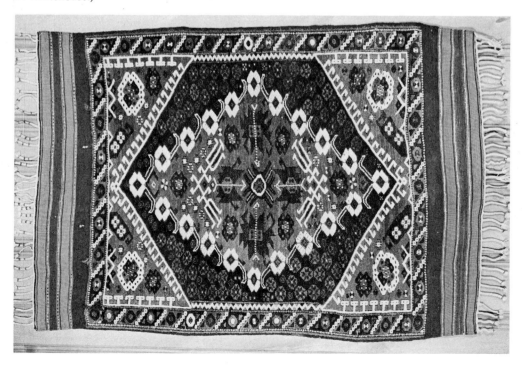

of art of Persian culture have been produced by these people. Made with fine-quality wool, their floral designs have intricate, flowing patterns representative of a sophisticated lifestyle. Identifying these designs, too, can be difficult. The people who make them are in contact with the outside world, know what designs are being made elsewhere, and know what designs may be wanted by the buying public; so it is very difficult even for an expert to tell which floral rug was made where. Because there is so much borrowing back and forth of floral designs throughout the rug-weaving world, in the end you can only rely on the technique and materials with which the rug was made. Leading floral rugs are the *Kirman*, the *Keshan*, the *Kazvin*, the *Meshed*, the *Tabriz*, the *Isfahan*, the *Nain*, the *Qum*, and the *Sarouk*. Almost all of these are names of Persian cities that have been capital cities in the past.

CONVENTIONAL RUGS. Made by townspeople, these tend to be repetitive, stylized, conventional rugs. These people are, for the most part, making their living from their weaving during the winter months. The townspeople are a little more sophisticated than the weavers of geometric designs; but they don't have the technical skill to make fine, flowing, floral rugs. They tend to make small motifs which they repeat over and over again. One practical aspect of this method is that the weaver can stop at any point in the design, weave the end border, take the rug off the loom, and sell it—whereas a rug with a medallion is woven from the beginning to the middle and from

Figure 18-16: An interesting example of gracious floral weaving, not from city looms but from the Bachtiari tribes people, who also make geometric designs. This rug borrows its designs from the nearby city of Isfaha, while retaining tribal simplicity. (Gregorian Rug Company, Joyce Ballou Gregorian.)

Figure 18-17: This Tabriz rug from Persia is a refined example of the "Herati" repetitive motif, here juxtaposed with a dramatic open field. This pattern, with its accompanying "turtle" border, dates back more than 2000 years in Middle East textile design. (Gregorian Rug Company, Joyce Ballou Gregorian.)

the middle to the end. Typical of these conventional designs are the *Saraband*, the *Herati*, the *Senna*, the *Fereghan*, the *Kandahar*, the *Hamadan*, the *Serab*, the *Bibikebad*, the *Enjelus*, and some of the *Bidjar* rugs.

GEOGRAPHIC DISTRIBUTION OF BASIC PATTERNS. Almost all rugs woven in Turkey are geometric; a very few are floral. In Persia and Iran, on the other hand, about half are floral. All of the great cities of Iran produce fine floral rugs, each named for its city; but Iran is also full of small villages and tribal people who make rugs named for the villages or their tribes. The tribal rugs of Iran greatly resemble in certain ways some of the Turkish geometric rugs. The floral rugs of Turkey, like almost all floral rugs the world over, are made in imitation of the city rugs of Iran. Even though they have been made for 300 years, most floral rugs are fundamentally derived from Persian Court art.

Classification of Oriental Rugs by Geographic Origin

The preceding classification—according to the pattern types produced by village, city, or town weavers—provides a helpful framework within which you can consider any Oriental rug, whatever country it comes from. Another frequently used system of classification, however, divides Orientals into six main groups, according to geographic area. Within the six groups are less than fifty common types, each named after its probable place of origin.

PERSIAN. These rugs generally have a delicately colored all-over pattern of flowers, vines, or leaves which start from a center medallion and almost completely cover the background color. Floral *Kirmans* and *Kirmanshahs* are noted for their fine pile and soft cream, rose, or light-blue colors. *Sarouk* rugs also have a fine pile, but in stronger colors of red and blue, mixed with lighter colors. *Isfahans* have a coarse pile, with a regal design on a deep red ground. Among more conventional Persian rugs, the *Fereghan* has a smart all-over design of flowers in rows; the *Hamadan* is made of coarsely woven camel's hair, in shades of light brown, red, and blue. Bidjar has a very thick pile. *Polonaise* antique silk rugs are delicately colored, and the *Sehna* is a small, tightly woven and minutely patterned rug.

INDIAN. Decorated, like Persian rugs, with motifs of flowers, vines, and animals, Indian rugs are characterized by more brilliant colors and a more naturalistic style. Their names echo the areas from which they come: the cities of *Agra*, *Lahore*, and *Srinagar*, and the state of *Kashmir*.

TURKOMAN. These rugs are woven by the nomadic tribes of *Boukara*, *Afghanistan*, *Belouchistan*, and *Turkestan*, and generally fall into the geometric category. Closely woven, with a short, firm pile, they are predominantly red and have designs including squares, diamonds, octagons, and other simple angular motifs.

CAUCASIAN. These small rugs with strong contrasting colors are also woven by nomadic tribal people, and have geometric designs, often incorporating stylized people and animals. Principal types include *Shirvan*, *Kuba*, *Soumak*, *Daghestan*, and *Ghendje* rugs.

TURKISH. Turkish rugs are woven in both geometric and floral designs, but with smaller patterns than the Persian or Indian, and brighter sharper colors than the Turkoman or Caucasian. A study of Turkish prayer rugs is vital to their identification; the most famous prayer rugs are from *Ghiordes*. Armenian and Anatolian rugs are also considered part of the Turkish classification.

CHINESE. Recognizable by their soft ground colors of yellow, rose, beige, and brown (like softened tones of the Chinese silk dyes), Chinese rugs usually have a pattern in one color, blue—in the reverse of the Persian system. Designs on Chinese rugs stem from Chinese religious symbols. The finest examples of antique Chinese rugs are those of the *K'ang Hsi* (1662–1723) and the *Ch'ien Lung* (1736–1796) periods; these types have been extensively copied since their original creation.

Purchasing Oriental Rugs

The purchasing of Oriental rugs is analogous to buying paintings or antique furniture or porcelains. You become knowledgeable by studying at great length. In the beginning, it is important to go to dealers who are experts and on whose word you can rely; then, gradually, your own confidence and knowledge will built to the point where you can go out to make the finds yourself.

As you look at an Oriental rug, the first questions you must ask are aesthetic. Does the rug appeal to you? Will it suit the space for which it is intended? Those are subjective questions; there are also objective ones. What type of pattern is it, and is it a good example of that type? Other questions have to do with the physical characteristics of the rug—its material and its construction.

QUALITY OF MATERIAL. The wearing quality of a rug has to do with the wool used more than with anything else: a finely made rug with a poor wool will not last nearly as long as a coarsely made rug with good wool. A good-quality wool is greasy, with a lot of lanolin still in it; it has a lot of strength because it hasn't been overboiled; and it has incredible wearing power. Very fine, soft, fluffy wools tend to deteriorate relatively quickly.

QUALITY OF CONSTRUCTION. Town (conventional) and city (floral) rugs should be evenly made, tightly woven, and finished along the sides and ends in a neat and orderly fashion. Primitive rugs, however, as is true of all primitive art, are frequently coarsely made and uneven—which is part of their charm. If you are uncomfortable with the crude quality of a primitive rug, then this type is not for you. Handling different types of rugs enables you to get a feeling of the differences in weights and weaves. The next step is to learn the basic elements of construction techniques in Turkey, Iran, Afghanistan, and so on, so that you can judge how successfully a rug meets the standards for its type and pattern.

PRICE. The price of an Oriental rug is not always related to the intricacies of its design, but depends on beauty, quality, construction—and supply and demand. In many cases, rare geometric rugs will cost more than much finer, but more readily available, city-made floral rugs. Therefore, knot counting is not the measure of value that many people think: it is only of importance after you have decided that the rug is of aesthetic worth. You can have a great rug that is very simply made; and you can have a very fine rug that is lifeless, has poor colors, and is even a bad choice of design.

Oriental rugs are defined as hand-woven or hand-knotted rugs originating in the Middle and Far East. The choices among them are vast; but there are also numerous other types of traditional hand-crafted area rugs to be used in interior settings. The following section lists (in alphabetical order) a selection of possible choices from around the world.

OTHER HAND-MADE AREA RUGS

Area rugs provide a wonderful way to accent a decorative scheme with individuality and color. These rugs do not cover an entire floor, but, placed in strategic locations, bring focus to a defined area. Sizes vary widely, depending on the type of rug and its origin. In both antique and contemporary hand-made rugs, fibers range from natural wool, cotton, and straw to the newer synthetics. For the interior designer today the options in area rugs are as varied as the countries and cultures that produce them. This sampling will be helpful as you go about selecting the right area rug for your specific space.

237

American Indian

Colorful Navajo rugs are hand-woven of wool in the Indian reservations of the Southwest. The motifs are primitive geometric patterns, stripes, and borders; the weave is flat.

Alpujjara

These coarse and heavy rugs, originally meant to be used as bedspreads, have been hand-loomed by peasants in the province of Alpujjara in southern Spain since the fifteenth century. The bold designs, woven in two to ten colors, include tree-of-life patterns, flowers, leaves, and grapes. The surrounding fringe is made separately and then sewn on.

Arraiolo

Arraiolos are Portuguese hand-embroidered accent rugs, made in either bright or pastel colors. The coarse cross-stitch is backed with linen.

Aubusson

Named for the French town of Aubusson, where a tapestry works existed during the Middle Ages, the carpets and rugs that later came to be produced there were made of wool, linen, and cotton. The weave resembles needlepoint and usually has a pale cream ground with floral designs and arabesques in pastel shades of rose, blue, lavender, green, and beige. The name *Aubusson* today is given to any rug resembling this type of heavy tapestry weave, even if it is not actually made in Aubusson.

Braided

Hand-made rugs of the Americans of the late eighteenth century consisted of many fabric scraps, braided and sewn together into colorful round or oval rugs of various sizes. The art of braiding rugs continues to be practiced among craftspeople in rural areas such as the Appalachians; and there are rug companies today that make mass-produced versions of braided rugs.

Dhurrie

A Tibetan carpet of Kelim weave (see following), these flat-woven and reversible rugs are very well adapted to today's decorating scene, relating to contemporary as well as to traditional furnishings. The old Dhurrie rugs, made by nomadic tribespeople, had bold geometric designs in bright colors; more modern ones have more subdued patterns and colors, varying with the individual rug. Old Tibetan Dhurries were made of cotton, but these are becoming increasingly hard to find; the later ones are usually made of wool (except by special custom order). These are extremely practical rugs.

Flokati

These shaggy wool area rugs are made in Greece, in solid colors as well as in wool's natural off-white shade.

Hooked

Hand-made hooked rugs are often associated with "early American" decor. They are made by pulling lengths of yarn (in any of a variety of fibers) through a heavy canvas mesh backing, and knotting them in back. The top can be cut to create a pile of various depths, or left looped, as desired. Designs can be anything, from the most primitive to the most contemporary theme. The making of hooked rugs is popular today as a craft project.

Kelim (also spelled Kilim or Kelem)

Kelims can come from Turkey, Italy, Romania, Persian Gulf states, Morocco, or Hungary. They are hand-woven rugs of all-over geometric patterns with a center motif. Sometimes more than one weaver works on a single rug. Colors are strong, usually deep red or blue; in old Kelim rugs the yarn is wool, although newer ones are made of cotton. The older rugs are very durable, and are hard to find at present because of heightened interest in them in the decorating market.

Moroccan

Hand-woven area rugs from Morocco have thick, shaggy pile and fringed edges. Geometric patterns dominate, and the strong contrasting colors used in Moroccan rugs include black and rust-brown, on white or bright orange on red grounds.

Needlework (Needlepoint or Gros-point)

Tapestry-stitch embroidery is worked with wool yarns on a canvas mesh backing; the tightness of the backing determines the tightness of the needlepoint or gros-point stitch. Quality in needlework rugs is judged according to the smallness and tightness of the stitches, because the smaller the stitches are, the finer and more detailed the design can be. The finest needlework rugs are made in France, where yarns of the highest quality are produced; the romance of old Aubusson and Savonnerie designs is captured in delicate wreaths and flowers. In Portugal, where needlework rugs have also been made for centuries, it is rug weavers who originate the designs that are reproduced in tiles. English needlework designs are bolder. In the United States, these rugs are usually made only by individual artisans.

239

Rya

Ryas are Scandinavian rugs of hand-knotted shaggy weave with alternating short and long pile, in abstract or contemporary peasant designs. In Ryas the colors are varied and vivid. Although they are made today by machine, their hand-made look has been retained. Ryas are very popular for contemporary settings.

Savonnerie

The Savonnerie is a hand-woven wool rug with a high pile, in pastel colors and floral and scroll patterns. Designed for eighteenth- and nineteenth-century houses and palaces, these rugs were produced at the rug and tapestry factory in the former soap works (*savonnerie*) outside Paris. Antique Savonneries are very much in demand and bring high prices; good copies can, however, be purchased for less.

Sisal

A natural product that grows like grass, Sisal is a light cream or oatmeal color and rough in texture. It is twisted into strands that then can be sewn into squares; the squares, attached together in any desired number, make up the finished rug. Other natural vegetable rug fibers are maize (made from corn husks) woven by Indians for their tents, or coconut hush, which is a hairlike fiber from coconut shells. Rugs made from these natural materials are strong, durable, and practical for today's interiors; their strawlike look is very suitable for our contemporary settings and color schemes.

Whether you decide to investigate custom-woven or custom-tufted rugs, to explore hand-crafted folk rugs, or to learn more about Oriental rugs, further study and visits to rug showrooms will be sure to reward you. The more you know, the more fully you will appreciate the craftsmanship and the fine materials that go into a hand-made, carefully designed modern or antique rug. What Joyce Gregorian says about Oriental rugs is also true of all hand-made rugs: they "can do more than any other single furnishing to set the tone for a room: it is certainly no accident that the ownership of one or more of these laboriously crafted masterpieces [is] a sign of good taste."

CARPET AND RUG TERMINOLOGY[4]

Acrylics: In the carpet industry, refers to the acrylic and modacrylic fibers. Acrylic fiber is a polymer composed of at least 85 percent by weight of acrylonitrile units. Modacrylic fiber is a polymer composed of less than 85 percent but at least 35 percent by weight of acrylonitrile units. Acrylics come only in staple form and are noted for their high durability, stain resistance, and wool-like appearance.

[4] Adapted from *The Carpet Specifier's Handbook*, 1974 ed.; Copyright © 1973 by The Carpet and Rug Institute. Used by permission.

American Oriental: This term is applied to loom-made American carpets of the Axminster or Wilton weave which have been manufactured in the color and pattern designs of Oriental rugs. Because they are without sizing, these American-made carpets are soft and pliable and can therefore be folded like an Oriental. The sheen or luster distinguishes this type of American carpet from the other weaves.

Axminster: One of the basic weaves used in making carpets. The pile tufts in this weave are mechanically inserted and bound to the back in a manner similar to the hand-knotting of Oriental rugs, making possible almost unlimited combinations of colors and patterns.

Backing: Material that forms the back of the carpet, regardless of the type of construction. (1) *Primary back*—In a tufted carpet, the material to which surface yarns are stitched. May be made of jute, kraftcord, cotton, woven or nonwoven synthetics. (2) *Secondary back*—Also called "double backing." Any material (jute, woven or nonwoven synthetics, scrim, foam, or cushion) laminated to the primary back.

Baseboard: A board skirting the lower edge of a wall.

Broadloom: An obsolete term originally used to denote carpet produced in widths greater than 6 feet. Was at one time used to identify "high quality." It is no longer an acceptable term in the carpet industry, the preferred word being simply "carpet."

Bullnose: Colloquial name for Step Return.

Carpet: The general designation for fabric used as a floor covering. It is occasionally used incorrectly in the plural as "carpets" or "carpeting." The preferred usage today is "carpet" in both singular and plural form. It may be used as an adjective, as in "carpeted floors."

Cut Pile: A fabric, the face of which is composed of cut ends of pile yarn.

Density: The amount of pile packed into a given volume of carpet, usually measured in ounces of pile yarn per unit volume.

Dyeing: The process of coloring materials; impregnating fabric with dyestuff.

1. Solution-dyed—Synthetic yarn that is spun from a colored solution; the filament is thus impregnated with the pigment.
2. Stock-dyed—Fibers are dyed before spinning.
3. Yarn- (or skein-) dyed—Yarn dyed before being fabricated into carpet.
4. Piece-dyeing unfinished carpet—Carpet dyed "in a piece" after tufting or weaving but before other finishing processes such as latexing or foaming.
5. Cross-dyeing—Method of dyeing fabrics with dyestuffs which have different affinities for different types of yarns.
6. Space-dyeing—Process whereby different colors are "printed" along the length of yarn before it is manufactured into carpet.
7. Continuous dyeing—The process of dyeing carpet in a continuous production line, rather than piece-dyeing separate lots. Most often done on Kusters continuous dyeing equipment which flows on dyestuffs, as distinguished from submerging carpet in separate dye becks.

241

Embossing: In carpet, the type of pattern formed when heavy twisted tufts are used in a ground of straight yarns to create an engraved appearance. Both the straight and twisted yarns are often of the same color.

Ground Color: The background color against which the top colors create the pattern or figure in the design.

High Low: A multilevel pile, sometimes combining cut and looped surface yarns.

Indoor/Outdoor: Obsolete term for outdoor carpet. The first carpet produced for outdoor use was named indoor/outdoor carpet. Over a period of time this term became erroneously defined by retailers and consumers, who assumed that if carpet was suitable for outdoor use it had superior qualities indoors. Since this is generally incorrect, the carpet industry wants to avoid perpetuating this term.

Jacquard: The pattern control on a Wilton loom. A chain of perforated cardboard "cards" punched according to the design elements, which when brought into position activates this mechanism by causing it to select the desired color of yarn to form the design on the pile surface. The unselected colors are woven "dormant" through the body of the fabric.

Jute: A fibrous skin between the bark and stalk of a plant native to India and the Far East. Shredded and spun, it forms a strong and durable yarn used in carpet backing to add strength, weight, and stiffness.

Kemp: Coarse, brittle white fiber occurring frequently in "nonblooded" carpet wools. These fibers do not accept dye and consequently an excess could be prominent and undesirable.

Leno Weave: Weave in which warp yarns, arranged in pairs, are twisted around one another between "picks" of weft yarn.

Looped Pile: Pile surface in which looped yarns are left uncut. In woven carpets, sometimes referred to as "round wire."

Mill End: The remainder of a roll carpet, generally described in the carpet industry as being between 9 and 21 feet in length, by the width of the roll from which it was cut.

Olefins: Any long chain synthetic polymer composed of at least 85 percent by weight of ethylene, propylene, or other olefin units.

Oriental Rugs: Hand-woven rugs made in the Middle East and the Orient.

Pile: The upright ends of yarn, whether cut or looped, that form the wearing surface of carpet or rugs.

Pilling: A condition in certain fibers in which strands of the fiber separate and become knotted with other strands, causing a rough, spotty appearance. Pilled tufts should never be pulled from carpet, but may be cut off with a sharp scissor at the pile surface.

Polyester: A manufactured fiber in which the fiber-forming substance is any long chain synthetic polymer composed of at least 85 percent by weight of an ester of a dihydric alcohol and terephthalic acid ($p - HOOC - C_6H_4 - COOH$).

Random-Sheared: Textured pattern created by shearing some of the top or higher loops and leaving others looped.

Remnant: The remainder of a roll of carpet, generally described in the carpet industry as being under 9 feet in length by the width of the roll from which it was cut.

Repeat: The distance from a point in a pattern figure to the same point where it occurs again, measuring lengthwise of the fabric.

Resilience: The ability of a carpet fabric or padding to spring back to its original shape or thickness after being crushed or walked upon.

Rug: A term used to designate soft floor coverings laid on the floor but not fastened to it. As a rule, a rug does not cover the entire floor.

Tunnel Test: A test method measuring flame spread, fuel contribution, and smoke density of building construction materials.

Twist Carpet: Surface texture created with tightly twisted yarns, resulting in a nubby or pebbly effect.

Velvet Carpet: A woven carpet made on a cam loom very similar to the Wilton loom, except that there is no Jacquard motion to control when each individual yarn rises to the surface. Today most velvet carpet produced is a level loop fabric in tweed or plain colors. Some cut pile plush or plush fabrics are also produced.

Weft or Woof: The threads running across a woven fabric from selvage edge to selvage edge, binding in the pile and weaving in the warp threads.

Wilton: Named after a town in England. This carpet-weaving process employs a Jacquard pattern-making mechanism, operating on the same principle as player-piano rolls, with punched pattern cards determining pile height and color selection; most often used for patterns and multilevel textures.

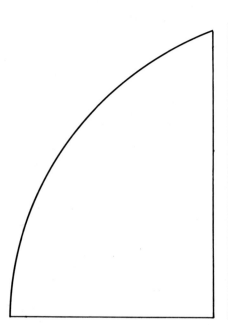

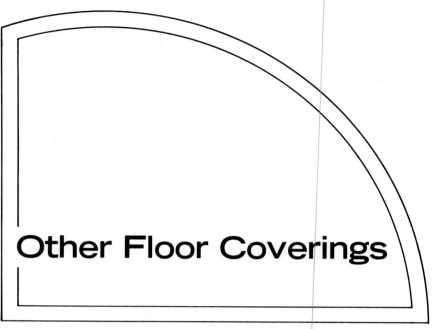

Other Floor Coverings

The preceding two chapters have concentrated on carpets and rugs, machine-made and hand-crafted, because they are a vitally important part of the floor covering plan in any house or commercial space. In many rooms, however, floor coverings other than carpeting are preferable. Some rooms require nonporous floor coverings for practical reasons—kitchens, bathrooms, laundry rooms, conservatories, family "mud rooms," for instance. Other rooms call for a shiny, smooth floor purely from an aesthetic standpoint. The glossy sheen of stone, tile, or polished brick can add reflected gleams of color and livelier lighting and acoustical effects to a room with many textures or patterns—and can set off area rugs in unparalleled style.

In this chapter we will look at varieties of ceramic tile and at some of the new floor-covering materials made of vinyl-treated wood. Available, too, are many familiar stand-bys as well as new additions. Floor coverings made of vinyls are most widely known and used. Because of the vast variety of floor coverings, however, the following two types were chosen as examples of flooring with both aesthetic appeal and practicality. Ceramic tile has been in use for many years, while vinyl-treated wood is a new addition to the scene.

CERAMIC TILE

Ceramic tile is one of the world's oldest building and design materials.[1] Decorative tile was used in the palaces of ancient Rome and the pyramids of Egypt. And anthropologists have evidence that even cave-dwellers produced crude ceramic tiles by baking riverbank clays in their fire pits.

Of course, today's sophisticated firing and blending techniques are a far cry from those used in prehistoric times. But ceramic tile

[1]Information provided by the Tile Council of America, and used by permission.

Figure 19-1: An assortment of sizes, shapes, and textures in ceramic tile. (Tile Council of America)

still consists of clays harvested from the earth and hardened at high temperatures, so it remains a truly natural medium. Today more than a thousand different types, designs, colors, and shapes of ceramic tile are available; but every ceramic tile fits into one of four general categories: glazed wall tile, ceramic mosaic tile, quarry tile, and pavers.

Glazed Wall Tiles

The glaze, which gives the tile its surface color and texture, is fused onto the body during firing. This category of tile boasts the largest range of colors, designs, and glazes, including a heavy-duty glaze that makes it suitable for counter-tops and floors as well as for walls.

Ceramic Mosaic Tiles

Unglazed or glazed tiles with a facial area of less than 6 square inches are called ceramic mosaic tiles. These small tiles are usually sold mounted on paper or mesh-backed sheets, for easier, quicker installation. Custom color combinations may be ordered. Unglazed mosaics come in a variety of earth colors, while the glazed versions are available in every color imaginable. Mosaics are extremely durable, and can be used for both interior and exterior walls and floors.   245

Figure 19-2: Ceramic mosaic tile adds its natural look to a contemporary interior. (Tile Council of America, Lis King.)

Quarry Tiles

Made from natural clay, quarry tile has become one of the most popular floor covering materials for both residential and commercial interior and exterior use. It is available in glazed or unglazed forms. The unglazed version comes in such colors as sand, caramel, and blue as well as the traditional earthen-red. The glazed type is made in fashion colors ranging from snow white, buttermilk, and birch gray to grass green, fire-engine red, and steel blue. Sizes range from 4-inch to 9-inch squares, plus a number of curved and other geometric shapes.

Pavers

Pavers are similar to ceramic mosaic tile in composition, but are thicker and larger and have a soft, unglazed-looking finish. Like quarry tile and ceramic mosaics, they can be used outdoors as well as indoors.

Ceramic tile is one of the most versatile materials you can use on floors and walls; and nothing beats it for durability. The ceramic tile palette now includes bright primaries, pastels, neutrals, and sophisticated black and browns. Even white has many new shades: no longer do we think of "institutional" white tile.

Figure 19-3: Brick-shaped ceramic tiles in brown, white, and beige make an elegant and efficient floor in this dining room. (Tile Council of America)

A tremendous number of sizes, shapes, and textures are also available. There are squares in sizes from 1 to 12 inches; rectangles, octagons; hexagons, and Moorish curves—all ranging in sizes from dainty to bold. Ceramic tile may look like brick, cobblestones, river-polished pebbles, tide-rippled sand, parquet, or bamboo. Some tiles are sculptured for interesting light and shadow effects, or decorated with motifs ranging from old Delft patterns to bold surrealistic images.

Uses of Ceramic Tile

Perhaps the only design problem with ceramic tile is its long life: since it is such a permanent improvement, colors and designs must be selected especially carefully. Future changes in decor, and even the possible tastes of future buyers of the house, have to be considered. Like most design materials harvested from nature, however, tile has the kind of lasting good looks that will adapt to styles ranging from French Provincial to Contemporary with perfect grace.

Adding to tile's versatility are the new colored grouts (the filler that goes into the joints between the tiles). The grout alone can change the appearance of an entire installation. White, brick-shaped tile on a floor might be an example. With matching white grout the effect will be one of cool serenity. With blue grout, the mood would change to old-world coziness. The same floor, with black grout,

247

Figure 19-4: Tile in a terrace, as a completely natural material, looks right in an outdoor setting. It also stands up under all kinds of weather and does away with constant paint jobs. (Tile Council of America)

Figure 19-5: This contemporary family room is planned for carefree living; everything in it, from tile floor to tweed-covered sofa, will withstand all sorts of wear. (Tile Council of America)

would create the sort of dramatic geometry associated with contemporary decor.

Here are some ideas for tile selections for a few home furnishing styles:

TRADITIONAL. For the floors in a traditional American house, effective treatments might be quarry tile in wood tones, laid parquet style; in medallion designs in deep harvest gold; or glazed to a dark leather or burgundy finish.

PROVINCIAL AND COLONIAL. Quarry tile in earthen-red, caramel, or antique white would work well in a French Provincial or American Colonial interior; as would brick shapes in white, red, brown, blue, or gold. A decorative wall tile might be used as well, below a dado of a dining room or to trim a fireplace.

MEDITERRANEAN. Moorish-shaped tile in white or in the richest colors could be used on both floors and walls. Or quarry tile floors might be selected in terra cotta, brown, or sand colors. Decorative tile on kitchen counters, backsplashes, or even entire walls is well suited to exotic styles.

CONTEMPORARY. For floors in a contemporary setting, good choices are: square glazed tile in white, black, beige, or brown: quarry tile in earth colors; white octagonal tiles with "dots" in bright primaries; or unglazed ceramics in natural earth colors. A custom mosaic mural can be very successful for indoor or outdoor use. And the sleek elegance of ceramic tile is perfect for the contemporary kitchen.

From ceramic tile—one of the oldest of floor covering materials—we move to vinyl-covered wood, one of the newest. The warmth, practicality, and elegance of a traditional hardwood floor are qualities now available in virtually indestructible machine-made products such as PermaGrain and GenuWood.[2]

VINYL-COVERED WOOD

PermaGrain

PermaGrain acrylic wood flooring is a composite material that combines the performance advantages of acrylic plastics with the aesthetic appeal of fine hardwoods. The product is extremely hard and wear-resistant; it requires little maintenance and thus is ideal for use in heavy-traffic installations such as shopping malls and office buildings, as well as in residential and multipurpose facilities.

Most hardwoods and softwoods are porous: they contain a large amount of void space. To produce PermaGrain, a liquid acrylic plastic is forced under pressure into the porous structure of the hardwood. The liquid plastic contains dyes for color, and flame-spread inhibitors for fire resistance. It is permanently hardened in the wood

[2]Information provided by PermaGrain Products, Inc. (Arco Chemical Company) and used by permission.

through the use of radiation. The result is a piece of wood that has the equivalent of Plexiglas or Lucite in the pore structure, giving exceptional resistance to abrasion and indentation, a soft luster, and a finish that permeates the wood.

PermaGrain is normally manufactured in oak, ash, or maple colors. The standard product is a 12-inch square in either a parquet or a one-dimensional pattern. Special patterns are made by combining the standard square with either pickets or bands. In addition, PermaGrain is manufactured in 2-by-12-inch strips which permit the construction of herringbone, brick, or ashlar patterns. (See Figures 19–6, 19–7, and 19–8.)

GenuWood™ II

GenuWood II flooring combines the maintenance-free and long-wear characteristics of vinyl with the beauty of hardwood veneers. In the manufacture of this product, hardwood veneers are permanently bonded between a thick wear surface of moisture-resistant vinyl and core layers of fiberglass and vinyl. The result is a showcase wood floor that can be maintained by sweeping, damp mopping, or an occasional buffing.

Figure 19-7: Another PermaGrain pattern is tough enough for the heavy traffic of a shopping mall. (Arco Chemical–Atlantic Richfield Company. Photo: D. Randolph Foulds.)

GenuWood II finds applications in commercial areas, offices, boutiques, and homes. It is available in walnut, oak, rosewood, teak, cherry, English brown oak, and mahogany and the new limed oak. These woods are manufactured in a wide range of shapes so that the designer can utilize all conventional wood-flooring patterns such as random plank, herringbone, or basket-weave.

These new treatments of wood reflect once again what makes interior design so exciting: technology is ceaselessly changing the ways we build and decorate our homes, and the materials available to the designer are more varied and numerous each year. Furniture, walls, windows, floors: these are the basic components of the room, and by now you have considered some of the infinite variety of ways to handle these essential elements. Art and accessories are the finishing touches. In Part VII, we will explore further ways to mesh the best of the old with the most current of the new.

[3]Information provided by Parkwood New England, Medford, Massachusetts, distributors of Grenwood.

Figure 19-8: Herringbone-patterned Per-maGrain flooring comes in oak, ash, maple, or other fine woods. (Arco Chemical–Atlantic Richfield Company. Photo: D. Randolph Foulds.)

VII
Art and Accessories

The chapters in this part of the book cover the major types of decorative additions that complete your carefully planned interior. Chapter 20 discusses mirrors—which, although they are used increasingly in major architectural roles, further fulfill a role of enhancing, brightening, and adding intrege by means of reflective and refracted images in an existing interior design. Thus it is as accessories that we include mirrors in this section of the book.

Chapters 21 and 22 are closely related. In Chapter 21 you will be introduced to the principal forms of graphic art, drawings, and paintings. This introduction is intended above all to direct you to work with professional art dealers and keep abreast of work in galleries and 253

ART AND ACCESSORIES   *shows in search of choices for your client's interior. Chapter 22 continues the exploration into the world of decorative accessories: fabric arts, sculptures, ceramics, antiques, and objets d'art.*

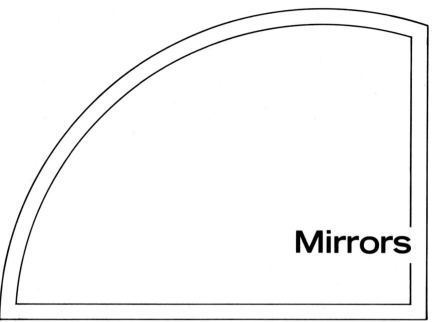
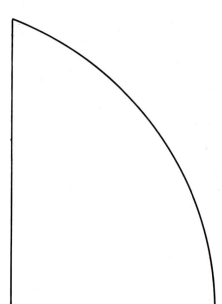

Mirrors

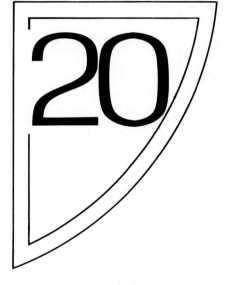

No other material has the versatility and appeal of a mirror; it offers beauty, function, and design qualities for today's interiors that are unsurpassed.

Mirrors provide sparkle and interest, enhance colors, reflect light, and add a look of greater space. But beyond all this, beyond the obvious use to reflect images or to enlarge space, they can be used also to refract images, adding intrigue and imagination to an already successful interior. They can be used on entire walls or in sections; angled to any degree, creating unusual designs of the room in conjunction with other mirrors on the walls, ceilings, or even floors. Mirrors today are used to cover furniture or to blend with other reflected surfaces, such as mirrored vertical drapes. The varieties of use make this material so versatile.

Thousands of years ago, the Egyptians polished bronze to a high gloss for use as mirrors. It wasn't until 1507 that the first glass mirrors were made in Murano, Italy, and sold at extremely high prices. But people wanted more and more mirrors, and this demand has prompted continued progress in mirror-making over the centuries since then.

Vast strides have been made in mirror manufacturing in the twentieth century. The silver backing, so common today, wasn't available in great-grandmother's day; nor were the wide range of styles, shapes, and sizes. Modern manufacturing methods, tools, machinery, and skills have made it possible for every home to make use of mirrors that can reflect form, line, and color with clarity and brilliance never before achieved.[1]

Individual mirrors are styled to accent any period you've chosen, whether it is Early American, English, French, Spanish, or contemporary. An important trend today is to have mirrors covering entire walls and ceilings, creating reflective surfaces that enhance any decor. Today we are finding ways to use mirrors to their full potential as architectural and design tools.

[1]Information provided by the National Association of Mirror Manufacturers and used by permission.

Figure 20-1: Mirrors on both wall and ceiling create the illusion of space in a sophisticated modern bedroom designed by Maurice Weir. (Maurice Weir, ASID. Photo: Louis Reens.)

USES OF MIRRORS

Properly used, mirrors are capable of expanding space, multiplying beauty, camouflaging structural flaws, and supplying a unique visual element that offers solutions to various design problems. The feeling of depth that a mirror creates—where no space exists—is of primary importance. Walls can be visually moved outward, ceilings pushed upward, and space generally manipulated through the placement of mirrors by the designer.

Spatial Effects

If an area is too long and narrow, a mirrored side wall visually broadens the space. When a room is short or boxy, a mirrored wall extends the depth. In too-low rooms, a mirror butted against the ceiling will seemingly raise the ceiling.

Not only can room dimensions be doubled by mirroring two adjacent walls, the room size is quadrupled. The reflection of a cher-

256

Figure 20-2: On reverse side: a unique bedroom with a mirrored wall, mirrored dressers, a modular mirrored platform bed, and a five-foot square flotation bed light fixture that seems to float free directly above the bed. Beige tones were used throughout, to give a neutral reflection. (Tomorrow Designs, Ltd.)

Figure 20-3: Above: Mirrors in an impressive bathroom, designed for Boston's ASID "Hope House" by ASID Associate members Ida Goldstein, Sylvia Sturm, and Celest Cooper. A too-high ceiling was lowered with squares of mirror, and the small bay window was enlarged by panels of mirror up its sides. (Ida Goldstein, ASID Associate; Sylvia Sturm, ASID Associate; and Celest Cooper, ASID Associate. Photo © Edward Jacoby.)

ished piece such as a chandelier, dining table, or sculpture can be doubled. Or a sculpture can be placed in front of a wall with two or more mirrors, to show all its sides to perfection. A mirror used in conjunction with light doubles your lighting image as well as creating light designs. For example, a chandelier mounted flush on a mirrored ceiling becomes a dazzling crystal globe creating an elegant effect.

Special Mirrors

Interior designers who think of mirrors only as clear, reflective surfaces are unaware of the full potential in color, pattern, texture, and styling variations modern production processes now make possible. In certain installations a clear mirror might be too bright, whereas a mirror made from a modern tinted plate glass might be perfect. Unlike the colored glasses of the past, today's neutral gray and bronze hues do not distort color values: they provide a muted effect while reflecting true colors of the room's decor.

Today's antique-style mirror also has been improved by production techniques. There are smoky and shadow effects, further highlighted by the application of random veining in one or more colors. Silk-screening can be used to apply a custom design to a mirror. Mirrors can be in squares, convex or concave, acid-etched, engraved, and so on. Your imagination will suggest ways of incorporating mirror in wall panels—with wood designs cut out, with trellis, between plaster or brick columns, or in arches, for instance. Angled or patterned mirrors give a unique impression.

Mirrored Furniture and Accessories

Mirror magic goes beyond wall and ceiling treatments. Today's market boasts of mirrored furniture, accessories, and lighting. Progressive companies such as Tomorrow Designs Limited are dedicated to designing and producing to suit the designer's particular needs. A wide variety of mirrored items include sofas, chairs, tables, chests, beds, bars, cubes, and dressers. Lamps are available with mirrored bases, as hanging mirrored globes, or as flotation light fixtures with individual light units inside. You will discover such accessories as mirrored placemats, napkin rings, candlesticks, planters, cubes, and frames. There have always been framed mirrors; today, however the frame itself is also made of mirror—in solid or in mosaic or random patterns, or even in a dimensional effect that has the look of sculpture.

Let your imagination go: creating with mirror is exciting and lends itself to innovative ideas.

Figure 20-4: *A collection of mirrored furnishings, mirrored lighting fixtures, and decorative wall mirrors in Tomorrow Designs' showrooms. (Tomorrow Designs, Ltd.)*

MIRROR INSTALLATION

Richard Becker, of Paris Glass in Boston, has set forth some very good points to keep in mind when installing mirror:

The proper installation of mirror is as important as the quality of the mirror itself.

People tend to misuse mirrors. They should be used for the proper reflection. Mirroring will defeat its purpose if the area that is reflected is undesirable, rather than a view of beautiful objects.

The most important single technical point of installation is the elimination of distortion: it is necessary to make up for the fact that walls are never even. You have to build out the mirror in the back to make it lay evenly. If the wall is very uneven, a plywood foundation would be necessary. In terms of degree, there should be as little distortion as possible; one-hundred percent perfection should not be expected.

For the most finished results, pencil-polished edges are much more desirable than a raw edge. As for thickness, all mirrors for home installation should be one-quarter of an inch float—giving better quality and better clarity than window-type mirrors.

The method of installation is a matter of the designer's preference. Installation methods do not affect the technical aspects of the mirror itself, which would not vary. The most common material used now is cement; in the past, rosettes were used. Moldings of mirror or wood, used top and bottom, also will hold the mirror in place.[2]

MIRROR TERMINOLOGY

To know mirrors and discuss them intelligently, it helps to familiarize yourself with the mirror terminology given here.[3]

Acid Etch: A process of producing a specific design or lettering on glass, prior to silvering, by cutting into the glass with a combination of acids. Process may involve either a frosted surface treatment or a deep etch.

Antique Mirror: A decorative mirror in which the silver has been treated to create a smoky or shadowy effect. The antique look is often heightened by applying a veining on the silvered side in any one or more of a variety of colors and designs.

Backing Paint: The final protective coating applied on the back of the mirror, over the copper, to protect the silver from deterioration.

Concave Mirror: Surface is slightly curved inward. Tends to magnify reflected items or images.

Convex Mirror: Surface is slightly curved outward to increase the area that is reflected. Generally used for safety or security surveillance purposes.

Door Mirror: Polished or beveled-edge mirror, usually cut to standard height dimension of 68'', with widths ranging from 16'' to 24'' in 2'' increments, attached to a room or closet door.

---

[2]Extracted from an interview with Richard Becker of Paris Glass, Boston, Mass.
[3]Information provided by the National Association of Mirror Manufacturers and used by permission.

Edge Work: Among numerous terms and expressions defining types of edge finishing, the five in most common usage are listed here:

○ *Clean-cut Edge:* Natural edge produced when glass is cut. Should not be left exposed in installation.
○ *Ground Edge:* Grinding removes raw cut of glass, leaving a smooth satin finish.
○ *Seamed Edge:* Sharp edges are removed by abrasive belt.
○ *Polished Edge:* Polishing removes raw cut of glass to give smooth-surfaced edge. Available in two basic contours.
○ *Beveled Edge:* A tapered polished edge, varying from ¼'' to a maximum of 1¼'' thick, produced by machine in a rectangular or circular shape. Other shapes or ovals may be beveled by hand, but the result is inferior to machine bevel. Standard width of bevel is generally ½''.

Electro Copper-Plating: Process of copper-plating by electrolytic deposition of copper on the back of the silver film, to protect the silver and to assure good adherence of the backing paint.

Engraving: The cutting of a design on the back or face of a mirror, usually accomplished by hand on an engraved lathe.

Finger Pull: An elongated slot cut into the glass by use of a wheel, so that a mirrored door or panel, for instance, may be moved to one side.

First-Surface Mirror: A mirror produced by deposition of reflective metal on front surface of glass, usually under vacuum. Principal use is as automobile rear-view mirror.

Float Glass: Glass formed by recently developed process of floating molten glass over molten metal. Considered to be the highest-quality glass available for mirrors.

Framed Mirror: A mirror placed in a frame that is generally made of wood, metal, or composition material and equipped for hanging. Many types of designs and styles are available.

Hole: A piercing of a mirror usually ½'' in diameter and generally accomplished by a drill. Generally employed in connection with installation involving rosettes.

Mastic: An adhesive compound used to secure mirrors to wall areas without mechanical fasteners such as clips or other hardware.

Mirror Glass: The type of glass most prevalent in mirror manufacturing.

Mitre Cutting: The cutting of straight lines by use of a wheel on the back or face of a mirror for design purposes. Available in both satin and polished finishes.

Pattern or Shape Mirror: A mirror cut to a pattern other than a rectangle.

Rosette: Hardware used for affixing a mirror to a wall. A decorative rose-shaped button used in several places on the face of a mirror. Holes are drilled through the mirror to accept fastening screws and rosettes.

Sand Blasting: Engraving or cutting designs on glass by a stream of sand usually projected by air.

Shadowbox Mirror: Mirror bordered or framed at an angle on some or all sides by other mirrors, making possible multiple reflections of an image.

Shock Mirror: Term used (incorrectly) to describe a sheet (window glass) mirror.

Silk-Screen: Stencil application of a design or lettering on the silvered side of a mirror prior to silvering. Many colors are available.

Stock-Sheet Mirrors: Mirrors of varying sizes over 10 square feet, and up to 75 square feet, from which all types of custom mirror are cut. Normally packed 800 to 1,000 square feet to a case.

Transparent Mirror: A first-surface mirror with a thin film of reflective coating. To insure most efficient use, the light intensity on the viewer's side of the mirror must be significantly less than on the subject side. Under such a condition, the viewer can see through the mirror as through a transparent glass, while the subject looks into a mirror.

The professional designer should consider the many uses of mirrors at the beginning of the room planning. The effects obtained by mirroring even small areas can add drama and intrigue to any setting. Used in conjunction with plants, sculpture, and works of art, mirrors can enhance the finest collections.

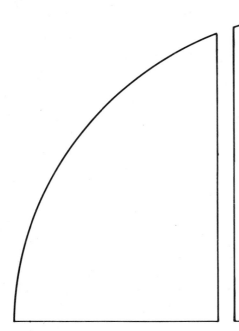
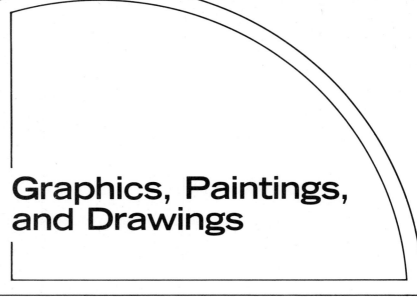

Graphics, Paintings, and Drawings

Completing your interior with the proper choice of art and accessories is as important as selecting the furnishings themselves. The art you choose can enhance or detract from the entire mood you have worked so hard to create. The room as a whole, conversely, can have a tremendous impact on the way the works of art appear.

Living with an art collection can impose certain demands that inevitably influence interior design. For one thing, walls ideally should be kept free for paintings, which in turn means that furnishings work best in a free standing arrangement rather than hugging the perimeter of the room. Turning these strictures into a decorative asset is not only possible but plausible, a feat deftly accomplished by Regina Lee,[1] an art consultant, whose penthouse apartment overlooking the Boston waterfront is a prize illustration of comfort and style, surrounded by art. This is not the usual interior setting, as she is an artist representative and does not own the art she lives with. But her solutions for incorporating this embarrassment of riches into her own personal decor could act as an invaluable guideline for private collectors.

Proper lighting and furniture arrangement are interchangeably important in making art an integral but subtle part of everyday living. Lighting is provided by adjustable cones that slide on ceiling tracks, with each wall on a separate dimmer for dramatic effects. Paintings are hung on notched rods from a wood molding, allowing for flexibility in height and layering, without banging a lot of nails into the walls. [See Figures 21–2 and 21–3.]

This living room is a handsome case in point, its island furniture arrangement floating within the larger space, leaving the walls free for paintings and a spectacular view as well.[2]

[1] Apartment of noted art consultant, Regina Lee.
[2] Excerpted by permission from an article by Estelle Bond Guralnick, design writer for several New England and national magazines.

Figure 21-1: Art in an interior: the home of potter Merna Canner Kalis displays her own exquisite pottery as well as sculpture, graphics, and silver. (Merna Canner Kalis. Photo: Peter Ficksman.)

Figure 21-2: The penthouse apartment of artists' representative Regina Lee, Boston. Art is the focal point of this interior setting. (Regina Lee. Photo: Jankow Photo Center.)

Figure 21-3: In Regina Lee's penthouse, walls are left free of furniture so that paintings can be seen. (Regina Lee. Photo: Jankow Photo Center.)

Figure 21-4: Collagraph and intaglio print: "Yama" ("mountain" in Japanese) (1972) by Helene Levenson, working in studio of Donald Stoltenberg. (Helene Levenson, ASID. Photo: Laban Whittaker.)

Figure 21-5: Collagraph and intaglio print: "Village" (1973) by Helene Levenson, (Helene Levenson, ASID. Photo: Laban Whittaker.)

It is important to learn a little about art before you buy. Remember that some works of art have more intrinsic quality than others; and price is not always commensurate with quality. Art, if purchased carefully, can be a wise investment—because good art continually increases in value. Many museums and libraries have rental programs, enabling you or your client to live with a piece of art to see if it is compatible with your taste—or if you will tire of it easily. The best way to learn about art, however, is to start frequenting the galleries in your area, for with proper exposure and advice comes greater knowledge of the subject. Gallery owners are happy to help you understand and appreciate the artworks they handle.

Before starting on your art search, you should be armed with some essential facts about different art forms. The following five categories are some of the more popular ones, although certainly not all of the art forms you will encounter.

DEFINITION OF ART FORMS[3]

The Graphic Arts: Limited-Edition Works

It is important to differentiate between an original "print" and a "reproduction." Reproductions are photographic copies of famous works of art. While these can be lovely additions to any interior, and

[3] This section was written by Leni Levenson-Wiener, whose expertise made it possible. Mrs. Wiener has degrees in Art History from: Simmens College, Boston, Mass. and Università Internazionale Dell'Arte, Florence, Italy. She has also aided Dr. Baldini of the Uffizi Gallery in Florence with the conservation and restoration of works of art. Under Drs. Becherucci and Berti, Directors of the Uffizi Gallery and the Palazzo Pitti (also of Florence), she has studied Museology. Ms. Levenson-Wiener is currently a professional photographer in New York City.

Figure 21-6: Collagraph and intaglio print: "Long Night's Journey into Day" (1791) by Renee Winick, working in studio of Donald Stoltenberg. (DeCordova Museum Collection.)

allow you to own a particular favorite that is well beyond your means in the original, it is important to know that reproductions as artworks do not increase in value because they are not original works. Therefore, they should not be bought as investments but purely for your own enjoyment.

Original prints on the other hand, are made by the artist in a series (of perhaps twenty, fifty, or one hundred, for example), each numbered and signed by the artist, and each an original work of art that will increase in value. This is called a "limited edition." The number that appears on the bottom of the print—for example, 25/53—means that the print was the 25th printed in a series of 53. It makes no difference whether the print was the first or the last in the series: each is an original and of equal quality and value. An "artist's proof" (A.P.) is generally the first of the series. Because they are all done in a series, prints are often reasonably enough priced for even the tightest budget and are, consequently, a good way to start an art collection.

An original print is a work of *graphic art.* There are general requirements governing the definition of a work of graphic art. First, the artist alone has to have made the image to be printed, whether it be in or upon wood, stone, or a metal plate. Second, only the original materal is used directly, either by the artist or under his or her guidance, to make the impression. Finally all prints have to be personally approved by the artist.

For easy reference, graphics are broken down into three categories: *intaglio, relief,* and *planographic* prints.

Intaglio Printing

This form of printing is produced by the means of incised or cut-into lines or textured areas on the copper, zinc, or other types of plate that hold the ink. When the plate is wiped clean, leaving the ink in the incised lines, the damp paper is placed over it; and the image is formed when the ink is picked up as the paper goes through the press. The following are varieties of intaglio printing methods:

ENGRAVING. No acid is used in an engraving; instead, the line is cut into the plate with a graver or burin, a special tool that makes a clean cut.

ETCHING. The artist begins with a copper plate covered with wax or varnish. He or she then scratches, or incises, the design into the surface with a sharp instrument. The plate is put into an acid bath, and

Figure 21-7: Collagraph and intaglio print: "Victorian Gothic" (1973) by Donald Stoltenberg. (DeCordova Museum Collection.)

Figure 21-8: Collagraph and intaglio print: "A Quiet Memory IV" (1973) by Ruth Rodman. (DeCordova Museum Collection.)

those areas left uncovered by wax are eaten away by the acid; the plate is then inked and printed onto paper. Both etchings and engravings are fine-lined and often resemble delicate pen-and-ink drawings.

AQUATINT. Large tonal areas of the plate may be done this way. Before being put into the acid bath, the plate is covered with a slightly porous dusting of rosin or spraying enamel. The amount used, along with the length of time the plate is etched in the acids, determines the final tone—which is created by the acid making many tiny marks through the resistant coating.

DRYPOINT. This is similar to engraving, but because a sharper needle is used, the cut line is shallower and creates a burr on the surface of the plate.

MEZZOTINT. In mezzotint, a tool is used which raises a texture or burr over the entire plate, so that when inked, the print would be solid black because the entire area would hold the ink. Lighter areas, therefore, are scraped or burnished away.

COLLAGRAPH. The artist uses a plate of metal or masonite board on which the designs are built up in some areas and incised (cut in) in other areas. The artist may also adhere materials of varied textures—each one holding the ink differently—in order to create various shades and textures in the print. Then relief (see below) and/or intaglio inking is done. Print board can be inked, wiped off, and then a roller used in one color or graded colors. Additional colors can then be added for accents; when printed, the paper will be embossed owing to the thickness of the materials on the plate. Lately a very popular technique, collagraphs can be strong and dramatic, or subtle and delicate. The variety of effects that can be obtained is unlimited.

Relief Printing

In relief printing, the artist carves away from the plate or block the areas that are *not* to be printed. The raised surface that is left is then inked and printed onto paper by means of pressure by hand—that is, by rubbing the paper with a hard object such as a spoon, or by using a letter press.

WOODCUTS. The artist begins with a block of wood and cuts away those parts of the surface he does not want printed. The design, which remains raised on the surface of the woodblock, is inked and printed onto paper. Because wood is so much harder than wax or varnish and is usually cut away in broad, sweeping chunks, woodcuts have none of the delicacy of etchings and engravings, but rather a strong, dramatic feeling.

WOOD ENGRAVING. A wood engraving is similar to a woodcut but, by using the end grain of the block, the artist can get a much finer line.

LINOCUTS. Linoleum may be used instead of wood, to produce prints in the same manner with a similar effect.

RELIEF ETCHING. In relief etching a metal plate is acid-etched; then its top surface is rolled with ink and printed, rather than the etched lines being inked and printed.

Figure 21-9: Woodcut: "Prophet–Isaiah: (1952) by Leonard Baskin. (DeCordova Museum Collection; Gift of Mr. and Mrs. Stephen Stone.)

Figure 21-10: Linoleum print (linocut): "Artist in Studio" (1963) by Pablo Picasso. (DeCordova Museum Collection; Gift of Mrs. Margaret Silberman.)

Planographic Printing

This is a process for printing from a plane, or flat, surface using a chemical basis.

LITHOGRAPHY. The artist begins with a highly polished stone plate (or sometimes a metal plate) on which he or she draws the design with a crayon or a greasy ink stick. Ink is applied directly to the stone and is repelled by those areas drawn on by the crayon. Paper is then pressed onto the stone; and the ink takes, leaving the crayoned areas the color of the paper. This method allows a larger range of tonal subtleties than some others, and it often resembles crayon or charcoal sketching.

Figure 21-11: Lithograph: "Speculative Passage" (1967) by Jack Coughlin. (De-Cordova Museum Collection.)

SERIGRAPHY (SILK-SCREEN). Silk fabric is stretched onto a square form—much like the frame for a canvas—and the design is cut with sharp instruments through the fabric, leaving an opened space through which the ink is applied onto the paper. A different "screen" is used for each color in the print. Producing hard-edged and crisp images, this medium is particularly suited to poster art and often even the printing of T-shirts and canvas bags. It reached the height of its popularity in the 1960s during the "pop" and "op" movements. Today it is considered a very serious art form.

MULTIMEDIA. Prints need not be confined to one method, and often the artist will employ two or more methods in one work to achieve the effect he or she desires. These are often referred to as multimedia prints.

Photography

Included in this section because of the ability of the artist to work in a series of photographic prints, photography is becoming increasingly recognized as an art form with great decorative potential. The photographer begins with a negative that can be blown up from small to relatively large sizes. Usually a photographer, like any other printmaker, will print only a limited series of each work and either destroy the negative or store it for future reference. Photos need not be realistic; some lovely abstract effects can be achieved, or two or more negatives can be printed on top of each other for interesting and spectacular results. There is also macro- (close-up) and micro- (microscopic) photography; and the prints can either be in color (not always realistic color) or in black and white for increased tonal contrast.

PAINTINGS AND DRAWINGS: UNIQUE WORKS OF ART

Paintings and drawings are unique works of art. Each one is one of a kind and wholly unlike any other. For this reason, and because of the time involved in these works, they are considerably more expensive than prints. Painting styles are as varied as the artists working on them: whatever your preference, from realism to abstraction, there are thousands of choices, and each one is unique.

Oil Paintings

Done on stretched canvas or canvas board, oil paintings are so named because the color pigments are ground with oil as a base. The canvas is prepared with a base layer, and the paint is applied with

Figure 21-12: Oil painting: "Figure 1956" (1956) by Franz Kline. (DeCordova Museum Collection; Anonymous gift in memory of Margaret Brown.)

273

brushes or palette knives. Paint can be smooth and flat or built up in heavy textures. Most of the great masters you are familiar with—from da Vinci to Van Gogh—painted in oils. Because oil paint can be painted over, paintings by old masters are often found underneath newer, less valuable works. New oil paintings must be handled with care, because oil paint takes up to 100 years to dry *completely* throughout (a fact that is often used to detect forgeries), and while new, will crack in extreme dryness. Oil paintings are expensive and therefore are often not the best way to start a collection.

Watercolors

Watercolor pigments are mixed with water as a base as opposed to oil, and the colors are transparent and delicate. The paper used is absorbent by nature, and the color of the paper comes through the paint color to form translucent tones and shade gradations. Unlike oil paint, watercolor cannot be painted over or built up; and the resulting work is subtle and delicately lovely.

Figure 21-13: Watercolor: "Summer Pattern" (1958) by Ruth Cobb. (DeCordova Museum Collection.)

Acrylics

A relatively new medium in the history of painting, acrylic paints are popular with artists because the paints are less expensive and easier to handle than oils. The colors are strong (sometimes even garish) and clear, and large areas of paint will not crack with age or fade, as oils sometimes do. Acrylics, like oils, are usually done on canvas or canvas board. Because the paint dries almost immediately, it has the advantage over oils in that it can be worked over at any time.

Drawings

PEN-AND-INK. Just as the name implies, pen-and-ink drawings are done with drawing pens of varying widths and India ink. The effect, like that of etching, is simple and fine-lined; although, unlike etchings, pen-and-ink drawings are one-of-a-kind works. Often these are

Figure 21-14: Pen and ink with watercolor wash: "Basket of Eggs" by Ben Black. (Ben Black, Photo by Charles Haggerty.)

embellished with watercolor "washes" (small areas of transparent color) for added interest.

Illustrations similar to pen-and-ink drawings are sometimes done in colored ink or felt-tip pen and have areas of sharp, clear, opaque color. Often more commercial in character, such illustrations have a bright, clean look and are usually strong and well-defined.

CHARCOAL AND PASTEL. Other popular drawing techniques are charcoal—in which a burnt wood pencil produces soft, black lines or gently graded tones—and pastel, which uses colored, chalky crayons that can create deep and luminous effects. These drawings are more textured than pen-and-ink drawings or felt-tip-pen illustrations, and less linear. It is important to frame any work on paper with glass, to protect the surface; but it is particularly important to cover charcoal and pastel drawings with glass because the color will rub off the paper if it is touched.

Collage

Not a form of drawing, but included here as one of the unique arts, collage was originally developed to a form of art in the early part of the twentieth century by Pablo Picasso. The artist starts with a flat surface—usually paper or board—and builds the composition up by pasting various papers and materials to the surface in overlapping patterns. The possibilities in collage are endless: newspaper, colored papers, wallpaper, fabrics, drawings, photos, and textured materials such as netting and screen are only some of the materials used. When the collage is made up only of pieces of photographs, it is often called *montage* or *photo montage*.

This chapter has emphasized the many kinds of art that are created primarily to be hung on walls to view. In the next chapter we will survey other kinds of art: accessories that can not only be looked at but often held, touched, walked around, and used.

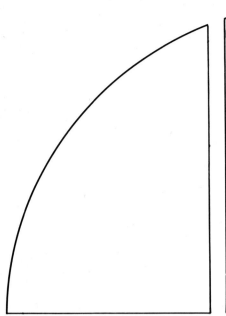
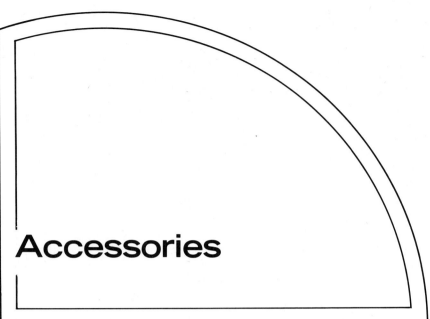

Accessories

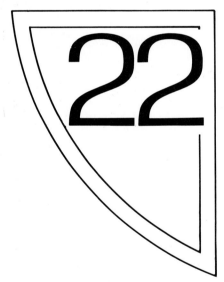

The wealth of accessories available to a designer today is practically infinite, and ranges from the most ancient pieces of craftsmanship to the newest products of the plastics industry. In this chapter we will not attempt to list every kind of vase, pillow, and bibelot known to the modern world; instead we will concentrate on major categories. Within the broad rubrics of the fabric arts, sculpture and the three-dimensional arts, antiques, and objets d'art, your best guide will be your own educated taste. Read, explore, ask questions; be aware when you visit homes and showrooms; and you will discover what your tastes are and what will be best suited to the room you have conceived.

THE FABRIC ARTS

The fabric arts include all works done on fabric, with yarn or rope, or any embroidery or stitchery. Today open-weaved wall hangings in natural colors and materials are popular and create handsome effects in homes and offices. A large weaving or tapestry can be the focal point of an entire room or the dramatic introduction of an entrance-way. The fabric arts add warmth and texture to any room. Four major kinds of fabric art are weaving, tapestry, needlepoint, and batik.

Weaving

Weavings can vary greatly, from the tightly woven work done on a loom all the way to the openness of knotted macramé. Loom-weaving and hand-weaving are alike in that the yarns or threads of the

This chapter was written by Mrs. Leni Levenson-Wiener, who is also responsible for the "Definition of Art Forms" section in Chapter 21.

piece are arranged parallel to one another in a vertical direction; horizontal yarns are then passed through these, alternating under some and over others, and in varying colors, to form patterns—the same way any cloth is woven. The difference is that decorative weaving can incorporate yarns, straw, strips of cloth, even dried plants, and can be used in your room in anything from rag rugs and woven pillow covers to wall hangings. Particularly lovely, too, are geometric weavings from some of the Mediterranean countries. Macramé, on the other hand, is done with ropes or twine in a series of intricate knots, often with glass, ceramic, or wooden beads woven into the piece. Macramé can encompass anything from belts to plant holders and beautiful wall hangings.

Tapestry and Appliqué

A tapestry is a tightly woven piece, usually large, with a pictoral design woven directly into the fabric, or embroidered into it. Very popular in earlier times, wall-sized tapestries and hangings were originally used to retain heat in large, drafty rooms before the advent of heating systems. Small ones were used for screens or upholstery covers. More popular today, however are appliquéd "tapestries"; that is, abstract or realistic works created almost like a fabric collage, with fabrics of different textures and/or colors sewn together with interesting stitchery techniques for truly spectacular results. Often spaces are left open, or fringes left hanging. There are a multitude of techniques that add dimension and can be used to exciting advantage.

Needlepoint and Bargello

Almost everyone is familiar with needlepoint—the process of drawing yarn in small stitches through a stiff netting material to form colorful designs. Bargello, developed in Florence, Italy and done by women sitting on the steps of the Bargello Tower (hence its name), is a special kind of needlepoint in which the yarn is drawn through one, two, three, or four squares of the netting (instead of only one square as in other needlepoint) to create zig-zag, geometric, flamestitch, or even "optical" patterns. Best suited for accessory pillows or chair seats and backs, small needlepoint and bargello works can also be framed and hung in picture groupings.

Batik

A kind of printing on fabric, the method of batik is especially popular in the Middle East and the Orient; but many artists employ the technique very successfully in this country as well. Wax is painted onto the fabric and the piece is dipped into dye, which colors the fabric everywhere but the waxed areas. When the wax is removed, the color of the fabric shows through. Many color dyes can be used; but each color must be waxed, dyed, and thoroughly dried separately. These works are quite unusual and make interesting hangings.

277

SCULPTURE AND THE THREE-DIMENSIONAL ARTS

The three-dimensional arts include any sculpture, silverwork (such as tea sets, vases, etc.), and pottery—the variations of which are too vast to list here. Sculpture, whether of stone, clay, wood, metal, bone, or ivory, large or small, is effective because it lends itself to every style and cultural background in the world. Eskimo, pre-Columbian, and African pieces are primitive and exciting. Modern sculpture takes many forms, from the smooth, sublime, and sensuous to welded, hard-edged realism. Abstract sculpture, in many moods and styles, includes mobiles, or hanging sculptures that move and change with the shifting air within the room.

Figure 22-1: Bronze relief sculpture: "Moon Worshippers" (1963-1969) by David Aronson. (DeCordova Museum Collection; Gift of the artist.)

CERAMICS. Emerging from a rich tradition, ceramics has grown to a point of even greater interest in current times. The potter is involved with the most basic elements in the world: earth, fire, and water. A lasting and enduring piece of art can be created when a piece made of clay and water comes into contact with the extreme heat of the kiln. Its special quality arises from the blend of the three-dimensional form with glaze, color, and texture. The artist has to master many areas of knowledge, from the many types of clay, to the technique of hand-throwing on a potter's wheel, to the chemistry involved in glazes and glaze techniques and decoration, to the complex uses of kilns—both gas and electric—which set the glaze and harden the ceramics at high temperatures. This art form has always been both an aesthetic and practical addition to the lives of civilized people through history.[1]

[1] Written from an interview with noted potter Merna Canner Kalis, Marblehead, Mass.

Figure 22-2: The creation of a pot on the wheel of potter Merna Canner Kalis, photographed in her studio as she worked. (Merna Canner Kalis. Photo: Peter Ficksman.)

Figure 22-3: Finished ceramic jars with covers, after firing in a gas kiln, photographed in the home of potter Merna Canner Kalis together with items from her own art collection. (Merna Canner Kalis. Photo: Peter Ficksman.)

ANTIQUES AND OBJETS D'ART

A search through antique dealers' shops and antique auctions can produce some interesting additions for the residential or commercial interior. China, clocks, crystal, pewter, brass, iron stoves, old photographs, metal toys, even the tins that used to house tea and tobacco, can add character and individuality to a finished interior. The culture and history of many generations can be recaptured in the treasures of the past. Furniture with aged patinas; silver, tarnished and polished to a luster; brass, mellowed and softly colored; straw; quilts; antique rugs; Wedgwood, China; cloissoné enameled boxes; pottery; old prints; and Tiffany glass are all valuable additions.

Individual collections, too, can be a focal point of a room—old glass medicine bottles, paperweights, Hummel figures, indentures (hand-written legal land-ownership documents on sheepskin), keys, leather-bound books, and seashells are only a few examples.

Fine antique shops are available in every city; however, some values can still be found at country auctions and flea-markets. Even if you don't know what the original function of a piece was, it can still be a worthwhile aesthetic addition to your room. One era's necessities can be another era's art. Remember, unless you have a strictly "restoration" room, depicting only one style, the art and ac-

Figure 22-4: In this interior designed by Karl Mann, carefully chosen accessories tie together all the elements of a finished room. (Karl Mann.)

cessories need not be all of the same period: a mixture is often more effective. A varied collection including, for instance, oil paintings, sketches, prints, Chinese wood carvings, African sculpture, and pottery both contemporary and traditional can be much more interesting than a collection of similar pieces.

Your search for art and antiques can bring you as much satisfaction as the pieces you eventually purchase. In your travels, for instance, hunting for one representative antique or artwork for your collection or your clients' will give a trip a special meaning beyond that of the pure pleasure of visiting new places. It helps to keep your exposure to these things current by leafing through art and antique magazines, reading the reviews in newspapers of new art openings, and browsing through the galleries. Art schools often have student shows where you can purchase new works of high merit for very reasonable prices. And who knows? You might discover one of the trendsetters of the next artistic generation.

Above all, always continue in your search for the art and antiques that best suit your room and your personality. It is the individuality of these pieces of art that, in the long run, make that particular interior a personal statement. The designer therefore has the responsibility of making the proper choices that best suit his or her clients' needs, budget, and taste.

Figure 22-5: A fine example of the use of objets d'art in an interior. This library designed by Philip Smith, ASID Associate, expresses a love of antiquities from the perspective of an antiquarian as well as from that of an interior designer. (Philip Smith, ASID Associate. Photo: William W. Owens, Jr.)

VIII Professional Interior Design

Insofar as this book was intended to be an introduction to the study of interior design, much further indepth study is needed. Now that you have learned the basic elements, this chapter deals with putting it all together for you—whether you are working on your own room plan, as a student of design, or as a professional designer.

First we will see many interested people taking an **interior design course** *in classes at Decordova Museum in Lincoln, Massachusetts. This course, directed primarily toward the layperson, has also been written and given by Helene Levenson as a refresher course by interior designers (not leading to a degree).*

Next we will see **students' work** *from an A.S.I.D.-accredited school for interior design, Chamberlayne Jr. College, Boston, Massachusetts, along with a statement from the student whose work is shown. This student is now an associate member of A.S.I.D. and working as a professional interior designer.*

Finally, as a summation of all aspects of knowledge in the field, we show a successful design project by a prominent architect, furniture designer, and interior designer. Warren Platner's "Windows on the World" was chosen as a classic demonstration of all the steps shown in this book that lead to a **finished interior space.**

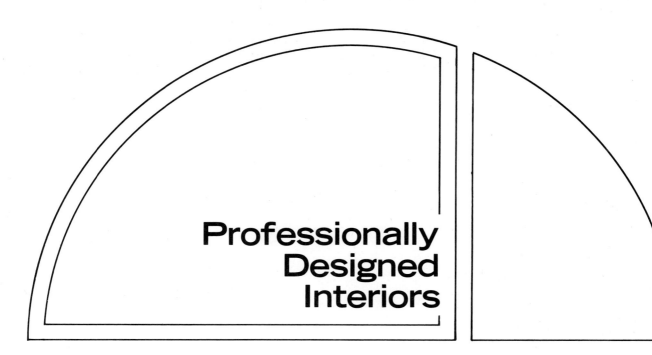

Professionally Designed Interiors

Today, people recognize the importance of having their surroundings express beauty and happiness; and they are finding that there is great satisfaction in creating such an image in interior design. Today's mode of living is very different from that of the past; and men and women know that the rooms in which they spend their time, whether at home or in the office, have a direct influence on their psychological well-being and that of their families. They are aware that color and light and the arrangement of space can affect their day-to-day life, mood, and happiness. *This is why professional interior designers are in demand.*

While there are many people enrolled in qualified schools of interior design, there are also many laypeople who are interested in understanding the basic elements of good interior design. The seminars shown in the illustrations on these pages are written and given by Helene Levenson, A.S.I.D., in Massachusetts as a refresher course both for people already in the field of design and for interested laypersons. I have advised many of the latter to enroll in an accredited school of interior design for future study toward a professional degree.

Material that I had written for these seminar groups, together with my studies for the NCIDQ exam, formed the basis for this book. And as this book has emphasized from its first pages, a carefully conceived overall plan is an absolutely vital element in the creation of an interior design. One of the subjects covered in any course on interior design is the method of presentation of the plan to the client.

Figure 23-1: Above: *A seminar in interior design: Helene Levenson, ASID, and Ida Goldstein, ASID Associate, with some of their display materials. (Photo © Warren Jagger.)*

Figure 23-2: Below: *Interior design seminars given by Helene Levenson, ASID, include basic information on furniture styles, floor plans, color, lighting, fabrics, floors, accessories. (Photo © Warren Jagger.)*

Figure 23-3: Above: Students and instructor Helene Levenson, *ASID*, during workshop portion of an interior design seminar. Many visual aids were used, as well as slide presentations of finished interiors. (Photo © Warren Jagger.)

Figure 23-4: Below: Presentation board for living and dining room: paint, fabric, and rug fiber samples; furniture schedule; finish schedule. (Student work of Ida Goldstein, *ASID* Associate.) (Photo: Laban Whittaker.)

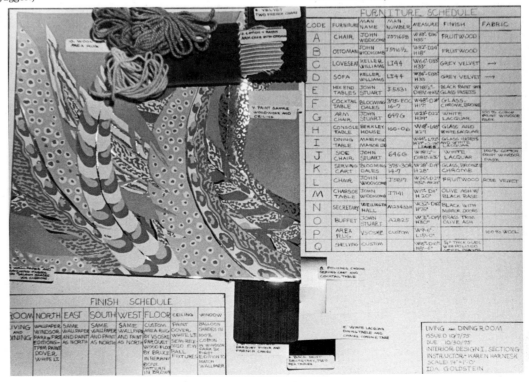

PRESENTATION OF A PLAN
Ex-Student Work

Ida Goldstein, Associate Member of ASID and a graduate of an A.S.I.D.-accredited school of interior design, Chamberlayne Jr. College, Boston, Massachusetts has described the way a designer should go about presenting a plan that will lead to the design and execution of a finished interior:[1]

Interior design must reflect the needs and personality of the individual client. A student or a professional designer must begin with a personality profile of the prospective client and that person's specific needs. After this initial step is completed, the area perimeters are drawn and all architectural details are noted on a floor plan. Then the furniture layout is drawn to scale on the floor plan. Elevations depicting the walls and ceiling heights are drawn to scale, in order to depict the proportions and details of the area.

Utilization of the proper type of lighting is now planned and shown on a reflective ceiling plan, drawn to scale as an overlay to the floor plan. The selected individual pieces of furniture are listed in the furniture schedule. The colors, fabrics, and materials, chosen to enhance the design, are shown in a separate schedule. Sketches, notes, or details depicting special design treatments and requirements are shown along with a swatch board demonstrating the relationship between the fabric and materials. The client can now readily visualize a completed interior through the total design presentation.

The plans and presentation boards illustrated on these pages show the kind of help a client should receive from a designer at the initial planning stage. From such a thorough and detailed presentation, the client and the designer can work together toward a wholly satisfying finished product. This work was done at Chamberlayne Jr. College as a student project.[2]

---

[1]This presentation from Chamberlayne Jr. College, Boston, Massachusetts, is reprinted by permission of the Director of the Interior Design Department, Mr. Herbert Anderson, whose constant encouragement to me and to his students is gratefully appreciated.

[2]Ida Goldstein is presently on staff of Helene Levenson Assoc. Inc.

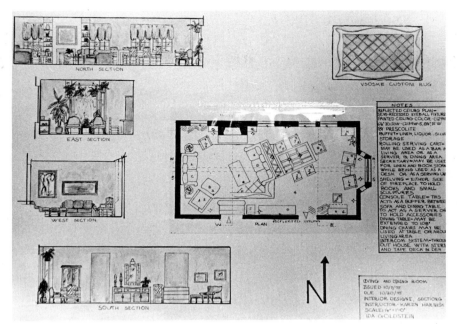

Figure 23-5: Presentation board for living and dining room; floor plan and four sections of room, with sketch of area rug. (Student work of Ida Goldstein, ASID Associate.) (Photo: Laban Whittaker.)

Figure 23-6: Presentation board for family room: carpet, upholstery, and wood finish samples; furniture schedule; furniture sketches; end view and storage unit sketches. (Student work of Ida Goldstein, ASID Associate.) (Photo: Laban Whittaker.)

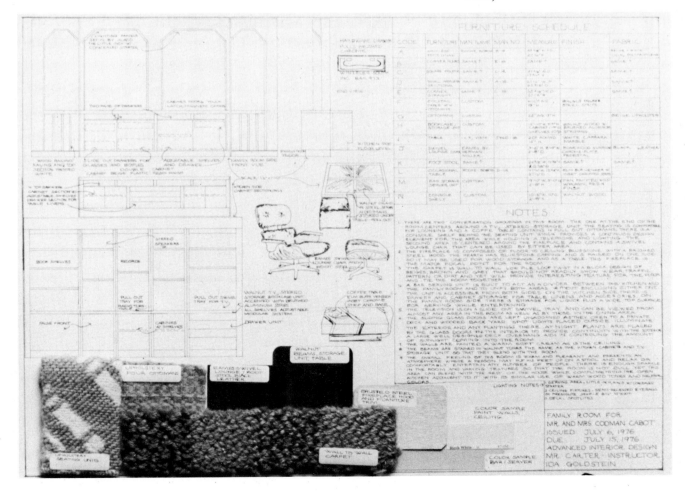

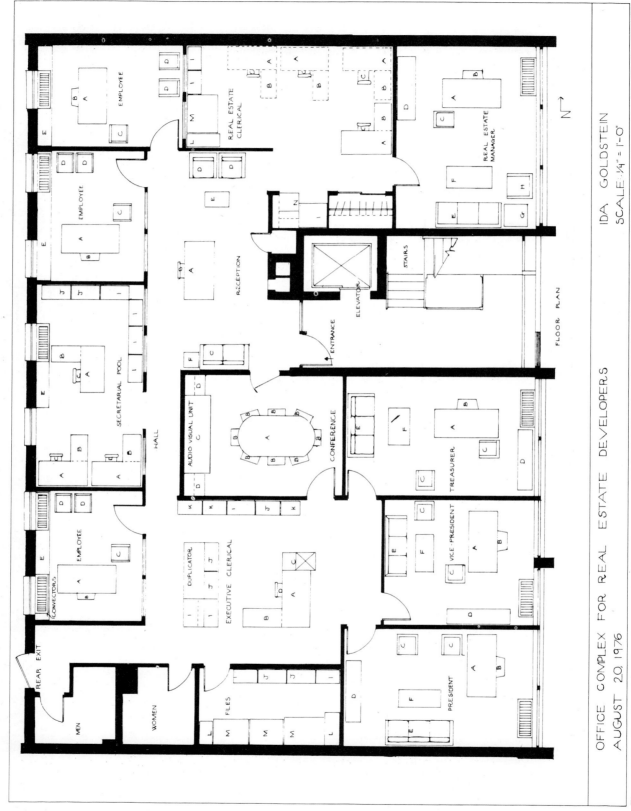

OFFICE COMPLEX FOR REAL ESTATE DEVELOPERS
AUGUST 20, 1976

IDA GOLDSTEIN
SCALE: 1/4" = 1'-0"

Figure 23-7: Furniture layout and space plan for office complex. (Student work of Ida Goldstein, ASID Associate.)

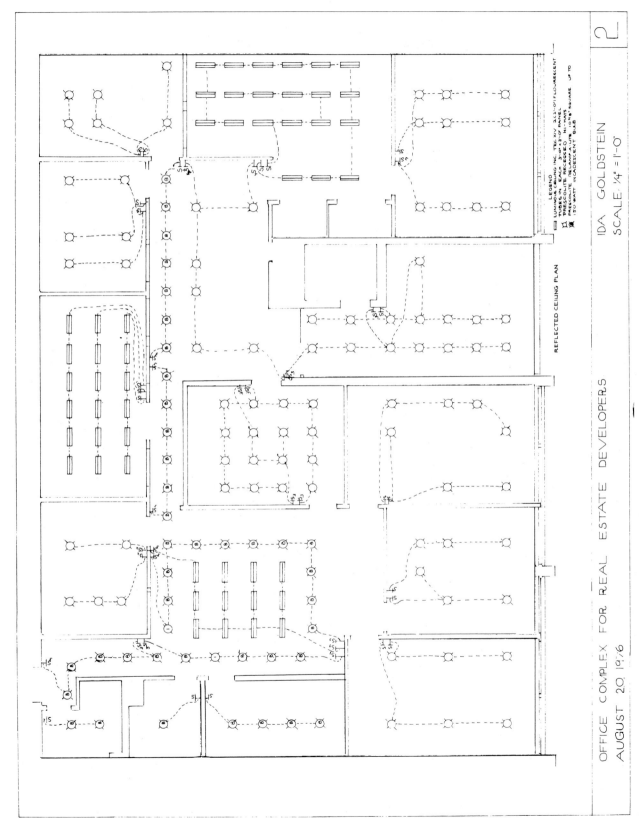

Figure 23-8: *Lighting plan for office complex. (Student work of Ida Goldstin, ASID Associate.)*

FINISHED INTERIORS

Figures 23–9 through 23–11 are examples of the finished interiors created by professional designers. Other such fine examples can be seen in the section of color plates. The quality of these designs reflects the years of training, study, and practice that develop a qualified ASID interior designer. (See Color Plates.)

Figure 23-9: A library in a Victorian spirit, designed for the ASID "Hope House" in Boston by Hal Langell, ASID. Cranberry carpet, gold-figured grasscloth walls, leather and velvet-covered furniture, books, and trophies combine to create a casual, traditional atmosphere. (Hal Langell, ASID, with Paine Furniture, Inc. Photo © Edward Jacoby.)

Figure 23-10: Another view of Hal Langell's "Hope House" library. (Hal Langell, ASID, with Paine Furniture, Inc. Photo © Edward Jacoby.)

Figure 23-11: An interesting Art Deco bed-sitting room by Noel Jeffrey, ASID. Dramatic focal point is the diagonally placed bed, a peach moiré shell clothed in fabric with a raw silk look. A pair of peach moiré chaises and a white leather-covered coffee-table form a conversation group at the foot of the bed; Graber vertical blinds are at the windows. (Window Shade Manufacturers' Association, Hilda D. Sachs.)

Warren Platner: architect; interior designer; and designer of furniture, art work, and decoration. The entrance hall to Windows on the World, at New York's World Trade Center, has a mirrored ceiling and floor. Glass arches subdivide the sixty-foot length of the space. Wall photographs of people and places of the world set the international theme. (Photo by Jaimé Ardiles-Arce)

WARREN PLATNER'S "WINDOWS ON THE WORLD"

I have chosen the interior space "Windows on the World" because of the versatility of its designer, architect Warren Platner, whose practice includes master planning, building structures, interiors, lighting design, furniture, and decoration. His success in synthesizing all these elements has resulted in a series of completed works that have had an important influence on his profession.

From the vast array of available literature and photos of interiors, furniture, lighting, and architecture, we will focus here on one space, designed and executed by Warren Platner, a leading professional in the field.

Windows on the World is a world-renowned restaurant that occupies the top floor of the World Trade Center, tallest building in New York City—an acre of space. While this is actually a contract interior, Platner explains, "it was designed with a residential feeling." In a personal interview he explained the concepts and intents behind his creation of this interior space.

It will be seen that the three central concerns of *Creating An Interior* are part of Mr. Platner's thinking, too: he evaluates the needs and tastes of his "clients" (the people from around the world who come to the restaurant); he works to make the most interesting possible use of the existing architectural space; and the functional requirements of the area define all his planning.

293

Basic Concepts

Platner's basic plan was to create the atmosphere of a fine residence, a gracious setting for entertaining, similar to that of a great manor house with many rooms. Though Windows on the World encompasses a huge area, the intimate scale of each individual space prevails; and individual interest gives variety while the whole is remembered as an entity. The ivory-white background color, used throughout for continuity, provides one common denominator. Another continued theme is that of *pointillism* (see p. 297).

Another continued theme is that of *pointillism* (see p. 297).

Figure 23-12: The entrance gallery to Windows on the World: Warren Platner gave interest to a 65-foot-long gallery with mirrored and clear glass spaces of varying widths. (Warren Platner, architect, interior designer, and designer of furniture, art work, and decoration.)

THE TASTES OF THE CLIENT. In residential design, creating a physical environment for a particular client is the goal; but in Windows on the World, the design had to appeal to the tastes of a broad spectrum of people—each one responding on a different level. The design had to

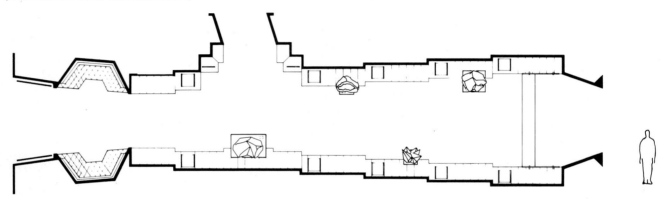

have literally universal appeal. There had to be a sense of elegance, yet the atmosphere had to be friendly rather than formidable. This effect was achieved through decorative elements that people would recognize as appropriate to hospitality, such as fruit and flowers.

A theme appropriate to the international clientele of the World Trade Center invites the guests into Windows on the World: photographs of the people and places of the world are set against the walls of the 65-foot-long entrance gallery, in panels between the mirrors and glass arches that subdivide the space. By means of the mirrored ceiling, walls, and floor, and a carpeted strip down the center of the floor that acts as a bridge through space, the visitor has the effect of "being inside a kaleidoscope."

Carrying out the international theme, also in the entrance hall, are four boulder-sized semi-precious stones: amethyst geode, rose quartz, clear rock crystal, and pegmatite. Beautiful in themselves, they represent the four corners of the earth. (See Color Plate 1.)

THE POSSIBILITIES OF THE ARCHITECTURE. To take full advantage of the superb view and high ceilings in the dining areas of Windows on the World, Platner decided to use terraces so that the people at the back of the room could have as fine a view as those sitting by the windows. There is another purpose to this terracing. Because of the enormous size of the dining rooms, each of which accommodates about 350 people (the full capacity of the whole restaurant is 900), the design had to solve a paradox, achieving an atmosphere of "con-

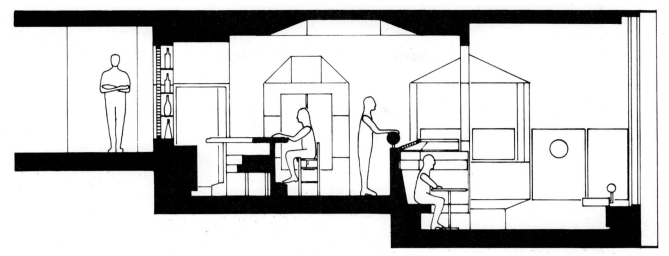

vivial intimacy" within a huge space. The changes of levels give each table a special vantage for enjoying the view, as well as a sense of privacy. Vertical separation is more effective than horizontal. (See Figure 23–13.)

The reception area has a raised floor, so that its ceiling is at an 8-foot rather than a 12-foot height. This creates an intimate space; it also heightens the drama of the changing levels that lie ahead. At the end of the glass entrance gallery the visitor steps up into the reception area—and the effect is that of standing on a balcony suspended above New York Harbor, looking down at a view which includes the Statue of Liberty. Other changes of level, occurring throughout the public areas, give a grace and interest to the succession of spaces. (See Figure 23–14.)

Figure 23-13: Terracing: an impression of greater height is created within the existing 12-foot ceiling height by terracing the floor levels. (Warren Platner, architect, interior designer, and designer of furniture, art work, and decoration.)

Figure 23-14: Levels: the grill in Windows on the World is on a level between those of the entrance gallery and the windows. (Warren Platner, architect, interior designer, and designer of furniture, art work, and decoration.

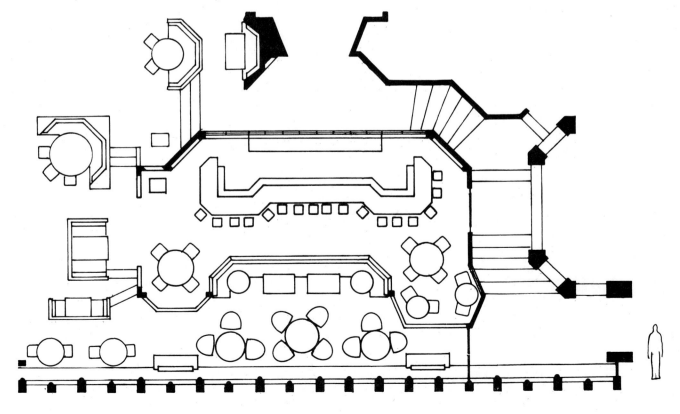

The largest rooms, including the bar and all the dining areas, are located around the exterior walls of the square area, to obtain the finest views. (See Figure 23–15.)

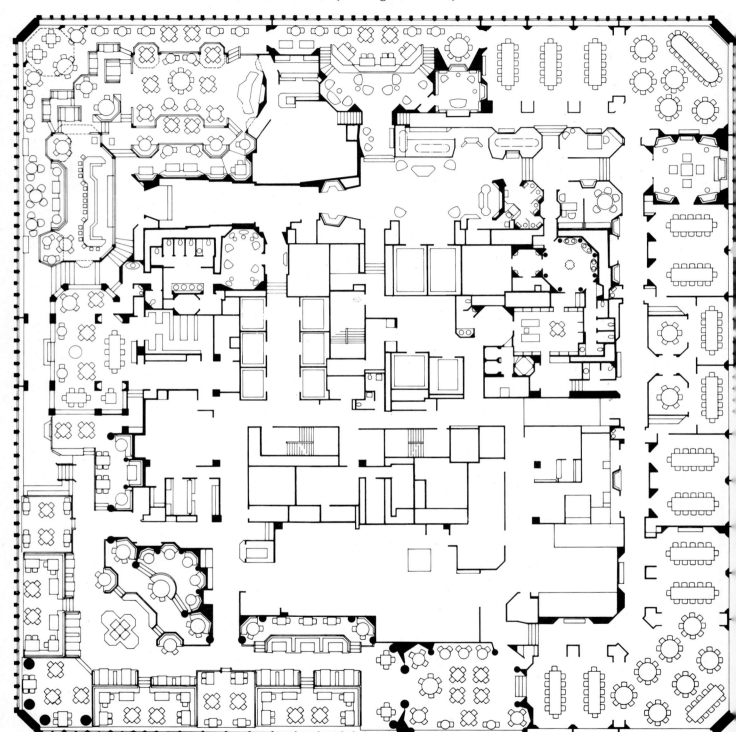

Figure 23-15: Floor plan of Windows on the World by Warren Platner. All dining areas are at the perimeter of the floor, allowing full view from the windows; the largest dining areas are at the four corners of the building. (Warren Platner, architect, interior designer, and designer of furniture, art work, and decoration.)

Decorative Elements of the Design

POINTILLISM. The background behind a console table in the reception area is a detailed wall. Small circular gold forms, repeated all over the wall, suggest spheres floating in space. This pattern is repeated in the carpet, in the fabric on the chairs, in the tufting on the banquettes, and in the gold tiles in the restaurant. Even in the gallery the photographs are treated with a screen process which produces a black-and-white pattern. The whole effect is described as *pointillism*—after the technique of the French Impressionist painters of the last century who created luminous images with thousands of tiny dots.

MIRRORS. The reflections in Windows on the World are charming— and they carry further the pointillist effect. There are no walls using flat mirror: rather than repeating images, mirrors are used to fracture them. The result could be compared to the visual equivalent of hearing the overtones in music. Images are enriched as the tones in music are enriched.

Mirrors are used extensively. They make the "kaleidoscope" in the glass entrance gallery; divided in sections and with beveled angles, they appear in the reception room and throughout the restaurant. (See Plates 1 and 22.) They extend space, reflecting and diffusing the light.

LIGHTING. In this triumph of design, lighting is used to create an aesthetically richer effect. With a great amount of available daylight, warm colors to offset daylight's blueness were sought. Because no task lighting was needed (see pp. 142–147), the interest lay in the creation of highlights and shadows, lighting the centers of interest.

The four large semi-precious stones in the glass gallery, for example, are lit by standard exhibition wall washers and framing projector fixtures, grouped in multiples and encased in shields of polished brass. In the Statue of Liberty Lounge, custom brass ornamental lighting fixtures start at the upper level and descend to light the dining alcoves below.

In the main dining room, ceiling-light boxes are set into the seating alcoves, creating high-relief shadows on the walls and upholstery. In the Cellar in the Sky, which has the ambiance of a wine cellar, a romantic lighting effect is achieved by the use of framing projectors. In the West Parlor, one of two lounge areas, the brass center ceiling chandeliers are reflected in triptych mirrors one above another, creating additional light. (See Color Plate 22.)

In total, the play of light and shadow works with the variety of textures, so that both reflective and absorbent surfaces help to create the magic of this interior.

It is the skillful combination of all the elements of interior design, used in an excitingly innovative manner, that distinguishes Warren Platner's Windows on the World. Here is a finished artwork that exemplifies the unlimited possibilities open to the creator of an interior.

297

In the next chapter, information on the history, the nature, the aims, and the ideals of America's professional design organizations has been assembled. These organizations are taking an increasingly important part in determining the requirements for professional qualification in interior design.

PROFESSIONALLY DESIGNED INTERIORS

These photos are examples of the finished results when the professional interior designer has completed all of the planning stages leading to the final design. Other such fine examples can be seen in the center section of color photos in this book. The years of training, study and practice will produce well qualified A.S.I.D. interior designers. Information on professional organizations and course of study is provided for you in the following chapter.

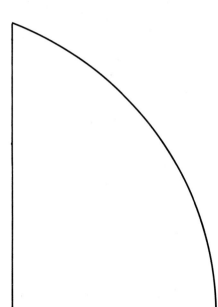

Professional Organizations

The standards of the interior design profession are constantly being evaluated and changed. The purpose of this chapter is to familiarize you with the history, the goals, and the achievements to date of each of the major organizations in the profession of interior design. As the years go by, new achievements will be added to those described here; but the central purposes of all these organizations can be expected to remain constant. Each of them is directed, in its own area of activity, to the improvement of the training and qualifications of the people who enter the field. And each of them is dedicated to the ultimate goal of excellence in the planning and construction of the spaces in which people live and work.

A.S.I.D. (AMERICAN SOCIETY OF INTERIOR DESIGNERS)

The American Society of Interior Designers is the largest organization of professional interior designers in the world. It was formed on January 1, 1975, by the consolidation of the American Institute of Interior Designers (A.I.D.) and the National Society of Interior Designers (N.S.I.D.).

The A.S.I.D. comprises forty-five chapters within the United States, and has International Members, with a total membership of over 24,000.

It is considered the standard-bearer and prolocutor for the interior designer because of its size, rigid membership requirements, and unflagging efforts to raise the level of professionalism in the practice of interior design. It is the main force behind the change in the roles and image of the professional interior designer since the early 1960s.

299

History of A.S.I.D.

The proliferation of the practice of interior design after World War II was vastly out of proportion to the number of adequate design courses being offered. There were professionals, to be sure, but flair and bravado were the tools of the trade for many others.

Designers at every level were seeking ways to become more professional, and found—short of European schools—that the continuing education seminars sponsored by the two constituent organizations of A.S.I.D. were the prime source. In 1966, A.I.D. and N.S.I.D. came to the full realization that interior design could not call itself a profession without improved educational programs in this country. After lengthy studies concerning guidelines for the teaching of interior design and methods of accreditation, they were joined in 1968 by the Interior Design Educators Council (I.D.E.C.) and together they created F.I.D.E.R. (Foundation for Interior Design Education Research) in 1970, with the major goal of improving the academic programs and establishing degrees in interior design.

F.I.D.E.R. has now been recognized by the U.S. Office of Education as the accrediting body for educational design programs offered in this country, and also by the Council of Post-Secondary Accreditation. Having taken this step to advance the qualifications of interior designers through improved educational programs, they turned their attention to gaining recognition for the professional designer. While public recognition has been surfacing since the 1940s, the members of A.S.I.D. came face to face with the fact that only a minority of Americans realize that there is a vast difference between the professional and the self-styled "professional" interior designer.

In 1973, both having had their own membership qualification programs previously, they agreed to establish common criteria for recognition of the interior designer and to examine the feasibility of legal qualification or licensing. This resulted in the formation of the N.C.I.D.Q. (National Council for Interior Design Qualification), which now comprises eight U.S. and Canadian organizations. Since early 1974, the first nationally recognized examination to qualify an interior designer has been administered under the Council's auspices. Successful completion of the N.C.I.D.Q. exam is one of the requirements for professional membership status in A.S.I.D., and it is hoped it will one day become a standard for all practicing designers.

This uniformity of standards is obviously in the public interest, since unless or until standards are established by legal requirements, *anyone can practice in the field!* The N.C.I.D.Q. has prepared a model state title act to aid its constituent organizations in the pursuit of licensing of the professional interior designers. Meanwhile, through self-regulation, the members of the A.S.I.D. are effecting the closest thing to universal standards for qualification of the professional designer.

Importance of Professionalism in Design

Few people realize the scope of the designers' influence, which touches virtually every area of life in this country. Their work extends to low-cost housing, and improves the efficiency and aesthetics of hospitals, schools, libraries, and other public buildings. Besides the better-known areas of designing homes, offices, restaurants, banks, hotels and motels, stores, and beauty shops, they design for the handicapped and the aged, design churches, theaters, funeral homes, and even sports stadiums.

Even when you add their involvement in advertising, magazine and newspaper editorials, model rooms in retail stores and real estate promotions, museums, TV, stage and movie sets, and the creation of tourist attractions, it does not complete the compilation of sources through which the work of the professional interior designer influences life in America.

Their work in historic preservation and restoration, a large part of which was and is on a volunteer basis, was one of the earlier means of bringing attention to their knowledge of architecture and engineering. This depth of knowledge has made them important in the growing and economical practice of remodeling homes and other buildings for private use or resale.

The layperson who was impressed in the past with the designer's grasp of periods, scale, and color will be dazzled by today's professional designer. A knowledge of new fibers and finishes, new materials and production techniques, electrical technology, building codes, as well as government regulations, psychology, flammability standards, product performance, and a host of other data are basic requirements.

A.S.I.D. represents interior design as a profession dedicated to serving all people. It embraces the entire interior design community, on the basis that the fundamental concepts of interior design apply to all professionals, regardless of their specialization, and the Code of Ethics is in the interest of all members and their publics.

Programs of A.S.I.D.

The member benefit programs of the A.S.I.D. include seminars, research, a library, audiovisual programs, information distribution and other professional development programs, referral systems, public relations and insurance programs, a benevolent fund, and group tours. In addition, the A.S.I.D. participates in numerous interprofessional programs and has representation in the National Forum on Growth Policy, Interior Environment Committee, Legislative Minuteman Program, U.F.A.C., National Trust for Historic Preservation, Illuminating Engineering Society, Resources Council, Federal Design Assembly, Inter-Society Color Council, both the Committee and the National Center for Barrier Free Design, and the President's Committee on Employment of the Handicapped.

Members are kept abreast of new government standards and regulations, are provided standard contract forms and other business documents, and receive periodic information on such topics as OSHA, flammability, and shipping.

A.S.I.D. has a national awards program, scholarships and grants, official competition standards, community affairs programs, an Industry Foundation, a Student Council, and year-round market programs designed to be of great benefit to retailers, specifiers, dealers, and designers.

301

Membership in A.S.I.D.

It should be noted that A.S.I.D. has eight membership categories: Professional, Associate, Design Affiliate, Education Affiliate, Press Affiliate, Public Relations Affiliate, and Student Member; plus Industry Foundation Participants. Only a Professional Member is permitted to use the A.S.I.D. appelation—or F.A.S.I.D., which indicates she or he has been elected a Fellow (the highest honor the Society can bestow on a member)—without further clarification.

F.I.D.E.R. (FOUNDATION FOR INTERIOR DESIGN EDUCATION RESEARCH)

The following are excerpts from a statement on design education and accreditation issued by the Chairman of F.I.D.E.R. Board of Trustees in 1977, Professor Richard A. Rankin, Interior Design Department, University of Kentucky, also a charter member of I.D.E.C.:

The opportunity to further the recognition of design education is a temptation no designer or educator can possibly ignore. The cause is so much an integral part of the continued struggle to preserve, enlighten, and enhance the life style and environment of the twentieth century, that responding to Helene Levenson's request for comment seems entirely natural and appropriate. Bearing in mind that it is difficult for print to appear timeless and meaningful to the reader when change and growth are an ongoing part of the general order of things, collective interpretations of a few significant events concerned with design, education, and accreditation will hopefully stimulate continued objectivity.

Design

The design profession has obviously emerged from the merits of decoration for the few to design for the many. In the growth process, a totally new posture has been forged: Individuals and collaborators specifically trained to solve problems encountered by a society determined to possess more than shelter and security from the elements of nature. What began historically with the client's visual and aesthetic needs, continued and flourished but with new and added dimensions: control aspects of function, action, behavior for specific purposes other than sheer beauty and pleasure.

Education

The time arrived when materials and symbols used by people were organized in various ways for any variety of purposes. These purposes became the touchstone for the curriculum of the emerging educational institutions whose singular aim became the amalgamation of theory and pragmatic experience for the student. Thus the needs were to be met for individuals desiring the acquisition of knowledge, skills, and competencies.

302

Where to experience the training was no more complex than how long, how much, and with what end proof of completion. The design profession, in realizing this need, observed the parallel disciplines and the monitoring systems devised by other professions. In 1968 the professional societies joined forces for purposes of investigating interior design accreditation procedures, leading to a possible certificate or degree. It is these pioneers who have given us a basis for professional service: organizational skills in interpreting needs and requirements based on a predetermined program supported by known and variable data.

Accreditation

With the quality of the profession in mind, the quality of education was the target of a joint effort in 1968. The American Institute of Interior Designers (A.I.D.), together with the National Society of Interior Designers (N.S.I.D.), prompted by the Interior Design Educators Council (I.D.E.C.), formed the Joint Committee on Accreditation: a study group made up of representatives and executive council members of the founding group. Its purpose was to investigate the feasibility of establishing accreditation procedures and processes for Interior Design Education. In 1971, the Joint Committee chartered the nonprofit Foundation for Interior Design Education Research: a pilot agency to accredit programs in the U.S. and Canada.

Referred to as F.I.D.E.R., the Foundation began the process of writing an entire series of guidelines and objectives of design education together with site and visitation procedures that would be acceptable to other established accreditation agencies. These agencies were the U.S. Office of Education and the Council on Post-Secondary Accreditation, known in the trade as U.S.O.E. and C.O.P.A. Both agencies had specific recognition criteria to be met, if provisional and continued recognition was to be granted, and membership restrictions for continued campus visitations. Prior to U.S.O.E. recognition in 1975 and the C.O.P.A. acceptance in 1977, F.I.D.E.R. refined its accreditation criteria, trained its volunteer observers and team chairmen, wrote a Procedures and Operational Manual, conducted the pilot program, published lists annually, and marshaled financial support from industry and the professional societies.

In summary, accreditation is the profession's insurance of continued expansion, accommodation, quality of training, and diversified experience as it relates to and is concerned with the near and proximate environment. The purpose of the educational monitoring is as varied as the number of schools offering programs: it insures that the program can be identified as contributory, protects the consumer and public from misrepresentation, insures that the discerning body conducting the review is legal, and that the program truly prepares for active participation in the stated aspect of the profession and identifies those individuals who have completed the required experiences and have attained known proficiencies required to render design service.

In retrospect, the design profession may have begun cosmetically, been juvenile in enduring controversy, suffered from diversity and rapid growth, but has triumphantly emerged malleable, mature, and a versatile adult.

303

F.I.D.E.R. has prepared a pamphlet listing programs accredited in the following categories:

1. Baccalaureate degree programs of at least four years' duration with major emphasis on education for professional interior design combined with general education in the liberal arts.
2. Certificate or diploma of no less than four years' duration with emphasis on intensive training for professional interior design. (Such programs are generally offered by professional design schools with little or no academic subject matter included.)
3. Certificate or associate degree programs of at least two years' duration with emphasis on either pre-professional (continuing) education or technical (terminal) training for interior design aids. (Such programs are generally given through junior colleges or technical institutes.)

This list indicates the programs that have been certified to be in conformance with the F.I.D.E.R. accreditation standards. The acceptance of these programs has been recommended by the full committee on accreditation and approved unanimously by the F.I.D.E.R. board of trustees.

N.C.I.D.Q. (NATIONAL COUNCIL FOR INTERIOR DESIGN QUALIFICATION)

N.C.I.D.Q. is a separately incorporated organization concerned with the development and maintenance of professional standards of practice in the field of interior design through professional performance testing and the establishing of national standards of legal qualification.

The Council, established in 1972 as a consortium of national design societies, pursues programs of information and research in two related areas:

○ Principles of legal qualifications and guidelines for statutory licensing
○ Testing methods for determining professional competency; development and administration of a national qualification examination

History and Membership of N.C.I.D.Q.

The N.C.I.D.Q. was incorporated in June of 1974. What had begun in 1972 as dialogue and discussions among national design organizations was formalized as a nonprofit organization. Initially, the Council received two charges or directions which were considered of concern and interest to all interior designers: to formulate and administer a mutually acceptable examination that would qualify the individual designer, and to investigate the advantages and disadvantages of pursuing legal registration or certification.

The member organizations of the Council are:

○ A.S.I.D.: American Society of Interior Designers
○ I.D.E.C.: Interior Design Educators Council
○ I.D.S.A.: Industrial Designers Society of America
○ I.B.D.: Institute of Business Designers
○ I.S.P.: Institute of Store Planners
○ NHFL: National Home Fashion League

They are joined by observers from:

○ A.I.A.: American Institute of Architects
○ I.D.B.C.: Interior Design Industry of British Columbia
○ I.D.O.: Interior Designers of Ontario

Progress of N.C.I.D.Q.

The first examination under the auspices of N.C.I.D.Q. was given in the fall of 1974. There is a spring and fall examination given in approximately thirty locations across the nation. The examination is under continuing re-evaluation and refinement funded by a research grant from the National Endowment for the Arts.

N.C.I.D.Q. retained the expertise of legal counsel highly qualified in the field of professional licensing to conduct the study into the advantages and disadvantages of pursuing registration of certification. The result was a 35-page report entitled "Guidelines for Statutory Licensing of Interior Design Professionals." The report also includes a model title act.

The N.C.I.D.Q. Examination

The present examination is the result of many years of development. All Council members require it as a prerequisite for their individual professional membership categories. It is given each April and October to those candidates who can furnish proof of the following:

1. Five-year degree in Interior Design or allied field of design plus one year practical experience or ...
2. Four-year degree in I.D. or allied field plus two years' practical experience or three-year certificate in I.D. plus three years' practical experience or ...
3. Two-year certificate in I.D. plus four years' practical experience or one year of I.D. education plus five years' practical experience or ...
4. High school diploma plus six years' practical experience.

The examination consists of two parts given on two consecutive days. The first part, or academic section, tests the candidate's knowledge of history, modern design, technical information, and business practices and ethics.

305

The second part is an eight-hour design problem testing the candidate's ability to arrive at a conceptual solution of a realistic design problem involving space allocation, furniture arrangement and selection, schedules, elevations, and a perspective.

The academic section of the examination is machine-graded, while each design section is graded by a panel of jurors consisting of three especially qualified interior design professionals—one educator and two practitioners. These panels are conducted in six metropolitan centers across the country.

Regardless of the individual goals and accomplishments of the Council, its reasons for existing have been to increase the professional level of competency of the individual designer by giving an examination, the content of which is based on the curricula of schools accredited by the Foundation for Interior Design Education Research in concert with the body of knowledge and expertise considered essential by qualified interior design practitioners. The Council also is prepared to advise and guide state groups of professional designers who wish to pursue legal certification or registration.

NHFL (NATIONAL HOME FASHIONS LEAGUE, INC.)

The National Home Fashions League, Inc. is a nonprofit service organization of women executives in the interior furnishings and related fields. Members work in fields of design, production, distribution, education, promotion, and communication, all related to total living environment.

Founded in 1947, the National Home Fashions League represents the major marketing and manufacturing centers of the United States with chapters from coast to coast. The League is the only organization that brings together all facets of the industry, fostering an interplay of ideas.

Through national and local programs and other activities, it circulates news in the industry, stimulates interest and growth in interior furnishings, spurs self-improvement, and recognizes excellence with special awards. It is also concerned with the consumer and the community.

Definition of NHFL

The National Home Fashions League and the Educational Foundation could not fulfill their goals without the partnership of industry itself. NHFL is

Professional: A nonprofit service organization of 1,800 woman *leaders* in the interior furnishings industry and related fields. Full membership is available only to those with executive standing in the field.

Established: Founded in 1947, it includes members with over twenty-five years of industry experience as well as bright newcomers who continually qualify and join.

National: With 1,800 members representing the major marketing and manufacturing centers in the United States. There are chapters in Arizona, Northern and Southern California, the Carolinas, Florida, Georgia, Illinois, New England, New York, North Central Ohio, Michigan, Philadelphia, the Southwest, and Washington, D.C. The N H F L is growing, with new chapters targeted for other locations.

Goals of NHFL

IMPROVING ENVIRONMENT. The National Home Fashions League has as its purpose the improvement of the quality of the human environment by serving as the communications catalyst between our industry and the public it serves.

CONSUMER SERVICE. Through educational programs in wise buying, the consumer is guided and motivated to improve his or her home. N H F L disseminates information, tailored to best serve the local community.

INDUSTRY STRENGTH. The healthy growth of the interior furnishings industry is important to the national economy and to career-minded members. The activities of N H F L stimulate interest in interior design and furnishings.

INDIVIDUAL GROWTH. When members from the many facets of the industry work together, they learn from each other and grow in their jobs. The N H F L membership Handbook, including the directory, facilitates communication.

NHFL Educational Foundation

The National Home Fashions League Educational Foundation, Inc., was incorporated in 1968 and carries out the educational and philanthropic activities of the National Home Fashions League, which was founded in 1947. It is a separate corporation with a separate board, and, because of its purposes and activities, may receive tax-deductible donations.

ITS PURPOSES. The purposes of the Foundation are "to encourage the development of programs and activities to improve the quality of living of the individual and the community; and to provide opportunities for continuing education in interior furnishings and related areas for students, faculty and the consumer."

N H F L is a member of the N.C.I.D.Q. whose concerns are the development and maintenance of standards of practice in the field of Interior Design through professional performance testing and the establishment of national standards of legal qualifications.

CONCLUSION

In conclusion, it is my hope that readers can now appreciate and better understand the complexity of the field of interior design. The fully designed interior is a sum total of its parts—and each part is a precise study in itself, changing and evolving daily to suit our present lifestyles.

We've unfolded the pages of history—to reveal man's plight
to *create* a better existence, to achieve a higher plateau of living.
In combining his function needs with his aesthetic values,
he evolved ever advancing goals to a suitable life style.
WHAT GREATER SATISFACTION CAN THERE BE THAN
TO BE IN TOTAL HARMONY WITH YOUR SURROUNDINGS?
We've come a long way, from the first small hovel
to the endless skyscraper heights.
With the help of technology and *creative* minds,
our advance will continue.

Glossary

ARMOIRE: A piece of furniture traditionally used to store clothes. In America the armoire is much more likely to be converted into a bar, a stereo shelter, or a china closet.

ATRIUM: Inner-oriented central court, open to the sky, around which the Greeks and Romans built their houses. This room-at-the-core now appears roofed or unroofed, according to its purpose and the prevailing climate.

AUBUSSON RUGS: Carpets and rugs woven in the French tapestry works at Aubusson during the Middle Ages. The name Aubusson is now given to any rugs with this type of heavy, coarse tapestry weave whether made in Aubusson or not, in both period patterns and contemporary designs.

BAKER'S RACK: Tiered iron or brass stand on which nineteenth-century bakers arranged their wares. Assume a modern role as a bar or display shelf.

BALUSTER: A small turned column found as a support for a stair rail.

BANDING: A narrow inlay of contrasting woods usually found on table or desk tops or inset around drawers.

BANQUETTE: An upholstered bench, with or without a back.

*BATIK: A method of decorating fabric that originated in the Dutch East Indies. In this method the design or pattern is applied to the surface with hot wax. When the cloth is dipped into vegetable dye, the wax-coated areas resist the color. When the cloth is then emerged in hot water, the wax is removed, leaving the design.

BAUHAUS: The famous school of art, architecture, and design established in Weimar, Germany in 1919 by Walter Gropius and others to explore the concept of total creative design that could be applied to all aspects of daily life.

BAY WINDOW: A window that projects from the wall of the house, forming an interior recess.

BERGÈRE: An upholstered armchair with closed, upholstered sides developed in France during the eighteenth century.

BERTOLA, HARRY: Modern sculptor remembered in the furniture field for his upholstered wire-mesh contour chairs manufactured by Knoll Associates.

BIEDERMEIER (1810–1850): Simplified bourgeois equivalent of the French Empire style that prevailed in German-speaking areas of Europe during the early and mid-nineteenth century.

BLOCK PRINTING: A pattern or picture is printed by hand on paper or fabric with a series of carved wood blocks coated with dye, each of which produces one part of the design in a single flat color.

BOISERIE: French word for the delicate eighteenth-century paneling and decorative woodwork.

BOMBÉ: Term for furniture with a surface that bulges or swells, either in the front, the sides, or both, such as in a commode.

BOUILLOTTE LAMP: The candle lamp of gilt bronze or brass with a painted tole shade.

BROADLOOM: Solid-color or patterned carpet woven on a broad loom in widths of 9, 12, 15, and 18 feet.

BURL: (Also burr.) Diseased or abnormal growth on trees, exalted to the status of a veneer wood when sliced into cross-sections that show up the beautifully mottled or figured patterns.

*CABRIOLE: A type of furniture leg or support shaped like an animal's leg, flaring out at the knee and narrowing to the ankle and foot. This leg style originated in the seventeenth century but became more pronounced during the eighteenth century. It is associated with the Queen Anne style in English, with the Louis XV style in French, and with the Georgian style in American.

CANE: Flexible furniture material from the rattan palm, split and woven into chair backs and seats and table tops.

CANOPY: The wooden frame and fabric hangings over a bed. Also, an indoor or outdoor awning of similar design.

CANTON: Oriental export china, usually blue and white.

CAPITAL: The head, or top, of a column that identifies the various orders or architecture—the three Greek: Doric, Ionic, Corinthian; and the five Roman: Tuscan, Doric, Ionic, Corinthian, and Composite.

CARYATID: The supporting column shaped like a female figure found in Greek architecture.

CASE GOODS: General term for storage pieces, as distinguished from upholstered seating pieces.

CATHEDRAL CEILING: An arched, vaulted, or gabled ceiling, at least one-and-a-half stories high, adapted from the ribbed construction of cathedrals.

CHEVAL GLASS: Portable full-length mirror that swings from two vertical posts fastened to a trestle.

CHINOISERIE: french term in the eighteenth century for things Chinese or reminiscent in decoration of the Chinese fashion.

CHROMA, or COLOR INTENSITY: The measurement of the intensity—or amount of pigment—in a color.

CLAMSHELL MOLDING: A single-curve molding commonly used for window and door trim.

CLOISONNÉ: A type of enamelwork in which different glaze colors in the design are separated by fine metal dividers, or cloisons.

310 *COLORWAY: When a manufacturer prints a fabric design, it is usually

available in more than one color combination, sometimes as many as 12. These combinations are referred to as "colorways."

COMMODE: French word for a chest of drawers.

CONTRACT: Trade term for interior designs executed for commercial firms on a price fixed by contract.

CONVERSATION PIT: A recess in the floor, padded for seating.

COROMANDEL SCREEN: A type of Chinese paneled screen, heavily lacquered in rich, dark tones and decorated with bas-relief patterns.

CREDENZA: Italian name for the French crédence, a side table of Gothic persuasion which developed into a sideboard for carving meat and displaying plate. Today, it may be used to hold books or a TV/hi-fi system.

CREWEL: A showy type of embroidery worked with colored worsted yarns and long, loose stitches on natural or white linen, cotton or wool grounds.

DADO: The lower part of a wall topped by a chair rail, decorated with a panel of wood, paper. or paint.

DELFT: The tin-slip or enameled faïence made in the town of Delft, Holland, since the seventeenth century. The blue-and-white pottery is the most familiar.

DELLA ROBBIA: Tin-glazed terra cotta reliefs modeled by the Della Robbia family of Florentine sculptors.

DISTRESSED: Finish designed to age furniture prematurely, achieved through beating with chains, stabbing with awls, shooting with BB's.

DORMER WINDOW: A window built out from a sloping roof to bring light to a top-floor or attic room.

DOVETAIL: A type of joint usually found in drawer construction in which two notched pieces of wood in the shape of a dove's tail interlock tightly at right angles.

DOWEL: A form of construction joint in which the sections are joined by fitting round pegs or pins into corresponding holes.

DROP REPEAT: A design technique for printing fabric and wallpaper in which the pattern on the left and right edges is not in direct horizontal alignment.

EBONY: A hard, fine-grained, brownish-black wood from tropical countries, mainly Africa, India, and Ceylon.

ECLECTICISM: The art of selecting the best from several sources, applied in decorating to an uninhibited mixture of styles of previous periods with designs of today.

EMBOSSING: Form of projecting surface decoration in which designs are stamped, molded, or hammered from the reverse side. Also known as repoussé work.

ENAMEL: A decorative colored glaze on ceramic or metal surfaces which becomes hard and shiny after firing.

*ENCAUSTIC: This technique, invented by the Romans in the fourth century B.C., entails a method of painting with pigments mixed with hot wax. This wax mixture is then heated and applied with a brush. Because marble is a porous material, the dyes sink into it and remain there for thousands of years.

ENTABLATURE: In architecture, the upper element of a classical order, made up of an architrave, frieze, and cornice.

311

ÉTAGÈRE: A pyramid of open shelves intended for the display of objects.

FACADE: The front elevation of a building.

FAUTEUIL: A French open-arm chair with either upholstered or caned seat and back.

FEDERAL (1780–1830): The patriotic style of the transitional era from the Revolution to Victorian-age America.

FENESTRATION: The arrangement of windows on the facade of a building.

FINIAL: An ornament, usually in the shape of a pineapple or knob, that adds a decorative finis to a post.

FLEUR-DE-LIS, or FLEUR-DE-LYS: A decorative motif originally based on the Egyptian stylized iris and adopted by the Bourbon kings as their royal standard.

FLOCK DESIGN: Raised design on fabric or wallpaper accomplished through felting.

FRANKLIN STOVE: A cast-iron, wood-burning, stove-cum-fireplace.

FRENCH DOOR, CASEMENT, OR WINDOW: Arrangement of two vertical side-hung windows, often multipaned, that reach to the floor and open like the halves of a double door.

FRESCO: A type of mural painting in which the colors are applied to the plaster while it is still wet and fresh.

GALLERY: Ornamental railing along the edge of a table, a shelf, or a serving tray. The term also describes a long hall that is hung with paintings.

GATE-LEG TABLE: Drop-leaf table popular in England and America during the seventeenth and early eighteenth centuries. The leaves are supported by a gate-type leg with stretcher that swings out from the center section.

GESSO: Finely ground plaster that is formed while wet into raised decorations on furniture, walls, or moldings, allowed to dry, and then gilded or painted.

*GIBBONS, GRINLING (1648–1720): A wood carver who became an associate of the architect Christopher Wen in the late seventeenth century. He created carved designs of fruit and festoons, and he was appointed Master Wood Carver to King George I in 1714.

GIMP: Flat decorative tape used as a finishing trim to conceal upholstery tacks or stitching in draperies.

GLAZE: The thin, transparent coating of glass fired on pottery, porcelain, and stoneware to give a hard, shiny, nonporous finish. Also, a liquid glaze applied to walls and furniture to produce a finish similar to that on china.

GLAZING: Hard finish with a softening influence on the color of the final coat of paint. Shellac or varnish with added color is applied as a thin wash, then wiped off, to subdue the base color.

GODDARD AND TOWNSEND: John Goddard and his son-in-law John Townsend, cabinetmakers of Newport, Rhode Island, during the latter half of the eighteenth century. Among their pieces are the distinctive block-front chest and desk and secretaries with shell carving.

GRASSCLOTH: A handsome wall covering of woven grass glued and stitched to a paper backing invented by the Chinese more than 2,000 years ago.

*GUÉRIDONS: A small French table from the Empire period, originally a holder for candelabra or decorative items. This occasional table was named after a Moorish galley slave whose likeness was used as a supporting pedestal for a table.

HADLEY CHEST: Early type of New England chest with a hinged top, short legs, and one, two, or three drawers.

HANDKERCHIEF TABLE: American drop-leaf table with a triangular top, like a handkerchief folded corner to corner. When the drop leaf is raised, the table becomes square.

HARD EDGE: A style of modern painting using strong contrasts of flat color without shading.

HARDWOOD: Generic term for the timber from any broad-leafed tree—such as oak, elm, chestnut, beech, birch, mahogany, walnut, or teak.

HIGH-RISER: A bed within a bed, similar to a studio couch, but different in that each of the mattresses, which are stored one under the other, is on separate springs. When the under-mattress and spring are pulled out, they raise to standard height.

HITCHCOCK CHAIR: Designed by Lambert Hitchcock, early nineteenth-century cabinetmaker and designer. His widely copied chair, based on a Sheraton original, has a broad pillow-back band, turned and splayed legs, and a rush or cane seat. It was usually painted and frequently stenciled.

HUNT TABLE: A crescent-shaped or long sideboard table with drop leaves to extend the serving surface, designed for hunt breakfasts. The distinguishing feature is the height, tall enough for everyone to stand around it comfortably.

HUTCH: Chest or cabinet on legs which supports an open-shelf deck.

IMARI: Style of decoration executed in blue, red, yellow, gold, and green on a white ground, originating on Japanese porcelain made solely for export.

IMPRESSIONISM: A nineteenth- and early twentieth-century school of painting in which visual impressions were expressed in broad, sweeping terms without minute detail or defined outline.

INLAY: A form of surface decoration in which one material—wood, metal, ivory, shell, or semi-precious stones—is set flush into the cutout surface of another.

*INTAGLIO: This form of printing is produced by incising lines or textured areas onto the copper zinc or onto other types of plates that hold the ink.

*INTARSIA: Designs inlaid in wood in many different colors and textures such as metal, ivory, shells, or stones.

JABOT: Valance heading, a pleated piece of fabric that hangs either over or under the swags or sides of the valance.

JALOUSIES: Shutters of wood or aluminum slats that adjust like Venetian blinds.

JAPANNING: A type of lacquerwork in which surfaces of wood or metal are coated with layers of varnish and then dried in heated ovens. May have high-relief, incised, or flat designs.

JARDINIÈRE: French term for a decorative wood, ceramic or metal container or stand for plants or flowers.

*JASPER: Wedgwood's fine stoneware, originally in the coloring of blue with white relief carvings, now in other colors.

JONES, INIGO (1573–1652): Leading English architect who studied in Italy and brought back the Palladian style.

KIDNEY SHAPE: The oval shape with concave front found on desks and dressing tables; a favored form of Sheraton's.

KLISMOS: The reclining chair of ancient Greece that inspired similar styles in the French Directoire and English Regency periods and in our own century.

KNIFE EDGE: The single-seam edge on a pillow or cushion. A box edge consists of a double-seam edge with space between.

KNOTTY PINE: Pine in which the knots are conspicuous. The fad for knotty-pine walls to simulate "Early American" is historically incorrect. Clear pine, free from knots, was originally used.

LACQUER: A laborious build-up of several layers of colored varnish on wood or metal objects, a process originated by the Chinese. The name is derived from the basic natural substance, a resin lac that becomes very hard when exposed to the air and polishes to a high, glossy finish. Lacquer has always been superior to paint both in color and in hard-wearing qualities. We have duplicated the colors—although not the patina—with synthetic lacquers.

LADDERBACK: A type of chair back with horizontal ladderlike slats, common in early American and provincial styles.

LAMBREQUIN: Shaped valance with fabric, bound or trimmed, which crowns a window, the top of a bed, or a chair back.

LAMINATES: A process in which thin layers of a given material are bonded to each other or to another material under great pressure. Plywood is a laminate, as are the plastics Formica and Micarta.

***LAMPAS:** A cloth of flowered silk, a damask-like design woven in many tones of one color on a different type of satin ground.

LAWSON SOFA: A completely upholstered sofa with a low, square back and flaring scroll arms.

LAYOUT: Interior designers' name for a plan or sketch of a room, showing furniture arrangement, color plan, and often swatches of fabrics and materials.

LIMOGES: Famous name in decorated porcelain, which has been made since the eighteenth century in the factory at Limoges, France.

LOGGIA: A room or area that extends on one side into an open arcade or roofed gallery projecting from the side of the house.

LOUNGE: Upholstered chaise with a headrest.

LOUVERS: Slatted system to control light and air at windows or doors. Louvers may be vertical or horizontal.

LUMINOUS CEILING: Installation of striplights behind translucent panels which diffuse shadow-free light.

MACRAMÉ: French word for the hand-knotted fringe in geometric designs introduced to Spain and the rest of Europe by the Turks.

MARQUETRY: Veneers inlaid with contrasting materials (wood, ivory), but retaining a flat surface.

McINTIRE, SAMUEL (1757–1811): American architect and wood carver from Salem, Massachusetts, famous for his mantelpieces and overdoors.

***MD. POMPADOUR:** The Marquise de Pompadour, the mistress of Louis XV of France, for whom he built the building Petite Trianon. She was instrumental in obtaining artisans who created many of the style highlights of this period.

MEISSEN: The first to make the true hard-paste porcelain at Dresden, Germany, in the early eighteenth century.

MERCERIZING: A chemical process that gives cotton fibers or fabrics body, strength, and greater ability to absorb dyes.

MITER: The joining of two pieces cut or beveled to fit together at right angles to form a corner.

MODERNE: Furniture style of the mid-1920s that was based on simplified Hepplewhite designs and stressed blond finishes, straight lines, tubular or strap metal frames, with wood grains and inlays to provide contrast. Exemplars of moderne were the architects and designers of the Bauhaus school.

MODULAR FURNITURE: Storage units based on standard modules, or sizes, that can be stacked vertically or grouped horizontally, and assembled in various combinations.

*MOIRÉ: A fabric with a wavy watermarked design, originated during the eighteenth century. Usually in silk, it is now available in other materials. The pattern is creased when it is pressed between cylinders engraved with the wavy line design.

MOLDED FURNITURE: Plywood, laminated woods or plastic molded into figure-conforming contours that, even when upholstered, reveal the underlying structure, an instance of form dictated by function rather than by precedent.

MOSAIC: Decorative inlay of small pieces of wood, marble, glass, semi-precious stones, and similar materials set in geometric or pictorial designs; a technique that dates back to the Romans.

MOUNTS: Metal fittings or decorations applied to furniture or objects.

NEEDLEPOINT: Cross-stitching done by hand on canvas, linen, or net with wool or silk threads which gives the look of tapestry.

NICHE: A wall recess for a statue or ornament.

ONION PATTERN: Popular blue-and-white pattern first produced at the Meissen factory around 1735.

OPALINE: Translucent glass that comes in lovely shades of blue, pink, green, and white.

*ORMOLU: Gilt, brass, or copper mounts for furniture; imitation gold originating in the eighteenth-century French pieces, used also during the English Regency.

PAD FOOT: Termination of a cabriole leg, generally in Queen Anne styles, that resembles a club foot, but without the disk at the bottom.

PALLADIAN WINDOW: A window design based on the work of Andrea Palladio. The window consists of three parts separated by columns, or pilasters; the outer sections have straight cornices, and the taller inner section is arched.

PALLADIO, ANDREA (1518–1580): Famous Italian architect who applied to houses his own interpretation of the classic orders and directly influenced much of the domestic architecture in England and America.

PANELING: Decorative detail on furniture, walls, doors, and ceilings consisting of a rectangular area enclosed in a frame and raised above or sunk below the surrounding surface.

PARQUET: Geometric shapes of wood inlaid, mosaic fashion, for flooring and for furniture.

PARSON'S TABLE: A square or rectangular table with apron and leg widths that measure the same.

PATINA: Mellowing of surface texture and color produced by age, wear, and rubbing.

PEACOCK CHAIR: Rattan chair from Hong Kong with a high, lacy fan back and a base that swells out like an hourglass.

PEDESTAL: A single—and singular—means of elevating chairs and tables without the support of legs.

PEDIMENT: An architectural triangle over a portico, window, door, or gable end of a house. Applies in furniture to the top of a cabinet or high piece.

PERIOD: Historical stretch of time when a certain style or influence prevailed in furnishings.

PEWTER: A dull-gray alloy of lead and tin.

PHYFE, DUNCAN (1768–1854): America's first great furniture designer whose name is synonymous with a style derived in part from the English and Fench design of the period.

PIECRUST TABLE: Descriptive name for a small, round eighteenth-century English table with a scalloped edge.

PIER GLASS: Tall Victorian wall mirror customarily hung between windows or in a narrow space over a low marble-topped console.

*PIETRA DURA: A design made by setting small pieces of marble or semiprecious stones into mortar and then usually buffing them to a high finish.

PILASTER: Half-round or rectangular columns used architecturally to decorate or divide a long wall surface or opening.

PILE: The surface of any fabric or carpet in which the ends of the fibers are upright rather than flat.

PIPING: A fabric-covered cord trim that finishes and disguises the seams of upholstery, slipcovers, draperies, and pillows.

PLINTH: Derived from architecture, this term describes a block of wood or stone employed as the base of a column or, decoratively, as a pedestal for sculpture.

POUF: Type of ottoman that is usually round and well upholstered.

PULLMAN KITCHEN: The straight line-up of minimum kitchen equipment that is set against the wall or in a shallow recess of a living area in a small house or apartment.

QUARRY TILE: Square or diamond-shaped unglazed paving tile or stone.

QUARTER ROUND: A molding with a quarter-circle profile.

QUATREFOIL: A decorative motif originating in Gothic architecture, art, and furniture composed of four circular arcs meeting at the cusps, suggestive of a four-leaf clover.

RABBET: In furniture, a step down on a wood section so that another piece may be snugly fitted in. A cabinet door is rabbeted to take a panel, or the side rails of beds to accommodate the box spring and mattress.

RÉCAMIER: French Empire chaise longue that resolves itself in a highly curved end.

REEDING: Raised parallel convex grooves carved to simulate a bunch of reeds; the reverse of concave fluting.

REFECTORY TABLE: Originally, a long, narrow table built close to the floor and supported by heavy stretchers. When this kind of table was later shortened and fitted underneath with pullout leaves, it became the first self-contained extension table.

RELIEF: A form of sculptured decoration in which the design is raised in relief from the flat surface.

RENDERING: Interior designer's hand-drawn illustration of proposed decoration of a room.

316 *RENT TABLE: This eighteenth-century design was the forerunner of

the filing cabinet. Designed in a round or octagon shape, this type of table has drawers that are marked alphabetically. Used by landlords when collecting the rent from tenants.

REPOUSSÉ: Decorative sheet-metal work. The design is projected in relief on the front through hammerings from the back.

RESTORATION: Term for furniture, china, rooms, or houses that have been restored to their original condition, with missing or damaged parts replaced or substitutions made.

REVEAL: The section between the face of a wall and the frame of a window or door.

RISER: The upright section of a step connecting the two treads.

ROMAN SHADE: A neat variation on the Austrian shade in which the folds of the flat fabric panel are horizontally accordion-pleated rather than being shirred in scallops.

RUNNER: Either the guide strip on the side or bottom of a drawer or the rocker of a rocking chair.

RUSH: Woven grass or reed, a traditional material for chair seats and backs.

SABER LEG: Simple tapered leg, curved like a scimitar, and found on furniture—mostly chairs—of the Empire, Biedermeier, and English Regency periods.

SANG DE BOEUF: French name (in translation, *oxblood*) for the Chinese porcelain glaze color developed during the K'ang Hsi period (1662–1722).

SAUSAGE TURNING: Simple lathe turning of repeated forms resembling a link of small sausages; similar to spool turning.

SAVONNERIE: French rug and tapestry factory that produced handwoven wool rugs with a high pile in pastel colors and floral and scroll patterns for eighteenth- and nineteenth-century houses and palaces.

SCAGLIOLA: Hard plaster surface embedded with small pieces of granite, marble, alabaster and other stones, and highly polished.

SCONCE: A wall bracket that is decorative and dispenses light.

SECTIONAL FURNITURE: Furniture made in units designed to fit together but also to function as single, separate pieces.

SELVAGE: The reinforced outer edges of a fabric; the plain vertical margins in wallpaper rolls or sheets.

SEMAINIER: A tall, narrow chest of drawers developed during the reign of Louis XV and so named because it contained seven drawers, one for each day of the week.

SERPENTINE FRONT: The sinuous shape of a commode, chest, or bureau that curves inward at the ends and outward at the center.

SETTEE: Long seat or bench with open arms and back, sometimes upholstered, sometimes caned.

SÈVRES: Porcelain from the factory established by Louis XV under the patronage of Mme. Pompadour, famous for its highly decorated and colorful glazed pieces.

SÈVRES BLUE: One of the first and most widely copied of the Sèvres enamel ground colors.

SHAKER (1776–1880): Simple, straightforward furniture, mainly of pine, maple, walnut, or fruitwoods, made by the Shakers, a self-sufficient religious sect that came to America from England in the late eighteenth century. The clean-lined functionalism of the Shaker style has sustained it in popularity.

317

SHIRRING: Fabric gathered or shirred on a rod, cord, or thread.

SHOJI: Japanese term for wood-framed translucent sliding panels used as room partitioning.

SIDEBOARD: Sixteenth-century serving table or board that developed through various ages and stages. Today's version seems to be reverting to the original, simple design of a shelf table sans storage space.

SINGERIE: Lively representation of monkeys.

SLAT-BACK CHAIR: A seventeenth-century English turned and carved chair with a high, open back crossed by three slats. It was the forerunner of the later American maple or pine slat or ladderback, which had as many as six slats and a rush seat.

SLEIGH BED: American version of the French Empire bed, named for the high, scrolled ends.

SLIPPER CHAIR: A low, luxurious little side chair or armchair, upholstered and skirted.

SOFFIT: The underside of a projecting cornice, beam, wide molding. Often a concealment for lighting.

SPADE FOOT: A tapering, quadrangular foot seen on Hepplewhite and Sheraton chairs and tables.

SPINDLE-BACK: Chair back in a series of slender, vertical, turned members, most often applied to Windsor chairs.

SPLAT: The central vertical member of a chair back.

SPOOL TURNING: A simple turning for table legs and bed and mirror frames that mushroomed in America during nineteenth century, after the invention of the power lathe. A continuous bulbous design resembling a vertical line of spools.

SPOON-BACK: A chair that is "spooned," or shaped, to complement the contour of the human body, specifically Queen Anne.

STENCILING: Surface decoration simply applied by brushing paint, stain or dye through the cutout openings of a paper pattern.

STERLING: Term for silver articles containing, by law, at least 92½ percent pure silver.

STIPPLING: A way of duplicating the rough texture of old plaster or stucco by rubbing a brush, piece of burlap, or crumpled paper on freshly plastered walls to simulate trowel marks.

STRETCHER: The horizontal support that braces and links the legs of chairs and tables.

STRIÉ: Woven fabric with streaks of different widths and lengths formed by varying tones in the warp thread.

SUITE: A complete set of matched furniture, at one time admirably conceived.

SWAG: A decoration representing hanging drapery, ribbons, or garlands of fruit and flowers.

TALLBOY: English name for the double chest (chest-on-chest) or the single chest on a stand. In America, it is called a highboy, from the French *haut bois* (high wood).

TAPESTRY: Originally, a hand-woven wool, linen or silk fabric, an all-purpose decorative material that has been used as a wall hanging or for upholstery.

TEA TABLE: A single table with pullout leaves to hold the tea service.

TEMPERA: A painting process in which powdered pigments are held together, or tempered, by egg yolks.

TEMPLET: A pattern or contour drawing for a decoration or object, of identical size and shape.

TENT CEILING: A trompe l'oeil re-creation in fabric or wallpaper of the peaked, draped top of a campaign tent, an effect much in vogue during the French Empire.

TERRA COTTA: A clay varying in color from light buff to deep red.

TÊTE-Á-TÊTE: A small loveseat for two or three, with seats facing in opposite directions.

TIFFANY GLASS: Fantastically colored iridescent glass produced by Louis Comfort Tiffany at the turn of the century.

*TOILE DE JOUY: A floral or scenic design usually printed on cotton or linen. Originally printed in Jouy, France, the fabrics were printed in single colors from engraved copper plates, the designs were characteristically classic scenic motifs of the French countryside.

*TOLE: Decorative objects made of tin with patterns of paint or enamel.

TONGUE AND GROOVE: A type of joint used for flooring, paneled walls and doors. A continuous narrow projection, or tongue, on one board fits into a rabbet or groove on another.

TORCHÈRE: A portable stand for lights, originally a stand to hold a great candelabrum in France.

TRESTLE TABLE: Early, primitive form of dining table composed of boards or planks laid across trestles, or horses, and removed when not in use.

TRICTRAC TABLE: Dual-purpose piece of seventh-century furniture.

TRIPOD TABLE: A pedestal table with three legs that flare out at the base.

TROMPE L'OEIL: In translation from the French, "to fool the eye," an ancient art form that makes things appear other than they are. Paint or paper can simulate dimension, architecture, or a view.

TRUMEAU: French combination mirror with a painting or carving over it.

TRUNDLE BED: Early, ingenious form of space-saving furniture, a low bed on casters designed to roll or trundle under a full-sized bed when it was not being used.

TUFTING: In upholstery, an indented surface pattern produced by sewing a series of self-covered buttons into the fabric. In fabrics, stitchery in rounds, squares or diamonds that form a puffed-up design.

TURKEY WORK: Handmade fabric that ingeniously imitated, in an inexpensive way, the appearance of Oriental pile rugs. To achieve the effect, worsted yarns were pulled through a coarse cloth, knotted and clipped.

TUXEDO SOFA: An American style of sofa with back and arms of the same height.

VALANCE: Shaped wood, stamped or pierced metal, or draped, gathered, or straight fabric used across the top of a drapery treatment or a canopied bed.

VENEER: A thin layer of decorative wood applied to solid wood to give it the face value of a fancy grain, or a similar facing of ivory, pearl, tortoise shell, or other decorative material.

VENETIAN BLIND: One of the earliest—and still one of the most effective—ways to control light at a window. Introduced from the East to Venice by Marco Polo. A simple construction of narrow or wide slats of wood, metal, or plastic strung on tapes or wires, the blinds can work either horizontally or vertically.

VENETIAN GLASS: Hand-blown Italian glassware noted for its delicacy, decoration and exquisite shapes.

VERMEIL: Gilded silver or bronze developed originally as a substitute for solid gold.

VITRINE: A combination display and storage piece for china and objets d'art. The French word describes a cabinet with glass doors and sometimes a glass top and sides as well.

VOLUTE: The three-dimensional spiral scroll of the Greek Ionic order, often found in furniture decoration and drawer pulls.

WAINSCOT: Geometrically designed wall paneling that stops short of the ceiling, sometimes terminated by a plate rail.

WEDGWOOD: One of the greatest of the English potteries. The name and the fame come from the eighteenth-century genius, Josiah Wedgwood. Fired by the discoveries at Pompeii and Herculaneum, Wedgwood took the forms of classical antiquity as his inspiration for pottery that in style and spirit echoed the interior designs and furniture of Robert Adam. Wedgwood's jasperware, with its beautiful ground colors and classical motifs, appeared not only in decorative objects but also as panels on walls and mantels and as plaques on Sheraton and Hepplewhite furniture.

WELSH DRESSER: A cabinet that begins as an enclosed storage piece, which is the base, and develops into a set-back upper part composed of open shelves.

WELTING: Lengths of cotton cord covered in matching or contrasting material sewed between upholstery and slipcover seams to give them strength and a more finished appearance.

WICKER: Generic term for an airy, woven furniture material of various natural or synthetic fibers like willow, reed, rattan, or twisted paper.

*WILLIAMSBURG RESTORATION: A total city restored to its original in Colonial Virginia, replica of 1699–1779. Included are many historic sites, a select group of furniture reproductions, accessories, and suitable examples of eighteenth-century craftsmanship.

WINDSOR CHAIR: Named for Windsor Castle in England and introduced during the reign of Queen Anne, Windsor chairs achieved their greatest prominence and most graceful styling in America from 1725 to 1800. The original chairs were made by wheelwrights who laced the bentwood back frames with spindles for support and pegged legs into saddle-shaped seats.

WING CHAIR: Sheltering side pieces, or "wings" add to the comfort of this large upholstered chair.

WORMY CHESTNUT: A strongly grained wood with multiple wormholes, real or simulated, showing on the surface.

ZEBRA WOOD: A highly decorative wood with bold reddish-brown stripes on a light-yellow ground, primarily used for inlays, bandings, and veneers.

ZIG-ZAG: The chevron or herringbone motif of Norman and Gothic architecture; a line of continuous V's.

The glossary is abridged from *Decorating Defined*, by Jose Wilson and Arthur Leaman, by permission of Simon & Schuster, Inc. Entries preceded by an asterisk (*) have been composed and interpolated by the author. [Ed. note]

Bibliography

BOOKS

Architecture

BLAKE, PETER, *Mies van der Rohe: Architecture and Structure*. Baltimore, Maryland: Penguin Books, 1964.

CAMESASCA, ETTORE, *History of the House*. Translated by Isabel Quigly. New York: G.P. Putnam's Sons, 1971.

GROPIUS, WALTER, *The New Architecture and the Bauhaus*. Newton Centre, Mass.: Charles T. Branford Company, 1959.

HEYER, PAUL, *Architects on Architecture: New Directions in America*. New York: Walker Publishing Co., 1966.

HORNUNG, WILLIAM J., *Architectural Drafting* (4th ed.). Englewood Cliffs, N.J.: Prentice-Hall, Inc., 1966.

PEHNT, WOLFGANG, ed., *Encyclopedia of Modern Architecture*. New York: Harry N. Abrams, 1964.

RICHARDS, JAMES MAUDE, *An Introduction to Modern Architecture*. London: Cassell and Co., 1961.

SCULLY, VINCENT JOSEPH, JR., *Modern Architecture: The Architecture of Democracy*. New York: George Braziller Co., 1967.

Space Planning

DREYFUSS, HENRY, *The Measure of Man*. New York: Whitney Library of Design, 1965.

HALL, EDWARD TWITCHELL, *The Hidden Dimension*. New York: Doubleday & Company, Inc., A Doubleday Anchor Book, 1969.

LIND, LOUISE T., *The Home You Love to Live In*. Cambridge, Mass.: Microglyphics, 1972.

PANERO, JULIUS, *Anatomy for Interior Designers* (3rd ed.), New York: Whitney Library of Design, 1962.

RAMSEY, CHARLES GEORGE, and H.R. SLEEPER, *Architectural Graphic Standards* (6th ed.). New York: John Wiley & Sons, Inc., 1970.

SOMMER, ROBERT, *Personal Space*. Englewood Cliffs, N.J.: Prentice-Hall, Inc., 1969.

Furniture and Design

ARONSON, JOSEPH, *Book of Furniture and Decoration: Period and Modern* (new rev. ed.). New York: Crown Publishers, 1941.

————, *Encyclopedia of Furniture*. New York: Crown Publishers, 1938.

D'ARCY, BARBARA, *Bloomingdale's Book of Home Decorating*. New York: Harper & Rowe, Publishers, 1973.

FAULKNER, RAY NELSON, and SARAH FAULKNER, *Inside Today's Home* (rev. ed.). New York: Holt, Rinehart & Winston, 1975.

FRIEDMANN, ARNOLD; JOHN F. PILE; and FORREST WILSON, *Interior Design* (rev. ed.). New York: Elsevier, 1976.

KORNFELD, ALBERT, *The Doubleday Book of Interior Decorating and Encyclopedia of Styles*. New York: Doubleday & Company, Inc., 1965.

WHITON, SHERRILL, *Interior Design and Decoration* (4th ed.). Philadelphia: J.B. Lippincott Company, 1974.

WILSON, JOSE, and ARTHUR LEAMAN, *Decorating Defined*. New York: Simon and Schuster, Inc., 1971.

Color

ALBERS, JOSEF, *The Interaction of Color*. New Haven, Conn.: Yale University Press, 1963.

BIRREN, FABER, *Color for Interiors*. New York: Whitney Library of Design, 1963.

————, *Creative Color*. New York: Reinhold Book Corp., 1961.

HALSE, ALBERT OTTO, *The Use of Color in Interiors*. New York: McGraw-Hill Book Company, 1968.

RAINWATER, CLARENCE, *Light and Color*. New York: Golden Press, 1971.

Lighting

ALLPHIN, WILLARD, *Primer of Lamps and Lighting* (3rd ed.). Reading, Mass.: Addison-Wesley Publishing Company, 1973.

ILLUMINATING ENGINEERING SOCIETY, *IES Lighting Handbook* (5th ed.). New York: Illuminating Engineering Society, 1972.

————, *Lighting Interior Living Spaces*. New York: Illuminating Engineering Society, 1969.

NUCKOLLS, JAMES L., *Interior Lighting for Environmental Designers*. A Wiley Interscience Publication. New York: John Wiley & Sons, 1976.

WILSON, FORREST, *Graphic Guide to Interior Design*. New York: Van Nostrand Reinhold Company, 1977.

Fabrics

HOLLEN, NORMA, and JANE SADDLER, *Textiles* (2nd ed.). New York: The Macmillan Company, 1964.

JOSEPH, MARJORY LOCKWOOD, *Introductory Textile Science* (2nd ed.). New York: Holt, Rinehart & Winston, 1972.

WINGATE, ISABEL, *Textile Fabrics and Their Selection* (6th ed.). Englewood Cliffs, N.J.: Prentice-Hall, Inc., 1970.

Rugs

THE CARPET AND RUG INSTITUTE, *The Carpet Specifier's Handbook* (1974 ed.). Dalton, Georgia: The Carpet and Rug Institute, 1974.

GREGORIAN, ARTHUR T., *Oriental Rugs and the Stories They Tell*. Boston: Nimrod Press, 1967.

LANDREAU, ANTHONY, *America Underfoot*. Washington, D.C.: Smithsonian Institution Press, 1976.

Art

GARDNER, HELEN, *Art Through the Ages* (6th ed.). New York: Harcourt, Brace, Jovanovich, Inc., 1975.

GOMBRICH, ERNST, *The Story of Art* (12th ed.). New York: E.P. Dutton Co., 1974.

JANSON, H.W., *History of Art*. Englewood Cliffs, N.J.: Prentice-Hall, Inc., New York: Harry N. Abrams, Inc.

PERIODICALS

Architectural Digest. Los Angeles: John C. Brasfield Publishing Corp.

The Designer. New York: H.D.C. Publication.

Interior Design. New York: Whitney Communications Corp., Magazine Division.

Interiors. New York: Billboard Publications, Inc.

Index

A general glossary of design terminology appears on pages 309–320; entries in that glossary are not separately indexed below. Specialized terminology lists are given on pages 182–186 (fabrics); 240–243 (carpets and rugs); and 261–263 (mirrors). A selected bibliography is on pages 321–323.

In the following index, references to black-and-white illustrations are given in **boldface** type. Color illustrations appear in a separate color section and are not individually indexed here.

Aalto, Alvar, 51, 103
Absorption of light, 139–140
Abstract designs, for rugs, 223
Abstract sculpture, 278
Accent lighting, 150–154
Accent pillows. See Pillows
Accent rugs. See Area rugs
Accessories, **56–57**, 87, 129, **200**, 230, 276–281, **278–281**; Georgian, 31; mirrored, 260, **260**
Accordion pleats, 199
Accreditation of interior designers, 303–306
Acetate, 172
Acrylic, 172; in carpets, 212, 218–219, 240; clear, in contemporary furniture, **109**; paints, 274; wood flooring, 249–250
Adam, Robert, 24, **25**, 30–31, **31**; influence of, on American Federal style, 40
Afghanistan, 231–232, 237
Afghanistan rugs, 236
African art, 278
Aging: of carpet, 219; of fabrics, 169
Agra rugs, 236
Alabaster, 89
Albers, (Josef), 51
Alpaca, 172
Alpujjara rugs, 238
Aluminum: in contemporary furniture, 48, 106, 114, **115**; as reflecting material, 140; in traditional furniture, 87
America: carpet industry in, 212; rug weaving in, 210, 239; wallpaper in, 188
American eagle, 40
American furniture, contemporary, 106–110, **107–109**
American Indian rugs, 238, 240
American Institute of Interior Designers (A.I.D.), 299–300, 303
American Oriental rugs, 241
American Society of Interior Designers (A.S.I.D.), 299–302
American style periods, 34–45, **34**; Colonial, 22, 35–37, 249; Early American, 22, 35–37; Federal, 35, 40–41, 230; Georgian, 35, 38–39,

American style periods (cont.)
38–39; Greek Revival, 35, 44; Victorian, 35, 44–45, **44**
Analogous color schemes, 127
Anatolian rugs, 236
Angora, 172
Aniline dyes: for alabaster, 89; in malachite finishes, 95
Aniline stains, 91, 100, **101**
Animal designs in Oriental rugs, 236
Animal prints in wallpaper, 190
Anne, Queen of England, 23, 28. See also Queen Anne style
Antiques, 280–281, **281**; primitive, 60
Antique settings, 230
Antiquing: of furniture, 92; of mirror, 259, 261; of paint, 195
Appalachia, 238
Appliqué, 277
Aquatint, 270
Arches, **294**; in American Federal style, 40; in English Norman style, 21; in English Tudor style, 21, 26; with mirrors, 259; in Romanesque style, 8
Architects, professional, 40. See also individual named architects; Contemporary furniture; Contemporary style
Architects, The, Collaborative, 51
Architectural changes, creating, 61–62
Architectural patterns in wallpaper, 190
Architecture: American Federal, 40; American Georgian, 38; American Greek Revival, 44; American Victorian, 45; classical, influence of, 10; contemporary, 48–53; Early American, 36; English Georgian, 30; English Tudor, 26; European, post-1900, 50–51; French Baroque, 12; French Empire, 19; French Neoclassic, 16; French Rococo, 14; and interior design, 46–47; mirrors used in, 255–256, 259; noted in planning, 1; organic, 48–50; Queen Anne, 28; Regency, 32; today, 53; of Windows on the World, 293–295
Area rugs, 129, 237–240; in Queen Anne style, 28

Arkwright, (Sir Richard), 210
Armchairs: American Victorian, **44;** contemporary, 110, **111;** Early American, **36;** French Baroque, **12;** French Empire (fauteuils), 18, **18;** French Neoclassic, 16; French Rococo (bergères), **14,** 15; polyurethane, 110, **111,** 113, **113;** Regency, **32**
Armenian rugs, 236
Arraiolo rugs, 238
Art, 264–275
Art Deco, 52, **293**
Art Nouveau, 48, 99–100, **99,** 188
Arts and Crafts Movement, 48, 98–99
Ash: in Early American style, 37; olive, 107; vinyl-covered, 252
Asia, central, 232
A.S.I.D. (American Society of Interior Designers), 299–302
Aubusson, France, 210
Aubusson rugs, 238; in American Greek Revival style, 44; in French Empire style, 19; in French Neoclassic style, 17; in French Rococo style, 15
Aubusson tapestries, 17
Auditorium Building, Chicago, 49
Austrian shades, 201, 203
Axminster, England, 210
Axminster carpet, 214–216
Axminster weave, 241
Azay-le-Rideau, Chateau de, 8

Bachtiari rugs, 232
Backing: of carpets, 213, 220, 241; of rugs, 227, 239, 241
Ballast, 136
Balloon shades, 203
Bamboo, 88, 129; tiles resembling, 247; on walls, 195; in window treatments, 201
Banquettes, **75,** 297
Barcelona chair, 51, 103
Bargello embroidery, 277

Barn room, 56–60, **58**, **59**
Barnsley, Ernest, 99
Barnsley, Sidney, 99
Baroque style, French, 8–9, 12–13, **12**; influence of, 45
Basket-weave patterns: in vinyl-covered flooring, 251; in wallpaper, 190
Baskin, Leonard, **271**
Bathrooms, **194**, 244, **258**
Batik, 175, 182, 277; in furniture finishing, 94
Bauhaus, The, 50–52, 86, 101–102, **102**, 110, 188
Beams, 61; in barn room, **58–59**, 59
Bedrooms, **165**, **200**, **202**, 256–257; American Georgian, **38–39**. See also Color plate section
Beds: day, Philadelphia Chippendale, **34**; four-poster, American, **34**, 37; French Empire, 18; sleigh, Regency, **32**; trundle, Early American, 37
Bed-sitting room, **293**
Beechwood, 98, 100, **101**; in Early American style, 37; Thonet's use of, 47; in traditional furniture, 85–86
Belgium, 99, 166
Bellini, Mario, 110, 113–114, **114**
Belouchistan, 232
Belouchistan rugs, 236
Belter, John Henry, 45
Bentwood, 47–48, 51, 86, 98
Bergamo rugs, **233**
Bergère. See Armchair, French Rococo
Beveled mirrors, 262, 297
Bibikebad rugs, 235
Bidjar rugs, 235
Bigelow, Erastus, 210
Birch, white: in contemporary furniture, 103; in furniture, 51
Bleaching of fabric, 168, 180
Blinds, 204–207. See also Vertical blinds
Block-printed wallpaper, 187–188
Block-printing, 167, **167**; of floor coverings, 210
Blois, Chateau de, 8
Board-and-batten wall treatment, **58**, 59
Bobbins, 166
Bogardus, James, 48
Boiserie. See Paneling, gilded
Bookcase, breakfront, Hepplewhite, **30**
Bookcases, lighting of, 151–152
Border designs in wallpaper, 190
Borders in area rugs, 238
Boston, Mass., 38, 40, 45, 49
Boucher, (François), 10
Boukara rugs, 232, 236
Box pleats, 198, 200
Braided rugs, 39, 210, 238
Brass, 129, 297; antique, 280; in Chippendale furniture, 29; poles, 200; in traditional furniture, **83**, 86
Breakfront bookcase, Hepplewhite, **30**
Breuer, Marcel, 47, 51, 86, 102–104, **102**, 110
Brewster, Sir David, 121
Brick, 61; in contemporary architecture, 49, 53; floors, 129, 230; herringbone-patterned, 59, 129; houses, English Tudor, 21; with mirrors, 259; patterns in acrylic wood flooring, 250; tiles shaped like, 247, **247**, 249; walls, 59, 195. See also Carpets
Broadloom, 241. See also Carpets
Brocade, 182; in American Georgian style, 39; in English Georgian style, 29; in French Neoclassic style, 17; in French Rococo style, 15; in Queen Anne style, 28
Bromley-by-Bow, England, 22
Bronze: in sculpture, **278**; in traditional furniture, 87
Brussels, 210
Bulfinch, Charles, 35, 40
Burl, wood, 107, 109
Burnishing, 95

Cabinetmakers: John Henry Belter, 45; Thomas Chippendale, 29; Dutch, under William and Mary, 23; Duncan Phyfe, 40
Cabinets: French Neoclassic, 17; Victorian, **33**
California, University of, at Berkeley, 53
California School, 53
Camel, 172
Candlepower, 138
Candle stands, 37
Cane, 88, **102**, **205**; pattern in ceramic tile, **194**
Cantilever chair, 103
Canton lacquer, **93**, 94

Canvas: in contemporary furniture, 102; floor coverings, 210; backing for rugs, 239
Care of fabrics, 172–173
Carpenter Hall, Cambridge, Mass., 52
Carpets, **165**, **200**, **202**, **205**, 210, **211**, 212–222, **212–218**, 241, **292**; terminology of, 240–243; in Windows on the World, 294, 297. See also Oriental rugs; Rugs
Carriage seat, **58**, 59
Cartridge pleats, 198
Cartwright, (Edmund), 210
Carved furniture: Chippendale, 24, 29; English Gothic, 21
Carved textures: in carpets, 215; in rugs, 227
Carving: Grinling Gibbons, 23, 28; linenfold, 21
Caryatids, 18, 19
Cashmere, 172
Cast iron in traditional furniture, 86
Cathedrals, Gothic, 21
Caucasian rugs, 236
Caucasus, 231–232
Cedar in Early American style, 37
Ceiling, reflective, plan, 156–157, 286
Ceiling beams, English Tudor, 26
Ceilings, 61–63; fabric-draped, 62, 163; in French Gothic style, 8; in French Neoclassic style, 16; high, 192, **258**, 294; low, 192, 256, 294–295; lowered, 62, 64, **64**; mirrored, 62, 255, 256, **256**, 258, 294; wallpapered, 56, **56–57**, 62, 128. See also American Georgian style; Early American style; French Baroque and Rococo styles; Late Georgian style
Center for Advanced Study in Behavioral Science, Calif., 53
Ceramic beads, incorporated in weavings, 277
Ceramic tiles, 129, 244–249; on floors, 128, 230; mosaic, 245, **246**; on walls, **194**, 195
Ceramics, 129, 278–279, **279**; in traditional furniture, 89
Chairs: American Georgian, 38–39, **39**; Barcelona, 51, 103; Bentwood, 47–48, 51; bergère, **56–57**; cantilever, 103; Chippendale, 29, **29**, **39**; contemporary upholstered, 111–114, **111–114**; ladderback, Early American, **36**, 37; Late Georgian, 31, **31**; lattice-back, **99**; lyre-back, 40; mirrored, 260; Newport Chippendale, **34**; red/blue, 100, **101**; Saarinen, 106, **107**; Sheraton, **31**; side, Newport Chippendale, **34**; splat-back, Queen Anne, 23, **28**; Thonet, 98; tubular steel, 51, **102**; Tugendhat, **103**; turned, Early American, 37; wainscot, Early American, 37; Wassily, 102; Hans Wegner, **105**; wing, Newport type, **60**; wing, Queen Anne, **39**; wood, Scandinavian, **105**; "zig-zag," **100**. See also Armchairs; Upholstered furniture; Upholstery
Chaise longue: contemporary, 112; in French Rococo style, 15; Le Corbusier, 104
Chambord, Chateau de, 8
Chandeliers, 259, 297
Charcoal drawings, 275
Charles I of England, 22; II of England, 22–23; VIII of France, 8; IX of France, 9
Charleston, South Carolina, 35
Chartres Cathedral, 8
Cherry wood: in American Federal style, 35; in Early American style, 37; in traditional furniture, 85; vinyl-covered, 251
Chest of drawers, Rhode Island Chippendale, **60**
Chests: Early American, 37; Italian, **229**; mirrored, 260
Chicago, Ill., 49
Chi'en Lung rugs, 236
Children's room, **192**, **205**
China, wallpaper in, 187
Chinese influence: on Chippendale furniture, 24, 29; on French Rococo style, 14; on Middle Georgian style, 29; on William and Mary style, 23
Chinese lacquer, 92–94
Chinese porcelain, 89
Chinese rugs, 232, 236; in Middle Georgian style, 29
Chinoiserie, 93; in Chippendale furniture, 29; in wallpaper, 190
Chintz, 170, **177**, 182; in American Georgian style, 39; in Queen Anne style, 28
Chippendale, Thomas, 23–24, 29; style, American, **34**, **60**; copied in America, 35; influence of, on American Georgian style, 38
Chiswick House, England, 23
Chlorofibers, 173
Chroma (intensity) of color, 121–124, **124**, 127–128

Chrome, 129; in furniture, 112, **112**, 230; on walls, 195
Chrysler Building, N.Y., 52
Circulation patterns, 71–72
Classical influence: in American Federal style, 35, 40; in French Baroque style, 12; in French Empire style, 18–19; in French Neoclassic style, 16; in Late Georgian style, 24, 30
Clay, in sculpture, 278
Cleaning of fabrics, 172–173, 181
Cloth. See Fabric
Coffee tables. See Tables, coffee
Cole, Henry, 99
Collage, 275; fabric, 277; on walls, 195
Collagraph, **266–269**, 270
Collections: of antiques, 60, 280–281; of art, 264
Colonial style, American. See Early American style
Color, 117–130; effect of, on apparent size of room, 123–125; of electric light, 135–137; in fabrics, 163; with mirrors, 255, 259; physics of, 119; psychological effects of, 120, 122; in Windows on the World, 294. See also Color plate section
Colors: in American Federal style, 45; in American Georgian style, 39; in American Greek Revival style, 44; in American Victorian style, 45; of area rugs, 237–240; of carpets, 214–217, 220–221; in ceramics, 278; of ceramic tile, 245, 247, 249; in contemporary style, 230; cool, 134, 192–193; in Early American style, 37; in English Tudor style, 26; in French Baroque style, 13; in French Empire style, 19; in French Neoclassic style, 17; in French Rococo style, 15; in Late Georgian style, 31; of Oriental rugs, 229–230, 232, 235–237; planning of, 286; in printing fabric, 169; in printmaking, 270, 272; in Queen Anne style, 28; in Regency style, 32; of rugs, 223, 227, 229; in Victorian style, 33; warm, 128, 134, 192–193; in weavings, 277. See also Color plate section
Color schemes, 126–130; blended by wallpaper, 188. See also Color plate section
Colorways, 165, 169, 182
Columns: in American Federal style, 40; in American Greek Revival style, 44; in American Victorian style, 35; in English Tudor style, 26; in French Empire style, 19; in Late Georgian style, 30; in Le Corbusier designs, 52; with mirrors, 259; in Regency style, 32
Commode, French Rococo, **15**
Comparative furniture styles, table of, 42–43
Complementary color schemes, 127–129
Concrete, use of, in contemporary architecture, 50
Console tables: American Federal, 40; Late Georgian, 31
Constantinople, 231
Contemporary furniture, **63**, 98–116, **99–105**, **107–109**, **111–115**, **189**
Contemporary patterns in Wallpaper, 190
Contemporary settings, 238, 240, 246, 249
Contemporary style, 46–53, 230, 247
Contrast: of fabric textures, 163; in light values, 140; in room design, **125**, 126–127
Contrasting color schemes, 127–129
Conventional rugs, Oriental, 234–235, 237
Copenhagen, 105
Copper, 129; engraving of, plate, 268; in upholstery, 96; on walls, 195
Corbusier. See Le Corbusier
Cordelan, 179
Cork, walls covered with, 195
Cornices, 201; in American Victorian style, **44**
Coromandel, 94
Cotton, 172; area rugs, 237–240; in carpet, 220; for floor coverings, 210; in rugs, 223, 227
Cotton fabric: in American Georgian style, 39; in French Neoclassic style, 17; in French Rococo style, 15; printed, **175**, **177**, 179; in traditional upholstery, 96
Counter-tops, 59, **59**, 163, 245; tiled, 249
Country look, 54–60, **56–59**, **189**, **204**, 230
Country print patterns in wallpaper, 190
Crewel embroidery, 182, 196; in Queen Anne style, 28
Crewel patterns in wallpaper, 190
Cromwell, Oliver, 22
Cromwell, Richard, 22
Crystal Palace, London, 25
Cupboards, Early American, 37
Curtains, 202. See also Window treatments
Curved line: in French Rococo style, 14–15; in Queen Anne style, 23, 28
Custom-made rugs, 223–229, **224–228**

Custom-tufted carpet, 213
Cut length of drapery fabric, 207
Cut-pile carpet, 214, 241

Dacron, 173; fiberfill, 112–114, **112**; foam, 97, 110–113, **111–113**, 195; wall upholstered with, **165**
Daghestan rugs, 236
Damask, 183; in American Georgian style, 39; in American Victorian style, **44**; draperies, 196; in French Baroque style, 13; in French Empire style, 19; in French Neoclassic style, 17; in French Rococo style, 15; in Late Georgian style, 31; in Middle Georgian style, 29; patterns, in wallpaper, 190; in Queen Anne style, 28
Daylight, 154, 297. See also Light, natural
Declaration of Independence, 40
Decorative lamps, 135
Deniers of yarns, 212, 217
Denmark, 105
Densities: of carpets, 214, 216–217, 241; of rugs, 223, 241
Designers, professional. See Professional designers
Desks: contemporary, **108**; writing, French Baroque, **13**
Dessau, Germany, 51
De Stijl, 50, 52, 100–102, **100**, 104
Dhurrie rugs, 238
Diamond tie in upholstery, 96
Dimmers for lighting, 154, 264
Dining area, **189, 194**; lighting of, 153, **156**
Dining room, **205, 229, 247**, 294, 297. See also Color plate section
Dining tables. See Tables, dining
Directoire style, French, 10, **82**; influence of on American Federal style, 35; influence of on Regency style, 25
Distressing of furniture, 92
Documentary patterns in wallpaper, **174–177**, 188
Doors, sliding glass, 60
Double-complementary color schemes, 127
Down, 97, 114
Downlights, 148
Draperies, 196–202; in French Empire style, 19; lighting of, 152; patterned, 129; terminology of, 207–208
Draw draperies, 201
Drawings, 264, 273–275, **275**
Dressers, mirrored, 260
Dry cleaning. See Cleaning
Drypoint, 270
Durability: of carpets, 212–213, 215–216, **217–218**, 218–219; of floors, 244–246, 249–251; of furniture, 85–90; of rugs, 227, 230, 237–240; of upholstery, 96–97
Dutch metal, 95
Dyeing: of carpets, 212, 219–221, 241; of fabrics, 169, 183; of rugs, 227, 229, 241. See also Aniline dyes

Eagle, American, 40
Eames, Charles, 106
Early American settings, 239
Early American style, 22, 35–37; floor coverings in, 210
Early Georgian style. See Georgian style, early
Early Renaissance style. See Renaissance style, early
Earth materials in traditional furniture, 89–90
Ebony furniture, French Empire, 18
Education of interior designers, 300–306
Edward VI of England, 21
Egypt, 244; floor coverings in, 210; furniture in, 87; influence of, on Regency style, 25; mirrors in, 255
Electrical outlets, 72, 156–159
Electrical wiring, 72, 154–156
Electric light. See Light, artificial; Lighting
Elizabeth I, Queen of England, 22, 188
Elizabethan style, English, 22
Elm wood, 107
Embossed carpet, 213, 242
Embossed textures in wallpaper, 190
Embroidered fabrics in American Victorian style, 45. See also Crewel embroidery

Embroidered rugs, 238–239
Embroidery, 276–277
Empire style, American, 40, 44
Empire style, French, 11, 18–19; influence of, on American Federal style, 35, **41**; influence of, on American Greek Revival style, 44; influence of, on Regency style, 25
Enamel: use of, in aquatints, 270; on boxes, 280; on traditional furniture, 92
Encaustic, 90
England, 20–33, 42–43, 210; wallpaper in, 188
English fabric pattern, **177**
English rugs, 239
English style periods, 20–33, 42–43, Late Georgian, 24, **25**, 30–31, **30–31**; Middle Georgian (Chippendale), 24, 29, **29**; Queen Anne, 23, 28, **28**; Regency, 25, 32, **32**; Renaissance, influence of, on American Georgian style, 38; Tudor, 21, 26, **27**; Victorian, 25, 33, **33**
Engraving, 259, 268; of mirrors, 262; of wood, 270
Enjelus rugs, 235
Entire room area lighting, 148–150, **149**
Equipment needs, allowing for, in planning, 72
Eskimo art, 278
Etching, 268
Etruscan alabaster, 89
Etruscan furniture, 87
European architecture, post-1900, 50–51
Exhibition Pavilion, Barcelona, 51

Fabric arts, 276–277
Fabrics, 163–186, **200**; in American Federal style, 41, **41**; in American Georgian style, 39; in American Greek Revival style, 44; in American Victorian style, 45; draperies, 196; in Early American style, 37; in English Tudor style, 26; fibers in, 170, 172–173, 179–180; finishing processes for, 180–181; in French Baroque style, 13; in French Empire style, 19; in French Neoclassic style, 17; in French Rococo style, 15; gathered, 163; in Late Georgian style, 31; making of, 164–170; in Middle Georgian style, 29; paper-backed, 163; patterned, 129, 174–179, **175–179**; planning of, 286; printed, 165, 167–170, **167–168**, 174–179, **175–179**; in Queen Anne style, 28; quilted, 163, **165**; shirred, 163; in Regency style, 32; terminology of, 182–186; in Victorian style, 33; on walls, 61, 193, 195; weaves, 170, **171**, 174; wet-look, 129; William Morris, 48; use of, in window treatments, 196–208; in Windows on the World, 297. See also Color plate section
Face weights, carpet, 214
"Falling Water," 50
Family rooms, **217**, 248. See also Barn room
Fanlight, 204
Farnsworth House, Plano, Ill., 51
Fauteuil. See Armchair, French Empire
Federal style, American, 35, 40–41, 230
Feininger, (Lyonel), 51
Felt, 195
Fereghan rugs, 235–236
Fiberglass, 173, 183, **204**
Fibers, 183; carpet, 218–220; fabric, 170, 172–173, 179–180; flame-retardant, 179; synthetic, 170, 172–173, 179, 183, 185, 216, **217**, 220, 237. See also Carpets, terminology of
Fieldstone, **58**, 59
Filling (weft) in fabric weaves, 170, **171**, 174, 183
Fireplaces, **58**, 59, 61, 65; in Early American style, 36; in English Tudor style, 21, 26; hoods for, 8, 55, **56–57**; lighting of, 152. See also Mantels
Finishes: for fabric, 180–181; for traditional furniture, 91–95
Finishing of fabrics, 169, 183
Fixtures, lighting, 142–144, **144**. See also Lighting
Flagstone, 26
Flameproof finishes, 180
Flame-resistance of carpets, 212
Flame-retardant fibers, 179–180
Flamestitch, **176**, 277
Flat-bed printing of fabric, 169
Flat-top draperies, 199
Flax, 166
Flemish influence in French style, 9
Flocking of wallpaper, 188, 190
Flokati rugs, 239

Floor coverings, 209–252; carpets as, 212–222, 240–243; ceramic tile as, 244–249; patterned, 129; rugs as, 223–240, 240–243; vinyl-covered wood as, 249–251. See also Carpets; Ceramic tile; Oriental rugs; Rugs; Color plate section
Floor plans, 72–81, **73–74**, **76–77**, 286, **289**; for Windows on the World, **294**, **296**
Floors: in American Federal style, **34**, 41; in American Georgian style, 39; in American Greek Revival style, 44; in American Victorian style, 45; brick, 8, 129; ceramic tiled, 8, 128, 245–249, **246–248**; in Early American style, 37; in English Tudor style, 26; in French Baroque style, 13; in French Empire style, 19; in French Neoclassic style, 17; in French Rococo style, 15; in Late Georgian style, 31; in Middle Georgian style, 29; mirrored, 255, 294; parquet, 13; in Queen Anne style, 28; stone, 8, 13; in Victorian style, 33. See also Color plate section
Floral patterns in rugs, 223, **226**, 238–240; in wallpaper, 190, **191**
Floral rugs, Oriental, 232, 234–237, **234**
Flowers as decorative theme, 294
Fluorescent lamps, 133, 136–137
Foam. See Dacron; Polyurethane; Rubber; Urethane
Foliage, 129
Folk rugs, 210
Fontaine, Pierre Francois Leonard, 11, 18
Fontainebleau, Chateau de, 8
Footcandles, 134, 138, 141–142, 145, 157
Footlamberts, 139
Forged iron in traditional furniture, 86
"Form follows function," 49, 71
Formal look, 60, **60**
Foundation for Interior Design Education Research (F.I.D.E.R.), 300, 302–304
Fox-edge, 96
Fragonard, (Jean-Honoré), 10
Frames: for drawings, 275; fabric, for pictures, 163, **165**; for mirrors, 260, 262; for needlepoint, 277; use of, in printmaking, 272
Framing projector fixtures, 297
France, 8–19, 42–43, 210, 238–240; concept of space in, 70; wallpaper in, 187
Francis I of France, 8; II of France, 9
Free-form designs in rugs, 223
French pleats, 198
French style, 8–19, 42–43; Baroque, 12–13, **12–13**; country, 55–56, **56–57**; Empire, 18–19, **18–19**; formal, 230; Neoclassic, 16–17, **16–17**; Provincial, 10, 247, 249; Rococo, 14–15, **14–15**
Frescoes, 90, 195
Fretwork in Chippendale furniture, 29
Frieze patterns in wallpaper, 190
Frieze textured carpets, 214
Fringes, **178**; on area rugs, 238; on Oriental rugs, **233**; on tapestries, 277; on draperies, in French Empire style, 19
Fruitwood, 10, 15
Fullness of drapery, 197, 208
Function: allied to form, 47; "form follows," 49, 71; in Le Corbusier style, 104; of space, in planning, 3, 69, 71, 293–295
Furniture: American Federal, 40, **41**; American Georgian, 38; American Greek Revival, 44; American Victorian, 45; antique, 280; arrangement of, 264; carved, 22; contemporary, 98–116; Early American, 37; English Tudor, 26; French Baroque, **12–13**, 13; French Empire, 18; French Neoclassic, 17; French Rococo, 15; Late Georgian, 31; layout of, **289**, **290**; Middle Georgian, 29; mirrored, 255, **257**, 260, **260**, **280**; molded, 106; Queen Anne, 28; Regency, 32; sizes of, 80; styles, comparative, 42–43; templates, 75, **76–77**; traditional, 82–97; tubular steel, 47–48; Victorian, 33; William Morris, 48. See also Armchairs; Beds; Chairs; Chippendale; Contemporary furniture; Sofas; Tables

Gage Building, Chicago, 49
General lighting, 141–142
General-use lamps, 135
Geometric patterns: in contemporary settings, 230; in rugs, 223, **224**, 238–239; in wallpaper, 190; in weavings, 277
Geometric rugs, Oriental, 232, **233**, 236
George I of England, 23; II of England, 23–24, 29; III of England, 24–25, 20–30; IV of England, 25
Georgian style, American, 35, 38–39, **38–39**

Georgian style, English, **60**; copied in America, 35; Early, 23; influence of, on American Georgian style, 38; Late, 24, 30–31; Middle (Chippendale), 24, 29
Germany, 50; concept of space in, 70
Ghendje rugs, 236
Ghiordes rugs, 236
Gibbons, Grinling, 23, 28
Gilded furniture: Chippendale, 29; French Baroque, 12–13; French Empire, 18; French Neoclassic, 17; Late Georgian, 31; Victorian, 33
Glare, 140, 207
Glass, 140, 207; antique, 280; beads, in weavings, 277; in contemporary architecture, 52–53; in contemporary design, 48–49; in contemporary furniture, 107, **206**; doors, sliding, 60; fiber, 173; in traditional furniture, 90; walls, 60, 230
Glaze: of ceramic tiles, 244–249; of paint, 195; in pottery, 278
Gold leaf: with lacquer, 93–94, **93**; on walls, 195
Gold in traditional furniture, 95
Gothic Revival: in England, 188; in Victorian style, 25
Gothic style: English, 21, 26, 196; French, 8–9; influence of, on American Federal style, 40; influence of, on American Victorian style, 45; used by Thomas Chippendale, 24, 29
Government regulations, 301, 303
Grained finish on walls, 195
Graphics, 264, **266–269**, 267–273, **271–272**
Grasscloth, 195, **292**; textures, in wallpaper, 190
Gray goods. See Greige goods
Grecian influence: on American Federal style, 40; on American Greek Revival style, 44; on American Victorian style, 25; on French Empire style, 11, 18–19; on Regency style, 25, 32
Greece, 239
Greek Revival style, American, 35, 44
"Green Room," William Morris's, 48
Gregorian, Arthur T., 231
Gregorian, Joyce Ballou, 229–232
Greige goods, 180, 184, 220–221
Grimson, Ernest, 99
Gropius, Walter, 51, 101–102
Guéridons. See Tables, marble-topped
Guggenheim Museum, New York, 50

Hackling, 166
Halogen lamps, 135
Hamadan rugs, 235–236
Hampton Court Palace, 21, 23
Hand-made rugs, 210–211, **224**, 237–240. See also Oriental rugs
Hansen, Johannes, 105
Hansen, Paul, 105
Harvard University, 51
Heal, Sir Ambrose, 99
Hems, drapery, 197, 202, 207–208
Henry VII of England, 21; VIII of England, 21, 26; II of France, 9; III of France, 9; IV of France, 9, 210
Hepplewhite, George, 24, 30–31; breakfront bookcase by, **31**; influence of, on American Federal style, 40; influence of, on American Georgian style, 38; style of, copied in America, 35
Herati rugs, 235, **235**
Herculaneum, excavations at, 10, 14, 16
Herringbone patterns: in acrylic wood flooring, 250, **251**; in brick, 59, 129; in vinyl-covered flooring, 251
Highboys: American Georgian, 38, **38**; Early American, 37; Queen Anne, 28
High-intensity discharge lamps (HIDs), 137–138
Hoban, (James), 35
Holland, wallpaper in, 187
Holland House, London, 22
Hoods, fireplace: in French country look, 55, **56–57**; in French Gothic style, 8
Hooked rugs, 210, 239
Horizontal blinds, 201
Houses, English Tudor, 26
Houston City Hall, Houston, Texas, 52
Hue of colors, 121–124, **122–124**, 126–129. See also Color plate section
Hungary, 239

Illinois Institute of Technology, 51
Illumination. See Light; Lighting

Immediate area lighting, 147–148
Imperial Hotel, Tokyo, 50
Incandescent Lamps, 133–136
India, 231, 236
Indian, American. See American Indian
Indian rugs, 236
Indirect lighting, 142, 148–153
Industrial Revolution, 33, 45–47, 86; in America, 40
Inlaid furniture: French Empire, 18; traditional, 95; Victorian, 33
Inlaid marble, 89–90
Inlaid wood, **83**
Installation of mirrors, 261
Insulating finishes, 180
Intaglio printing, 188, **266–269**, 268, 270
Intarsia, 89
Intensity (chroma) of color, 121–124, **124**, 127–128
Interior Design Educators Council (I.D.E.C.), 300, 303, 305
Interior designers. See Professional interior designers
International Style, 51, 53, 103–104
Iran (Persia), 231, 235, 237. See also Persia
Ireland, 227
Iron in traditional furniture, 86
Isfahan, 232, 234; rugs, 234, **234**, 236
Italian contemporary furniture, 110–115, **111–115**
Italian influence: on English Renaissance style, 21; on English Tudor style, 26; on French style, 8–9
Italy, 239, 277; mirrors in, 255
Ivory: inlaid, 95; in sculpture, 278

Jacobean style, English, 22; influence of, on Early American style, 37
Jacquard, (Joseph Marie), 210; design, 184; pattern, 215, 242; weave, 174
James I of England, 22, 36; II of England, 23
Japan, concept of space in, 70
Japanese lacquer, 92
Japanese style, influence of, on Frank Lloyd Wright, 50
Japanning, 94
Jeanneret-Gris, Charles Edouard. See Le Corbusier
Jefferson, Thomas, 40
Johnson Wax Tower, Racine, Wisc., 50
Jones, Inigo, 22
Jones, Owen, 99
Juhl, Finn, 105
Jute, 242; in carpet, 220; in upholstery, 96–97

Kandahar rugs, 235
Kandinsky, (Wassily), 51
K'ang Hsi rugs, 236
Kashmir, 236
Kauffman, Angelica, 30–31
Kazak rugs, 232
Kazvin rugs, 234
Kelim rugs, **228**, 238–239
Keshan rugs, 234
Kidderminster, England, 210
Kilim. See Kelim
Kiln, use of, in pottery, 278–279
Kiln drying of wood, 86, **100**
King, Rufus, House, Albany, N.Y., 35
Kirman rugs, **60**, 234–235
Kirmanshah rugs, 236
Kitchens, **204**, 244
Klee, (Paul), 51
Kline, Franz, **273**
Klint, Kaare, 105
Knitted carpet, 216, 220
Koufman House, Bear Run, Pa. ("Falling Water"), 50
Kraftcord, use of, in carpet, 220
Kronish House, Calif., 53
Kuba rugs, 236

Lacque de Chine, 93–94
Lacque gravée, 93–94
Lacquer: on contemporary furniture, 100, **101**; in French Neoclassic style, 17; in French Rococo style, 15; on metal furniture, 87–88; in Queen Anne style, 28; on traditional furniture, 92–94, **93**; on walls, 195

Lacquered furniture, 129
Lahore, India, 236
Lake Shore Apartments, Chicago, 51
Lambrequins, 201
Laminated fabric, 163
Laminated shades, 201, **202**, 203
Lampas, 184; in French Empire style, 19
Lamps: mirrored, 260, **260**; portable, 147, **147**. See also Light; Lighting
Larking Building (Buffalo), 49
Late Georgian style, English, 24, 30–31, **30–31**
Late Renaissance style: English, 24; French, 9
Lattice-back chair, **99**
Lattice patterns in wallpaper, 190
Laundering. See washing
Leather, 129, 184; coffee-table covered with, 293; in contemporary furniture, 107; on door, 109; in Middle Georgian style, 29; in traditional furniture, 90–91, **91**; upholstery, **58**, 59, 63, **64**, **103**, **206**, **292**; wallcoverings, 187, 195; on windows, 196
Le Corbusier (Charles Edouard Jeanneret-Gris), 47, 52, 104, **104**, 110
"Less is more," 51, 103
Libraries, **211**, 230, **292**
Light, 119, 131–159; artificial, 119, 134–159; control of, 140; cool, 119–120; natural, 132–134, 154; warm, 119–120. See also Daylight; Sunlight
Lighting, 72, 131–159, **257**, 259, 264, **265–266**; accent, 150–153; classification of, types, 141–142; fixtures used in, 142, **144**, 147–149, **206**, 260, 264, **265–266**, 297; lamp types used in, 134–138; plans, 62–63, 71, 81, 154–159, **155–156**, 286, 291; symbols, 144, 157–159, **158–159**; in Windows on the World, 297
Light meter, 139–140
Line preparing, 166
Linen, 166, 172; in American Georgian style, 39; in area rugs, 238; in carpet, 214; in draperies, 196; as floor covering, 210
Linenfold. See Carving, linenfold; Paneling, linenfold
Linocuts, 270–271, **271**
Lithography, 272, **272**
Living rooms, **201**, 203–204, **206**, 213, 264–266. See also Color plate section
Local lighting, 142, 150–153
London, 48
Looms, 166, 184; carpet, 214–216; rug, 210, 238; for weavings, 276–277
Looped pile, in carpet, 210, 214, 216, 242
Lost wax technique (batik), 94, 277
Louis XII of France, 8; XIII of France, 8
Louis XIV of France, 9–10; influence of, on William and Mary style, 23; style, 12–13
Louis XV of France, 9–10, 14–17; style, copied in Victorian style, 33
Louis XVI of France, 10; style, **13**, 16–17
Louvers, 204
Louvre, Palace of the, 9, 18, 210; influence of, on American Victorian style, 45
Lowboys: American Georgian, 38; Newport Queen Anne, **34**; Queen Anne, 28
Lucite panels for walls, 195
Lumens, 138
Luminaries as decorative accents, 153. See also Light; Lighting
Luminous panels, 152–153

Machine-made carpets, 210–211
Machine-made materials, 47
Machine-made wallpapers, 188
Machine manufacture in French Restoration style, 11
"Machine to live in," 52, 104
McIntire, Samuel, 35, 40
Mackintosh, Charles Rennie, 99–100, **99**
Macramé, 204, 276–277
Magistretti, Vico, 113, **113**
Mahogany: Age of, in English style, 20, 29; in American Chippendale style, **34**; in American Federal style, 35, 40; in American Georgian style, 38; used by Thomas Chippendale, 24, 27; in Early Georgian style, 23; in French Empire style, 18; in Regency style, 32; vinyl-covered, 251
Malachite, 95
Malewitsch, 50, 100

Man-made. *See* Synthetic

Mannerism, 8

Mantels, 55, **56–57**; in American Federal style, 40; in French Neoclassic style, 16; in French Renaissance style, **12**; in French Rococo style, with over-mantel (trumeau), 14; in Late Georgian style, 30

Manufacture: of carpets, 212–216, 220–221; of mirrors, 255. *See also* Industrial Revolution; Mass production

Maple wood: in American Georgian style, 35; in Early American style, 37; vinyl-covered, 252

Marble, 129; in contemporary furniture, 109, **109**; in Late Georgian furniture, 31; in table tops (guéridons), 18, **19**; in traditional furniture, **83**, 89; on walls, 195

Marbled wallpaper, 187

Marble floors: in French Baroque style, 13; in French Empire style, 19; in French Rococo style, 15

Marble patterns in wallpaper, 190

Marbling, 95; on walls, 195

Marquetry, 95; in French Neoclassic style, 17; in French Rococo style, 15; in Queen Anne style, 28

Mary, Queen, of England, 21; II, Queen, of England, 23

Mass production, 47, 102; in contemporary furniture, 114

Massachusetts Institute of Technology, 53

Master carrier for drapery, 201

Materials: in contemporary furniture, 107, 109; planning of, by designer, 286; of rugs, 227; in traditional furniture, 84–91. *See also* Fabrics; Glass; Iron; Leather; Metal; Plastic; Wood

Measurement of light, 138–140

Measurements: of drapery, 207–208; for floor plan, 72

Mediterranean settings, 249

Meshed rugs, 234

Metal: in contemporary furniture, 103, 106; use of, in printmaking, 268, 270, 272; in sculpture, 278; in traditional furniture, 86

Metallic fibers, 172

Metallic wallpapers, 195

Mezzotint, 270

Miami Beach, Fla., 52

Middle Ages: in England, 21; in France, 8–9

Mies van der Rohe, Ludwig, 47, 51, 86, 103–104, **103**, 110

Mildew-resistant finishes for fabric, 181

Military motifs: in French Directoire style, 10; in French Empire style, 11, 18

Mirrors, **63**, 129, 255–263; American Chippendale, **34**; on blinds, 204, **205**; in Chippendale furniture, 29; in French Rococo style, 14; Georgian, **60**; in Late Georgian style, 31; terminology of, 261–263; in traditional furniture, 90; on walls, 61, 193, 230; in Windows on the World, 297; in window treatments, 201. *See also* Color plate section

Mitered corners in drapery, 208

Mobiles, 278

Modacrylic, 173, 179, 212; for carpet, 218–219

Modern Art, Museum of, 103, 106

Modular furniture, 110–115, **111–115**

Mohair, 172; in contemporary furniture, 109

Moiré textures, 185; in French Empire fabrics, 19; in French Neoclassic fabrics, 17; in Late Georgian fabrics, 31; in upholstery, **293**; in wallpaper, 190

Molded furniture, 110, **111**, 114, **115**

Moldings, 61–64, **63**, 195; in American Federal style, 40; in Chippendale furniture, 29; in Late Georgian style, 30; with mirrors, 261; for hanging paintings, 264, **265–266**

Mondrian, Piet, 50, 100

Monochromatic color schemes, 126–127

Montage, 275

Monticello, 35, 40

Moorish patterns in ceramic tiles, 247, 249

Moroccan leather, 90

Morocco, rugs in, 239

Morris, William, 48, 99, 188

Mosaic mirror, 260, **260**

Mosaic tiles, ceramic, 245, **246**, 249

Mother-of-pearl, inlaid, 95

Multimedia prints, 272

Munsell, Albert, 121

Murals, 61, 195; lighting of, 150

Museum of Modern Art, 103, 106

Mylar, 172; on ceilings, 62; on walls, **63**, 64, 190, 193, 195

Nain rugs, 234

Napoleon Bonaparte, Emperor, of France, 11, 18; influence of, on American Victorian style, 45

National Council for Interior Design Qualification (N.C.I.D.Q.), 300, 304–307

National Home Fashions League, Inc. (N.H.F.L.), 306–307

National Society of Interior Designers (N.S.I.D.), 299–300, 303

Natural fibers, 170, 172, 183, 185; used in traditional furniture, 88–89

Navajo rugs, 238

Needlepoint, 277; Florentine, **60**; in French Neoclassic style, 17; in Middle Georgian style, 29; in Queen Anne style, 28; rugs, 210, 238–239

Needle-punched carpet, 216, 220

Neoclassic style: American, 40; French, 10, 16–17, **16–17**

Nesbitt, J. B., House, Calif., 53

Neutra, Richard, 53

New England, country style of, 57–60, **58–59**

Newport, R.I., furniture made in, **34**, 38, **60**

Newton, Sir Isaac, 119

New York, N.Y., furniture made in, 38

Niches, lighting of, 151

Norman style, English, 21. *See also* Romanesque style

Nylon, 173, 212; in carpet, 218–219

Nytril (fiber), 173

Oak: Age of, in English style, 20, 21; in Early American style, 37; in English Early Renaissance style, 22; in English Gothic style, 21; in English Tudor style, 26; in French Baroque style, 13; vinyl-covered, 251–252

Oilcloth floor coverings, 210

Oil paintings, 273–274, **273**

Oil stains for furniture, 92

Olefin (fiber), 173, 212, 246; in carpet, 218–219

Organic architecture, 48–50

Oriental influence on French Rococo style, 10, 14. *See also* Chinese influence

Oriental patterns: in rugs, 223, **228**; in wallpaper, **193**

Oriental rugs, **60**, 129, **206**, **228–230**, 229–237, **233–234**, 242, 281; American, 241; in American Georgian style, 39, **39**; classifications of, 232–236; in French Neoclassic style, 17; in Middle Georgian style, 29; purchasing of, 236–237

Ormolu, 17

Ostwald, Wilhelm, 121

Ottoman, contemporary, 112

Ottoman Empire, 23

Oval rooms, Late Georgian, 30

Overdrapes, 201, **202**

Overlap of drapery, 208

Over-mantel (trumeau): in French Neoclassic style, 16; in French Rococo style, 14

Painted floors, 210

Painted furniture, **83**, 92; in French Neoclassic style, 17; in French Rococo style, 15

Painted paneling in Queen Anne style, 28

Painted walls, 195. *See also* Color plate section

Paintings, 264, **265–266**, 273–274, **273–274**, 280; in Late Georgian style, 31; lighting of, 150

Paisley patterns, 59–60, **59**, **175**, 190

Palais Royal, Paris, 11

Palladio, (Andrea), influence of: on American Federal style, 40; on English Elizabethan style, 22

Paneling, **83**, 195; in American Georgian style, 38; of barn floor boards, 59; board-and-batten, **58**, 59; in English Tudor style, 21, 26; in French Baroque style, 9; in French Empire style, 19; in French Gothic style, 8; in French Neoclassic style, 16; in French Rococo style, 14

Panels: drapery, 207; linenfold, 8; luminous, 152–153; in window treatments, 201

Paris, 48, 210. *See also* France; French style periods

Parliament, Houses of, 25

Parquet: in French Empire style, 19; in French Neoclassic style, 17; in French Rococo style, 15; tiles resembling, 247, 249

Parson Capen House, Topsfield, Mass., 35

Parthenon, influence of, on American Greek Revival style, 44

Pastel drawings, 275

Patchwork patterns in wallpaper, **189**, 190

Pattern repeat, 45, 168–169, 207, 243

Patterns: of area rugs, 238–240; Art Deco, 52; of carpets, 213, 215–216, 221; and color, 127–129; fabric, in American Federal style, 41; fabric, in English Tudor style; fabric, in French Baroque style, 13; fabric, in French country style, **56–57**; fabric, in French Empire style, 19; fabric, in French Rococo style, 15; fabric, in Regency style, 32; of fabrics, 163, 174–179, **175–179**, 185; machine (TAK), 220; with mirrors, 259; of Oriental rugs, 229–237; of rugs, 223–229, **224–228**; of rugs, in American Federal style, 41; of rugs, in American Victorian style, 45; of rugs, in Middle Georgian style, 29; of tiles, 247; of vinyl-covered wood, 250–251; in wallpaper, **189–193**, 190, 192–193; in weavings, 277. *See also* Color plate section

Pauferro wood, 107

Pavers, ceramic tile, 245–246

Pedestal chairs, 106, **107**

Pediments in American Greek Revival style, 44

Pen-and-ink drawings, 274–275, **275**

Penthouse, 264, **265–266**

Percier, Charles, 11, 18

Perpendicular style, contemporary, 99–100, **99**

Perret, Auguste, 50

Persia (Iran), 210, 232, 234–236. *See also* Iran

Persian Gulf, 239

Personal space, 70–71

Petit Trianon Chateau, 10, 16

Petrochemicals, carpet fibers made from, 212

Pewter in traditional furniture, 87

Philadelphia, Pa., 35; furniture made in, 38

Phillip II (Duke of Orleans), Regent of France, 9

Photographic engraving, 169, 188

Photographs, 273, 294, 297

Phyfe, Duncan, 40; furniture in the style of, **40–41**

Picasso, Pablo, **271**, 275

Picture frames. *See* Frames

Piece dyeing, 220, 241

Pietra dura, 89

Pigment: theories of, 120–125; for wallpaper, 187. *See also* Color; Color plate section

Pilasters, **60**; in English Tudor style, 26; in French Empire style, 19

Pile: of carpets, 212, 214–215, 220; of Oriental rugs, 236; of rugs, 223, 239–240, 242

Pillow shams, **165**

Pillows: accent, **56–58**, 60, 128, 280; woven covers for, 277

Pinch pleats, 198, 200

Pine in Early American style, 37

Plain weave, 170, **171**, 174

Planning, overall, 1–3, 161, 196–197, 209; of space, 69–81

Planographic printing, 272

Plans: bubble (circle), 71; floor, 72–81, **73–74**, **76–77**, 286; floor, for Windows on the World, **294**, **296**; lighting, 62–63, 71, 81, 154–159, **155–156**, 286, 291; presentation of designer's, 286, **288–291**

Planters, **206**; lighting of, 151

Plants, **213–214**

Plaster: in French country style, 55, **56–57**; with mirror, 259; walls, 195; walls, Early American, 36; walls, Late Georgian, 30

Plastic: furniture, 48, 106, **107**, 114, **115**; in lighting fixtures, 140

Platner, Warren, 286, 293–297

Pleats, drapery, 198–199

Plush: carpet texture, 212, 214; fabrics, in American Victorian style, 45

Ply of yarns, 210, 217

Plymouth Hotel, Miami Beach, Fla., 52

Plywood, 100, **101**, 201; in contemporary furniture, 51, 106, 112, **112**; lumber core, 85

Pointillism as decorative theme, 297

Pole screen, New England Chippendale, **60**

Pole treatments of windows, 200

Polka-dots in wallpaper, 190

Polonaise rugs, 236

Polyester, 173, 212, 242; in carpet, 218–220; in silk-screen printing, 169

Polypropylene carpet fiber, 220

Polyurethane: to coat rattan, 88; in contemporary furniture, 110–113, **111**, **113**; foam used in upholstery, 97

Pompadour, Madame de, 14, 16

Pompeii, excavations at, 10, 14, 16, 19, 30

Poncing paper, 94

Porcelain, use of, in traditional furniture, 89

Portable lamps, 147, **147**
Portugal, 238
Pottery, **265**, 278–280, **279**
Prayer rugs, 236
Pre-Columbian art, 278
Presentation board, designer's, 286, **288–289**
Primitive art, 278
Primitive rugs, 232, 237, 239
Printed wallpapers, 188–193, **189–193**
Printing: of carpets, 221; of fabric, 167–169, 185
Prints, antique, 280. *See also* Graphics
Prisms, 119, 119
Professional architects, 40. *See also* individual named architects; Contemporary furniture; Contemporary style
Professional interior designers, 1–3, 6, 40, 72, 118, 120, 126, 132, 140, 143, 154, 163–165, 170, 174, 196, 204, 211–212, 263, 282–308. *See also* Color plate section
Proportion, consideration of, in planning, 72, 81
Psychology: of color, 120, 122; in space planning, 69–71
Public space, 70
Puerto Rico, wool from, 227
Pull cord, drapery, 201

Qualification of interior designers, 304–306
Quarry tile, ceramic, 245–246
Queen Anne style, 23, 28, **28, 60**; American, **34**, 35; influence of, on American Georgian style, 38
Quilting of fabric, 185
Qum rugs, 234

Radio City Music Hall, 52
Rag rugs, 210, 277
Random plank patterns, in vinyl-covered wood, 251
Rattan, 88–89, **213, 265–266**
Rayon, 172, 212; in carpet, 220
Recessed luminaires, 148
Redgrave, Richard, 99
Redwood furniture, French Empire, 18
Reflection: of light, 119, 129, 139–140, 142, 154, 163; in mirrors, 255–261; in Windows on the World, 297
Reflective ceiling lighting plan, 156–157, 286
Reflectorized lamps, 135
Reflectors, 148
Regency, French, 9–10
Regency style, English, 25, 32; influence of, on American Greek Revival style, 35
Regent's Park, London, 25
Reinforced concrete, 50
Related color schemes, 126–127
Relief: printing, 270–271, **271**; sculpture, **278**
Renaissance, English: Early, 21–22; Late, 24; Middle, 22
Renaissance, French: Early, 8; Middle, 9; Late, 9
Renaissance, Italian, 232; influence of, on American Victorian style, 45
Repeat, pattern, 45, 168–169, 207, 243
Resin, 181; textures in fabric, 180
Restoration, French, 11, 87
Restoration style, English, 23; influence of, on Early American style, 37
Return, drapery, 208
Revolution, American, 40, 232
Ribbon: patterns, in Chippendale chairs, 29; trims, in Late Georgian fabrics, 31
Richardson, Henry Hobson, 35, 45, 49
Richmond, Va., Capitol, 35, 40
Rietveld, Gerrit, 50, 100–101, **100–101**
Ripplefold pleats, 199
Robie House, Chicago, 49
Rococo style, French, 10, 14–15, **14–15**; influence of, on Chippendale style, 24, 29; marquetry, 95; Revival, American Victorian, **44**
Rods, use of in window treatments, 202, 204
Roller printing of carpets, 221
Romanesque style, French, 8–9; influence of, on American Victorian style, 45; influence of, on H. H. Richardson, 49
Roman frescoes, 90
Romania, 239
Roman influence: in English Elizabethan style, 22; in French Empire style, 11, 18–19; in French Neoclassic style, 10; in Regency style, 25
Roman shades, 201, 203
Rome, tile used in, 244

Room dividers, 204
Rooms: architecture of, 1, 54–65; children's, **192, 205**; circular, 30; family, 120, 129; 56–60, **58–59**; formal, 60–61, **60**; function of, 3; informal, 55–60, **56–57**; oval, 30; planning of, 1–3, 54–65, 70–81; size of, 70–72, 81, 123–125, 156, 163–164, 192–193, 203, 255–256, 259, 293–296. *See also* American style; Bedrooms; Contemporary settings; Country look; Dining rooms; English style; Floor plans; Formal look; French style; Living rooms; Libraries, etc.; and Color plate section
Rosewood: in American Federal style, 35; in American Victorian style, **44**; vinyl-covered, 251
Rosin, use of, in aquatints, 270
Rotary screen-printing of fabrics, 169
Rotogravure printing of wallpaper, 188
Royal Pavilion, Brighton, England, 25
Rubber; foam, 106, 213; sponge, 216
Rugs, 210, 223–243, **224–229, 231, 233–235**; antique, 280; pile of, 129; terminology of, 240–243; on walls, 195. *See also* Area rugs; Carpets; Floor coverings; Floors; Oriental rugs
Rush seating, 88, **189**
Rya rugs, 240

Saarinen, Eero, 106, **107**
St. Martin's-in-the-Fields, Church of, London, 24
St. Paul's Cathedral, London, 23
St. Paul's Chapel, New York, 35
Salem, Mass., 35, 40
Salisbury Cathedral, England, 21
Samuel Powel House, Philadelphia, Pa., 35
Saraband rugs, 235
Sarouk rugs, 234, 236
Satin, 129; in French Baroque style, 13; in French Empire style, 19; in French Rococo style, 15; in Late Georgian style, 31; weave, 170, **171**, 174
Satinwood: Age of, in English style, 20, 24; in American Federal style, 40; in American Georgian style, 38; in Late Georgian style, 24, 31
Savonnerie, 210; carpets, in French Baroque style, 13, **13**; rugs, 239–240; rugs, in American Greek Revival style, 44; rugs, in French Neoclassic style, 17; rugs, in French Rococo style, 15
Scagliola, 90
Scale, consideration of, in planning, 81
Scandinavian furniture, 103, 105, **105**
Scandinavian rugs, 240
Scarpa, Afra and Tobia, 110, **111–112**, 112
Scenic patterns in wallpaper, 190
Schuman, I., House, Calif., 53
Scotland, 166
Screen-printing: of carpets, 221; of fabric, 168–169
Screens for walls, 195
Sculpture, 257, 259, 278, **278**; lighting of, 150–151
Sculptured textures: in carpet, 213–214; in tiles, 247; in wallpaper, 190
Seagrams Building, New York, 51
Seating system, contemporary, **108**
Secretary, Queen Anne, 28, **28**
Sehna rugs, 236
Senna rugs, 235
Serab rugs, 235
Serigraphy, 272
Shades, window, **200, 202–204**, 203–204
Shag carpet, **214**, 217
Sheer draperies, 197, 201
Shell motifs in French Rococo style, 10, 14–15
Sheraton, Thomas, 24, 30–31, **31**; influence of, on American Federal style, 35, 40; influence of, on American Georgian style, 38
Shinering of fabric, 170
Shiraz, 232
Shirring: of draperies, 199; of poles, 200; of rugs, 210. *See also* Fabrics
Shirvan rugs, 236
Showcase lamps, 135
Showrooms, 97, 165, 170, 212, 227, 276
Shrinkage control, fabric finishes for, 181
Shutters, 201, **204**
Shuttles, 210
Sideboards, Chippendale, 29
Siena, Cathedral of, 89
Silk, 172; in American Federal style, 41; in American Greek Revival style, 44; in draperies, 196; in French Empire style, 19; in French

Silk (cont.)
Neoclassic style, 17; Oriental rugs made of, 236; in Rugs, 227; Shiki, texture in wallpaper, 190; in silk-screen printing, 169, 272; on walls, 195
Silk-screen printing, 272; of fabric, 168–169; of mirrors, 259, 263; of wallpaper, 190
Silver, 140; antique, 280; furniture, French Baroque, 13; leaf, 93–94, **93**; plate, 87; in traditional furniture, 95; on walls, 195
Silverwork, 278, **280**
Sisal rugs, 240
Skein-dying of yarns, 220, 227, 241
Skyscrapers, 48–49
Slate in traditional furniture, 90
Slipcovers, zippered, in contemporary furniture, 110, 113–114
Smocking of drapery, 199
Soane, Sir John, 32
Social space, 70
Sofas, **58**, 59; American Federal, 40, **41**; American Georgian, **39**; American Victorian, **44**; Chippendale, 29; contemporary, **108**, 112–113; French, **56, 57**; mirrored, 260; Victorian, **33**
Solution dyeing of fibers, 220, 241
Somerset House, London, 24
Soumak rugs, 236
Space dyeing of yarn, 220, 241
Space planning, 69–81, **73–74, 76–80, 290**. *See also* Plans
Spain, 238
Spanish influence in French style, 9
Spinning, 166
Splat-back chairs: Chippendale, 29; Philadelphia Chippendale, **34**; Queen Anne, 23, **28**
Split-complementary color schemes, 128
Sponge, 213, 216
Spotlights, 148
Spring-and-down upholstery filling, 97, 114
Srinagar, India, 236
Stain removal for rugs, 221–222
Stain repellent finishes, 181
Stains used in traditional furniture, 91–92
Steel, 129; in contemporary architecture, 49, 53; in contemporary furniture, 106, 109–110, 112–114, **112**; in traditional furniture, 86, **87**; in traditional upholstery, 96–97, tubular, 47–48, 51, 102, 103–104, **104**
Stenciling: of fabrics, 169; of floor coverings, 210
Stencil patterns in wallpaper, 190
Stentering of fabric, 168
Stippled textures: of paint, 195; of wallpaper, 190
Stock dyeing of fibers, 220, 241
Stock Exchange Building, Chicago, 49
Stone: floors, 8, 13; houses, in English Norman style, 21; use of, in lithography, 272; in sculpture, 278; walls, 195
Straw, 129; area rugs, 237, 240; matting, 210; in weavings, 277; in window treatments, 201
Strawberry Hill, England, 22
Stripes: in area rugs, 238; in wallpaper, 190
Stucco, 61; on walls, 195
Study-workshop, **218**
Sturbridge Village, Mass., 35
Styles: adapting a room to suit, 54–65; American, 34–45; contemporary, 46–53; English, 20–33; French, 8–19; furniture, comparative (table), 42–43; universal, 116
Suede, 129, 185; door covered in, 109
Sullivan, Louis, 49
Sunlight, 119, 133–134, 207, 219. *See also* Daylight
Sun-porch, **214**
Surface printing of wallpaper, 188
Swags, drapery, in French Empire style, 19
Swatch board, designer's, 286, **288**
Swiss Pavilion, Paris, 52
Switches, lighting, 154, 156
Synthetic (man-made) fibers, 170, 172–173, 183, 185, 216, **217**, 220, 237. *See also* Carpet terminology

Tables: butterfly trestle, Early American, 37, **37**; chair, Early American, 37; Chinese Chippendale, **34**; Chippendale, 29; coffee, **58**, 59, **206, 280, 293**; coffee, Oriental, **189**; console, American Federal, 40, **40**; console, Late Georgian, 31; contemporary, **109**; dining, Chippendale, 29; drop-leaf, Chippendale, 29; drop-leaf, Early American, 37; extension, Chippendale, 29; French Neoclassic, 17; gate-leg, Early American, 37; glass-topped, **104**; lacquered, **93**; Le Corbusier, **104**;

329

Tables (cont.)
  marble-topped (guéridons), 18, **19**; mirrored, 260; piecrust pedestal-base, **39**; tea, French Rocco, 15; tea, New England Queen Anne, **60**; tea, Queen Anne, **39**; tilt-top piecrust, 29; tilt-top Queen Anne, 34; rent, Chippendale, 29
Tabriz rugs, 234, **235**
Taliesin houses, 49–50
Tamo wood, 107
Tapestries: in English Gothic style, 21; in French Baroque style, 9; in French Gothic style, 8; lighting of, 150; in Middle Georgian style, 29
Tapestry, 186, 210, 276–277; furniture upholstered in, in French Baroque style, 13, **13**; weave, 238
Task lighting, 142–147, 154
Tassels: with Late Georgian fabrics, 31; on window drapery in French Empire style, 19
Taste: of client, 2, 286, 293–294, 302; in purchasing Oriental rugs, 236–237
Tea chest wallpaper, 190
Teak, vinyl-covered, 251
Templates: furniture, 75, **76–77**; use of, in printing carpets, 221
Tent bag, **233**
Terra cotta in traditional furniture, 90
Terminology. See Carpets; Fabrics; Mirrors; Rugs
Terrace, **248**
Terracing, 294–295, **295**
Territories, individual, 69–70
Tetrad color scheme, 128
Textiles. See Fabrics; Rugs
Textures, 126, 129; of carpet, 212–217, **217–218**; of ceramics, 278, **279**; of fabrics, 163; of floors, 244–249, **245–248**; with mirrors, 259; of rugs, 223–229, **224–228**, 238–240; of wallpaper, 190; of weavings, 277
The Architects Collaborative (TAC), 51
Thonet, Michael, 47–48, 51, 86, 98
Thread, spinning and weaving of, 166–167
Three-dimensional arts, 278, **278–279**
Tibet, 238
Tie-back curtains, **165**, 200
Tie-backs, **178**, 201, **202**
Tiffany, Louis, 48
Tiffany glass, 280
Tiles, 297; carpet, 213; ceramic. See Ceramic tile
Toile de Jouy, **175**, 186; in American Georgian style, 39
Toile patterns in wallpaper, 190, **190**, 193
Toiles: in French Baroque style, 13; in French Rococo style, 15
Top treatments of windows, 200
Track lighting, 148, **206**, 264, **265–266**
Traditional furniture, 82–97, **83**, **87**, **91**, **93**, **96**
Traditional patterns in rugs, 223
Traditional settings, **190**, 230, 238, 249
Transmission of light, 139–140
Traverse rod for drapery, 199, 201
Trellis: with mirror, 259; on walls, 195
Triacetate, 172
Triad color schemes, 128
Trimmings for fabrics, 175, **178**
Trinity Church, Boston, 35, 45, 49
Trumeau. See Over-mantel
Tubular steel. See Steel, tubular
Tudor style, English, 21, 26–27, **27**; windows in, 196
Tugendhat chair, **103**
Tugendhat House, Brno, Czechoslovakia, 51
Tufted carpet, 220, 221
Tufting: carpet, 212–213; custom, 213; rug, 223, 225–227, **226–227**; upholstery, **44**, **63**, 64, 91, **91**, 112, **112**, **206**, 297. See also Carpet terminology
Tuileries, Paris, 11
Turkestan rugs, 236
Turkey, 231, 233, 237, 239
Turkish carpet in French Empire style, 19
Turkish rugs, 236
Turkoman rugs, **233**, 236
Twill weave, 170, **171**, 174
Twist of yarn, 218
Twist carpet, 214, 243

Unity: in color scheme, 128–129; of design, in style of Robert Adam, 24, 30–31
Unity Church, Chicago, 49
University of California at Berkeley, 53
Upholstered furniture, **87**, **293**; in American Victorian style, 45; contemporary, 108, 111–114, **111–114**; traditional, **96**, **200**. See also Chairs; Contemporary furniture; Sofas; Traditional furniture
Upholstered poles for drapery, 200, **200**
Upholstered walls, 195
Upholstery, 163; leather, **63**, 64; machine, for carpet-weaving, 216; patterned, 129; traditional, 96–97; vinyl, 64, **64**, 186; urethane, 186. See also Fabrics; Tufting
Uplights, 148
Urethane: to coat marble, 90; in contemporary furniture, 110–113, **111–113**; upholstery, 186

Valances, 200, **201**, **206**; in French Empire style, 19
Value of color, 121–124, 127–128
Van der Rohe. See Mies van der Rohe
Van de Velde, Henri, 48, 99
Varnish, use of, in engraving, 268, 270
Velour, 186; in Middle Georgian style, 29
Velvet, **58**, 59, 186; carpet, 214, 243; draperies, 196; in French Empire style, 19; furniture upholstered in, **292**; in Middle Georgian style, 29
Veneer, 98; in contemporary furniture, 107; in French Rococo style, 15; rosewood, in American Victorian style, 45; in traditional furniture, 85; in vinyl-covered flooring, 250
Venetian blinds, 204
Venetian rugs, 210
Versailles, Palace at, 9, 12, 18
Vertical blinds, 201, **201**, 203–207, **205–206**, **293**; mirrored, 255
Vertical design in French Gothic style, 8
Victoria, Queen of England, 25, 33
Victoria and Albert Museum, London, 48
Victorian style, 25, 33; American, 35, **44**, 45; fabric patterns in, **176–177**
Vicuna, 172
Villa Savoye, Poissy, France, 52
Vinyl, 204; carpet backing, 213; upholstery, 64, **64**, 186; wallcoverings, 190, **192**, 195; wood covered with, as flooring, 249–252, **250–252**
Vinyon (fiber), 173
Voltage of lamps, 135–136
Voysey, Charles F. Annesley, 99
V'Soske Rug Co., 223–229

Walker Warehouse, Chicago, 49
Wallcoverings, 187–195. See also Wallpaper; Walls; Wall treatments; Color plate section
Wall hangings, 276–277
Wallpaper, 61, 175, 187–193, **189–193**; in French Empire style, 19; in French Neoclassic style, 16; in French Rococo style, 14; patterned, 129; wet-look, 129; William Morris, 48; in window treatments, 200–201, **205**. See also Wall treatments; Color plate section
Walls: glass, 61–62; textured, lighting of, 152
Wall-to-wall carpet, 211, 213, **213**, **215**, **217–218**. See also Carpet
Wall treatments, 187–195; lacquer, 129; mirror, 61, 255–256, **256–257**, 261, 294; tile, 245, 249; upholstery, 61, 163, **165**. See also American style periods; English style periods; French style periods; Color plate section
Wall washers, 148, 297
Walnut: Age of, in English style, 22–23, 28; in American Georgian style, 35; in American Victorian style, **44**; in Early American style, 37; in Queen Anne style, 28; in traditional furniture, 85; vinyl-covered, 251
Warp, 166, 170, **171**, 174, 186; in carpet, 214

Wash-and-wear fabrics, 180
Washing of fabrics, 172–173, 181
Washington, George, 40
Wassily chair, 102
Watercolors, 274, **274**
Waterproof finishes, 181
Water stains for furniture, 91
Watteau, (Jean-Antoine), 10
Wax: in engraving, 268, 270; in fabric printing, 277
Weaving of fabric, 167, 170, **171**, 174, 184
Weavings, 129, 276–277
Webb, Philip, 48
Wedgwood, Josiah, 30–31; china, 280
Weft (woof): of carpet, 210, 214, 243; of fabric, 166, 168, 170, **171**
Wegner, Hans, 105, **105**
Weight: of carpet yarn, 217; in drapery, 208
Weimar, Germany, 51
White House, The, 35, 40
Wicker, 88–89, **200**, **213–214**
William III of England, 23; IV of England, 25
William and Mary style, English, 23
Williamsburg, Va., 35
Willow, 88
Wilton, England, 210
Wilton carpet, 214–215, **216**, 241, 243
Windows, 61; in American Victorian style, **44**; in Early American style, 36; in English Tudor style, 26, **27**; in French Empire style, 19; mirrored, **258**
Window shades, 203; fabric-laminated, **59**, 60, **165**
Windows on the World, 293–297
Window treatments, **60**, 196–208, **197–206**, **280**. See also American style periods; English style periods; French style periods; Color plate section
Windsor Castle, 23
Wing chairs, Queen Anne, 28
Wood, 129; in contemporary architecture, 49, 53; in contemporary furniture, 103, 107; cornices, 201; floors, 230; floors, in Queen Anne style, 28; furniture, 230; kiln-dried, 100, **101**; paneling, 61; poles for drapery, 200; in Scandinavian furniture, 105, **105**; sculpture, 278; shades, 203; in traditional furniture, **83**, 84–86; vinyl-covered, 249–252, **250–252**. See also American style periods; Beechwood; English style periods; Floors; French style periods; Mahogany; Oak; Plywood; Satinwood; Walnut
Woodcuts, 270–271, **271**
Wooden beads, 277
Wood engraving, 270
Woof. See Filling; Weft
Wool, 129, 172, 210; in carpets, 212, 214, **216**, 218–219; in American Georgian style, 39; in draperies, 196; in Oriental rugs, 232, 234, 237; in rugs, 223–224, 227–228, **228**, 237–240; spinning of, **164**
World Trade Center, New York, 293
Woven carpet, 214–216, 220–221
Woven rugs, 210, 238–240
Woven textures in wallpaper, 190
Wren, Christopher, 23
Wright, Frank Lloyd, 49–50, 53
Writing tables, Queen Anne, 28
Wurster, William Wilson, 53

Yarns: in carpet, 214–218, 220–221; in fabric arts, 276–277; in rugs, 227. See also Carpet terminology
Yarn-sewn rugs, 210
Yomut rug design, **233**
"Zig-zag chair," **100**
Zig-zag patterns, 277
Zippered slipcovers, contemporary, 110, 113–114
Zonal cavity method for lighting, 157
Zone plan, 71
Zones, lighting, 142